OXFORD STUDIES IN EUROPEAN LAW

Series Editors

PAUL CRAIG

Professor of English Law at St John's College, Oxford

GRÁINNE DE BÚRCA

Professor of Law at the European University Institute,
and Florence Ellinwood Allen Professor of Law at New York University

Legal Mobilization for Migrant Rights

OXFORD STUDIES IN EUROPEAN LAW

Series Editors:

Paul Craig, Professor of English Law at St John's College, Oxford
and Gráinne de Búrca, Professor of Law at the European University Institute,
and Florence Ellinwood Allen Professor of Law at New York University

The aim of this series is to publish important and original research on EU law. The focus is on scholarly monographs, with a particular emphasis on those which are interdisciplinary in nature. Edited collections of essays will also be included where they are appropriate. The series is wide in scope and aims to cover studies of particular areas of substantive and of institutional law, historical works, theoretical studies, and analyses of current debates, as well as questions of perennial interest such as the relationship between national and EU law and the novel forms of governance emerging in and beyond Europe. The fact that many of the works are interdisciplinary will make the series of interest to all those concerned with the governance and operation of the EU.

OTHER TITLES IN THIS SERIES

Saving the European Union from its Illiberal Member States
András Jakab and Lando Kirchmair

Constitutional Disintegration and Disruption
Withdrawal and Opt-Outs from the European Union
Oliver Garner

Business Freedoms and Fundamental Rights in European Union Law
Niall O'Connor

Compliance with European Consumer Law
The Case of E-Commerce
Felix Pflücke

Legislative Authority and Interpretation in the European Union
Martijn van den Brink

Secession and European Union Law
The Deferential Attitude
Núria González Campañá

Fiscal State Aid Law and Harmful Tax Competition in the European Union
Dimitrios Kyriazis

The Abuse of Constitutional Identity in the European Union
Julian Scholtes

Judging European Democracy
The Role and Legitimacy of National Constitutional Courts in the EU
Nik de Boer

EU Values Before the Court of Justice
Foundations, Potential, Risks
Luke Dimitrios Spieker

Postnational Constitutionalism
Europe and the Time of Law
Paul Linden-Retek

The Legislative Priority Rule and the EU Internal Market for Goods
A Constitutional Approach
Eadaoin Ní Chaoimh

The Jurisprudence of Constitutional Conflict in the European Union
Ana Bobić

Reflexive Governance in EU Equality Law
Emma Lantschner

Enhanced Cooperation and European Tax Law
Caroline Heber

Legal Pluralism in European Contract Law
Vanessa Mak

Legal Mobilization for Migrant Rights

Opportunities and Barriers at the European Court of Justice

VIRGINIA PASSALACQUA
Assistant Professor, Law Department, University of Turin, Italy

OXFORD
UNIVERSITY PRESS

OXFORD
UNIVERSITY PRESS

Great Clarendon Street, Oxford, OX2 6DP,
United Kingdom

Oxford University Press is a department of the University of Oxford.
It furthers the University's objective of excellence in research, scholarship,
and education by publishing worldwide. Oxford is a registered trade mark of
Oxford University Press in the UK and in certain other countries

Published in the United States of America by Oxford University Press
198 Madison Avenue, New York, NY 10016, United States of America

British Library Cataloguing in Publication Data
Data available

Library of Congress Control Number: 2025931459

ISBN 9780198942979

DOI: 10.1093/9780198943006.001.0001

Printed and bound by
CPI Group (UK) Ltd., Croydon, CR0 4YY

FSC
www.fsc.org
MIX
Paper | Supporting
responsible forestry
FSC® C013604

The manufacturer's authorised representative in the EU for product safety is
Oxford University Press España S.A. of El Parque Empresarial San Fernando de Henares, Avenida de Castilla, 2 – 28830 Madrid (www.oup.es/en or
product.safety@oup.com). OUP España S.A. also acts as importer into Spain
of products made by the manufacturer.

To those who fight for the rights of others

Series Editors' Preface

This is a fine scholarly work that brings together two broad and important sets of issues within European Union law and policy. The first is the policy issue of migration, which has rarely been off the EU agenda or out of the news headlines over the past decade. The second is the legal process of the preliminary reference procedure that connects national courts and the European Court of Justice.

The preliminary reference procedure has been a subject of fascination for lawyers and others ever since its introduction by the original EC treaties, not just because of its role in the (uneven) "Europeanization" of the national judiciary and of areas of national law but also because of the way it has enabled important legal and policy questions of trans-European interest to be brought before the European Court of Justice. Equally, the issue of migration has been of high importance for the EU—and for EU scholars—not just due to the greatly increased flows of refugees seeking to enter the EU in 2015 but also due to its salience within the Brexit debate and in the politics of the right and the far-right across Europe.

This book contributes to those literatures in interesting and novel ways. In the first place, it contains a thorough study of preliminary references to the Court of Justice in the specific field of migration, looking at who is using EU law for these purposes, who requests a preliminary reference, and with what aims and results. The study tells us about differences across various jurisdictions: the Member States whose courts have more frequently referred questions on these issues to the European Court of Justice, as well as those (including most prominently and surprisingly, given its role at the center of events in relation to migration and refugee flows: Greece) whose courts have not made references, and explores some of the reasons why. Further, the book contributes to a burgeoning literature on legal mobilization in Europe, which focuses less on judicial actors or on substantive rulings but more on those who are choosing to use the national and eventually the EU courts to advance their causes and cases: who they are, who are their lawyers, why they litigate, and how they do so.

The book adopts a sociolegal methodology including selected empirical studies, and is based not only on documentary research and on coding of cases but also on selected interviews with relevant actors in the various Member States under scrutiny. It provides a novel set of insights into the world of civil society mobilization for migrants' rights across Europe, adding also to the literatures on the relation between the European Court of Justice and national courts as well as to that on EU migration law and policy.

It is a work which should be of considerable interest to lawyers, legal and policy scholars, and activists alike within the fields of EU law and migration law.

Paul Craig
Gráinne de Búrca

Acknowledgments

This book has been a long way coming. In 2012, with my newly issued law degree, I started volunteering at a lawyers' association, giving free legal advice to migrants in Bologna. By watching my senior colleagues advising persons on the most disparate problems, I learned that law could truly change people's lives, but only if they have a good lawyer by their side. Tariq was among the people that I first met, a man who came by foot from Pakistan to Italy; on the way, he was bitten by a snake and developed a bad and debilitating disease. He was the first "case" I took charge of and I wanted to do whatever was in my power to help him. He finally obtained a permit in 2018, six years after my intervention.

While my experience as a volunteer prompted me to study law and migration, the idea for this book would have never arisen without my EUI supervisor Bruno de Witte. He read in me a passion for law in action and sent me the first article I read on legal mobilization. I am very grateful to Bruno for his mentorship and support during and after my PhD, and also for being a great example of how to undertake an academic career happily and ethically.

In Florence, I was lucky to meet several people who believed in and supported my project over the years, among which I wish to thank Dia Anagnostou, Claire Kilpatrick, and Elise Muir. I also had a wonderful group of legal mobilization colleagues, with whom I exchanged reflections and readings: Mario Pagano, Raphaële Xenidis, Lilla Farkas, and Jeffrey Miller. My journey continued to New York, where Gráinne de Búrca and the amazing fellows at NYU further helped me to strengthen my project. In Turin, I concluded this long writing journey with the support of my new, big, and supportive academic community, *Stanza 19.* I am especially grateful to Francesco Costamagna, Alberto Miglio, and Stefano Montaldo for their constant feedback and support. And to Ludovica Poli for telling me to go on holiday when I needed a break.

I am grateful to all the lawyers, judges, activists, and academics who agreed to be interviewed by me and who shared their thoughts and experiences. Each interview enriched my view of EU law in action and was a source of inspiration. Thanks also to the OUP editors, Peter Daniell and Paulina Dos Santos Major, and to the production editor, Victoriya Sherly, for their great support and help during the submission of the manuscript. And to the Oxford Studies in European Law editors for welcoming my book in the series.

Throughout this journey, I was lucky to have many friends and a caring and loving family by my side. Without their support, I would not have found the way. I am happy that this book will see the light now that our family is becoming bigger.

Contents

Figures

Tables

Table of Cases

EUROPEAN COMMISSION ON HUMAN RIGHTS

EUROPEAN COURT OF JUSTICE/COURT OF JUSTICE OF THE EUROPEAN UNION

EUROPEAN COURT OF HUMAN RIGHTS

NATIONAL CASES

Greece

Italy

Netherlands

United Kingdom

United States

Table of Legislation

EU LEGISLATION

REGULATIONS

NATIONAL LEGISLATION

British Legislation

STATUTES

Dutch Legislation

Greek Legislation

Irish Legislation

Italian Legislation

Abbreviations

AFSJ	Area of Freedom, Security and Justice
The AIRE Centre	Advice for Individual Rights in Europe
ASGI	Associazione per gli Studi Giuridici sull'Immigrazione
CJEU	Court of Justice of the European Union
CUKC	Citizens of the United Kingdom and the Colonies
DRC	Dutch Refugee Council
ECHR	European Convention on Human Rights
ECJ	European Court of Justice
ECRE	European Council on Refugees and Exiles
ECtHR	European Court of Human Rights
EEC	European Economic Community
GRC	Greek Refugee Council
HIAS	Hebrew Immigrant Aid Society
HRA	Human Rights Act
IAS	Immigration Advisory Service
IND	*Immigratie-en Naturalisatiedienst*
IOT	*Inspraak Orgaan Turken*
ILPA	Immigration Law Practitioners' Association
JCWI	Joint Council for the Welfare of Immigrants
LASPO	Legal Aid, Sentencing and Punishment of Offenders Act 2012
LOS	legal opportunity structure
NGO	non-governmental organization
PLP	Public Law Project
RSA	Refugee Support Aegean
TCN	third-country national
TEU	Treaty on European Union
TFEU	Treaty on the Functioning of the European Union
UK	United Kingdom
USA	United States of America
UKIAS	United Kingdom Immigrants Advisory Service
UNHCR	United Nation High Commissioner for Refugees
WRV	*Werkgroep Rechtsbijstand in Vreemdelingenzaken*

1

Legal Mobilization, Resistance, and Contestation through EU Law

1. Introduction

In the summer of 2019, Stefan was doing a PhD in international law at the University of Graz. When reading about the Schengen Borders Code, he realized that the Austrian practice of routinely reintroducing and prolonging border controls was blatantly in conflict with EU law and the abolition of internal borders between the Member States.[1] He thought: "There should be something done about this."[2] A few months later, he was driving his old red car, going back to Austria from his holidays in Croatia; as he approached the Slovenian–Austrian border, he could see a long line of cars waiting to be checked, and his anger rose. It took him forty-five minutes in the line to reach the border, and by then he had decided that he would contest the controls. When the police officer stopped Stefan and asked him to show his passport, he refused and got a fine of 36 euros.

Stefan appealed the fine before an Austrian court, where he contested the legitimacy of the national decree reintroducing border controls.[3] In his written statement, he asked the court to submit his case to the European Court of Justice (ECJ) through the preliminary reference procedure, which allows national courts to ask the EU Court for advice on the interpretation or the validity of an EU norm.[4] During the hearing, the Austrian court asked him only questions about EU law (How does the Schengen Borders Code function? Are

[1] Regulation (EU) 2016/399 of the European Parliament and of the Council of 9 March 2016 on a Union Code on the rules governing the movement of persons across borders (Schengen Borders Code). Stefan Salomon and Jorrit Rijpma, 'A Europe Without Internal Frontiers: Challenging the Reintroduction of Border Controls in the Schengen Area in the Light of Union Citizenship' (2023) 24 German Law Journal 281, 284.

[2] Interview with Stefan Salomon, 12 September 2024, via phone.

[3] Decree of the Federal Minister for the Interior on the temporary reintroduction of border control at internal borders of 9 May 2019 (BGBl. II, 114/2019).

[4] Under the preliminary reference procedure, a national court can submit a request for a preliminary ruling to the ECJ in case it has doubts regarding the interpretation or the validity of an EU norm, art 267 TFEU.

Legal Mobilization for Migrant Rights. Virginia Passalacqua, Oxford University Press.
 DOI: 10.1093/9780198943006.003.0001

there any other similar cases before the ECJ?). The judge eventually was convinced of the illegality of the Austrian practice but could not understand why a preliminary reference was necessary since the law was clear. Stefan sought the reference because, while a positive national judgment would have displayed effects only in the Austrian legal order, a ruling of the ECJ saying that this type of border check is illegitimate would have had an impact on the whole of the Union.[5] Thus, Stefan argued that EU law is not completely clear as we still did not know whether illegally prolonging border controls could be considered a breach of EU citizens' free movement rights. He persuaded the judge.

At the hearing before the ECJ in Luxembourg, Stefan was assisted by Christoph Tometten, a Berlin-based immigration lawyer in his first experience with preliminary references. "We were little fishes against all the powerful Member States' lawyers."[6] But despite the five Member States' interventions against him, the ECJ ruled in Stefan's favor. He obtained a landmark ruling declaring illegitimate the Member States' widespread practice of prolonging border controls without there being any new threat to public policy or internal security.[7] Having won the case before the Austrian court too, Stefan was reimbursed the legal cost of the case, except for the travel to Luxembourg.[8] The case received much attention, and Stefan was enthusiastic, at least initially. He soon realized that some Member States, including Austria, decided to reiterate border controls despite the ECJ judgment.[9] This pushed Stefan into a greater

[5] Alberto Trabucchi, L'effet "erga Omnes" Des Decisions Prejudicielles Rendues par la Cour de Justice des Communautes Europeennes' (1974) 10 Revue trimestrielle de droit europeen 56.

[6] Interview with Stefan Salomon, 12 September 2024, via phone.

[7] Joined cases C-368/20 and 369/20 *NW v Landespolizei Steiermark* (26 April 2022) CJEU, ECLI:EU:C:2022:298; Pola Cebulak and Marta Morvillo, 'Backtracking or Defending Free Movement within the Schengen Area? *NW v. Landespolizei Steiermark*' (2023) 60 Common Market Law Review; Angelo Marletta, 'Nulla di più definitivo del provvisorio? La Corte di giustizia sui limiti alla reintroduzione temporanea dei controlli alle frontiere interne' (*ADiM Blog*, 31 May 2022) <https://www.adimblog.com/2022/05/31/nulla-di-piu-definitivo-del-provvisorio-la-corte-di-giustizia-sui-limiti-alla-reintroduzione-temporanea-dei-controlli-alle-frontiere-interne/> accessed 29 October 2024; Jonas Bornemann, 'Reviving the Promise of Schengen' (*Verfassungsblog*, 28 April 2022) <https://verfassungsblog.de/reviving-the-promise-of-schengen/> accessed 29 October 2024; Francesco Luigi Gatta, 'Enough is enough! La Corte di Giustizia interviene sull'(il)legittimità delle proroghe "a catena" dei controlli alle frontiere interne. Ma lo Spazio Schengen rimane a rischio' (*Diritti Comparati*, 18 May 2022) <https://www.diritticomparati.it/enough-is-enough-la-corte-di-giustizia-interviene-sullillegittimita-delle-proroghe-a-catena-dei-controlli-alle-frontiere-interne-ma-lo-spazio-schengen-rimane-a-rischio/> accessed 29 October 2024.

[8] It is not rare that the legal cost of the case does not cover the proceedings in Luxembourg, which is often excluded by legal aid too. To be sure, since 2012, the parties of the preliminary reference procedure can ask for economic support from the ECJ in the case they are "wholly or in part unable to meet the costs of the proceedings" (art 115 of the Rules of Procedure of the Court of Justice). Chiara Enrica Tuo, Regolamento di procedura della Corte di giustizia. Titolo III, Capo IV, Gratuito patrocinio' in Chiaro Amalfitano, Massimo Condinanzi, and Paolo Iannuccelli (eds), *Le regole del processo dinanzi al Giudice dell'Unione europea. Commento articolo per articolo* (Editoriale Scientifica 2017).

[9] Cebulak and Morvillo, 'Backtracking or Defending Free Movement within the Schengen Area?' (n 7) 1092.

stage of rebellion: he now refuses to show his passport at any illegal border check. A new case is pending before the Bavarian Administrative Court.

In its own small way, Stefan's case presents some of the features that often characterize legal mobilization against national migration policies. First, the case reveals the crucial role that preliminary references play in contesting Member States' violations of EU law: Austria was renewing its border controls with Slovenia since 2016, with the complicity of the European Commission that turned a blind eye to them;[10] it took Stefan's initiative to mobilize the ECJ and raise the border checks' illegal nature. Second, this case also shows that, contrary to common assumptions, you do not need significant financial resources or renowned lawyers to reach the ECJ and obtain a landmark ruling. You do, however, need skillful EU legal experts who have the capacity to see the opportunities that EU law offers to contest national policies. As the book will show, this blend of EU legal expertise and activism is the hallmark of EU legal mobilization.

The debate around the ECJ migration case law often revolves around who accuses the Court of overstepping its boundaries and who demands from it a more prominent role, while scarce attention is paid to how migration cases arrive in Luxembourg. Who brings migration cases to the ECJ and how? And why these cases and not others? The ECJ, like any other court, needs to be mobilized.[11] This book tells the story of the civil society actors who, from behind the scenes, organized the litigation and persuaded national judges to refer preliminary questions to the ECJ. Litigation for migrant rights represents in itself an interesting case because most accounts depict the ECJ as a Court that the legal elite and affluent stakeholders mobilize. This book shows that, given some conditions, the ECJ can be relied upon by less powerful groups too.

Today the ECJ is arguably the most important court to adjudicate migration and asylum law in Europe. One judgment of the ECJ can change the lives and destinies of thousands of people forever: it can rule on their right to enter and reside in the EU, their right to be freed from detention, their right to reunite with their family members, and their right to work and to be treated equally. It often takes an ECJ judgment to ensure EU migration law is respected and correctly enforced. But the condition for having the ECJ decide on these cases

[10] Pola Cebulak and Marta Morvillo, 'The Guardian Is Absent' (*Verfassungsblog*, 25 June 2021) <https://verfassungsblog.de/the-guardian-is-absent/> accessed 29 October 2024.

[11] Frances Kahn Zemans, 'Legal Mobilization: The Neglected Role of the Law in the Political System' (1983) 77 The American Political Science Review 690, 691; Harm Schepel and Erhard Bankenburg, 'Mobilizing the European Court of Justice' in Gráinne De Búrca and Joseph HH Weiler (eds), *The European Court of Justice* (OUP 2001) 12.

is that they are first mobilized before national courts and then referred. This makes it very important to understand why some cases are referred and not others, why there are references from certain Member States and not from others, and why a certain case has been referred at one time and not earlier. Believing that these are pressing questions for EU constitutional law and judicial enforcement in general, this book contributes to our understanding of the structural and subjective factors that facilitate or hamper the activation of EU justice for migrant rights.

2. The uneven mobilization before the European Court of Justice

The EU is a community of law.[12] However, EU law is not applied and enforced in the same way across all the Member States. This becomes evident when we look at the cases brought to the ECJ over the years. Despite being the supreme judicial body of the EU,[13] litigation rates before the ECJ vary greatly between countries, and so does the enforcement of EU law provisions.[14] An eminent example is the preliminary reference mechanism, the most consequential procedure for EU legal integration,[15] which however is used with considerable variation between Member States.[16] The procedure is initiated by domestic courts during national proceedings: in case of doubt about the interpretation or validity of an applicable EU norm, national courts may refer the case to the ECJ along with their questions, and if they are last-instance courts, they have

[12] *Partie écologiste 'Les Verts' v European Parliament* (1986) CJEU, case 294/83, ECLI:EU:C:1986:166; Riccardo Luzzatto, 'L'Unione Europea in Quanto Comunità Di Diritto: Il Ruolo Del Sistema Giurisdizionale' in Maurizio Maresca (ed), *Valori e Principi nella costituzione europea: Il diritto alla mobilità* (Il Mulino 2004); Rafał Mańko, 'The EU as a Community of Law: Overview of the Role of Law in the Union' (2017) PE 599.364 <https://www.europarl.europa.eu/RegData/etudes/BRIE/2017/599364/EPRS_BRI(2017)599364_EN.pdf> accessed 17 December 2024.

[13] Roberto Adam, 'Il Rinvio Pregiudiziale Tra Tutela Dei Diritti Soggettivi e Controllo Delle Inadempienze Statali' (2023) 1 Il Diritto dell'Unione Europea 2.

[14] For examples of uneven enforcement and litigation in the field of environmental law: Tanja A Börzel, 'Participation Through Law Enforcement. The Case of the European Union' (2006) 39 Comparative Political Studies 128; Andreas Hofmann, 'Left to Interest Groups? On the Prospects for Enforcing Environmental Law in the European Union' (2019) 28 Environmental Politics 342.

[15] Catherine Donnelly and Thomas De la Mare, 'Preliminary Rulings and EU Legal Integration: Evolution and Continuity' in Paul Craig and Gráinne de Búrca (eds), *The Evolution of EU Law* (OUP 2021) 228; Adelina Adinolfi, 'I Fondamenti del Diritto Dell'UE Nella Giurisprudenza della Corte di Giustizia: Il Rinvio Pregiudiziale' (2019) I I Post di AISDUE 197, 198.

[16] Morten Broberg and Niels Fenger, 'Variations in Member States' Preliminary References to the Court of Justice—Are Structural Factors (Part of) the Explanation?' (2013) 19 European Law Journal 488; Jacopo Alberti, 'I rinvii pregiudiziali italiani dall'entrata in vigore del trattato di Lisbona al 31.12.2021: uno studio sulla prassi e sulle sue prospettive' [2022] Eurojus 124.

an obligation to refer. The ECJ, in response, will issue a preliminary ruling that indicates to the judge how to interpret EU law or whether the EU norm at stake is invalid.[17]

Over the years, many theories have tried to explain why the courts of some Member States refer more cases to the ECJ than others. Most theories have focused on the role of national judges, examining their legal education, policy preferences, workload, or attitude toward higher courts.[18] While this court-centric perspective might seem natural in the context of the preliminary reference procedure, which is initiated by national judges, it has two shortcomings. First, it assumes that the proportion of cases related specifically to EU law heard by courts in different countries is broadly similar, as if there were not huge variations in the number of EU cases that arrive on the docket of national courts. Second, by focusing only on judges, it overlooks the question of who initiates a case at the national level and why, thus erasing lawyers, litigants, and other aspects of the national legal framework from the picture. This is particularly problematic in the EU context, where the decentralized enforcement of norms depends highly on the initiative of private litigants mobilizing before national courts and asking for their case to be referred to the ECJ.[19]

This book takes a different perspective. It decenters courts and redirects the focus onto those who initiate the action at the national level, the lawyers and civil society actors who support litigation and the sociopolitical environment in which they operate. In a nutshell, the book adopts a legal mobilization approach. The term "legal mobilization", on the one hand, denotes an empirical

[17] Koen Lenaerts, Kathleen Gutman, and Janek Tomasz Nowak, *EU Procedural Law* (OUP 2023) 235.

[18] Jasper Krommendijk, *National Courts and Preliminary References to the Court of Justice* (Edward Elgar Publishing 2021); Monika Glavina, 'Reluctance to Participate in the Preliminary Ruling Procedure as a Challenge to EU Law: A Case Study on Slovenia and Croatia' in Clara Rauchegger and Anna Wallerman (eds), *The Eurosceptic Challenge: National Implementation and Interpretation of EU Law* (Hart Publishing 2019); Karin Leijon and Monika Glavina, 'Why Passive? Exploring National Judges' Motives for Not Requesting Preliminary Rulings' (2022) 29 Maastricht Journal of European and Comparative Law 263; Juan Mayoral, Tobias Nowak, and Urszula Jaremba, 'Creating EU Law Judges: The Role of Generational Differences, Legal Education and Judicial Career Paths in National Judges' Assessment Regarding EU Law Knowledge' (2014) 21 Journal of European Public Policy 1120; Alec Stone Sweet and Thomas L Brunell, 'The European Court and the National Courts: A Statistical Analysis of Preliminary References, 1961–95' (1998) 5 Journal of European Public Policy 66; Maria Cristina Reale and Marco Borraccetti, *Da Giudice a Giudice. Il Dialogo Tra Giudice Italiano e Corte Di Giustizia Delle Comunita' Europee* (Giuffrè Editore 2008); Urszula Jaremba and Juan A Mayoral, 'The Europeanization of National Judiciaries: Definitions, Indicators and Mechanisms' (2019) 26 Journal of European Public Policy 386; Marlene Wind, 'The Nordics, the EU and the Reluctance towards Supranational Judicial Review' (2010) 48 Journal of Common Market Studies 1039; Urszula Jaremba and Marleen Kappé, 'The Unfolding Story of Judicial Dialogue in the EU: The Coercive and Persuasive Motives Behind the Participation of Belgian Highest Courts in the Preliminary Ruling Procedure' [2024] German Law Journal 1; Karin Leijon, 'Active or Passive: The National Judges' Expression of Opinions in the Preliminary Reference Procedure' (2020) 5 European Papers 871.

[19] Daniel Kelemen, *Eurolegalism: The Transformation of Law and Regulation in the European Union* (Harvard University Press 2011).

phenomenon: "any type of process by which individual or collective actors invoke legal norms, discourse, or symbols to influence policy or behavior;[20] on the other hand, legal mobilization also indicates a theoretical approach that studies courts as mainly reactive institutions.[21] As Galanter noted, courts "do not acquire cases of their own motion, but only upon the initiative of one of the disputants."[22] This shift in focus (from the courts to the legal subjects) is the main characteristic of legal mobilization studies, which for this reason are also sometimes referred to as bottom-up studies.[23]

The book uses migration as its central case. This field is broadly understood as comprising all the norms that are directed at regulating the status of third-country national (TCN) migrants in the EU: asylum seekers, refugees, migrant workers, family members of EU citizens, etc. For the sake of brevity, I refer to them generally as "migrants" or "TCN migrants" and to the field as "migration law" or "migration and asylum law." Through the analytical lenses of legal mobilization theory, the book asks: Are preliminary references in the migration field a result of legal mobilization efforts? Under what circumstances is EU litigation used for political reasons? What are the enablers of and constraints against the use of EU litigation for migrants?

The legal mobilization perspective uncovers the role that civil society actors play in the emergence of preliminary references to the ECJ by showing that these actors can persuade judges to refer and can create circumstances that are conducive to a reference. However, the book also reveals the precarious nature of such legal mobilization. In most cases, EU legal mobilization is not supported by large international non-governmental organizations (NGOs) but rather it depends on the initiative of small local associations, Eurolawyers, academics, and legal aid firms, most of which lack financial resources but capitalize on their EU legal expertise. The book thus shows that, contrary to the first stage of European legal integration,[24] today EU legal mobilization does not always need to be supported by legal elites, European entrepreneurs, or

[20] Lisa Vanhala, 'Legal Mobilization' <http://www.oxfordbibliographies.com/abstract/document/obo-9780199756223/obo-9780199756223-0031.xml> accessed 17 December 2024; Michael McCann, 'Law and Social Movements: Contemporary Perspectives' (2006) 2 Annual Review of Law and Social Science 17; Lisa Conant and others, 'Mobilizing European Law' (2017) 25 Journal of European Public Policy 1.

[21] Zemans (n 11) 691.

[22] Marc Galanter, 'The Radiating Effects of Courts' in Keith O Boyum and Lynn Mather (eds), *Empirical Theories about Courts* (Longman Inc 1983) 122.

[23] Michael McCann, "Litigation and Legal Mobilization" in Caldeira, Kelemen, and Whittington (eds), *The Oxford Handbook of Law and Politics* (OUP 2008) 524.

[24] Antoine Vauchez, *Brokering Europe: Euro-Lawyers and the Making of a Transnational Polity* (CUP 2015).

"deep pocketed clients."[25] EU legal mobilization can emerge with a low budget but skilled actors.

The book relies on the analysis of an original database of 505 preliminary references which I assembled by selecting and coding all the migration and asylum cases that were referred to the ECJ from 1981, the year of the first preliminary reference on the rights of a TCN migrant, until December 2022.[26] The database allowed me to identify litigation patterns, the countries that generate most of the references, and the most litigated topics. Moreover, the database provides another crucial insight: it allows us to identify the EU countries the courts of which have never given origin to preliminary references in the migration field (Figure 1.1).

The first part of the book focuses on positive cases, the countries in which legal mobilization through preliminary references took place. Using the database, I selected Italy, the Netherlands, and the United Kingdom (UK) as the most likely countries to present instances of legal mobilization because they not only present a considerable amount of litigation but their references were also substantially characterized by their focus on specific EU legal provisions (more on this in Section 6). Then, I traced the presence of legal mobilization via preliminary references, identifying the actors involved, the goals pursued, and the conditions that made EU litigation emerge. Each chapter tells a story of contestation and/or resistance through EU law, narrating how civil society actors became aware of the potential of EU law to challenge and set aside restrictive national migration policies. The political goal of the mobilization varied across the three countries: in Italy, associations of lawyers and judges mobilized against the criminalization of undocumented migrants; in the UK, NGOs and Eurolawyers mobilized against the deportation of family members of Union citizens; and in the Netherlands, NGOs and academics mobilized against the assimilationist policy of the government. Interestingly, each of the three countries presented very different judicial settings, legal frameworks, and actors involved. Nevertheless, it was possible to discern common patterns that I identified as enablers of legal mobilization via preliminary reference.

[25] Tommaso Pavone, *The Ghostwriters: Lawyers and the Politics behind the Judicial Construction of Europe* (CUP 2022) 212.

[26] I consider the first preliminary reference on migrant rights the case of Case C-53/81 *Levin* (1982) CJEU, ECLI:EU:C:1982:105. At that time, the European Economic Community still did not have the competence to adopt migration law, but third-country national migrants were subjects of EU law in case they were family members of mobile workers. In this case, the litigation focused on whether a UK national qualified as a "worker" under EEC law to exercise her free movement rights in the Netherlands and resist the deportation of her South African husband.

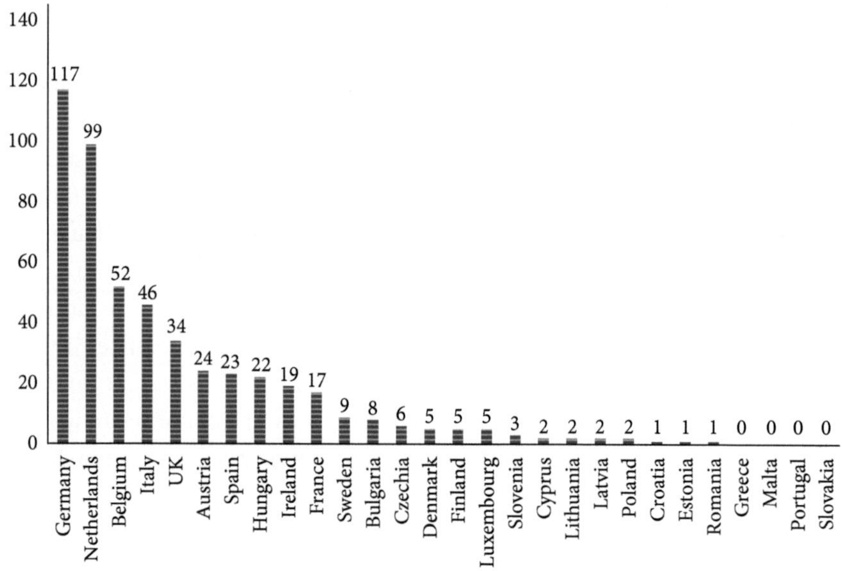

Figure 1.1 Preliminary references in the migration field per referring country from 1981 until December 2022.

Source: author's original database based on Curia and NEMIS, NEAIS, and NEFIS newsletters. These newsletters contain up-to-date lists of migration, asylum, and free movement cases before the Court of Justice. They are published regularly on the website of the Migration Law Center of Radboud University: <https://www.ru.nl/en/center-for-migration-law/research/background-documentation> accessed 17 December 2024.

These enablers were at the actor level (type of actors and resources) and at the structural level (applicable norms and judicial receptivity).

The fifth chapter of the book studies a country where EU litigation for migrant rights was absent. Among the zero-reference countries, I have selected Greece as a crucial case. Since 2008, the country has been crossed by large migration flows and has thus attracted a significant presence of NGOs and migrant rights defenders. However, quite surprisingly, Greek courts did not make a single preliminary reference in the migration and asylum fields until February 2023. The Greek case is crucial to test the findings of the positive cases; in particular, it allows us to understand whether the lack of EU litigation was due to the absence of one of the enabling factors identified in the Italian, British, and Dutch case studies. The investigation confirmed the findings of the previous chapters but also added further nuances: Greece presents a major access-to-court problem, which led me to change and enrich my definition of the EU "legal opportunity structure" (more on this shortly). Moreover, the Greek case confirms the importance of awareness of EU rights and litigation opportunities, which was lacking in Greece at the time. Finally, it shows the importance of civil society actors' perceptions: among Greek migrant rights defenders, the European Court of Human Rights was the natural court before which to seek justice for migrant rights violations. On the contrary, the road to the ECJ was perceived as less important or foreclosed.

By looking at the positive and negative cases of legal mobilization via the preliminary reference mechanism to the ECJ, I was able to identify three main factors that facilitated the emergence of legal mobilization via preliminary references:

1) the presence of altruistic actors who, despite not being migrants, mobilized on their behalf;[27]
2) the availability of crucial intellectual resources such as EU legal expertise;
3) the presence of an open "EU legal opportunity structure." This is a concept derived from the legal mobilization literature that indicates the structural factors pertaining to a legal system that hamper or enable legal mobilization.[28] I have adapted this concept to the EU context to suggest that a national system is open to EU litigation when EU law provides a comparative advantage vis-à-vis national law, and litigants have access to national courts who are willing and able to refer.

The positive cases confirm that civil society actors are not helpless in the face of the legal opportunity structure, but they can create and shape opportunities for action.[29] In the specific EU litigation case, they can set up conferences and training for judges to make them aware of the incompatibilities between EU and national law and make them more prone to refer. However, the Greek case study also reveals important limits: in a context in which activists and migrant rights defenders have limited EU litigation expertise, and in which access to courts is impaired, it is very difficult to generate legal mobilization before the ECJ.

[27] Paul Statham, 'Political Opportunities for Altruism? The Role of State Policies in Influencing Claims-Making by British Antiracist and Pro-Migrant Movements' in Marco Giugni and Florence Passy, *Political Altruism? Solidarity Movements in International Perspective* (Rowman & Littlefield 2001).

[28] Chris Hilson, 'New Social Movements: The Role of Legal Opportunity' (2002) 9 Journal of European Public Policy 238; Gianluca De Fazio, 'Legal Opportunity Structure and Social Movement Strategy in Northern Ireland and Southern United States' (2012) 53 International Journal of Comparative Sociology.

[29] Lisa Vanhala, 'Is Legal Mobilization for the Birds? Legal Opportunity Structures and Environmental Nongovernmental Organizations in the United Kingdom, France, Finland, and Italy' (2018) 51 Comparative Political Studies 380.

This book, combining original empirical research with doctrinal research, locates the significance of EU law for the national legal and judicial frameworks and reveals that for EU legal mobilization to emerge, several conditions must align. These are both structural and subjective, as well as deeply embedded in the local judicial and sociopolitical landscape.

3. Migration as a central case for EU legal mobilization

EU legal mobilization in the migration field has seldom been an object of study; in comparison other fields such as anti-discrimination and environmental law have attracted more attention.[30] But as Sterett argued, migration is a central case for the study of EU legal mobilization and juridification because on the one hand, courts play a pivotal role in protecting the rights of non-citizens, and on the other hand, the activation of legal protection is highly dependent on organizations protecting migrant rights.[31]

When in the 1990s the EU was endowed with new competences in the migration and asylum fields,[32] many scholars looked at this development with

[30] Some examples: Catherine Hoskyns, *Integrating Gender: Women, Law and Politics in the European Union* (Verso 1996); Claire Kilpatrick, 'Effective Utilisation of Equality Rights: Equal Pay for Work of Equal Value in France and the UK' in Frances Gardiner (ed), *Sex Equality Policy in Western Europe* (Routledge 1997); Hilson (n 28); Rachel A Cichowski, *The European Court and Civil Society: Litigation, Mobilization and Governance* (CUP 2007); Terri Givens and Rhonda Evans Case, *Legislating Equality: The Politics of Antidiscrimination Policy in Europe* (OUP 2014); Lilla Farkas, *Mobilising for Racial Equality in Europe: Roma Rights and Transnational Justice* (EUI Law PhD Thesis 2020); Jeffrey Miller, *The European Disability Rights Revolution* (EUI Law PhD Thesis 2020); Vanhala, 'Is Legal Mobilization for the Birds?' (n 29); Hofmann (n 14); Mario Pagano, 'Overcoming Plaumann in EU Environmental Litigation: An Analysis of NGOs Legal Arguments in Actions for Annulment' [2019] Diritto e processo 311; Stefan Thierse and Sanja Badanjak, *Opposition in the EU Multi-Level Polity: Legal Mobilization against the Data Retention Directive* (Palgrave Pivot 2021).

[31] Susan Sterett, 'Legal Mobilization and Juridification: Migration as a Central Case' (2016) 38 Law & Policy 273, 273.

[32] Initially, some cooperation in the field of visa, border checks, asylum, and immigration was foreseen by the Maastricht Treaty (Treaty on European Union, signed on 29 July 1992, OJ C 191) in the Area of Justice and Home Affairs, but this was characterized by intergovernmental method and led to the adoptions of few bindings measures. The competence was more significantly conferred on the Union by the Treaty of Amsterdam, within the newly established Area of Freedom, Security and Justice (Treaty of Amsterdam amending the Treaty on European Union, the Treaties establishing the European Communities and certain related Acts, signed on 10 November 1997, OJ C 340). Notably, some laws of the then European Economic Community were already deeply impactful on the rights of certain categories of migrants, such as the norms on mobile workers, which concerned their TCN family members, or association agreements with third countries such as Turkey. Stefano Amadeo and others, *Il diritto dell'immigrazione e dell'asilo dell'Unione europea* (Giappichelli Editore 2022); Evangelia Tsourdi and Philippe De Bruycker, 'The Evolving EU Asylum and Migration Law' in Evangelia Tsourdi and Philippe De Bruyckere (eds), *EU migration and Asylum Law* (Edward Elgar 2022) 1; Daniel Thym, 'Institutional and Constitutional Framework' in ibid 58; Chiara Favilli, 'Le Politiche Di Immigrazione e Asilo: Passato, Presente e Futuro Di Una Sovranità Europea Incompiuta' (2022) Annali AISDUE, Sezione "Atti convegni AISDUE" 100; Damian Chalmers, Gareth Davies, and Giorgio Monti, *European*

skepticism. Guiraudon argued that this was part of the European governments' strategy to conduct "venue shopping": Member States shifted migration policies to the EU level to avoid national constraints that were affecting their capacity to control migration.[33] At the national level, Member State governments had to face judicial scrutiny by high courts and political opposition by pro-migrant NGOs and national parliaments; these represented important obstacles to the executive's discretion and to the possibility of implementing restrictive migration policies.[34] At the EU level, governments could instead organize asylum and migration law-making with more margin for manoeuvre, at least at the beginning when it was decided under the intergovernmental method: the Council voted according to the unanimity rule, the European Parliament had a limited role, and the ECJ had only partial jurisdiction.[35] Obviously, after having escaped national constraints, governments did not want to be subjected to the European ones and were trying to "maintain national discretion at all costs."[36] Givens and Luedtke agreed to this view of the EU-level being less favorable to the migrant cause: they noted that contrary to other fields of EU policy-making, in the migration field "TCNs and their

Union Law: Text and Materials (3rd edn, CUP 2014) 519; Bruno Nascimbene, 'Lo Spazio Di Libertà, Sicurezza e Giustizia a Due Anni Dall'entrata in Vigore Del Trattato Di Lisbona' (2011) 4 Diritto, Immigrazione e Cittadinanza 13, 14. According to Elspeth Guild, the period before the Amsterdam Treaty was characterized by intergovernmental cooperation on migration and asylum policies which led to many 'resolutions, recommendations and conclusions the legal effect of which was deeply unclear'. Elspeth Guild, 'Competence, Discretion and Third Country Nationals: The European Union's Legal Struggle with Migration' (1998) 24 Journal of Ethnic and Migration Studies 613, 624. The Dublin Convention, which is the first milestone of what became the EU asylum system, also entered into force in 1997. 'Dublin Convention, Convention determining the State responsible for examining applications for asylum lodged in one of the Member States of the European Communities' OJ C 254, 19 August 1997.

[33] Virginie Guiraudon, 'European Integration and Migration Policy: Vertical Policy-Making as Venue Shopping' (2000) 38 Journal of Common Market Studies 251.

[34] ibid; on the important role of constitution and the judiciary in constraining migration control, see Christian Joppke, *Immigration and the Nation-State: The United States, Germany, and Great Britain* (OUP 1999); James Hollifield, Philip L Martin, and Pia Orrenius, *Controlling Immigration: A Global Perspective, Third Edition* (Stanford University Press 2014).

[35] The Maastricht Treaty of 1992 had explicitly excluded Justice and Home Affairs from the jurisdiction of the European Court of Justice. This exclusion was partially confirmed in the Treaty of Amsterdam which gave the ECJ the power to rule on preliminary references coming only from last-instance courts, neglecting to lower courts the possibility to submit a preliminary question on immigration and asylum issues. Thym (n 32) 59; Vassilis Hatzopoulos, 'Casual but Smart: The Court's New Clothes in the Area of Freedom, Security and Justice (AFSJ) after the Lisbon Treaty' in Jörg Monar (ed), *The Institutional Dimension of the European Union's Area of Freedom, Security and Justice* (Peter Lang 2010); Antonietta Damato, 'L'incidenza Sul Terzo Pilastro Di Principi e Regole Di Diritto Comunitario' in A Cannone and others (eds), *Studi in onore di Vincenzo Starace* (Editoriale Scientifica 2008) 1009; Mark A Pollack, *The Engines of European Integration: Delegation, Agency, and Agenda Setting in the EU* (OUP 2003) 182.

[36] Guild (n 32) 623.

political allies have been denied the ability to make rights claims in most areas of immigration policy."[37]

Things have changed consistently since these first accounts. In the last fifteen years, migration cases before the Court of Justice have increased exponentially (Figure 1.2) and many of them represented challenges to Member States' migration policies, transforming the Court into a new, serious judicial constraint on governments' discretion. This happened in part because of institutional reforms. As mentioned, while initially the ECJ was given only limited jurisdiction over migration and asylum (and the whole Area of Freedom Security and Justice), the Lisbon Treaty expanded the Court's jurisdiction, enabling national courts from any Member States and of any degree to send references to Luxemburg. Pro-migrant actors in some Member States started uncovering the opportunities offered by EU migration legislation and leveraging resources to use the preliminary reference procedure as an instrument to challenge the legitimacy of national restrictive policies. This was not a quick process but rather a slowly growing awareness among pro-migrant actors of the opportunities offered by EU law and the preliminary reference procedure, that arose thanks to attempts by some pioneers in selected Member States.

To make a prominent example, the United Nation High Commissioner for Refugees (UNHCR, the world leader international organization for asylum and refugee rights), since the case of *Elgafaji* in 2008,[38] regularly publishes on its website "informal amicus curiae," or online interventions that they write hoping to influence the Court's adjudication. According to UNHCR's internal reports, their interventions yielded positive or partially positive results in 93 percent of cases, which suggests that the organization holds the ECJ in high consideration and looks at its decisions favorably.[39] Clearly, positive ECJ rulings do not automatically yield a positive impact in practice, and sometimes they can even lead to backlash, which pushes civil society to be very cautious about the use of litigation for migrant and refugee rights.[40]

[37] Terri Givens and Adam Luedtke, 'EU Immigration Policy: From Intergovernmentalism to Reluctant Harmonization' in Tanja A Börzel and Rachel A Cichowski (eds), *The State of the European Union, 6: Law, Politics, and Society* (OUP 2003) 292.

[38] Case C-465/07 *Meki Elgafaji and Noor Elgafaji v Staatssecretaris van Justitie* (17 February 2009) CJEU, ECLI:EU:C:2009:94.

[39] Interview with UNHCR lawyer, 24 February 2023.

[40] Moritz Baumgärtel, *Demanding Rights. Europe's Supranational Courts and the Dilemma of Migrant Vulnerability* (CUP 2019); Helen Duffy, *Strategic Human Rights Litigation: Understanding and Maximising Impact* (Hart Publishing 2018).

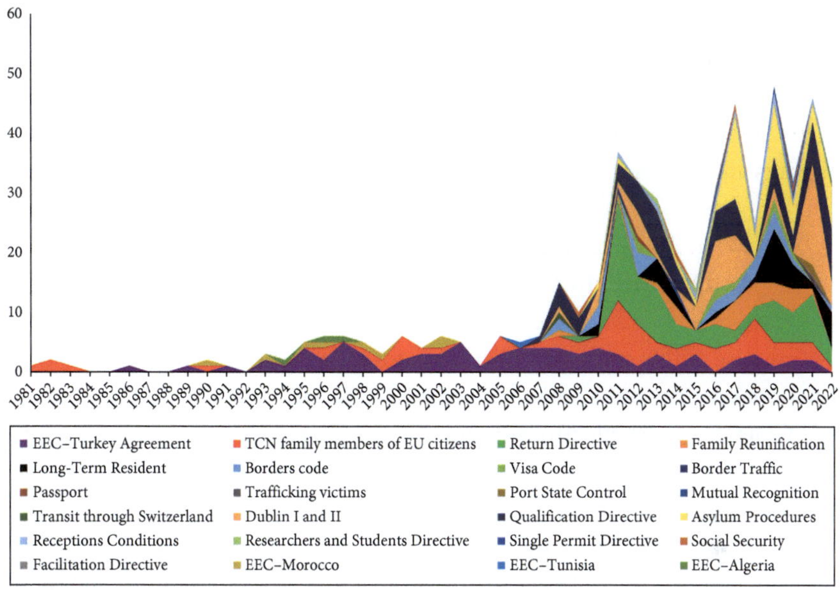

Figure 1.2 Migration references across time and legislation.
Source: author's original database.

If taken together, Figure 1.1 and Figure 1.2 give a two-sided picture of the phenomenon of EU litigation for migrant rights. On the one hand, they show that it is a relatively new and growing phenomenon; on the other, they show that it is extremely uneven, with some countries being at the forefront and others lagging behind in their reference rates. This suggests that EU-level institutional reforms, such as the expansion of the ECJ's jurisdiction to the migration and asylum field, do not fully account for the rise in EU migration litigation, as they would lead to an even increase in litigation across Member States. Instead, such "variable geography" of (migration) preliminary references can be explained by the local embeddedness of EU enforcement practices and the site-specific development of EU legal consciousness.[41] Along these lines, the book argues that in order to understand the uneven mobilization of EU law, we need to consider local sociolegal factors behind the rise of EU litigation for migrant rights by situating the preliminary references within the national social and legal context in which they emerge and that gives them

[41] Tommaso Pavone, 'Putting European Constitutionalism in Its Place: The Spatial Foundations of the Judicial Construction of Europe' (2020) 16 European Constitutional Law Review 669, 676.

a particular political meaning. Moreover, such contextual analysis allows us to uncover the local actors behind the domestic enforcement of EU law, namely the actors that in some Member States have been able to perceive and capitalize on EU litigation to contest and resist negative changes into the legal status of migrants and refugees.

4. Decentering and contextualizing EU law judges

The premise of this study on litigation before the ECJ is that we ought to look at national courts, but also go beyond them. Scholars have widely celebrated the ECJ as "the most effective supranational judicial body in the history of the world"[42] and the "hero" of European integration.[43] Being the Court widely studied, its cross-country variation in reference rates attracted much attention. For instance, Wind argues that the low number of references from Nordic countries can be explained by their lack of a judicial review culture and their propensity for majoritarian democracy;[44] Golub instead focused on domestic political factors, arguing (long before the Brexit referendum) that UK courts are less prone to refer because of the 'Euro-pessimism' that dominates British public debates;[45] more recently, studies relying on surveys and interviews with national judges argued that educational and organizational factors might have an impact on whether national judges are willing to refer or not.[46] To be sure, so far, it seems that "[g]rand theories are unlikely to explain the intricacies of different national patterns of mobilization of [EU] law" as no single factor exhaustively explains the variation in judges' reference rates.[47] Rather, these studies suggest that there is a variety of interacting factors, partly structural (national legal culture, judicial organization) and partly subjective (policy preferences, education) which influence judges' behavior.

All these studies have one thing in common: their focus on the ECJ and on national courts. Judges, however, cannot choose the cases they hear; thus, more recently, a new awareness started to emerge. A growing body of EU scholarship

[42] Alec Stone Sweet, *The Judicial Construction of Europe* (OUP 2004) 1.

[43] Anne-Marie Burley and Walter Mattli, 'Europe Before the Court: A Political Theory of Legal Integration' (1993) 47 International Organization 41, 41.

[44] M Wind, 'The Nordics, the EU and the Reluctance towards Supranational Judicial Review' 48 Journal of Common Market Studies (2010) 1039–63.

[45] Jonathan Golub, 'The Politics of Judicial Discretion: Rethinking the Interaction between National Courts and the European Court of Justice' (1996) 19 West European Politics 360, 377.

[46] Mayoral, Nowak, and Jaremba (n 18); Glavina (n 18) 197; Jasper Krommendijk, 'It Takes Two to Tango: An Introduction' (2020) 5 European Papers 745.

[47] Schepel and Bankenburg (n 11) 36.

shows some dissatisfaction with the mainstream way of depicting litigation before the ECJ. Authors increasingly challenge the classical approach that pictures the ECJ as an activist and isolated body, as if it were "always already there, out of history, independent from the sociopolitical contexts in which it successively operated."[48] These scholars started pointing out the existence of other actors and factors playing a pivotal role in the judicial law-making of the ECJ.[49]

Vauchez's study on Eurolawyers was pioneer in revealing the important role played by legal practitioners, academics, and legal counsels who have prepared the European legal revolution from behind the scenes.[50] His study sparked two new trends in EU studies. The first can be defined as the historical turn: relying on archival research, scholars are discovering new actors and factors that have been crucial for the development of EU integration.[51] The second trend is that of sociolegal and political science studies, which unveils how some of the ECJ landmark rulings were the outcome of the strategic action of Eurolawyers and collective actors that wanted to use EU law to promote or contest a certain policy.[52] Together, these two trends are revisiting the neo-functional account of EU integration and are looking at the history of "integration through law" through different lenses.

The literature offers some eminent examples of how legal mobilization has shaped the EU legal order. Gian Galeazzo Stendardi engineered the *Costa v ENEL* case, prompting the ECJ to expressly affirm the primacy of EU law in domestic legal orders.[53] Éliane Vogel-Polsky, a lawyer and academic, tested her feminist convictions in the *Defrenne* saga, where the Treaty provision on equal pay was invoked for the first time to advance women's rights and strike down national discriminatory legislation.[54] These works shed light on the actors, the legal strategies, and the personal and political incentives driving the legal revolution that transformed Europe into what we know today. However, the

[48] Antonin Cohen and Antoine Vauchez, 'The Social Construction of Law: The European Court of Justice and Its Legal Revolution Revisited' (2011) 7 The Annual Review of Law and Social Science 417, 418.

[49] Antoine Vauchez and Bruno de Witte (eds), *Lawyering Europe: European Law as a Transnational Social Field* (Hart Publishing 2013); Conant and others (n 20); Mikael Rask Madsen, Fernanda Nicola, and Antoine Vauchez (eds), *Researching the European Court of Justice: Methodological Shifts and Law's Embeddedness* (CUP 2022).

[50] Vauchez (n 24).

[51] Fernanda Nicola and Bill Davies, *EU Law Stories* (CUP 2017); Pavone, *The Ghostwriters* (n 25).

[52] Cichowski, *The European Court and Civil Society* (n 30); Thierse and Badanjak (n 30); Madsen, Nicola, and Vauchez (n 49); Pavone, *The Ghostwriters* (n 25).

[53] Amedeo Arena, 'From an Unpaid Electricity Bill to the Primacy of EU Law: Gian Galeazzo Stendardi and the Making of Costa v. ENEL' (2019) 30 European Journal of International Law 1017.

[54] Rachel A Cichowski, 'Women's Rights, the European Court, and Supranational Constitutionalism' (2004) 38 Law & Society Review 489; Hoskyns (n 30) 60.

reasons why Eurolawyers and civil society actors decide to mobilize before the Court of Justice and why they succeed or fail are still largely to be explored.

To understand the political use of the preliminary reference mechanism and its potential as a participatory tool, a classical doctrinal legal approach that focuses mainly on the text of the judgments would not be enough. For this reason, the book combines legal research with a more contextual and bottom-up analysis, redirecting the focus on the litigants and the national context, using what is known as the legal mobilization approach, according to which in order to understand the logic and dynamics of litigation, we need to look at who invokes the law and why, studying the social and political context around it.[55]

The legal mobilization approach was first developed by scholars in the United States interested in studying law and litigation as tools for political participation. One of the most cited definitions of legal mobilization was set forth by Zemans in 1983: the law is mobilized "when a desire or want is translated into a demand as an assertion of one's rights."[56] If read out of context, this definition may sound rather vague but Zemans' article laid down the basis for a new understanding of litigation as an intrinsically political activity that offers the individual a means to participate in policy-making. Litigation, even when conducted between private parties in pursuit of personal interests, consists of the action of invoking states' powers and participating in law enforcement.[57] With her article, Zemans challenged the mainstream understanding of the role of law and courts in society and started a new reflection on litigation as a tool for democratic participation.

Race discrimination offers an example of how litigation for the private interest can be a form of political participation; this is indeed the field where litigation was most famously used as a tool for social change.[58] When an individual brings a lawsuit against a private company because, say, it refuses to hire Black people, the lawsuit is privately motivated (the individual wants to be hired) but has a clear political impact (having a labor market free from race

[55] McCann, 'Litigation and Legal Mobilization' (n 23).

[56] Zemans (n 11) 700.

[57] 'The legal system . . . provides a uniquely democratic (as opposed to republican) mechanism for individual citizens to invoke public authority on their own and for their benefit. The bulk of this activity takes place among private citizens who, in the process of involving legal norms, employ the power of the state and so become state actors themselves.' Zemans (n 11) 692.

[58] I am referring here to the US Supreme Court's case of *Brown v Board of Education*, 347 US 483 (1954) and the related legal and political struggle to end the policy of "separated but equals" that justified race segregation in US public schools. Even if the decision's impact and the role of lawyers in the movement are contested, the case remains the symbol of litigation for political change and minorities' rights. Gerald N Rosenberg, *The Hollow Hope: Can Courts Bring about Social Change?* (University of Chicago 1991); Risa L Goluboff, *The Lost Promise of Civil Rights* (Harvard University Press 2010); Scott L Cummings, *Lawyers and Movements: Legal Mobilization in Transformative Times* (OUP 2025).

discrimination). Thus, by invoking anti-discrimination provisions in court, the litigant is participating in law enforcement and in the advancement of equality.

The concept of legal mobilization does not have a univocal definition in the literature, and scholars have long adopted different definitions.[59] In its narrowest sense, legal mobilization indicates high-profile legal action initiated with the purpose of achieving social change, much akin to strategic litigation.[60] In its broader sense, it includes any use of the law, like lobbying or rights advocacy, regardless of whether a legal action is initiated.[61] Also Zemans' legal mobilization definition lends itself to the criticism of being too vague as it can be used to describe any type of litigation, even one conducted to pursue exclusively one's personal interest. While the malleability of her definition is certainly intentional, such a broad concept risks losing analytical value and thus falling into "conceptual stretching," becoming too extensive and amorphous.[62]

For all these reasons, for my empirical analysis I decided to adopt a narrower definition of legal mobilization which draws from the political science literature on social movements and the "group-based legal mobilization."[63] In this book, the term "legal mobilization," if referred to as an empirical phenomenon, will indicate any instance in which litigation is used by collective actors to achieve a political goal. I thus look at legal mobilization before courts and not just at any use of the law. A court proceeding can be considered as a case of legal mobilization if it presents two main features: first, litigation must have a purpose beyond the mere interest of the parties, that is, to achieve a legal reform or political change; and second, litigation must have a collective character. By collective, I do not mean that the litigation must feature a class action or a collective lawsuit; for the litigation to have a collective character, it suffices that it is promoted, sponsored, or supported by a plurality of actors different from the private party in the case. Importantly, such actors do not need

[59] Emilio Lehoucq and Whitney K Taylor, 'Conceptualizing Legal Mobilization: How Should We Understand the Deployment of Legal Strategies?' (2020) 45 Law & Social Inquiry 166, 166; Vanhala, 'Legal Mobilization' (n 20).

[60] For a definition of strategic litigation: Kris Van der Pas, *The 'Strategy' in Strategic Litigation: The Why and How of Strategic Litigation by Civil Society Organizations in the Field of Asylum Law in Europe* (Europa Law Publishing 2024) 28.

[61] Vanhala, 'Legal Mobilization' (n 20).

[62] Giovanni Sartori, 'Concept Misformation in Comparative Politics' (1970) 64 The American Political Science Review 1034. Arguably, Zemans' main contribution is indeed not in the definition of legal mobilization as an empirical phenomenon (although she is mainly quoted for that) but in the elaboration of a new method and perspective to look at courts and law. She advanced what McCann called a "user perspective" on litigation, which inaugurated a new strand of bottom-up studies. McCann, 'Litigation and Legal Mobilization' (n 23) 524.

[63] Vanhala, 'Legal Mobilization' (n 20); McCann, 'Litigation and Legal Mobilization' (n 23) 533.

to be a party in the case as they can support the case from behind the scenes. Moreover, collective actors can be either organized groups or individuals, as long as they are a plurality and they are motivated by collective interest (not their private interest).

The presence of collective actors, as understood here, can be difficult to detect because it may not result from the documents of the case.[64] This is probably one of the reasons why most scholars have disregarded or downplayed the role of collective actors in the preliminary reference procedure. By resorting to in-depth case studies and interviews, I could detect the presence of collective actors in cases where it was not immediately evident from the documents of the case. The next two sections will expand on these methodological issues, explaining how the unique legal framework of the preliminary reference procedure impacts on opportunities for legal mobilization.

5. Preliminary references as a place for contestation and resistance: Legal opportunity structure and resources

The ECJ has a rather poor reputation in the field of legal mobilization and public interest litigation. Scholars have denounced its "general lack of openness" toward civil society[65] and defined it as "hostile to collective action."[66] This criticism largely originates from the fact that the Court is difficult to access for individuals, also thanks to the ECJ's restrictive interpretation of its legal standing rules, and particularly of the Treaty provisions on direct actions that created "a formidable barrier of standing for private parties."[67] Moreover, individuals cannot bring a Member State before the Court of Justice for EU law violations as this possibility is reserved to the Commission and the other Member States.[68] As if this was not enough, the ECJ does not admit *amicus curiae* briefs

[64] See eg the preliminary references analysed in the Italian case study (Chapter 2): from the official documents of the case, we would say that these proceedings do not feature the participation of any group or NGO. However, thanks to the interviews and in-depth contextual research, I could trace the presence and important role of groups and associations.

[65] Effie Fokas, 'Comparative Susceptibility and Differential Effects on the Two European Courts: A Study of Grasstops Mobilizations around Religion' (2016) 5 Oxford Journal of Law and Religion 541, 553.

[66] Carol Harlow and Richard Rawlings, *Pressure Through Law* (Taylor and Francis 1992) 525.

[67] Albertina Albors-Llorens, 'Remedies against the EU Institutions after Lisbon: An Era of Opportunity?' (2012) 71 The Cambridge Law Journal 507, 513; Hjalte Rasmussen, 'Why Is Article 173 Interpreted against Private Plaintiffs?' (1980) 5 European Law Review 112. This is an obstacle especially for environmental organizations that tried to challenge the ECJ's *Plaumann* doctrine: Pagano (n 30).

[68] Art 258 ss TFEU; Koen Lenaerts, Ignace Maselis, and Kathleen Gutman, *EU Procedural Law* (OUP 2014) 145.

and has strict rules for third-party interventions: private parties can intervene only in "contentious proceedings," meaning that preliminary references are excluded.[69] Plus, third party interventions are not admitted in direct actions between the Member States, the Union institutions, and between Member States and Union institutions;[70] in the remaining cases, a private intervener needs to prove that it "has a direct and certain interest in the outcome of the proceedings," as a general interest is not sufficient.[71]

All this considered, the ECJ is not the most obvious venue to pursue litigation for social change. Other European courts, such as the European Court of Human Rights, may seem more friendly or open to civil society actors.[72] And yet despite this apparently hostile legal framework, the preliminary reference procedure has enormous potential for legal mobilization. This mechanism, even if originally conceived as an instrument for the uniform interpretation of EU law, thanks to the judicial doctrines of supremacy and direct effect, soon started to be used by domestic courts to review whether national law is compatible with EU law.[73] National courts, often prompted by the litigants in the case, rather than asking pure questions of interpretation, ask the ECJ to rule on whether a certain national law or practice is in line with EU law. This is why scholars have described Article 267 as an instrument for the "decentralized enforcement of EU law,"[74] the "citizens' infringement procedure,"[75] and a crucial

[69] The ECJ has long ruled that third-party interventions are not admitted in preliminary reference procedures unless they were already a party in the national case. Order of the President, 3 June 1964, *Costa v Enel*, Case 6/64, ECLI:EU:C:1964:34. Lenaerts, Gutman, and Nowak (n 17) 175; Ilaria Anrò, 'L'amicus Curiae Presso La Corte Di Giustizia Dell'Unione Europea: Qualche Riflessione per l'apertura Delle Porte Del Kirchberg' (2023) 1 Rivista del Contenzioso Europeo 62; Jasper Krommendijk and Kris van der Pas, 'To Intervene or Not to Intervene: Intervention before the Court of Justice of the European Union in Environmental and Migration Law' (2022) 26 The International Journal of Human Rights 1394; Massimo Condinanzi, 'La partecipazione al pregiudiziale: tertium non datur' (2023) 1 Rivista del Contenzioso Europeo 1.

[70] Art 40 of the Statute of the Court of Justice of the European Union.

[71] Order of the President of The Court, Case C-26/23 P *Minority SafePack—one million signatures for diversity in Europe v Commission* (27 July 2023) CJEU, ECLI:EU:C:2023:616.

[72] This is mainly because individuals can directly file applications to the ECtHR for human rights violations committed by the Member States. The ECtHR has also more generous rules on third-party interventions, which civil society actors widely use: Nicole Bürli, *Third-Party Interventions before the European Court of Human Rights: Amicus Curiae, Member-State and Third-Party Interventions* (Intersentia 2017); Laura Van den Eynde, 'An Empirical Look at the Amicus Curiae Practice of Human Rights NGOs Before the European Court of Human Rights' (2013) 31 Netherlands Quarterly of Human Rights 271.

[73] Joseph HH Weiler, 'A Quiet Revolution. The European Court of Justice and Its Interlocutors' (1994) 26 Comparative Political Studies 510, 514; Karen Alter, 'Who Are the "Masters of the Treaty"? European Governments and the European Court of Justice' (1998) 52 International Organization 121; Bruno De Witte, 'The Impact of Van Gend En Loos on Judicial Protection at European and National Level: Three Types of Preliminary Questions' in Antonio Tizzano and Sacha Prechal (eds), *50th Anniversary of the Judgment in Van Gend en Loos, 1963–2013* (Office des Publications de l'Union Européenne 2013).

[74] Pollack (n 35) 123.

[75] De Witte (n 73) 95.

instrument for the protection of individual rights vis-à-vis Member States' violations.[76] As this book will show, the procedure, if initially conceived as a tool for interpretation, is today a crucial means for enforcing EU law, contesting illegal Member States' policies, and resisting national legal reforms.

The described EU legal and procedural framework importantly affect the capacity of actors to rely on the ECJ and mobilize EU justice. For instance, the fact that the preliminary reference procedure was conceived as a tool for judicial cooperation and for dialogue between judges importantly limits parties' ability to obtain a reference: the decision to refer is one for the national court alone, "whether or not the parties to the main proceedings have expressed the wish that it do so."[77] This means that parties do not have an individual right to have their case referred to the ECJ and while courts of last instance, if faced with a doubt regarding the interpretation of EU law, have an obligation to refer, lower courts have a broader margin of discretion and can avoid making a reference, potentially disappointing parties' expectations. But the preliminary reference procedure also presents some important advantages. First of all, given that the ECJ's authoritative interpretation is binding on all the Member States, its rulings display legal effects in the whole EU and have enormous importance for directing the implementation of EU law. Moreover, compared to the European Court of Human Rights (ECtHR) that can take ten years to issue a judgment, the ECJ normally makes its decisions in about eighteen months.

To analyze these legal and procedural factors and understand how they impact on actors' capacity to mobilize the law, the literature offers the concept of legal opportunity structure (LOS).[78] The latter is the legal equivalent of the political opportunity structure concept, which is based on the idea that the political environment, by providing incentives or disincentives to act, affects groups' expectations for the success of a collective action.[79] Since we still lack an agreed-upon definition of LOS, scholars have used it to indicate anything that affects opportunities for mobilization.[80] However, I argue that, for the

[76] Adam (n 13) 8; Morten Broberg, 'Preliminary References as a Means for Enforcing EU Law' in András Jakab and Dimitry Kochenov (eds), *The Enforcement of EU Law and Values: Ensuring Member States' Compliance* (OUP 2017).

[77] Court of Justice of the European Union, 'Recommendations to national courts and tribunals in relation to the initiation of preliminary ruling proceedings' (2019/C 380/01 of 8 November 2019) para 10. Recent case law of the ECtHR suggests that while national courts have the power, and a certain discretion, to refuse to submit a reference upon a party's request, they must motivate their decision. ECtHR *Dhahbi v Italy*, no 17120/09, judgment of 8 April 2014, para 31.

[78] Hilson (n 28) 243; Ellen Ann Andersen, *Out of the Closets and into the Courts: Legal Opportunity Structure and Gay Rights Litigation* (University of Michigan Press 2006) 12; De Fazio (n 28) 6.

[79] Sidney G Tarrow, *Power in Movement: Social Movements and Contentious Politics* (3rd edn, CUP 2011) 163.

[80] For example, Rhonda Evans Case and Terri E Givens, 'Re-Engineering Legal Opportunity Structures in the European Union? The Starting Line Group and the Politics of the Racial Equality Directive' (2010) 48(2) *Journal of Common Market Studies* 224.

sake of conceptual clarity, we should consider part of the LOS only the factors *external* to collective actors (ie legal stock, judicial receptivity, and rules on access to court), while *internal* factors, such as the actors' professional background, are to be considered mobilization resources.[81]

Regarding structural factors, I reformulated the concept of EU LOS to reflect the specifics of Article 267 TFEU. Despite being used to enforce EU rights, this remains "a procedure from court to court" that seats between the national and the supranational level.[82] This means that the national structure of opportunities heavily determines the EU one, as national rules decide whether a party can initiate a claim before a national court, whether third-party interventions are admitted, whether collective actors have legal standing, etc. In my study, I could trace the national factors that, by affecting access to justice and the legal stock, created or frustrated opportunities for EU litigation. Moreover, I identified the techniques used by pro-migrant actors to make national judges more prone to refer, which is an indispensable condition for a case to reach the ECJ.

Besides structural factors, the concept of mobilization of resources helps us understand why, in instances where EU legal opportunities remain the same, some actors seize them, and others do not, thus critically affecting the enforcement of EU migration law. In this respect, we first need to consider the special position of TCN migrants in Europe. They are often underrepresented in our institutions and parliaments, either because of institutional barriers to their democratic participation (eg depending on their status, they have limited right to vote) or because they are more exposed to social exclusion. This is especially true for countries where migration is a relatively new phenomenon and the foreign population has still not developed professional skills in the legal field.[83]

For these reasons, legal mobilization for migrants often depends on the support of interest groups that provide key resources for litigation, such as lawyers and legal expertise.[84] Sociolegal and legal mobilization scholars focused at length on the importance of those actors, referred to at that time as support structure,[85]

[81] Hilson (n 28) 270; Tarrow (n 79) 16.

[82] Pierre Pescatore, *Court of Justice of the European Communities: References for Preliminary Rulings under Article 177 of the EEC Treaty and Cooperation between the Court and National Courts* (Office for Official Publications of the European Communities 1986) 33.

[83] Maurizio Ambrosini, 'NGOs and Health Services for Irregular Immigrants in Italy: When the Protection of Human Rights Challenges the Laws' (2015) 13 Journal of Immigrant & Refugee Studies 116, 321.

[84] On the role of collective actors in the emergence of EU litigation before the ECJ: Elise Muir and others, *How EU Law Shapes Opportunities for Preliminary References on Fundamental Rights: Discrimination, Data Protection and Asylum* (European University Institute 2017).

[85] Charles R Epp, *The Rights Revolution: Lawyers, Activists, and Supreme Courts in Comparative Perspective* (1st edn, University of Chicago Press 1998) 3.

translators,[86] compliance constituency,[87] strategy entrepreneurs,[88] etc. Felstiner, Abel, and Sarat explain the importance of—what they call—reference groups in this way: "The movement from law to politics, and the accompanying expansion of the scope of disputing, are prompted and guided by the reaction of a wide social network to individual instances of injustice. Absent the support of such a network, no such movement is likely to occur."[89]

This is certainly true for the migration and EU law field, where the mobilization promoters are usually not migrants but rather individuals and groups who mobilize on behalf of migrants. To describe these actors supporting litigation for the rights of others, I relied on the concept of "altruistic actors" as they are by and large not the beneficiaries of the action themselves but actors that mobilize on behalf of migrants;[90] the concept of "Euro-expertise" describes instead the intellectual resources, the professional legal work, and the legal expertise that they provide.

While altruistic actors provide resources that facilitate the mobilization of EU justice, many scholars have pointed out how limited financial and intellectual resources can hamper the mobilization through law and courts. There is widespread agreement that litigation is characterized by a structural imbalance between different kinds of parties: the "haves" ("in terms of wealth, status and power") and the "have-nots", the "repeat players" (who use the courts more often) and the "one shotters."[91] The former have "a position of advantage in the configuration of contending parties," and this advantage may perpetuate or augment in a formally neutral legal system.[92] Litigation for social change is not immune of power imbalance between parties. It has been noted that the "ability to mobilize resources [widely understood as funding, allies, professional support etc.] decisively affects interest groups'" choice of resorting

[86] Sally Engle Merry, *Human Rights and Gender Violence Translating International Law into Local Justice* (University of Chicago Press 2006) 193 ss. She defined translators: "The translators were people who helped the members of one layer reframe their grievances in the language of others." And then: "Local women's groups translated the grievances into a rights language that the legislature and political leaders could hear. They taught rural women how to frame their inheritance problems in the language of rights and to talk to reporters this way. This example shows the importance of translators, people who navigate between more or less separate social worlds, helping each group to understand the perspectives of others."

[87] Karen Alter, *The New Terrain of International Law: Courts, Politics, Rights* (Princeton University Press 2014) 19.

[88] Vanhala, 'Is Legal Mobilization for the Birds?' (n 29) 18.

[89] William LF Felstiner, Richard L Abel, and Austin Sarat, 'The Emergence and Transformation of Disputes: Naming, Blaming, Claiming...' (1980) 15 Law & Society Review 631, 644.

[90] Statham (n 27).

[91] Marc Galanter, 'Why the "Haves" Come out Ahead: Speculations on the Limits of Legal Change' (1974) 9 Law & Society Review 95.

[92] ibid 103.

to litigation strategies or not, and their chances of success.[93] This is very true for the procedure before the ECJ, which is structurally unbalanced toward some parties that enjoy privileged status, namely the Member States and the Commission, while being rather closed to individuals and groups.[94] Moreover, ideological considerations might lead a movement to prefer non-institutional ways to pursue its political goals and, therefore, to avoid legal mobilization.[95] Resources, access to justice, and ideological considerations are all factors that can influence positively or negatively the feasibility of legal mobilization before the ECJ, and they are further explored in the empirical chapters of this book.

6. Methodology and case selection

Narrowing down the focus of analysis to one policy domain, migration, has methodological advantages. First, it avoids far-fetched comparisons; one may be skeptical of contextualized studies that put subjects as disparate as antitrust, cooperation in criminal matters, and labor law in the same box. Instead, focusing on one policy field gives adequate relevance to the specific legal framework, power structures, and political dynamics that underpin and characterize that area of law and society. Second, focusing on migration also allows us to better detect "meso-factors," which are the attributes of a national legal system that contribute to or hamper legal mobilization.[96] Indeed, by studying only migration references we can keep constant the EU legal stock, thus illuminating Member States' distinct features and differences, such as the organization of their judicial system, the national implementation of EU norms, their political debates, etc. The shortcoming of this focus on migration is that the book leaves open the question of whether the findings in this area of the law can be translated and remain valid in other areas.[97]

Doctrinal analysis is often not enough in a legal mobilization study. The text of the judgment provides only limited information on the context of the case

[93] Andersen (n 78) 4.

[94] Rasmussen (n 67); Christoph Krenn, *The Procedural and Organisational Law of the European Court of Justice: An Incomplete Transformation* (CUP 2022) 59–80; Virginia Passalacqua and Francesco Costamagna, 'The Law and Facts of the Preliminary Reference Procedure: A Critical Assessment of the EU Court of Justice's Source of Knowledge' (2023) 2 European Law Open 322, 335.

[95] Hilson (n 28); Vanhala, 'Is Legal Mobilization for the Birds?' (n 29).

[96] Conant and others (n 20) 4.

[97] Even if we have already some evidence that what observed in the migration field can be used to explain legal mobilization in the field of antidiscrimination law: Jeffrey A Miller, 'Peering Inside the Preliminary Reference Box: Coleman v Attridge Law' (2022) 2021 6 European Papers—A Journal on Law and Integration 1553.

and does not report information such as who had the idea to refer the case to the ECJ, what was the initial goal of the litigation, or who supported the migrant in the case. To find this information, I relied on empirical, qualitative analysis. I conducted interviews with the lawyers involved in the cases before the ECJ, relevant national and international migrant rights defenders, EU and migration lawyers, legal academics, and, when possible, with judges that have accepted or denied requests to submit a preliminary reference (a total of forty interviewees plus several informal conversations).[98] I combined this empirical data with the analysis of the national legal and judicial framework and the study of secondary sources describing the migration history and political debates.

The first methodological challenge of this study consists in the fact that legal mobilization in the migration field is often not visible. In many instances, civil society actors construct a litigation strategy and bring a case before national courts by legally representing an individual applicant, without their name being on the case file. This means that the documents of the judgment do not present any trace of legal mobilization, and from the outside it seems an ordinary case of a migrant against the public administration. To understand whether and to what extent legal mobilization for migrants existed before the ECJ, I selected three countries that were most likely to feature the phenomenon that I wanted to study, legal mobilization for migrant rights: Italy, the UK, and the Netherlands. I selected these three countries because they presented peaks or spikes in references, which I could trace thanks to my database with all the preliminary references submitted in the migration field through December 2022.[99] My intuition, at that time, was that a high number of preliminary references on a single migration issue could be an indicator of the presence of a legal mobilization. Italy, the UK, and the Netherlands present peaks in references regarding three pieces of EU migration legislation, meaning that they account for about half of all the references submitted on, respectively, the Return Directive,[100] the Family Reunification Directive,[101] and TCN family members of Union citizens (Figure 1.3).[102]

[98] When possible, to increase transparency, the interviews report the real names of the interviewees; names were anonymized upon the interviewees' request and/or when I feared that my research could negatively affect them.

[99] Information on preliminary references was obtained through the consultation of the Court of Justice's online case law search tool and its official annual reports (<https://curia.europa.eu/> accessed 17 December 2024); the results were confronted with the NEMIS, NEAIS, and NEFIS newsletters (<http://cmr.jur.ru.nl/nemis/> accessed 17 December 2024).

[100] Directive 2008/115/EC on common standards and procedures in Member States for returning illegally staying third-country nationals, OJ L 348, 24 December 2008.

[101] Council Directive 2003/86/EC on the Right to Family Reunification, OJ L 251, 3 October 2003.

[102] These are the first rights that TCN migrants acquired under EU law, and they stem from primary and secondary law provisions, such as arts 18, 20, and 21 of the TFEU; Regulation (EEC) No 1612/68

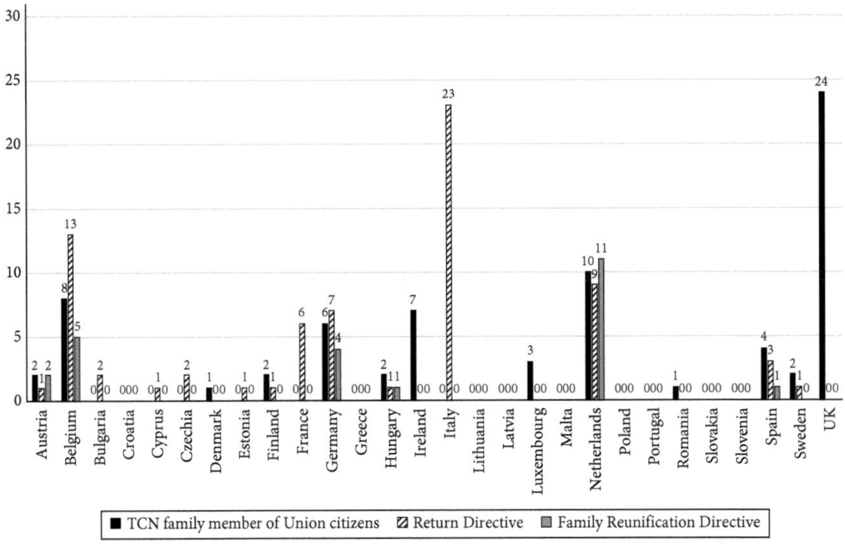

Figure 1.3 All preliminary references submitted by December 2022 on the Return Directive, TCN family members of Union citizens, and the Family Reunification Directive, by country of reference.

All references were considered, regardless of their admissibility. For example, of the twenty-three Italian preliminary reference requests on the Return Directive, only three led to a judgment. This is because the references were part of the same mobilization and they all asked the same questions: once the ECJ provided an answer, all the other references were withdrawn (Chapter 2).

When looking at the three countries' peaks in references, one could argue that demographic and structural factors, such as migrant population or countries' propensity to refer, can account for them. This explanation is ruled out by cases like Germany, which has the highest propensity to refer and the largest migrant population in Europe (both EU and TCN),[103] and yet it referred comparatively little on the single migration issues examined (Figure 1.3). Conversely, Germany accounts for most of the references on the EU–Turkey Association Agreement, also called the Ankara Agreement (forty-five references out of a total of seventy-seven),[104] but this figure is heavily influenced

on Freedom of Movement for Workers within the Community, OJ L 257, 19 October 1968; Directive 2004/38/EC on the right of Citizens of the Union and their Family Members to Move and Reside Freely within the Territory of the Member States, OJ L 158, 30 April 2004.

[103] See Eurostat, 'Migration and migrant population statistics' <https://ec.europa.eu/eurostat/statistics-explained/index.php?title=Migration_and_migrant_population_statistics>, accessed 17 December 2024.

[104] Agreement Establishing an Association between the European Economic Community and Turkey, signed in Ankara, 12 September 1963, OJ L 361/29, 13 December 77.

by structural factors. Germany hosts the largest Turkish community in the EU. This makes it problematic to compare the German case to other countries where the presence of Turkish nationals is rather slim. All this suggests that structural factors must be taken into account, but arguably alone they cannot explain the peaks in references in the three selected countries.

Rather than demographic factors, with regard to Italy, the UK, and the Netherlands, the qualitative research conducted confirmed that their peaks in references are largely due to legal mobilization efforts, that is, collective actors decided to mobilize the three EU migration provisions before national courts and the ECJ to achieve their policy goals. By comparing these case studies, I could identify the conditions that facilitated the emergence of EU legal mobilization in the three countries. For future studies it may be important to understand that even if in these three cases the number of references constituted a good hint that legal mobilization took place, there are instances of legal mobilization via preliminary references that were initiated and concluded with one single reference brought to the ECJ.[105] Thus, a selection criterion that exclusively considers the number of references as a proxy for legal mobilization, despite having the advantage of being objective and rather easy to apply to a large database, presents the limit of not being able to capture small-scale legal mobilization.

After identifying the factors that facilitated legal mobilization in Italy, the UK, and the Netherlands, I tested whether any of these factors were missing in a case without migration references: Greece. As explained at length in Chapter 5, Greece has been on the frontline of the EU migration policies in the last decades. There are many NGOs and pro-migrant organizations that operate there to support migrant rights, and yet, before 2023, Greece had never given rise to a preliminary reference in the whole migration field (which includes asylum, labor migration, and family members of EU citizens). The in-depth qualitative case study allowed me to test whether one of the factors facilitating legal mobilization in the positive cases was missing in Greece, concluding that, indeed, access to courts and awareness of EU legal opportunities were scarce.

7. The structure of the book

The rest of the book develops via four empirical chapters; the first three deal with cases of EU legal mobilization, while the fourth presents a case where

[105] Joined cases C-411/10 and C-493/10 *NS and ME and Others* (2011) CJEU, ECLI:EU:C:2011:865; Case C-133/15 *Chavez Vilchez* (2017) CJEU, ECLI:EU:C:2017:354.

references were missing. The first empirical chapter, Chapter 2, is about the Italian case study, and it tells the story of how associations of lawyers and judges teamed up to promote a mass legal mobilization against the criminalization of undocumented migrants. The second case study concerns the UK, a former EU country that, over the years, has generated more cases than any other Member State on the rights of TCN migrants who are family members of Union citizens, especially thanks to the crucial help of Eurolawyers and specialized legal charities. The third empirical chapter, Chapter 4, deals with the Netherlands, where I investigated the use of the Family Reunification Directive to contest the introduction of a civic integration test from abroad: this case study is smaller in scale because many of its references turned out to be a spill-over effect of the initial legal mobilization. Finally, Chapter 5 investigates the case of Greece and its puzzling lack of migration references. Here, using the insights of the positive cases, I take a more deductive approach and test the theories on legal mobilization to identify the areas where we would expect preliminary references to emerge and to investigate the structural and subjective reasons behind the non-mobilization. Chapter 6 draws some conclusions from these chapters, summarizing the enabling factors and the obstacles that civil society encounters on the way to the mobilization of justice before the ECJ.

2

Italy

Mobilizing EU Justice against Crimmigration

JUDGE: If you read the first three lines of the preliminary reference, you immediately realize that I didn't write it. I couldn't have written it . . .

VIRGINIA: It seemed like an excellent reference to me.

JUDGE: Precisely!

(laughs)

JUDGE: But you can tell the reference was not written by me, not because I'm a stupid judge, but because I don't write like that. This isn't my stuff.[1]

1. The puzzle: An exceptional number of references

In only one year, from January 2011 to February 2012, the Italian courts referred twenty-two requests for preliminary rulings concerning the Return Directive 2008/115.[2] This means that Italy, in only a year, has produced a third of all the preliminary references submitted by all the Member States since the adoption of the Directive in 2008 (see Figure 2.1). Why did Italian judges devote so much attention to the Return Directive?

This chapter argues that this extraordinary number of referrals cannot be understood using traditional doctrinal or court-centric perspectives that focus exclusively on the European Court of Justice (ECJ). Theories on decentralized enforcement fail to capture the real meaning and target of the litigation. Instead, only by looking at the references' local context, together with the resources and the legal opportunities that enabled their emergence, can we understand their real meaning. The chapter shows that the references resulted from a mobilization that used EU law to contest the "crimmigration" reforms

[1] Interview with Italian Judge, March 2016. Translation by the author.

[2] Directive 2008/115/EC of the European Parliament and of the Council of 16 December 2008 on common standards and procedures in Member States for returning illegally staying third-country nationals, OJ L 348, 24 December 2008.

Legal Mobilization for Migrant Rights. Virginia Passalacqua, Oxford University Press.
 DOI: 10.1093/9780198943006.003.0002

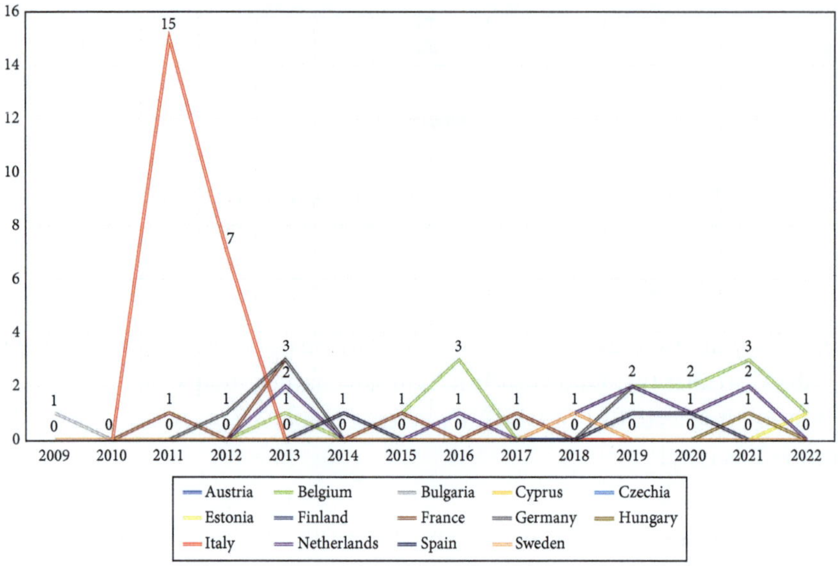

Figure 2.1 Number of preliminary reference requests submitted to the ECJ on the Return Directive from the adoption (2008) until December 2022.

approved by the Italian government a few years earlier. These reforms introduced harsh criminal sanctions and long detention for undocumented migrants and transformed what earlier were administrative offenses into serious crimes. Migrants became criminals merely because they did not have documents, and as a result, they risked spending several years in jail. These harsh rules sparked resistance and contestation among civil society actors in solidarity with migrants, and this movement led, among other things, to the legal mobilization that is the subject of this chapter.

Of the twenty-two references sent by Italian judges, only three cases obtained a judgment by the ECJ: *El Dridi*, *Sagor*, and *Celaj*.[3] These led to considerable changes in the Italian legal framework. First, they induced the reticent Italian lawmakers to transpose the Return Directive into the Italian legal system.[4] More importantly, the judgments led the legislator to partially repeal the crimmigration norms.[5] To be sure, some provisions criminalizing migrants

[3] Cases C-61/11 PPU *El Dridi* (2011) CJEU, ECLI:EU:C:2011:268; C-430/11 *Md Sagor* (2012) CJEU, ECLI:EU:C:2012:777; C-290/14 *Skerdjan Celaj* (2015) CJEU, ECLI:EU:C:2015:640.

[4] Chiara Favilli, 'L'attuazione in Italia Della Direttiva Rimpatri: Dall'inerzia All'urgenza Con Scarsa Cooperazione' (2011) 3 Rivista di Diritto Internazionale 695.

[5] Andrea Natale, 'La direttiva rimpatri, il testo unico immigrazione ed il diritto penale dopo la sentenza El Dridi' (2011) 2 Diritto, immigrazione e cittadinanza 17; Luca Masera and Francesco Viganò, 'Addio articolo 14' (2011) Diritto Penale Contemporaneo <https://archiviodpc.dirittopen

still exist in the Italian legal system, but the EU rulings played a significant role in compelling Italian lawmakers to abandon the idea of using criminal justice to tackle irregular migration.

Rather than focusing on the impact of the preliminary rulings, this chapter investigates the factors that facilitated the emergence of legal mobilization via preliminary references. It explores why Italian courts devoted so much attention to the Return Directive, which political forces on the ground influenced the emergence of the preliminary references, and how they managed to convince so many judges to refer these cases to the ECJ. The chapter shows that the legal mobilization counted on the valuable alliance between an association of lawyers (Association for Juridical Studies on Immigration (ASGI)), legal academics, and a professional association of judges (*Magistratura Democratica*), which was an essential vehicle for a pro-migrant interpretation of EU law. Moreover, some contingent characteristics of the Italian justice system offered fertile terrain for the mobilization: Italian criminal courts were unhappy with the crimmigration reforms, which overloaded them with migration cases to enforce returns. This diversion of the criminal justice branch for migration control purposes inadvertently created an opening in the legal opportunity structure: criminal judges, dissatisfied with the reform, were more receptive toward pro-migrant claims, and many of them decided to submit preliminary references to the European Court of Justice. The chapter thus provides evidence of how, under structural and subjective conditions, preliminary references can become useful tools for the contestation of restrictive national norms.

2. Crimmigration: The target of the legal mobilization

The decade between 2001 and 2011 was crucial for Italy because three parallel events changed its migration landscape forever.[6] First, Italy quickly passed from being a country of emigrants to a destination for immigrants.[7] According to official figures, 1.3 million foreign-born people lived in Italy in 2001, while

aleuomo.org/d/572-addio-articolo-14> accessed 17 December 2024; Favilli, 'L'attuazione in Italia Della Direttiva Rimpatri' (n 4); Elisa Fornalé, 'The European Returns Policy and the Re-Shaping of the National: Reflections on the Role of Domestic Courts' (2012) 31 Refugee Survey Quarterly 134.

[6] For a more comprehensive analysis of Italian law and policy of migration in those years, see Chiara Favilli, *Migration Law in Italy* (Kluwer Law International 2013); Alessia Di Pascale, 'Italy and Unauthorized Migration: Between State Sovereignty and Human Rights Obligations' in Ruth Rubio-Marín (ed), *Human Rights and Immigration* (OUP 2014).

[7] Wayne A Cornelius, Philip Martin, and James Frank Hollifield (eds), *Controlling Immigration: A Global Perspective* (1st edn, Stanford University Press 1994) 24.

by 2011 this increased to 4 million, about 7 percent of the entire population.[8] Second, during the same period, there was a transformation in how people migrated, with an intensification in the number of migrants trying to reach Italy and Europe across the Mediterranean Sea. For the first time, the now familiar pictures portraying boats overcrowded with men, women, and children circulated on Italian and international media. The small island of Lampedusa symbolized the failure of the Italian and European attempts to control migration flows. Third, during this transformative period, Italy was ruled by a right-wing coalition that stayed in power for eight years, almost without interruption.[9] This coalition was led by Silvio Berlusconi and included two far-right parties, *Lega Nord* and *Alleanza Nazionale*, which respectively were "xenophobic and extremist in their rhetoric" and had "neo-fascist roots."[10] During the electoral campaigns, they successfully framed the problem of undocumented migrants as a security issue, which significantly influenced the following reforms.

The Berlusconi government adopted two important migration reforms. The first, in 2002, became known as the Bossi–Fini Law, after the name of its authors, the leaders of the *Lega Nord* and *Alleanza Nazionale*.[11] Unsurprisingly, the law reflected the views of its authors: its declared goals were *lotta alla clandestinità* ("fighting irregular migration") and facilitating the expulsions of undocumented migrants via the introduction of new coercive procedures. The Bossi–Fini Law amended the Italian Immigration Law by introducing harsher sanctions for undocumented migrants on the Italian territory.[12] The second reform was completed in 2009 by the same government coalition and was composed of a series of norms known as the Security Package.[13] These norms officially inaugurated a new era of securitization of migration and criminalization of undocumented migrants.[14]

These reforms are central to our analysis because they introduced the criminal law provisions in the Italian system that were then contested before the

[8] The official report on Italian foreign population is available at <http://www.istat.it/it/files/2012/12/scheda_stranieri.pdf> accessed 17 December 2024.

[9] From 2006 to 2008, the country was ruled by a short-lived center-left government.

[10] Ted Perlmutter, 'Italy. Political Parties and Italian Policy, 1990–2009' in James Hollifield, Philip Martin, and Pia Orrenius (eds), *Controlling Immigration: A Global Perspective* (3rd edn, Stanford University Press 2014) 348.

[11] Law 189 of 30 July 2002, *Modifica alla normativa in materia di immigrazione e di asilo.*

[12] Art 13 of the *Testo Unico Immigrazione*, Legislative Decree 286/1998.

[13] In Italian '*Pacchetto Sicurezza*': a group of provisions including a law decree, two laws, and three legislative decrees adopted from 2008 to 2009. The two most relevant measures for the aims of this chapter are DL 92/2008 (*Misure urgenti in materia di sicurezza pubblica*), which was transposed into Law 125/2008, and the Law no 94/2009 (*Disposizioni in materia di sicurezza pubblica*).

[14] Di Pascale (n 6); Lorenzo Miazzi, 'Detriti di una legislazione: cosa resta della normativa sull'immigrazione' (2013) 5 Questione Giustizia 129, 137.

ECJ. The new crimes specifically targeted undocumented migrants and turned preexisting administrative fines into criminal sanctions. As such, these policies can be ascribed to a broader trend among European lawmakers that was described as "crimmigration": "criminal law mechanisms and imagery being heavily resorted to as part of a general political strategy for managing migration flows."[15] Crimmigration policies align with the idea that a foreign citizen who is undocumented is, as such, a threat to public security.

In Italy, the symbol of the crimmigration policies was the notorious Article 10bis of the Immigration Law, also known as clandestinity crime (*reato di clandestinità*).[16] This provision sanctions as a crime the irregular entry and stay of third-country nationals (TCNs) in Italian territory and provides fines ranging from 5,000 to 10,000 euros, which can be converted into an order of immediate expulsion upon validation by the competent court, the *Giudice di Pace*. The jurisdiction of this court, which is the lowest in the Italian judicial hierarchy, has been highly controversial: it is composed of single-panel honorary judges appointed for five years and whose stipend was a function of the number of judgments they issue. In the view of many experts, these circumstances make Giudici di Pace not competent enough to rule on administrative detention and return, which has significant repercussions for individual liberties and human rights.[17] We will discuss this issue later in this chapter.

The clandestinity crime was not the only crimmigration provision introduced by the Bossi–Fini and the Security Package Laws. They also introduced a crime that punishes any TCN who refuses to show their identification documents to public authorities with up to one year of imprisonment or a fine of 2,000 euros;[18] they extended the maximum period of migrants' administrative detention from 30 to 180 days;[19] and finally, and importantly for this chapter,

[15] Luisa Marin and Alessandro Spena, 'Introduction: The Criminalization of Migration and European (Dis)Integration' (2016) 18 European Journal of Migration and Law 147, 147.

[16] Art 10bis was introduced by an amendment to the Immigration law enacted by art 1(16) of the Security Package Law, Law no 94 of 2009.

[17] The Law 271/2004 conferred upon the *Giudice di Pace* the competence to rule on appeals against return decisions and to confirm the decision to detain an irregular migrant. Angelo Caputo and Livio Pepino, 'Giudice Di Pace e Habeas Corpus Dopo Le Modifiche al Testo Unico Sull'immigrazione' [2004] Diritto, Immigrazione e Cittadinanza 13; Alberto Di Martino and others, *The Criminalization of Irregular Immigration: Law and Practice in Italy* (Pisa University Press 2013) 86; Andrea Pugiotto, 'La "galera Amministrativa" Degli Stranieri e Le Sue Incostituzionali Metamorfosi' (2014) 34 Quaderni costituzionali 588.

[18] Art 22(h) of the Security Package Law 94/2009: ""A foreigner who, at the request of public security officials and agents, does not comply, without justified reason, with the order to show his passport or other identification document and residence permit or other document certifying his regular presence in the territory of the State is punished with arrest of up to one year and with a fine of up to 2,000 euros."

[19] First, the Bossi–Fini Law doubled the maximum term of administrative detention (from thirty to sixty days), then the "Pacchetto Sicurezza" further increased it to a maximum of 180 days. See art

the Bossi–Fini Law created a new crime against undocumented migrants who do not comply with the police order to leave Italian territory. This last crime is provided by Article 14(5) of the Immigration Law and is particularly harsh. It provides that any undocumented migrant found on Italian territory, despite having received a removal order, should be immediately arrested and punished with one to five years of detention.[20]

The crimmigration reforms were received with public outcry by the opposition in Parliament and pro-migrant organizations, both at the national and international levels.[21] In the academic realm, several public statements and articles were published denouncing the risks that the crimmigration reforms posed for migrants' rights and the rule of law in Italy.[22] One of the common critiques was that norms such as the clandestinity crime punish migrants for what they are, not because they committed any offense.[23] Importantly, judges and prosecutors too expressed negative views about the migration reforms: the National Association of Magistrates raised several doubts about whether it was convenient to adopt the clandestinity crime that was literally defined as a useless and detrimental norm.[24] These objections, predictably, led many judges to trigger the constitutional review procedure, under which ordinary courts and tribunals have the power to raise a question of constitutionality to the Italian Constitutional Court that can declare

1(22) of the Law 94/2009. Gianluca Bascherini, 'A Proposito Delle Più Recenti Riforme in Materia Di Trattenimento Dello Straniero Nei Centri Di Identificazione Ed Espulsione' (2012) 1 Rivista Associazione Italiana dei Costituzionalisti 5.

[20] See art 14(5) letter c of the Immigration Law: "A foreign national who is the recipient of the expulsion order referred to in paragraph 5b and a new removal order as referred to in paragraph 5a and who remains illegally on the territory of the State shall be liable to a term of imprisonment of between one and five years. In any event, the provisions of the third and last sentences of paragraph 5b shall apply." And art 14(5) letter d of the same law: "Where the offences referred to in the first sentence of paragraph 5b and paragraph 5c are committed, the *rito direttissimo* [expedited procedure] shall be followed and the arrest of the perpetrator shall be mandatory."

[21] For an overview: Redazione Melting Pot, "Speciale 'Pacchetto Sicurezza' - Le Nuove Norme Tra Applicabilità Ed Efficacia" (23 May 2008) <http://www.meltingpot.org/Speciale-pacchetto-sicurezza-Le-nuove-norme-tra.html> accessed 17 December 2024. Commissioner for Human Rights of the Council of Europe, Annual Activity Report of 2009, CommDH(2010)53, 7.

[22] Di Martino and others (n 17); Thomas Hammarberg, 'It Is Wrong to Criminalize Migration' (2009) 11 European Journal of Migration and Law 386; Luigi Ferrajoli, 'La Criminalizzazione Degli Immigrati (Note a Margine Della Legge n. 94/2009)' [2009] Questione Giustizia 9; Massimo Merlino, 'The Italian (In)security package: Security vs. Rule of Law and Fundamental Rights in the EU' CEPS Research Paper 2009 <https://cdn.ceps.eu/wp-content/uploads/2009/08/1809.pdf> accessed 25 January 2025.

[23] Massimo Donini, 'Il cittadino extracomunitario da oggetto materiale a tipo d'autore nel controllo penale dell'immigrazione' (2009) Fascicolo 1 Questione giustizia 101, 118.

[24] The ANM President defined the reform that introduced the clandestinity crime "inutile e dannosa": <http://www.associazionemagistrati.it/doc/1416/immigrazione-anm-bene-stop-a-reato-clandestinit-ma-non-dimenticare-problemi-come-situazione-minori-e-sfruttamento.htm> accessed 17 December 2024.

a law unconstitutional and strike it down (more in Section 8.1).[25] Some of these proceedings ended with the Italian Constitutional Court declaring unconstitutional parts of the Bossi–Fini and the Security Package Laws,[26] but with two famous judgments of 2004 and 2010, the Italian Constitutional Court eventually ruled that the two most prominent crimmigration norms, Article 14(5) and the clandestinity crime, were compatible with the Italian Constitution.[27]

To understand the subsequent developments, it is important to look at the impact that the crimmigration reforms had on the Italian criminal justice system. Indeed, the criminalization not only affected migrants' rights but also negatively compromised the overall functioning of the Italian criminal justice system. By criminalizing actions that were sanctioned with administrative fines before, the Bossi–Fini and the Security Package Laws transferred a huge amount of cases from administrative bodies to public prosecutors and criminal judges. Public prosecutors' desks were swamped with cases of undocumented migrants detected by the police. This was a direct consequence of the new Article 14(5) of the Immigration Law, providing that every undocumented TCN who does not comply with the order to leave Italian territory shall be immediately arrested and sentenced to prison. Official data from the Ministry of Justice reveals that, in 2006 alone, more than 18,000 migrants were tried for this crime, of which 14,000 were convicted.[28] This massive amount of cases clogged up the criminal justice system, overcrowding prisons with migrants who could spend up to five years in jail. This (perhaps unforeseen) consequence of crimmigration was consequential on judges' attitudes toward the preliminary references, as we shall explain in the next sections.

[25] Art 134 of the Italian Constitution. In Italy, only the Constitutional Court can review the constitutional legitimacy of a law, upon request of a national court; the doubt regarding the legitimacy of the norm should arise during an ongoing procedure and should be relevant to determine the outcome of the case (the procedure is very similar to the EU preliminary reference mechanism, and indeed, it was its blueprint). Amedeo Arena and Alessandro Rosanò, 'Nicola Catalano (1910–1984): padre del rinvio pregiudiziale d'interpretazione e apostolo del primato del diritto comunitario' [2024] Eurojus 89, 92.

[26] Corte Costituzionale, judgment no 223, 15 July 2004.

[27] Corte Costitizionale, judgment no 5, 13 January 2004, red Flick; Corte Costituzionale, judgment no 250, 8 July 2010, red Frigo; and Corte Costituzionale, judgment no 249, 8 July 2010, red Silvestri. Luca Masera, 'Costituzionale il reato di clandestinità, incostituzionale l'aggravante: le ragioni della Corte costituzionale' (2010) 3 Diritto, Immigrazione e Cittadinanza 37; Guido Savio, 'Prime riflessioni sulle modifiche penali introdotte dalla legge no 271 del 2004' (2004) 3 Diritto, Immigrazione e Cittadinanza 71.

[28] Di Martino and others (n 17) 68.

3. An opening in the EU legal opportunity structure: The Return Directive

In the early 2000s, while Italy was reforming its migration policy, an important change in the EU legal opportunity structure occurred, namely in the legal stock.[29] The EU negotiated and adopted the first legislative tool that would harmonize national procedures for repatriating migrants. This was adopted in 2008 and is known as the Return Directive because it provides for a uniform set of standards and procedures regulating the return of undocumented TCN migrants.[30] The text of the Directive reflects the underlying struggle to strike a balance between the position of the Council, aimed at "the establishment of an effective removal and repatriation policy," and the position of the EU Parliament which stressed the necessity to guarantee that people are returned to their country of origin "in a humane manner and with full respect for their fundamental rights and dignity."[31] As a result, many provisions of the Directive embody this compromise. For instance, Article 15 establishes that undocumented migrants can be detained in order to implement a deportation order but only if such a deprivation of liberty complies with the proportionality principle and only for a maximum duration of eighteen months.[32]

The Return Directive was adopted on December 16, 2008, and European Member States were supposed to implement it by December 24, 2010. Since the very beginning, however, the Italian government publicly stated that it would not transpose the Directive into Italian national law and, instead, it would keep its own return system, deemed already to be in line with EU standards. Some public statements made by the government reveal the motivation behind this decision: the then Interior Minister (Roberto Maroni, member of the *Lega Nord* party), at an audit before the Italian Parliament prior to the adoption of the Security Package Law, asserted that the procedure of the Return Directive was inefficient in implementing deportation because it was based on the principle that voluntary returns should be preferred over forced returns.[33] In his

[29] Chris Hilson, 'New Social Movements: The Role of Legal Opportunity' (2002) 9 Journal of European Public Policy 238; Gianluca De Fazio, 'Legal Opportunity Structure and Social Movement Strategy in Northern Ireland and Southern United States' (2012) 53 International Journal of Comparative Sociology 3.

[30] Directive 2008/115/EC of the European Parliament and of the Council (n 2) 98–107.

[31] See the Preamble of the Return Directive, 2. On the negotiation process of the Return Directive, see Anneliese Baldaccini, 'The EU Directive on Return: Principles and Protests' (2009) 28 Refugee Survey Quarterly 114, 125.

[32] Return Directive, art 15.

[33] Declaration of the Italian Interior Minister during an audit before the Parliament: 'Audizione del Ministro dell'interno, Roberto Maroni, in merito alle misure avviate per migliorare l'efficacia della normativa in materia di immigrazione' 15 October 2008.

view, the Italian procedures were more efficient because they provided for an immediate and coercive deportation.

Intending to elude the application of the Return Directive, the Italian government decided to rely on the exemption provided by Article 2.2(b) of the Directive. This states that Member States may decide not to apply the Directive to undocumented migrants who "are subject to return as a criminal law sanction or as a consequence of a criminal law sanction, according to national law, or who are the subject of extradition procedures." The article was intended for those convicted of a crime, independently from their regular or irregular status, to preserve Member States' discretion in criminal law matters. However, as mentioned earlier, the Bossi–Fini and the Security Package Laws with their crimmigration aim introduced new crimes: first, the clandestinity crime (Article 10bis of the Immigration Law), and second, the crime sanctioning undocumented migrants who did not comply with the police's removal order (Article 14(5) of the Immigration Law). In the view of the government, these two crimes fell within the exemption of Article 2 and therefore made the Directive virtually non-applicable to all the cases of undocumented migrants sanctioned under those criminal provisions.

Several commentators noted that the Italian government adopted the Security Package Law in 2009, when the Directive had already been adopted (it was published in the EU Official Journal in December 2008), but the deadline for transposition was yet to pass. This points to the fact that the introduction of the clandestinity crime was probably a deliberate strategy to elude Italy's obligations to comply with EU law.[34]

Even if we accept the position of the then government and assume that the exemption of Article 2 was applicable, the Italian legal order was still not in line with many aspects of the new EU administrative procedure of removal.[35] Let me give three examples: First, the Return Directive clearly stated that voluntary departure should be preferred, while the Italian norms provided for immediate forced return as the general rule;[36] this is in breach of Article 7 of the Return Directive requiring that undocumented migrants are guaranteed "an appropriate period for voluntary departure of between seven and thirty days."[37] Second, Italian law foresaw an entry ban for the

[34] Favilli, 'L'attuazione in Italia Della Direttiva Rimpatri' (n 4) 702; Baldaccini (n 31) 128.

[35] Rosa Raffaelli, 'Criminalizing Irregular Immigration and the Returns Directive: An Analysis of the El Dridi Case' (2011) 13(4) European Journal of Migration and Law 467–89.

[36] Immigration Law, art 13(3). Giuseppe Amato, 'Un Sistema Incompatibile Con La Direttiva Ue Perché Non Privilegia Il Rimpatrio Volontario' (2011) 5 Guida al Diritto 24.

[37] Return Directive, art 7(1).

returned migrant that could last for up to ten years, while the Directive provided for a maximum duration of five years.[38] Third, in Italy, the administrative detention of undocumented migrants was the rule and was supposed to always take place, provided that there were places available in detention facilities; the Return Directive, instead, set up a system of case-by-case evaluation where the restriction of migrants' liberty should comply with the principle of proportionality and can be enacted only when necessary to implement the return and when no other less restrictive measure is available.[39]

We can draw two conclusions from this short overview: First, the Return Directive, although considered by national and international organizations supporting migrants a "shameful" piece of EU legislation[40] in many respects, granted migrants a higher level of protection than Italian laws in 2009. Second, despite the Interior Minister's declarations, there were many evident frictions between Italian law and the Return Directive, and the deadline for its transposition was approaching.

4. The support structure: Actors and resources

The tensions between the EU and the Italian migration return systems became apparent when the term for transposing the Return Directive expired, on December 24, 2010. After this date, migrant rights defenders started mobilizing the Directive and brought the crimmigration norms before the ECJ.

In the Italian case, many actors were the protagonists of the legal mobilization. As stated earlier, the two crimmigration reforms had been highly criticized by pro-migrant groups and a huge part of civil society. But among these, a network of a diverse group of subjects, including non-governmental organizations (NGOs), lawyers, judges, and activists, decided to respond using EU law. To be sure, not all of them directly participated in the proceedings but each contributed from inside or outside the courtroom.

[38] ibid art 11.

[39] ibid art 15.

[40] The Directive was accused of not guaranteeing the respect of migrants' fundamental rights, as emerges from the manifesto '*Directive de la honte*' <http://www.migreurop.org/article1336.html?lang=fr> accessed 17 December 2024. Indeed, the Return Directive, by setting a "minimum standard" of protection, had the consequence of making Member States lower their standards where higher. Italy is an example: maximum detention was 60 days and it was extended to 180 days as soon as it was confirmed that that was the maximum period allowed by the Directive. EU Directives might have the effect of turning a floor into a ceiling, especially in the migration field.

4.1 The protagonists: Judges and lawyers' associations

The most prominent actor was surely ASGI, a membership-based association that focuses on various aspects of migration (asylum, antidiscrimination, xenophobia, citizenship, etc) from a legal perspective.[41] Among ASGI's members, there are many lawyers, academics, consultants, and civil society representatives. The Association was founded by a group of lawyers and legal scholars in 1990 and soon it became famous as a prominent network of experts and a reference point for all those interested in migration law issues. In 1999, ASGI and *Magistratura Democratica*, an association of judges, founded a legal journal on migration studies, Diritto, Immigrazione e Cittadinanza, still considered one of the most prominent in the field.

The *Magistratura Democratica* is another important actor in the mobilization. This is an Italian association of magistrates (similar to a trade union for judges and public prosecutors) founded in 1964 in the wake of the transformative and disruptive movements that characterized that period. *Magistratura Democratica* was born with the intent of radically rethinking the profession of the judge by dismantling hierarchies and increasing popular control over the members of the judiciary. Today on its website, *Magistratura Democratica* states that its primary objectives are to promote a culture of democracy, rule of law, protection of minorities (including migrants), and social justice.[42] While the idea of having politically positioned associations of judges may come as a surprise, this type of judicial association is very much embedded in the Italian tradition of strong judicial independence and thorough judicial review, and similar associations exist in southern European states, like France and Spain.[43] These progressive-leaning judicial associations have created a transnational network, *Medel*, of which *Magistratura Democratica* is also part.[44]

In 1998, when lively debates were taking place around the enactment of the first important migration reform,[45] a new sub-group was created within the criminal law group of *Magistratura Democratica* that was interested specifically in immigration, the so-called *gruppo immigrazione*. It was this sub-group that, together with ASGI, created the journal Diritto, Immigrazione e

[41] ASGI website: <http://www.asgi.it/chi-siamo/> accessed 17 December 2024.

[42] *Magistratura Democratica*'s statute can be read here: <http://www.magistraturademocratica.it/chi-siamo> accessed 17 December 2024.

[43] Carlo Guarnieri, 'Courts and Marginalized Groups: Perspectives from Continental Europe' (2007) 5 International Journal of Constitutional Law 187, 199.

[44] *Magistrats Européens pour la Démocratie et les Libertés*, <https://www.medelnet.eu/> accessed 17 December 2024.

[45] This eventually led to the adoption of the 'Turco-Napolitano' Law no 40/1998, adopted on 6 March 1998.

Cittadinanza and promoted debates around the topics of immigration and justice. Alongside the publication of the journal, *Magistratura Democratica*'s immigration group spread information and disseminated opinions, blogs, and articles among its members and through their privileged internal channels like its mailing list or via the organization of conferences and education events for judges. This, we will see, was crucial for the legal mobilization before the ECJ.

4.2 The platforms

As stated in Section 1 of this chapter, the special character of the Italian mobilization is the volume of requests made within a relatively short period (twenty-two in a single year). This would be difficult to understand without considering the role played by educational institutions and training initiatives that provided courses and lectures for legal practitioners on the new developments of EU law. Among them, particularly significant were the training programs organized specifically for judges. These were held either in the framework of judicial trainings, organized by the *Consiglio Superiore della Magistratura* (Higher Council of Judiciary), or by independent judicial associations, like *Magistratura Democratica*, that organized several events to raise awareness on the Return Directive.

Blogs and online journals also contributed significantly to the debate by disseminating information about the impact of the Return Directive on the Italian migration system. See, for instance, the website of *Melting Pot*, which specializes in migration law and policy.[46] A platform for debate that was particularly influential was an online legal journal specializing in criminal law: Diritto Penale Contemporaneo.[47] On its website, papers and judicial decisions related to the application of the Return Directive in the Italian legal system were uploaded, almost in real time.[48] The blog posts were read by many

[46] <http://www.meltingpot.org/> accessed 17 December 2024.

[47] <http://www.penalecontemporaneo.it/> accessed 17 December 2024.

[48] Some examples: Filippo Focardi, 'Ancora Sull'impatto Della Direttiva Comunitaria 2008/115/CE Sui Reati Di Cui All'artt. 14 Co. 5-Ter e 5-Quater d.Lgs. 286/1998' [2011] Diritto Penale Contemporaneo <https://archiviodpc.dirittopenaleuomo.org/d/313-ancora-sull-impatto-della-direttiva-comunitaria-2008115ce-sui-reati-di-cui-all-artt-14-co-5-ter-e-5> accessed 17 December 2024; Francesco Viganò, 'Il Dibattito Continua: Ancora in Tema Di Direttiva Rimpatri e Inosservanza Dell'ordine Di Allontanamento' [2011] Diritto Penale Contemporaneo <https://archiviodpc.dirittopenaleuomo.org/d/328-il-dibattito-continua-ancora-in-tema-di-direttiva-rimpatri-e-inosservanza-dell-ordine-di-allontanam> accessed 17 December 2024; Gian Luigi Gatta, 'Art. 10 bis T.U. Imm. e "Direttiva Rimpatri": un'altra ordinanza di rimessione alla Corte di Giustizia' (2012) Diritto Penale Contemporaneo <https://archiviodpc.dirittopenaleuomo.org/d/1229-art-10-bis-tu-imm-e--direttiva-rimpatri--un-altra-ordinanza-di-rimessione-alla-corte-di-giustizia> accessed 17 December 2024.

academics, lawyers, and judges who engaged in heated discussions on the correct interpretation of the Directive. The close connection that exists between Diritto Penale Contemporaneo (blog and journal) and legal mobilization is also demonstrated by the fact that one of the members of its board, Professor Luca Masera, acted as a legal representative in the cases of both *El Dridi* and *Sagor* before the ECJ.

Equally important, if less direct, was the role played by NGOs, social movements, and individual activists supporting the migrants' cause. After the adoption of the Security Package Law in 2009, many people and groups mobilized and campaigned against the law and in solidarity with migrants. A national march was held in Rome on October 17, 2009, when migrants and their supporters protested against the government's reforms and its pushback operations in the Mediterranean Sea.[49] The dramatic events that brought about the shipwreck and death of hundreds of people near the island of Lampedusa[50] constitute the backdrop to this period of heated debate and intense political contestation on migration.

5. Before the transposition deadline: The framing stage

Having described the actors, this section focuses on how they created the conditions that led to the emergence of so many preliminary references to the ECJ. The mobilization happened in three stages: the first, before the Return Directive's transposition deadline, was the framing stage during which the organized actors prepared the upcoming proceedings; the second stage, from January to April 2011, consisted of the mobilization against Article 14(5) that led to the emergence of twelve preliminary references and the *El Dridi* judgment; and the third stage, from July 2011 to February 2012, is the mobilization against the clandestinity crime that saw ten preliminary references and led to the case of *Sagor*. Here, I will describe the first stage.

The Return Directive's transposition deadline of December 24, 2010, was a decisive turning point. Already in 2008, the Italian government had publicly announced that it considered it unnecessary to transpose the Directive.[51] This

[49] In Rome, 200,000 people marched i on 17 October 2009: <http://www.repubblica.it/2009/05/sezioni/cronaca/immigrati-8/manifestazione-razzismo/manifestazione-razzismo.html?ref = search> accessed 17 December 2024.

[50] 'Strage di migranti a Lampedusa' *La Repubblica* (20 August 2009) <http://www.repubblica.it/2009/08/sezioni/cronaca/immigrati-10/lampedusa-strage/lampedusa-strage.html> accessed 17 December 2024.

[51] Section 2 of this chapter.

gave time to migrant supporters to explore possible ways to use the Directive and its provisions having direct effect. It is important to note that, for the group of lawyers, legal academics, and judges from ASGI and *Magistratura Democratica*, the Directive represented the last chance to strike down the Italian crimmigration legislation. They had already tried several times to obtain a declaration of unconstitutionality by the Constitutional Court but these proceedings had not brought the results they had hoped.[52]

Under the traditional definition, a legal mobilization starts by framing a will or a desire in legal terms.[53] Accordingly, migrant supporters first needed to frame their aim, that is declaring the crimmigration policy illegitimate, using EU law jargon and the provisions of the Return Directive. To this aim, as we shall see, migrant supporters embarked on the work of reinterpretation of the Directive, proposing a reading that emphasized its role as an instrument for defending migrants' rights, rather than for implementing expulsions.

Under the EU law doctrine of direct effect, all the provisions of a directive that are sufficiently clear, precise, and unconditional would become directly enforceable by individuals against the State once the deadline for transposition has passed, regardless of whether the directive had been transposed or not.[54] This means that, from December 24, 2010, the Return Directive's norms that were clear, precise, and unconditional became directly enforceable by public authorities and judges, who had to set aside all incompatible national provisions too. Given the open and deliberate refusal by the Italian government to implement the Directive, its direct effect was anticipated and studied by the different stakeholders.

In this context, an influential article published by Viganò and Masera deserves special mention.[55] At that time, both authors were criminal law professors

[52] Corte Costitizionale, sentenza 5, 13 January 2004, red. Flick; Corte Costituzionale, sentenza 250, 8 July 2010, red. Frigo; Corte Costituzionale, sentenza 249, 8 July 2010, red. Silvestri.

[53] More in Chapter 1. Zemans wrote that the law is mobilized "when a desire or want is translated into a demand as an assertion of one's rights." See Frances Kahn Zemans, 'Legal Mobilization: The Neglected Role of the Law in the Political System' (1983) 77(43) The American Political Science Review 690–703. Other scholars developed the role of legal consciousness in the process of legal mobilization further and deeper. See eg William LF Felstiner, Richard L Abel, and Austin Sarat, 'The Emergence and Transformation of Disputes: Naming, Blaming, Claiming . . .' (1980) 15(3/4) Law & Society Review 631–54.

[54] The idea behind this principle is that Member States should not be able to elude their EU obligations simply by not transposing Directives. Case C-41/74 *Yvonne Van Duyn* (1974) CJEU, ECLI:EU:C:1974:133. Despite this being a classical principle of European integration, it still raises important questions regarding its application: Grazia Vitale, *Principi generali e diritto derivato. Contributo allo studio del sistema delle fonti dell'Unione europea* (Giappichelli Editore 2013) 53; Daniele Gallo, 'Rethinking Direct Effect and Its Evolution: A Proposal' (2022) 1 European Law Open 576.

[55] Francesco Viganò and Luca Masera, 'Illegittimità Comunitaria Della Vigente Disciplina Delle Espulsioni e Possibili Rimedi Giurisdizionali' (2010) 53(2) Rivista Italiana Diritto e Procedura Penale 560.

and members of the board of the journal Diritto Penale Contemporaneo; shortly before the deadline for transposition, they published a thorough analysis of the Return Directive vis-à-vis the Italian legislation, arguing that Article 14(5) of the Immigration law (as well as other norms) was irremediably in conflict with Articles 15 and 16 of the Return Directive.[56] The authors supported their claim with two different arguments. The first was principle based: punishing undocumented migrants with up to five years of detention would disproportionally restrict their human right to liberty. The second argument was concerned with the efficiency and effectiveness of the Directive: keeping migrants in jail for five years would not facilitate their return; quite the opposite, it would force migrants to stay in Italy. According to Viganò and Masera, due to these incompatibilities between EU and Italian norms, after December 24, 2010, Italian judges had two options: they could recognize the supremacy of EU law and set aside Article 14(5), or they could stay the proceedings and make a preliminary reference request to the ECJ. For this second option, they even provided the text of the question to refer to the Court.[57] When the article was published on Diritto Penale Contemporaneo, a long and heated debate followed on the pages of the blog, which saw the participation of legal academics, judges, lawyers, and prosecutors writing comments and opinions and also sending documents (decisions and other materials) from ongoing proceedings.[58]

Meanwhile, the Italian government was preparing itself for the Return Directive's transposition deadline. The Interior Minister made the first move through the national police chief, Manganelli. On December 17, 2010 (a week before the deadline), he circulated a communication to all the police stations and offices, making them aware of the content of the (un-transposed) Directive and of the possible "future scenario" they might have to face.[59] In the communication, the police chief warned his colleagues to give adequate motivations to their removal orders to show clearly that they comply with EU law, foreseeing possible judicial review requests.[60] This communication can be read, on the

[56] As we saw in Section 3, art 14(5) letter c of the Immigration Law provides that if undocumented migrants fail to comply with the police order to leave the country voluntarily, they should be sentenced to a term of one to four years of detention. This term may increase to up to five years in case of reiteration (art 14(5) letter d).

[57] Viganò and Masera (n 55) 33.

[58] Francesco Viganò, 'Direttiva Rimpatri e Delitti Di Inosservanza Dell'ordine Di Allontanamento Del Questore' [2010] Diritto Penale Contemporaneo <https://archiviodpc.dirittopenaleuomo.org/d/284-direttiva-rimpatri-e-delitti-di-inosservanza-dell-ordine-di-allontanamento-del-questore> accessed 17 December 2024; Focardi (n 48); Viganò, 'Il Dibattito Continua' (n 48).

[59] Ministero dell'Interno, Dipartimento di Pubblica Sicurezza, 'Cittadini Stranieri in Posizione Di Soggiorno Irregolare' 17 December 2010, Prot 400/B/2010.

[60] ibid 2.

one hand, as an implicit admission of guilt: the police chief acknowledged that the removal orders could be contested for conflicting with the Directive. On the other hand, it could be seen as an attempt to bring Italian expulsion procedure in line with EU standards. As we will see, many courts, lawyers, and scholars deemed the police chief's communication not sufficient to remedy the defects of the Italian procedure with respect to Union law.[61]

The ball was now in the hands of Italian public prosecutors and criminal judges. They were at a crossroads: after December 24, should they uphold the government's position or raise the incompatibility between Italian and EU law? The underpinning legal issue was not trivial and consisted of two main evaluations. First, given that the Directive had not been transposed, they had to assess whether any of its norms was sufficiently clear, precise, and unconditional; only if they were would they be compelled to apply it directly in the Italian legal order. Second, they had to assess whether the EU norms enjoying direct effect were also in conflict with the Italian norms on return.

To help prosecutors and judges prepare to deal with these legal issues, the *Scuola Superiore della Magistratura* and other educational institutions organized several courses and events throughout Italy. Many of the experts invited to speak happened to be members of ASGI or *Magistratura Democratica*, thus they had a clear view of the issue and what was at stake, and these associations organized their own informative events as well.[62] In general, the issue of the direct effect of the Directive and its consequences on the Italian legal order were widely debated.

After the deadline for transposing the Directive expired, Italian judges followed three different paths. Some continued to apply the Italian Immigration Law as it stood, without identifying any conflict with EU law: they upheld the government view under which the Directive did not apply to criminal law provisions.[63] Others considered the Directive directly applicable, found a conflict between EU and Italian norms, and, in compliance with the principle of EU law supremacy, decided to set aside the conflicting articles of the Immigration law.[64] Among those, it is worth noting the position taken by

[61] Fulvio Vassallo Paleologo, 'Direttiva Rimpatri e Stato Di Diritto - Un Commento Alla Luce Della Circolare Manganelli Del 17 Dicembre' (*Melting Pot Europa*, 7 January 2011) <http://www.meltingpot.org/Direttiva-rimpatri-e-stato-di-diritto-Un-commento-alla-luce.html> accessed 17 December 2024.

[62] For instance *Magistratura Democratica* and ASGI organized a conference together in Verona, just a few days before the transposition deadline, on 15 January 2015: <http://www.meltingpot.org/Direttiva-Rimpatri-I-materiali-del-Convegno-di-Studi-On.html#.W1r_1NgzZol> accessed 17 December 2024.

[63] A list of these cases is available on the website of *Diritto Penale Contemporaneo*. For instance: Judgment of Tribunale di Verona, 20 January 2011, Judge Piziali.

[64] Among them: Judgment of the Tribunale di Aosta, 28 January 2011, Judge Tornatore; Judgment of the Tribunale di Nola, 17 February 2011, Judge Napolitano.

many chief prosecutors (the *Procuratori della Repubblica* of Lecce, Florence, Rome, and Milan) who issued communications directed to their teams recommending them not to initiate criminal cases under Article 14(5) because this norm should be set aside.[65] Finally, from January 2011 to April 2011, twelve courts found a problem of interpretation and filed a request for a preliminary ruling to the ECJ (among these was the Italian Supreme Court).[66]

Remarkably, all the twelve requests for preliminary rulings had been submitted by criminal courts and concerned Article 14(5), although this was not the only friction between Italian and EU law. Only one request, the thirteenth one, came from a *Giudice di Pace*[67] and addressed the legitimacy of Article 10bis, the clandestinity crime; however, this was declared inadmissible by the ECJ because it lacked sufficient description of the facts of the case.[68] These circumstances deserve attention because they reveal that not all national judges are equally willing and able to make references, and their rank and specialization may play a role. Section 8 of this chapter will address this further.

6. The second stage: The *El Dridi* reference

The first Italian reference regarding the Return Directive decided by the ECJ was *El Dridi*.[69] Despite not being the first one submitted, this reference was granted precedence over the others because the referring Appeal Court of Trento required the application of the urgent procedure as the accused person was in jail.[70]

[65] Being internal communications they are not public, but some were made available on the pages of *Penale Contemporaneo*: 'Nota del Procuratore della Repubblica di Lecce' 10 February 2011, Prot no 556/2011 <https://archiviodpc.dirittopenaleuomo.org/d/396-nota-del-procuratore-della-repubblica-di-lecce--10-febbraio-2011-inottemperanza-dello-straniero-all> accessed 17 December 2024; 'Nota del Procuratore della Repubblica di Milano' 11 March 2011, Prot no 54/11 <https://archiviodpc.dirittopenaleuomo.org/upload/Direttiva%20Proc%20Milano.pdf> accessed 17 December 2024.

[66] *Assane Samb* (2011) Tribunale di Milano, Order for reference in case C-43/11; *Lucky Emegor* (2011) Tribunale di Ivrea, Order for reference in case C-50/11; *Mohamed Mrad* (2011) Tribunale di Ragusa, Order for reference in case C-60/11; *El Dridi* (2011) Corte d'Appello di Trento, Order for Reference in case C-61/11; *John Austine* (2011) Tribunale di Rovereto, Order for reference in case C-63/11; *Survival Godwin* (2011) Tribunale di Bergamo, Order for reference in case C-94/11; *Mohamed Ali Cherni* (2011) Tribunale di Ragusa, Order for reference in case C-113/11; *Yeboah Kwadwo* (2011) Tribunale di Santa Maria Capua Vetere, Order for reference in case C-120/11; *Demba Ngagne* (2011) Corte Suprema di Cassazione, Order for reference in case C-140/11; *Ibrahim Music* (2011) Tribunale di Bergamo, Order for reference in case C-156/11; *Patrick Conteh* (2011) Tribunale di Frosinone, reference in case C-169/11, OJ 2008 L 348, p 98; *Elena Vermisheva* (2011) Tribunale di Treviso, Order for reference in case C-187/11.

[67] As explained, this is a single-judge court at the bottom of the judicial hierarchy. A *Giudice di Pace* rules on a variety of small proceedings in administrative, civil, and criminal law.

[68] Case C-144/11 *Asad Abdallah* (2011) CJEU, ECLI:EU:C:2011:565.

[69] *El Dridi* (n 3).

[70] Art 104b of the ECJ's Rules of Procedure.

The reference was made in the context of criminal proceedings against Mr. Hassen El Dridi, a TCN migrant with a history of convictions for drug dealing and unfulfilled repatriation orders. He received his first repatriation order in May 2004 in Turin but continued to stay in Italy without documents until May 2010, when he received the second order. The police attempted to forcibly deport him, but they faced practical obstacles (the detention center was full, and there were no vehicles available).[71] Thus, Mr El Dridi was, de facto, free again. However, the police caught him once more a few months later, in September 2010, and prosecuted him under the crime defined in Article 14(5) for failing to comply with the removal order; this time, he was swiftly sentenced to one year of imprisonment by the Trento Tribunal. On February 2, 2011, during the appeal, the Trento Appeal Court decided to stay the proceedings and refer a preliminary reference to the ECJ.

The questions asked in the case of *El Dridi* were remarkably similar to those asked in the other eleven referrals and they all reproduced the questions suggested in the article by Viganò and Masera, namely the Italian courts asked whether Articles 15 and 16 of the Return Directive should be interpreted as precluding a Member State's legislation that provides for a sentence of a term of imprisonment of up to four years passed to undocumented migrants solely on the ground that they have failed to comply with a deportation order. Moreover, the Trento Appeal Court asked whether the Italian legislation violated the principle of sincere cooperation between the EU Member States,[72] since it provided for criminal sanctions during the return procedure to avoid the application of the Return Directive.

Remarkably, the judges of the Trento Appeal Court were not part of the migrant supporters' network described earlier, and in fact, the *Magistratura Democratica*–ASGI group was surprised by the news of the referral. As one of the judges in the *Magistratura Democratica* group told me:

> We were thinking about whether to make the preliminary reference or not, when a Trento court anticipated us. They were not connected to the group, they had studied and read something on the [mailing] lists[73] and they made a preliminary reference request. Then, we had to make up for it. Once the procedure [before the ECJ] started, we tried to join through our lawyers, and we went to support the reference as a group.[74]

[71] *El Dridi* (n 3) para 19. This is in line with the procedure of immediate coercive removal provided for by art 13 of the Immigration Law, as explained in Section 3.

[72] Art 4(3) TEU.

[73] The mailing lists of judges from *Magistratura Democratica* cited in the previous section.

[74] Interview with *Magistratura Democratica* Judge, March 2016. Translation by the author.

The news that an Italian preliminary reference on Article 14(5) had been sent to the ECJ under the urgent procedure reached an EU law professor and ASGI member who immediately contacted Masera, one of the authors of the influential article mentioned earlier.[75] They understood that *El Dridi* was likely to become the first ruling on the legitimacy of Article 14(5) and they wanted to make sure that it would go well. They contacted Mr El Dridi's lawyer and offered their support; they came to the agreement that Masera would act as the defense lawyer before the ECJ.

On April 28, 2011, the ECJ delivered its judgment declaring Article 14(5) partially at odds with the principles stated in the Return Directive. The Court dismissed the argument of the Italian government but did not completely adopt the line of reasoning brought forward by Mr El Dridi's defense and the referring Court.

In its ruling, the ECJ started by confirming the direct effect of the Return Directive in the Italian legal order. As the Italian government had failed to transpose the Directive into national law by the prescribed time, individuals could invoke its provisions given that they are sufficiently clear, precise, and unconditional.[76] Among these there are also Articles 15 and 16 of the Directive. The ECJ dismissed the argument of the Italian government that wanted to rely on Article 2 to exclude the application of the Directive; the Court noted that, even if Mr El Dridi was sanctioned with a criminal penalty, his proceedings originated from an administrative order of removal which falls entirely within the scope of the Directive. On this point, the Advocate General, in his Opinion, highlighted the paradox within the Italian government's argument: "a Member State which has not adopted the provisions transposing a directive . . . cannot rely on the application of a right deriving from that directive."[77] In other words, having not transposed the Directive, the government cannot rely on the derogation under Article 2 therein.

As anticipated, the ECJ's decisive argument diverged from the one proposed by the defense and the referring court. Their main claim of the defense was that the Italian norm was illegitimate because it was exceptionally severe in its sanctions and thus it breached the principle of proportionality and the migrant's right to liberty.[78] Instead, the Court's reasoning was not rights based

[75] Interview with Luca Masera, 26 January 2016, Brescia.
[76] *El Dridi* (n 3) para 46.
[77] See Opinion of the Advocate General Mazák, Case C-61/11 PPU, 1 April 2011, 28.
[78] Pleading of the Defence Counsel Luca Masera, Case C-61/11 PPU, Hearing of 30 March 2011, 23.

but effectiveness based:[79] Article 14(5) of Italian Immigration Law risked "jeopardizing the attainment of the objective pursued by that directive, namely, the establishment of an effective policy of removal and repatriation of illegally staying third-country nationals."[80] In the ECJ's view, long imprisonments are unlawful because they might delay the enforcement of the return decision and thereby undermine the effectiveness of the Return Directive.[81] On these grounds, the ECJ declared that the Return Directive precludes Member States' legislation providing for custodial penalties against undocumented migrants because this would keep them on the territory of the state, thus impeding their removal.

Even if the ECJ did not uphold the argument of the defense, the judgment's result was nevertheless the one they hoped for. On the very same day of the publication of the *El Dridi* judgment, the Italian Supreme Court acquitted three undocumented migrants prosecuted under Article 14(5), stating that the ECJ's ruling amounted to an *abolitio crimini* and its effects are equivalent to those deriving from the adoption of a new law.[82] Regarding the other preliminary references submitted by Italian courts on Article 14(5), all were removed from the ECJ's register because of their substantial overlap with *El Dridi*, which definitively solved the issue.

The *El Dridi* ruling had a big impact on the political sphere too. A couple of months after its publication, in June 2011 the Italian government passed a new law, under the urgent procedure, to make the national return system in line with the principles established by the Return Directive and the ECJ's judgment.[83] The reason behind such a prompt reaction has probably to do with the government's intention to avoid an infringement procedure for transposition delay. However, instead of a proper reform, the Italian lawmakers introduced a few adjustments; for instance, they did not repeal Article 14(5) crime but only changed the sanction by substituting detention with a large fine (from 10,000 up to 30,000 euros), so that the return procedure would not be delayed. For this and other reasons, the new law failed to convince migration supporters and experts, and the mobilization continued.

[79] Raffaelli, 'Criminalizing Irregular Immigration and the Returns Directive' (n 35) 482; Fabio Spitaleri, 'L'interpretazione della direttiva rimpatri tra efficienza del sistema e tutela dei diritti dello straniero' (2013) 1 Diritto, immigrazione e cittadinanza 15, 27.

[80] Judgment in the Case of *El Dridi* (n 3) 55.

[81] ibid 59.

[82] Corte Suprema di Cassazione Sez. I Penale, Notizie di Decisione (su questione nuova), sentenze 1590/2011, 1594/2011, 1606/2011, Cam Cons 28 April 2011. Natale (n 5) 20.

[83] Law Decree no 89/2011, Disposizioni urgenti per il completamento dell'attuazione della Direttiva 2004/38/CE sulla libera circolazione dei cittadini comunitari e per il recepimento della direttiva 2008/115/CE sul rimpatrio dei cittadini di Paesi terzi irregolari, 23 June 2011, 11G0128.

7. The third stage: Preliminary references against the clandestinity crime

The late transposition of the Return Directive in July 2011 could have marked the end of the mobilization. However, migration experts immediately pointed out that the transposition was still incomplete because the new Decree failed to incorporate all the necessary amendments to set the Italian law in line with European standards.[84] For instance, the Italian lawmaker did not provide for a period of voluntary return or for alternative measures to pre-removal detention, as required by the Return Directive.[85] Also, one of the most contested provisions of the Italian Immigration Law had survived unscathed: Article 10bis, known as the clandestinity crime. As the figure at the beginning of the chapter shows, after the judgment of *El Dridi*, Italian judges kept referring preliminary questions to the ECJ on the Return Directive and the clandestinity crime was the target.

The clandestinity crime sanctions any TCN who enters and stays in Italy irregularly with a large fine (from 5,000 to 10,000 euros).[86] It is arguable that this crime bothers more migrant supporters than migrants themselves. Indeed, its sanction is hardly enforced: most irregular migrants do not have traceable resources or a bank account. To be sure, if the fine is not paid the judge may substitute it with community work or house detention. But again, these are also difficult to enforce against somebody who has no fixed address and is interested in fleeing.

Despite its little practical relevance, the clandestinity crime was considered heinous by migrant rights defenders who saw it as the example of a type of criminal law that punishes you for who you are, a foreigner, rather than for your actions.[87] And yet, this symbol of crimmigration policies proved exceptionally resilient: it has survived several constitutional challenges before the Italian Constitutional Court[88] and proposals for amendment by the

[84] Guido Savio, 'La nuova disciplina delle espulsioni dopo la legge 129/2011' (*Melting Pot Europa*, 30 August 2011) <http://www.meltingpot.org/La-nuova-disciplina-delle-espulsioni-dopo-la-legge-129-2011.html> accessed 17 December 2024.

[85] Art 7 and art 15 of the Return Directive.

[86] Art 10bis of the Immigration Law 286/98 provides for the crime of irregular entry and stay of foreign nationals; the article was introduced by the Security Package Law in 2009.

[87] In Donini's words: "a criminal law where the reason for punishability (or for an aggravated sanctioning response) does not consist in the act committed, but in the type of perpetrator... it is true that the commission of the act is not desired, but because in reality it is its perpetrator who is undesirable." Donini (n 23) 118, author's translation. This critic was explicitly refused by the Italian Corte Costituzionale, Judgment 250 of 8 July 2010, Judge Frigo, 6.2.

[88] Section 4.1.

Parliament.[89] Between 2011 and 2012, the crime was also the object of ten preliminary references which asked the ECJ whether it was compatible with the Return Directive. As we shall see, seven out of ten referrals came from the same judge (Revere's *Giudice di Pace*) and were all declared manifestly inadmissible. This means that in reality, only four Italian judges submitted preliminary references to the ECJ on the clandestinity crime, and this circumstance makes the mobilization against Article 10bis much smaller in scale than the one against Article 14(5). The following subsections examine the preliminary references submitted by the Italian courts from the perspective of the actors on the ground, in order to shed some light on the origins of the judges' decision to refer.

7.1 *Sagor*

The case of Mr Sagor came before the Rovigo Tribunal by coincidence. Normally, the clandestinity crime is under the competence of the *Giudice di Pace*, a lay judge who occupies the lowest rank in the Italian courts' hierarchy. However, in this case the public prosecutor charged Mr Sagor with an additional crime (refusal to show identity documents to the police);[90] this joint accusation brought the case of *Sagor* under the competence of the Rovigo Tribunal giving it the chance to rule on the clandestinity crime, something that the judge had always wanted:

> I was fighting against Article 10bis since years. I wrote a series of journal articles and I went several times to Rome to give talks before the Superior Council of the Judiciary[91] to explain them why the crime should not be applied. In sum, I was very engaged. But the real problem of Article 10bis was that it falls under the competence of the *Giudice di Pace*. We, professional

[89] The Law no 67 of 2014 titled "*Deleghe al Governo in materia di pene detentive non carcerarie e di riforma del sistema sanzionatorio*" contained a delegation of powers by the Parliament to the government to enact a law that would have decriminalized certain crimes, among which there was also the "clandestinity crime." In spite of this, the Italian government decided not to implement the decriminalization for reasons of "political opportunity," ie the mutated international scenario after the so-called refugee crisis. Fatto Quotidiano, 'Reato Di Clandestinità, Governo Rinvia Abolizione: "Prima Valutazione Di Opportunità Politica" *Il Fatto Quotidiano* (8 January 2016) <http://www.ilfattoquotidiano.it/2016/01/08/reato-di-clandestinita-governo-rinvia-abolizione-prima-valutazione-di-opportunita-politica/2358988/> accessed 17 December 2024.

[90] Article 6(3) of Legislative Decree No 286/1998 which states: 'A foreign national who . . ., without valid grounds, does not comply with the order to present his passport or other identification document, and his residence permit or other document to prove legal presence in the national territory, shall be imprisoned for up to a year and fined up to EUR 2.000.'

[91] *Consiglio Superiore della Magistratura*, the Italian magistrates' governing body: <https://www.quirinale.it/page/csm_en> accessed 17 December 2024.

judges, meet with them [lay judges] only on rare occasions. So, we couldn't catch the 10bis.[92]

The Rovigo Tribunal judge was a member of *Magistratura Democratica* and of the board of Diritto Immigrazione e Cittadinanza.[93] He described the preliminary reference in *Sagor* as a "collective effort." For the drafting of the preliminary reference, he was assisted by experts in the ASGI–*Magistratura Democratica* network, and in particular by an EU law professor, Chiara Favilli. This is the same network of lawyers, judges, and scholars who were behind the *El Dridi* case and that mobilized once again to obtain the preliminary reference in the case of *Sagor*, with the goal of challenging another piece of the Italian crimmigration policy. The network's involvement is also evident by the fact that Professors Favilli and Masera represented Mr Sagor before the ECJ in Luxembourg.

But let us take a step back. The case for the incompatibility of Article 10bis with the Return Directive was not an easy one. The clandestinity crime sanctioned migrants with a fine; where they could not pay the fine or undertake alternative community work, the sanction would be transformed into house detention or, at the discretion of the judge, into an immediate expulsion from Italian territory. As explained in Section 3 of this chapter, the clandestinity crime was introduced in part for its high symbolism and in part to elude the application of the procedures provided by the Return Directive.[94]

The strategy to contest it consisted of two different arguments. The first was to use the same reasoning of *El Dridi*: Article 10bis sanctioned undocumented migrants with house detention, thus it kept migrants in Italy and undermined the effective enforcement of return decisions. The problem was that house detention was not the main sanction but only an alternative one. Even if the referring judge argued that undocumented migrants often cannot pay the fine, admittedly this was not the strongest argument.

The second argument claimed that the clandestinity crime violated the duty of sincere cooperation between Member States, a key EU law principle enshrined in Article 4(3) TEU. According to the referring court, Italian lawmakers introduced Article 10bis to rely on the criminal law exemption provided by Article 2.2(b) of the Return Directive. Under this exemption, Member States can decide not to apply the Return Directive to undocumented migrants

[92] Interview with Magistratura Democratica Judge, March 2016. Translation by the author.

[93] The journal was founded by *Magistratura Democratica* and ASGI. Discussed further in Section 4 of this chapter.

[94] Viganò, 'Il Dibattito Continua' (n 48).

who "are subject to return as a criminal law sanction" (more detail in Section 3 of this chapter). According to the referring court, the Italian government only introduced the clandestinity crime to avoid the application of the Return Directive, thus breaching its duty of sincere cooperation.

Two things complicated the *Sagor* challenge further. The first was that, a few months after the *Sagor* reference was submitted, the ECJ issued its judgment in *Achughbabian*, a similar case from France.[95] In *Achughbian*, the Court stated clearly that Member States were free to criminally sanction undocumented migrants for their illegal stay, provided that this would not imperil "the realisation of the aims pursued by the said directive, thus depriving it of its effectiveness."[96] The second complication came from the intervention of two Member States in support of the Italian government. While no Member State intervened in *El Dridi*, probably because of the tight schedule dictated by the urgent procedure, in *Sagor*, the German and Dutch governments filed observations. They stated that Article 10bis does not affect the goals of the Directive since it provides for the criminal proceedings to be discontinued should the return become immediately enforceable.

This time, the ECJ, in its judgment, gave Italy significant leeway.[97] The Court confirmed its findings in *Achughbabian* and held that Member States are free to enforce criminal sanctions against undocumented migrants; moreover, they can also issue return decisions in the form of criminal sanctions but these have to comply with the same procedural requirements stated in the Return Directive, otherwise they would become a tool to circumvent its application. Therefore, sanctioning the clandestinity crime with a removal is possible only in cases where the period for voluntary returns and other guarantees do not apply for one of the reasons stated in the Directive. Finally, the ECJ confirmed its finding in *El Dridi* and declared the use of house detention in conflict with the Directive since it might delay the removal.[98]

The judgment of *Sagor* was rather disappointing for migrants' supporters. Nevertheless, the *Magistratura Democratica*–ASGI network worked to frame

[95] C-329/11 *Achughbabian* (2011) CJEU, ECLI:EU:C:2011:807; The timing of the reference was no coincidence, the French preliminary reference was inspired by the decision in *El Dridi*. Rosa Raffaelli, 'Immigration and Criminal Law: Is There a Judge in Luxembourg?' in Bruno de Witte and others (eds), *National Courts and EU Law: New Issues, Theories and Methods* (Edward Elgar Publishing 2016) 217.

[96] *Achughbabian* (n 95) para 33. According to the ECJ, the Return Directive "does not preclude the law of a Member State from classifying an illegal stay as an offence and laying down penal sanctions to deter and prevent such an infringement of the national rules on residence." (para 28)

[97] Niovi Vavoula, 'The Interplay between EU Immigration Law and National Criminal Law—The Case of the Return Directive' in Valsamis Mitsilegas, Maria Bergström, and Theodore Konstadinides (eds), *Research Handbook on EU Criminal Law* (Edward Elgar Publishing 2016) 312.

[98] *Md Sagor* (n 3) para 35 ss.

and communicate the message of the decision in a way that was beneficial to their cause:

> We sold it as a partial victory, even if it was a partial defeat; but we were mostly interested in the political message. That is, that once again the Court of Justice declared another piece of the Security Package Law in contrast with EU law.[99]

Their message went through: the *Sagor* judgment triggered a new debate on the opportunity to abolish the clandestinity crime and Parliament voted for its repeal (it also helped a change in the ruling majority, which was now in the hands of a center-left coalition).[100] However, for reasons of "political opportunity,"[101] the center-left government did not follow the project to abolish the clandestinity crime and, although partially mutilated, the crime is still in force today.

7.2 *Mbaye* and the preliminary references from the Giudici di Pace

Although *Sagor* was the most impactful, it was not the only reference to the ECJ regarding the clandestinity crime. A total of ten preliminary references were submitted, and all but Sagor were from *Giudici di Pace*. At first glance, the number seems similar to the mobilization against Article 14(5) but at second look, we realize that only three judges referred: one request was submitted by the *Giudice di Pace* of Mestre, one by the *Giudice di Pace* of Lecce, and seven by the *Giudice di Pace* of Revere.[102] This consistently reduces the size of the mobilization.

[99] Interview with Magistratura Democratica Judge, March 2016. Translation by the author.

[100] Sara Anastasio and Salvatore Centonze, *Ingresso e Soggiorno Illegale Nel Territorio Dello Stato* (Key Editore 2016) 17.

[101] 'Reato di clandestinità, governo rinvia abolizione' *Il Fatto Quotidiano* (8 January 2016), <https://www.ilfattoquotidiano.it/2016/01/08/reato-di-clandestinita-governo-rinvia-abolizione-prima-valutazione-di-opportunita-politica/2358988/> accessed 17 December 2024.

[102] *Asad Abdallah* (2011) Giudice di Pace di Mestre, Order for Reference C-144/11; Case C-522/11 *Abdoul Khadre Mbaye* (2013) CJEU, ECLI:EU:C:2013:190; *Xiaomie Zhu and others* (2012) Giudice di Pace di Revere, Order for reference in case C-51/12; *Ion Beregovoi* (2012) Giudice di Pace di Revere, Order for reference in case C-52/12; *Hai Feng Sun* (2012) Giudice di Pace di Revere, Order for reference in case C-53/12; *Liung Hong Yang* (2012) Giudice di Pace di Revere, Order for reference in case C-54/12; *Ahmed Ettaghi* (2012) Giudice di Pace di Revere, C-73/12; *Tam* (2012) Giudice di Pace di Revere, Order for reference in case C-74/12; *Majali Abdel* (2012) Giudice di Pace di Revere, Order for reference in case C-75/12.

Were these references in some way connected to the mobilization described earlier? According to the interviews with the members of the *Magistratura Democratica*–ASGI network, *Giudici di Pace*, in general, were not involved in judicial associations and did not take part in their meetings and debates. This is because *Giudici di Pace* are not ordinary magistrates but honorary judges: they are temporarily appointed, do not follow the same career path, and have a different background and experience than professional judges. Also, at that time, *Giudici di Pace* did not take part in judicial training programs (addressed only to ordinary judges), which excluded them from many initiatives organized to raise awareness about the new Directive. Arguably, this had a clear impact on the quality of the preliminary references too: four out of nine were declared manifestly inadmissible by the ECJ because they lacked a basic description of the facts of the case.[103]

The case of *Mbaye* is partially different.[104] This, rather than a test case, was an individual lawyer's crusade against the clandestinity crime. During the proceedings, the defense lawyer challenged the clandestinity crime before three different top courts, in order, the Italian Constitutional Court, the ECJ, and the Supreme Court, and none of these challenges brought the hoped result.[105] Behind this litigation strategy was the lawyer Salvatore Centonze, an expert in migration law and the author of a monograph on the clandestinity crime.[106] As far as I can tell, he was a lone wolf and acted independently from the *Magistratura Democratica*–ASGI network.[107] The ECJ declared the *Mbaye* preliminary reference admissible but it reached Luxembourg just after *Sagor*, thus the Court only restated the same conclusion.

Although of apparently limited concrete impact, the *Giudici di Pace* references are important to understand what conditions determine the success of a legal mobilization. Although the *Giudici di Pace* were probably prompted to refer by the same discussions on blogs, conferences, and journals, they

[103] *Asad Abdallah* (n 102); *Tam* (n 102); *Majali Abdel* (n 102); *Ahmed Ettaghi* (n 102).

[104] *Mbaye* (n 102).

[105] Both the references to the ECJ and to the Constitutional Court were submitted too late: the two courts had already decided on the issue before (Corte Costituzionale, judgment no 250/2011 and Court of Justice, *Sagor*). The text of the constitutionality question to the Constitutional Court can be found at this link: <https://www.personaedanno.it/articolo/gdp-lecce-19-aprile-2010-est-c-rochira-il-reato-di-clandestinita-in-odore-di-incostituzionalita-sc> accessed 17 December 2024.

[106] Anastasio and Centonze (n 100).

[107] I only had an email exchange with lawyer Centonze, since he was not available for an interview. He can be described as the "loner" strategic litigant who "has extensive knowledge of EU law but is only weakly if at all embedded in anetwork." Pola Cebulak, Marta Morvillo, and Stefan Salomon, 'Strategic Litigation in EU Law: Who Does it Empower?' (2024) 25 German Law Journal 800, 811.

lacked the support of the network of lawyers, academics, and judges behind *El Dridi* and *Sagor*. As the next section will argue, these are crucial factors in a mobilization.

8. Contesting crimmigration through EU law enforcement

After this overview of the actors and the strategies behind the preliminary references, we can answer the starting question of this chapter: Why did Italian judges devote so much attention to the Return Directive?

One possible reading of the Italian case study is that it is an example of "decentralized enforcement" of EU law.[108] The Italian government, in 2010, refused to transpose the Directive despite the national return system not being in line with European standards. As a response, the Italian courts triggered the preliminary reference procedure, and the consequent rulings in *El Dridi* and *Sagor* highlighted the inconsistencies between the national and the supranational frameworks, forcing the Italian government eventually to transpose the Return Directive into national law. In this light, the judgments are a strong example of how domestic courts help the ECJ to enforce EU norms against their national government. However, this account leaves an important question unresolved: given that most of the EU Member States had not transposed the Directive by the deadline, why did only Italian courts refer this issue to the ECJ?[109]

By comparing Italy to the other Member States, the exceptional nature of its references becomes visible. These, it is argued, amount to a mass legal mobilization that did not aim to enforce the Directive but instead to strike down national legislation. We can explain the exceptional number of references only by considering the special sociopolitical context of those years and the specific opportunity structure created by the criminal law reforms. The target of the mobilization was not, or not mainly, enforcing EU law but contesting the criminalization of migrants, for ideological and practical reasons.

[108] Mark A Pollack, *The Engines of European Integration: Delegation, Agency, and Agenda Setting in the EU* (OUP 2003) 163; Raffaelli (n 95); Fornalé (n 5) 144.

[109] See Commission Press Release, 'An effective and humane return policy: 8 Member States have yet to comply with the Return Directive' of 29 September 2011 <http://europa.eu/rapid/press-release_IP-11-1097_en.htm?locale=en> accessed 17 December 2024.

8.1 The ideological reasons

Starting from ideological reasons, progressive legal experts and practitioners felt that the Italian crimmigration norms conflicted with the normative principles that underpin criminal justice in liberal democracies and that are safeguarded by the Italian constitution.[110] Because of their discriminatory character, the norms were "radically compromising the democratic identity" of Italy.[111] Another recurring criticism was the violation of the "harm principle":[112] the legislator criminalized undocumented migrants because of their status and nationality, not because their conduct was harmful toward other people or rights.[113] According to this view, the criminal justice system was transformed into a tool of oppression that prosecuted persons for what they are and not for what they do.[114] Plus, the criminal laws did not aim at the redemption and inclusion of the criminals but at their prompt removal.[115]

But the political choice of using criminal law tools had unexpected consequences: criminalizing a conduct has so much "symbolic power" that "it inevitably and forcefully catalyzes the energies of jurists."[116] In response to this criminalization, a network of lawyers, academics, and judges emerged and started organizing; they triggered a vibrant debate about how to contest the crimmigration norms and which laws or courts could be used. Their first legal challenge took place before the Italian Constitutional Court, years before the Directive was adopted, which is further evidence that their main concern was not EU law enforcement.

The Italian Constitutional Court was the first recipient of the mass legal mobilization against crimmigration: a huge number of requests for constitutional review reached the Court which declared them only partially in conflict with

[110] Masera, Luca, "Immigrazione" in Oliviero Mazza and Francesco Viganò (eds), *Misure urgenti in materia di sicurezza pubblica* (Giappichelli 2008) 4.
[111] Ferrajoli (n 22) 13.
[112] Nina Peršak, 'Principles of EU Criminalisation and Their Varied Normative Strength: Harm and Effectiveness' (2021) 27 European Law Journal 463, 466.
[113] Donini (n 23) 123. Donini, in line with the Italian tradition, calls this criminal policy choice *diritto penale d'autore*: "This aspect reveals the emergence of a new type of diritto penale d'autore: the target is no longer Blacks, Jews, communists, terrorists, born criminals, heretics and the like. They are, much more simply, non-EU citizens, all human beings of non-EU origin". Translation by the author.
[114] Angelo Caputo, 'Diseguali, Illegali, Criminali (Una Guida Alla Lettura)' (2009) 1 Questione Giustizia 83, 85.
[115] Alessandro Spena, 'Resisting Immigration Detention' (2016) 18 European Journal of Migration and Law 201, 206.
[116] Natale (n 5) 17. Translation by the author.

the Italian constitution, leaving in place two of the most important criminal provisions, Article 14(5) and the clandestinity crime.[117] After this first partial defeat, the adoption of the Return Directive represented a new opening in the legal opportunity structure (LOS) for pro-migrant groups, that understood its potential to bring yet another challenge to a heinous national provision. This is quite ironic for a Directive that saw the light under the stigma of being the symbol of "Fortress Europe."[118]

8.2 The practical reasons

Beyond ideological reasons, the legal mobilization was facilitated by practical circumstances that made Italian judges more prone to refer. The work of Italian criminal judges had been heavily impacted by the crimmigration norms, which basically imposed the criminal prosecution of every undocumented migrant on national territory. Soon Italian prosecutors and criminal courts became swamped with thousands of cases concerning the clandestinity crime and Article 14(5), with negative consequences on the regular processing of other crimes. In some municipalities, like Rome and Milan, it was reached the point where up to 40 percent of all the arrests were made under Article 14(5).[119] Prosecutors and criminal judges openly criticized the crimmigration policy, claiming it was an ineffective system that was damaging the entire justice system.[120] This general discontent facilitated the role of migrant

[117] For instance, the following are all decisions from the Constitutional Court on the constitutionality of the clandestinity crime: Sentenza 250/2010, Ordinanza 252/2010, Ordinanza 253/2010, Ordinanza 318/2010, Ordinanza 320/2010, Ordinanza 321/2010, Ordinanza 329/2010, Ordinanza 343/2010, Ordinanza 3/2011, Ordinanza 6/2011, Ordinanza 13/2011, Ordinanza 32/2011, Ordinanza 64/2011, Ordinanza 65/2011, Ordinanza 72/2011, Ordinanza 75/2011, Ordinanza 84/2011, Ordinanza 86/2011, Ordinanza 95/2011, Ordinanza 100/2011, Ordinanza 131/2011, Ordinanza 135/2011, Ordinanza 144/2011, Ordinanza 149/2011, Ordinanza 154/2011, Ordinanza 158/2011, Ordinanza 161/2011, Ordinanza 162/2011, Ordinanza 193/2011, Ordinanza 200/2011, Ordinanza 252/2011, Ordinanza 306/2011, Ordinanza 65/2012, Ordinanza 84/2012, Ordinanza 175/2013.

[118] Diego Acosta Arcarazo, 'The Good, the Bad and the Ugly in EU Migration Law: Is the European Parliament Becoming Bad and Ugly? (The Adoption of Directive 2008/15: The Returns Directive)' (2009) 11 European Journal of Migration and Law.

[119] Miazzi (n 14) 138.

[120] Liana Milella, 'Roberti: "Il reato di immigrazione clandestina? Legge che ha solo ostacolato le indagini sui trafficanti"' *La Repubblica* (Rome, 8 January 2016) <https://www.repubblica.it/politica/2016/01/08/news/roberti_il_reato_di_immigrazione_clandestina_legge_che_ha_solo_ostacolato_le_indagini_sui_trafficanti_-130835471/> accessed 7 June 2024; Alessandra Ziniti, 'Il procuratore di Agrigento, Renato Di Natale: "Con il reato di clandestinità abbiamo gli uffici ingolfati"' *La Repubblica* (Palermo, 29 May 2016) <https://palermo.repubblica.it/cronaca/2016/05/29/news/il_procuratore_di_agrigento_renato_di_natale_con_il_reato_di_clandestinita_abbiamo_gli_uffici_ingolfati_-140854592/> accessed 7 June 2024.

supporters, who had an easier job in convincing criminal judges to challenge the crimmigration norms as soon as the opportunity arose.

The attitude of criminal judges also helps to explain why some norms were mobilized instead of others. Overall, several Italian norms conflicted with the Directive and their challenge would have led to a better protection of migrant rights. To mention just a few: Italian law provided an entry ban of ten years for returned migrants, while the Directive set a maximum of five years;[121] Italian procedures did not grant a term for voluntary departure[122] and neither provided for alternative measures to detention, as provided instead by the Directive.[123] Despite all these inconsistencies, the legal mobilization focused exclusively on challenging Article 14(5) and the clandestinity crime, the norms criminalizing migrants. On the one hand, this is explained by the much mentioned "catalyzing power" of criminal norms, which have awakened the conscience of criminal judges. On the other, this is further evidence that judges were particularly inclined to challenge the norms responsible for their overload of cases. If some judges acted under ideological considerations, others probably mobilized under more selfish or practical considerations.

8.3 The tail of the legal mobilization: *Celaj*

The mobilization targeting Article 14(5) and the clandestinity crime ended in 2012, with the half victory of the case of *Sagor*. For the sake of completeness, we should mention that a couple of years later, in 2014, a judge of the *Tribunale di Firenze* referred a new case on crimmigration, the *Celaj* case. Again, the case focused on one of the crimes introduced by the Bossi–Fini Law, Article 13(3) of the Italian Immigration Law, which provides for the immediate arrest of the undocumented migrant who violates an entry ban and punishes the crime with a prison sentence from one to four years.[124] The norm follows the blueprint of the Article 14(5) crime and for this reason, the Florence judge used the same argument of *El Dridi*: this norm, too, delays the return procedure and should be declared incompatible with the Directive.[125] However,

[121] Art 13(14) of the Italian Immigration Law, vs art 11.2 of the Return Directive.
[122] Art 13(3) of the Italian Immigration Law, vs art 7 of the Return Directive.
[123] Art 14(1) of the Italian Immigration Law, vs art 15 of the Return Directive.
[124] Art 13(3) of the Immigration Law provides: "A foreign national against whom a removal order has been made may not re-enter the territory of the State without special authorization issued by the Ministry for the Interior. In the event of infringement, the foreign national shall be liable to a term of imprisonment of between one and four years and shall be expelled by immediate deportation."
[125] *Celaj* (n 3) para 20.

the ECJ adopted a different interpretation this time: it differentiated between the case of a migrant that enters the territory of a Member State irregularly for the first time (*El Dridi*) and that of a migrant that enters a second time by violating an entry ban (*Celaj*); in the Court's view, Member States are free to inflict a prison sentence for this second conduct.[126] The ECJ's reasoning was criticized for being too weak and simplistic; commentators underlined the incongruences between the different approaches taken by the ECJ in its case law.[127] Remarkably, the case of *Celaj* was in no way connected to the legal mobilization that led to the emergence of *El Dridi* and *Sagor*.[128] The referring judge decided to refer the case autonomously and was not helped by the network of migrant supporters we saw in action.[129] Also, Mr Celaj's lawyer was not an ASGI member and did not participate in the proceedings before the ECJ. This leaves us with the question of whether a better supported case would have reached a more favorable conclusion for the migrant, especially because although nobody represented the migrant before the ECJ, five Member States intervened in support of the legitimacy of the Italian criminal provision.[130]

To conclude, the many preliminary references that reached the ECJ cannot simply be explained as EU law enforcement but neither as simply pro-migrant mobilization. They were part of a larger mobilization, started before national courts, and conducted by lawyers, migrant supporter groups, and progressive judges who wanted to contest the legitimacy of provisions contrasting with Italian constitutional principles and European liberal values. The network of lawyers and judges that we have seen in action stood up not only to protect migrants but also to defend an idea of justice in which they believe. The key to the success of their mobilization was the enhanced propensity to refer of common criminal judges, who wanted to get rid of a costly and inefficient crimmigration system.

[126] *Celaj* (n 3) para 28.

[127] Anna Magdalena Kosińska, 'The Problem of Criminalisation of the Illegal Entry of a Third-Country National in the Case of Breaching an Entry Ban. Commentary on the Judgment of the Court of Justice of 1 October 2015 in Case C 290/14, Skerdjan Celaj' (2016) 18 European Journal of Migration and Law 243; Andrea Romano, '"Circumstances . . . Are Clearly Distinct": La Detenzione Dello Straniero per Il Delitto Di Illecito Reingresso Nella Sentenza Celaj Della Corte Di Giustizia' [2015] Diritto, Immigrazione e Cittadinanza 109; Mario Savino, 'Irregular Migration at the Crossroads, between Administrative Removal and Criminal Deterrence: The Celaj Case' (2016) 53 Common Market Law Review 1419.

[128] *Celaj* (n 3).

[129] Interview with the Tribunale di Firenze Judge, 26 March 2016, Florence.

[130] *Celaj* (2015) Opinion Advocate General Szpunar, case C-290/14 [46].

9. Immigration lawyers and criminal judges against crimmigration

The visionary forces of law oppose matter-of-fact forces. The law is not insulated from the rest of the world. It maintains multiple relationships with politics, morale, history....

Introduction to MEDEL (Magistrats Européens pour la Démocratie et la Liberté)

Between 2011 and 2012, a network of lawyers, judges, legal experts, and migration activists decided to mobilize the Return Directive before the ECJ to challenge Italian immigration law. The EU law mobilization aimed at contesting the crimmigration norms introduced a few years before in the Italian legal framework, in defense of migrant rights and justice principles.

The Italian case study stands out in many ways in terms of both the mobilizing actors and the structure of legal opportunities. First of all, due to its scale, it can be defined as a mass mobilization: in about a year, sixteen courts decided to submit a reference to the ECJ regarding the compatibility between Italian norms and the Return Directive. Second, whilst legal mobilization often takes the form of "bringing a claim, representing a claimant, and also submitting written briefs (*amicus curiae*) as third parties,"[131] things went differently this time. The proceedings cannot be described as strategic litigation because they were initiated by public prosecutors and not by mobilizing actors. Yet, migrant supporters managed to find a way to be present before the Court of Justice and represent the migrants. Third, the mobilization counted on a high level of judicial receptivity, being very well received by criminal judges. This is partly explained by the role that judicial institutions and associations such as *Magistratura Democratica* had in the mobilization: they contributed to disseminating ideas and creating capabilities and resources within the judiciaries that were crucial to shifting judges' legal visions.[132] Because of their political preferences, some of these judges were sensitive to arguments regarding the respect of the legality principle and of the accused's rights; other judges just wanted to contest the crimmigration norms that overloaded them with migration cases. From this emerges the uniqueness of the Italian judicial context

[131] Rachel Cichowski, 'Mobilisation, Litigation and Democratic Governance' (2013) 49(3) *Representation* 322.

[132] Ezequiel A González-Ocantos, *Shifting Legal Visions: Judicial Change and Human Rights Trials in Latin America* (CUP 2016).

that, because of tangential jurisdictional factors, created an opening in the legal opportunity structure that greatly helped the mobilization.

While judges are usually seen as institutional actors, self-interested, or even active defenders of the status quo, in Italy, they stand out as active motors in the legal mobilization. The judges were not just open to receiving reference requests but, especially in their professional organizations, they were proactively working toward the mobilization of EU law. Despite being quite exceptional, this type of activist judge blurs the distinction between the actors and the structure of the mobilization.

Eventually, the mobilization before the ECJ did not completely prevent the criminalization of migrants in Italy. The judgments in the cases of *El Dridi* and *Sagor* were amplified by civil society and had an impact on the Italian legal framework but in a limited manner. Still today, in Italy, an undocumented migrant can be prosecuted and condemned for the clandestinity crime, and if he/she does not comply with a removal order, will also incur criminal sanctions. However, these sanctions are less onerous than earlier, and a long period of imprisonment is no longer admitted, neither in Italy nor in the rest of the EU. If mobilizing actors did not succeed in completely striking down the crimmigration norms, at least migrant supporters were able to reduce their relevance significantly.

3
The UK
Mobilizing EU Citizenship to Protect Third-country Nationals

There is a very strong and committed immigration bar. I guess [there are] thirty people who specialized in immigration, who always represent immigrants and never represent the government, conscious about trying to advance migrants' rights.[1]

1. The uneasy relationship between the UK and EU migration policy

One may ask why a book on the European Court of Justice devotes a chapter to the UK since this is no longer an EU Member State. British preliminary references have crucially shaped EU justice in many ways and a relevant part of their emergence is due to legal mobilization for migrant rights. This chapter will show that the mobilization of EU free movement law has shaped and has been shaped by Britain's colonial past and the UK's troubled European integration.

When still a Member State of the EU, the UK tried its utmost to shield its migration policy from EU influence. The UK enjoyed a special Treaty opt-out: it was not bound by any EU law adopted under the chapter on "border check, asylum, and immigration" unless it decided to opt in.[2] The UK was not bound either by the so-called *Schengen aquis*, the system of norms that regulates the abolition of internal border controls between the EU Member States. This means that the UK was exempted from the majority of EU rules on migration and visas, and British lawmakers could autonomously regulate the entry

[1] Interview with Simon Cox, London, 18 November 2016.

[2] See Protocol 21 on *The Position of the United Kingdom and Ireland*, annexed to the EU Treaties. The UK opted in to most of the norms on criminal matters and police cooperation, but it did not to measures regarding migration and asylum. An important exception is the UK's opt-in to the Dublin Regulation and its recasts. The list of UK's opt-ins is available at <https://www.gov.uk/government/publications/jha-opt-in-and-schengen-opt-out-protocols--3> accessed 17 December 2024.

Legal Mobilization for Migrant Rights. Virginia Passalacqua, Oxford University Press.
 DOI: 10.1093/9780198943006.003.0003

and residence of third-country nationals (TCNs) in their territory. Yet, despite these efforts, this chapter shows that migrant rights defenders managed to subject an important part of UK migration law to the judicial scrutiny of the European Court of Justice (ECJ): the free movement rights of TCN family members of Union citizens.

The UK, despite its many exemptions, was bound by EU primary law which comprises the norms on Union citizenship and free movement of persons. These norms regulate the rights of Union citizens to move, work, and reside in the EU. Union citizenship provisions grant free movement rights also to the family members of Union citizens, regardless of their nationality. This means that if Union citizens move to the UK with their TCN family members, the latter are also covered by Union citizenship law and enjoy "derived" free movement rights.[3] The focus of this chapter is precisely on these derived rights and on the mobilization of EU justice to use, expand, and defend them.

There is another reason that makes the UK an interesting case study. The UK was historically a country of weak judicial review and lenient judges, but when it joined the EU it had to adjust to the mutated constitutional context. Thanks to the principles of supremacy, direct effect, and the preliminary reference mechanism, British courts acquired new judicial review powers, strengthening individuals' position vis-à-vis the executive. On the one hand, this judicial empowerment was used and fostered by Eurolawyers and legal non-governmental organizations (NGOs) who learned how to use EU law to challenge British norms and mobilized in court against the executive. On the other hand, judicial empowerment was met with criticism from those who suspected it would threaten the doctrine of parliamentary sovereignty.[4] This shows how being an EU Member State had profoundly shaped the UK's judicial culture and legal opportunity structure, creating opportunities for legal mobilization.

As explained in the Introduction of the book, the case studies analyzed in this book were selected according to quantitative data on the preliminary references submitted to the ECJ. Before leaving the EU, the UK was the Member State that had referred most questions regarding the rights of TCNs who are family members of Union citizens. The Court of Justice received seventy-two

[3] Case C-413/99 *Baumbast and R* (2002) CJEU, ECLI:EU:C:2002:493; Case C-310/08 *Ibrahim* (2010) CJEU, ECLI:EU:C:2010:80; Case C-529/11 *Alarape and Tijani* (2013) CJEU, ECLI:EU:C:2013:290.

[4] TRS Allan, *The Sovereignty of Law: Freedom, Constitution and Common Law* (OUP 2013) 133. Catherine Barnard, 'Brexit and the [Rule of] Law' (2019) Policy Brief 10, Bennett Institute for Public Policy, <https://www.bennettinstitute.cam.ac.uk/wp-content/uploads/2020/12/Policy_brief_BIPP_Catherine_Barnard_Nov_19.pdf> accessed 18 March 2025.

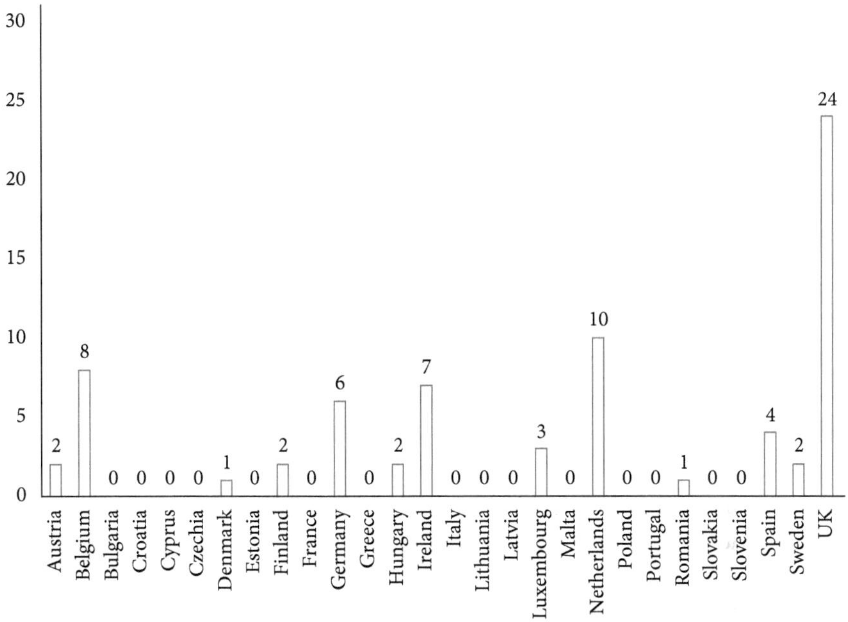

Figure 3.1 Number of preliminary references regarding TCN family members of Union citizens by country of reference (up to December 2022).

requests for preliminary rulings on this topic. Of these, twenty-four came from the UK (Figure 3.1).

These data raise interesting questions. Why did British judges refer so many questions in such a specific field? Was there any role for civil society actors?[5] And how does litigation relate to the migration debates in the UK? Relying on doctrinal and empirical research conducted in the UK, this chapter sheds light on the mobilization behind the references. By analyzing the actors, the resources, and the legal opportunity structure, the chapter unveils the internal and external factors that enabled and facilitated the mobilization of EU justice.

The first part of this chapter analyzes the British context for legal mobilization by focusing in particular on the migration field and explaining the local meaning that EU free movement law takes in the UK. The second part closely

[5] As explained in Chapter 1, the number of preliminary references is used as an indicator, a hint that a legal mobilization could have occurred. Notably, we can have legal mobilization consisting of only one test or strategic case. For instance, this was the case of *Chavez*, a case referred from the Netherlands, that was brought strategically to the attention of the ECJ to extend the rights of TCN family members of static Union citizens. Case C-133/15 *Chavez Vilchez* (2017) CJEU, ECLI:EU:C:2017:354.

traces the origin of the preliminary references, focusing on the conditions that led British judges to refer questions and on the role of civil society. The chapter illustrates who were the main promoters of EU litigation and what factors enabled or constrained them.

The UK case study shows that migrant supporters used preliminary references as a legal strategy to resist the deportation of TCN family members. Given the lack of protection offered by UK law and the European Convention on Human Rights (ECHR), migrant supporters turned to EU free movement law, trying to stretch its boundaries to cover TCN family members of British citizens too. The presence of a "support structure"[6] of EU lawyers and NGOs was a key resource: they understood the potential of free movement law for defending migrants' rights and they seized the opportunities offered by supranational litigation. This chapter shows that these preliminary references on TCN free movement rights should be read within the broader context of migrant supporters' long struggle to hold the executive (the Home Office) accountable for its violations of migrant rights.

2. Legal mobilization in the UK: Lessons from other fields

Legal mobilization has been widely studied in the UK context, probably more so than in any other EU country. Harlow and Rawling noted that in the UK, legal mobilization as a social phenomenon experienced a relevant expansion during the 1970s and 1980s, when groups representing minorities "had shifted their attention . . . towards the use of legal techniques to secure given objectives."[7] The authors interpreted this shift as a reaction to the closure demonstrated by Conservative governments, and especially Thatcher's, toward their campaigns. In their account, because the most traditional ways of lobbying and campaigning proved unsuccessful, organizations supporting minorities have resorted to litigation strategies. In the legal mobilization field, this is known as the "political disadvantage" argument.[8] Hilson too, in his comparative analysis of three UK cases (in the fields of environment, animal rights, and gender equality), stated that the lack of political opportunities might have influenced

[6] Charles R Epp, *The Rights Revolution: Lawyers, Activists, and Supreme Courts in Comparative Perspective* (1st edn, University of Chicago Press 1998).

[7] Carol Harlow and Richard Rawlings, *Pressure Through Law* (Taylor and Francis 1992) 48.

[8] Richard C Cortner, 'Strategies and Tactics of Litigants in Constitutional Cases' (1968) 17 Journal of Public Law 287.

the choice of social movements to adopt a litigation strategy, together with other factors such as resources and ideology.[9]

However, scholars offer contradictory accounts of the legal opportunity structure in the UK. Vanhala describes it as "an inhospitable environment for legal mobilization" because of the lack of constitutional rights, the doctrine of parliamentary sovereignty, "the slow nature of social movements," and the "conservative" nature of the English judiciary.[10] Kilpatrick, on the contrary, in a comparative study about the application of the EU Equal Pay Directive for men and women in the UK and France, takes Britain as a successful case of using the law to advance a specific cause. In her account, trade unions relied on the institutional support of the UK Equal Opportunity Commission which offered crucial expertise during litigation.[11] This is confirmed by other authors, according to whom the use of an EU litigation strategy yielded important results in this field: the equality body gained access to the ECJ through preliminary references and obtained the enforcement of the more protective EU law standards into the British legal system.[12]

At the same time, EU legal opportunities have not been seized in other policy fields. For instance, studies conducted in the environmental sector led to a less positive assessment. Golub pointed out that in general, the UK is one of the EU Member States that refer the least, given its size; he analyzed a series of cases in the field of environmental protection to show how British courts often do not apply EU law and refrain from making references to the ECJ (even courts of last instance).[13] In Golub's view, the reason behind the lack of references lies in the special attitude of British judges who are "loathe [sic] to make referrals" and are "unwilling to co-operate with the ECJ in promoting European integration."[14] According to his account, British judges' particular disposition toward EU law and the ECJ is a result of domestic political factors and in particular of the "Euro-pessimism" that dominates the political debate in the UK.[15]

[9] Chris Hilson, 'New Social Movements: The Role of Legal Opportunity' (2002) 9 Journal of European Public Policy 238, 239.

[10] Lisa Vanhala, 'Legal Opportunity Structures and the Paradox of Legal Mobilization by the Environmental Movement in the UK' (2012) 46 Law & Society Review 523, 529.

[11] Claire Kilpatrick, 'Effective Utilisation of Equality Rights: Equal Pay for Work of Equal Value in France and the UK' in Frances Gardiner (ed), *Sex Equality Policy in Western Europe* (1997) 41.

[12] Kilpatrick (n 11); Catherine Barnard, 'A European Litigation Strategy: The Case of the Equal Opportunities Commission' in Jo Shaw and Gillian More (eds), *New Legal Dynamics of European Union* (Clarendon Press 1995); Karen Alter and Jeannette Vargas, 'Explaining Variation in the Use of European Litigation Strategies: European Community Law and British Gender Equality Policy' (2000) 33 Comparative Political Studies 452.

[13] Jonathan Golub, 'The Politics of Judicial Discretion: Rethinking the Interaction between National Courts and the European Court of Justice' (1996) 19 West European Politics 360, 369.

[14] ibid 368.

[15] ibid 377.

These opposite findings suggest that in the UK, reliance on the ECJ is field specific. While in the gender equality field, the ECJ has been successfully used as a means for enhancing women's rights; in the environmental field, access to the Court has been denied. This is confirmed by the fact that the number of British references varies greatly depending on the subject matter. This also dismisses the argument that British courts are generally unwilling to refer: how can British judges be averse to referring in certain fields and not in others? If the British hostility lies in Eurosceptic discourses, do these not affect all judges equally?[16]

The fact that British references vary from field to field further confirms the need to overcome the approach that considers only national judges' behavioral factors to explain references,[17] that is, whether judges are "reference prone" or "reference averse." This approach assumes that the decision to refer depends entirely on the national court, which is true in the law (Article 267 of the Treaty on European Union (TFEU)) but arguably disproved in practice. Even if data on the general reference rate in the UK confirms Golub's hypothesis that British courts are among the most reference-averse in Europe,[18] this does not hold with regard to the issue covered in this chapter where UK courts referred more than any other courts in the EU. Alter's hypothesis on lower courts being more prone to refer is not confirmed either (only two out of twenty-four references came from first-instance courts). By adopting a bottom-up approach, this study takes a different perspective on how the preliminary mechanism works, emphasizing the role of the parties, the political context behind litigation, the resources that litigants have, and the legal opportunity structure.

3. Understanding migration in the UK: The historical and political context

The UK's migration policy, its colonial past, and its relationship with the EU are three pieces of the same puzzle: we cannot understand one without the others. This becomes evident if we place British migration and citizenship laws in their

[16] Stone Sweet and Brunell argue: "UK judges are not 'loath' to co-operate with the ECJ compared with judges in other member states. UK judges refer more references in some areas than some other national judges, and fewer references in some areas than some other national judges." Alec Stone Sweet and Thomas L Brunell, 'The European Court and the National Courts: A Statistical Analysis of Preliminary References, 1961–95' (1998) 5 Journal of European Public Policy 66, 88.

[17] Morten Broberg and Niels Fenger, 'Variations in Member States' Preliminary References to the Court of Justice—Are Structural Factors (Part of) the Explanation?' (2013) 19 European Law Journal 488, 489.

[18] ibid 500.

historical context. In the UK, the main instruments regulating people's movement were introduced as part of the process of emancipating the British nation from its imperial past, which mostly took place in the years from 1948 to 1981.[19] The next subsections of this chapter outline the main historical stages of British migration policy: the constitutive phase, the regulation of secondary movement and marriage migration, and the shift in migration policy that took place from 1997 on.

The historical and political overview points out the significance of the advent of European rights in the British context. As Joppke argued, Britain's initial success in controlling migration was largely because the government's restrictive policy did not encounter any judicial challenge; the UK does not have a written constitution and its judiciary is rather "docile" toward the executive.[20] This means that the government enjoyed great discretion in controlling migration, often at the expense of migrant rights. Against this background, the mobilization of EU rights before the ECJ constituted a powerful tool for resisting and opposing the British executive's migration policy.

3.1 The constitutive phase of British migration and citizenship law

The end of the Second World War marked the start of the process that redefined the British identity as a nation state. This process consisted mainly in dealing with decolonization and "shedding the vestiges of [the British] empire."[21] An important part of this process consisted of providing citizenship to the subjects of the empire. Until then, all people born or naturalized in the territory of the empire enjoyed the status of being British "subjects" and, interestingly, there was no such thing as British citizenship.[22]

The situation changed with the British Nationality Act of 1948, which turned the imperial subjects into Commonwealth citizens.[23] All people from the UK and its colonies enjoyed equal status with equal political, social, and residence rights in the UK, regardless of whether they came from London or from Delhi.[24] Remarkably, Commonwealth citizenship was granted also to

[19] The first citizenship reform was adopted in 1948, the last in 1981, which completed this period of citizenship and nation building.

[20] Christian Joppke, *Immigration and the Nation-State: The United States, Germany, and Great Britain* (OUP 1999) 103.

[21] JM Evans, 'Immigration Act 1971' (1972) 35 The Modern Law Review 508, 508.

[22] Rieko Karatani, *Defining British Citizenship: Empire, Commonwealth and Modern Britain* (Frank Cass 2003) 1.

[23] Randall Hansen, *Citizenship and Immigration in Postwar Britain* (OUP 2000) 35.

[24] Anja Wiesbrock, *Legal Migration to the European Union* (Martinus Nijhoff Publishers 2010) 79.

imperial subjects from former colonies, like Canada, to maintain a relationship between the UK and its Commonwealth. Within the broad group of Commonwealth citizens, some also enjoyed the status of Citizens of the United Kingdom and the Colonies (hereinafter CUKC). This status was granted only to the people from the UK and its present colonies. Remarkably, the status of CUKC does not correspond to modern British national citizenship because it recognized equal status and rights to all the people under the British government, from the UK to Jamaica.

The establishment of such an expansive citizenship reflects the resilience of the British imperial mentality: decolonization was a serious setback in the minds of British policymakers. However, the idea to grant equal status to all the citizens of the UK and the colonies came with unforeseen costs: the Nationality Act of 1948 virtually opened the UK's door to hundreds of millions of people coming from the Commonwealth who had the right to enter and reside as citizens. Apparently, British "[p]olicy-makers accepted the transformation of the United Kingdom into a multicultural society as the price of supporting the ties between Britain and the Old Dominions."[25]

The British post-war liberal attitude toward its borders can also be explained by the serious labor shortage that the UK was experiencing, which made it very attractive for people from the colonies in search of work. Between 1951 and 1971, the census registered an exponential increase in the foreign-born population, especially from Jamaica and India.[26] Clearly their migration was facilitated by the residence and movement rights they enjoyed as Commonwealth citizens or CUKC.

The first problems emerged in the 1960s when an economic recession hit the UK and the unemployment rates grew. Confronted with these new difficulties, the British attitude toward migration changed and public opinion became more openly hostile toward non-white immigrants.[27] The racist component of this new sentiment emerged also from the fact that white immigrants, such

[25] Hansen, *Citizenship and Immigration in Postwar Britain* (n 23) 19.

[26] Home Office and Office for National Statistics, 'Immigration Patterns of Non-UK Born Populations in England and Wales in 2011' (2013) 14. See also Stephen Small and John Solomos, 'Race, Immigration and Politics in Britain: Changing Policy Agendas and Conceptual Paradigms 1940s–2000s' (2006) 47 International Journal of Comparative Sociology 235, 239.

[27] The tensions between British and immigrant minorities became evident during the so-called race riots of 1958 in Nottingham and Notting Hill but also through polls that consistently proved population anti-migration stance. Marcus Collins, 'Immigration and Opinion Polls in Postwar Britain' (2016) 18 Modern History Review 8. At that time, nationalist and racist conceptions of the British state were gaining consensus, especially thanks to the campaign of Enoch Powell, a Member of Parliament, who heavily shaped public perceptions and ultimately influenced conservatories policy. See David Dixon, 'Thatcher's People: The British Nationality Act 1981' (1983) 10 Journal of Law and Society 161, 172 and Small and Solomos (n 26) 243.

as the Irish or East Europeans, who also moved to the UK in high numbers during the post-war period, did not face the same hostility.[28] Such public aversion toward non-white immigrants first led the Conservative and then the Labour government to endorse a reduction in the number of immigrants coming from certain Commonwealth countries; they embraced the idea that being a Commonwealth citizen, a CUKC, or holding a British passport were not enough to enter the UK, and they started introducing new migration controls aimed at distinguishing between wanted and unwanted citizens.[29] The UK experience was pretty unique as it introduced migration controls to be enforced against its own citizens, intending to differentiate between those who fully belonged and those who did not.

The process of immigration reform aimed at reducing the number of people moving to the UK started in the 1960s. Under this goal, several acts were adopted: the 1962 Immigrants Act, the 1968 Commonwealth Immigrants Act, the 1969 Immigration Appeals Act, and the 1971 Immigration Act. These laws did not formally affect the mechanism of citizenship allocation, but they de facto took away citizenship rights from many non-white Commonwealth citizens and CUKC. The 1971 Act was the culmination of this process: under these norms, the rights to enter and reside in the UK depended on whether a person was a "patrial" or not. The notion of "patriality" served to designate those born in the UK territory or with an ancestral connection with the UK. Hardly anyone from, say, Jamaica or Zimbabwe had British ancestors, therefore, like aliens, they became subject to migration controls.[30] On the contrary, many "white" citizens from the Old Commonwealth (ie Australia, New Zealand, and Canada), despite not being CUKC, had British ancestors and easily acquired rights to reside in the UK.

Some authors read this backlash toward CUKC newcomers as a direct consequence of the flaws present in the previous citizenship regime. The 1948 Nationality Act had included "ethnolinguistically diverse people" under the same status, and this created a discrepancy between citizenship and national identity: "Britishness had to be detached from the institutions of citizenship.

[28] The conclusion by the Committee on Social and Economic Problems 1955, reported by Layton-Henry, openly argued that problems arising from non-white migration do not arise in case of Irish migration because the last are not "a different race" [sic] from ordinary UK inhabitants. See Zic Layton-Henry, 'Britain: The Would-Be Zero-Immigration Country' in Wayne Cornelius, Philip Martin, and James Hollifield (eds), *Controlling Immigration: A Global Perspective* (Stanford University Press 1994) 274.

[29] Conservative and Labour governments adopted two Commonwealth Immigrants Acts, one in 1962 and a second in 1968.

[30] Joppke (n 20) 108. For a definition of "patriality" under the Immigration Act and a detailed description of the provisions in the law, see Evans (n 21) 509.

... It was thus only through migration control, whose purpose was to denote who belonged to Britain, that Britishness was gradually taking shape in the 1960s and 1970s."[31] However, this emerging concept of "Britishness" implicitly conveys the idea that the British identity cannot be one of many colors but can only be of just one: white. It is not by accident that the need to redefine "Britishness" emerged as a reaction to so-called colored (sic) Commonwealth citizens moving to Britain.

The 1971 Act represented a significant step forward in the process of definition of the British nation state, but it also attracted much criticism for grounding the idea of British identity on racist premises.[32] In the UK, however, such criticisms remained confined outside Parliament and did not result in any institutional political opposition to anti-immigration policies. The reason probably lies in the fact that both Labour and Conservative parties, at different stages, supported the tightening of controls over who can enter the UK. As Hansen noted, the Labour Party "has criticized restrictive migration policies in opposition and extended them in office."[33]

The debates that took place from 1948 to 1981 are important also because for the first time, migration became an issue of great political salience in the UK, capable of determining electoral results by itself. The "numbers game" started then: politicians began to check migration statistics obsessively, promising their electorate a significant reduction in the migrants' inflow.[34] Their tough policies proved successful: in the 1980s, net migration was close to zero, earning Britain the title of the "zero-immigration country."[35]

Joppke explained the effectiveness of the UK migration policy with the broad powers enjoyed by the executive and the interior minister (ie the Home Office). Notably, the Immigration Act of 1971 conferred on the Home Office the power to make Immigration Rules: norms that regulate how border controls are conducted and how immigration-related decisions are taken by immigration officials.[36] Moreover, compared to continental states like Germany, the UK presents "docile courts and the lack of constitutional protections for immigrants";[37] this "absence of constitutional and judicial constraints on the executive ... allows the Home Office to devise and execute immigration

[31] Karatani (n 22) 4.

[32] In the words of Dixon: "Patriality was justified as defining those who 'belonged to Britain': but this was no more than the corollary of a racist definition of those who did not 'belong.'" Dixon (n 27) 162.

[33] Hansen, *Citizenship and Immigration in Postwar Britain* (n 23) 222.

[34] Joppke (n 20) 102; Small and Solomos (n 26) 247.

[35] This is the title of the chapter by Layton-Henry (n 28).

[36] S 1(3) of the Immigration Act 1971.

[37] Joppke (n 20) 104.

policy as it sees fit."[38] In sum, the Home Office enjoys huge discretion and little accountability.

Because political opposition to anti-migration policies struggled to emerge at the national level, migrant supporter groups resolved to challenge the migration reforms using international law. Around 300 CUKC, thanks to the support of organizations like the Joint Council for the Welfare of Immigrants (JCWI),[39] lodged complaints against the UK's immigration policy before the Council of Europe, bringing the case that became famous as the *East African Asians* case.[40] The European Commission on Human Rights declared British immigration legislation discriminatory on the grounds of race and color[41] because it treated the CUKC as "second-class citizens."[42] However, because of a political deadlock, the international proceedings never reached a formal conclusion and the case was removed from the register in October 1977, leaving the UK government unpunished.[43]

The described seminal period of British migration and citizenship policies ended in 1981 when the newly elected Thatcher's government adopted the British Nationality Act. The 1981 Act fixed the inconsistencies present in the previous system, such as the fact that immigration controls were enforced against who was formally a citizen. The 1981 Act established the patriality test as the main criterion to acquire citizenship in the UK and abolished the *ius soli* principle. Eventually, the British nation arrived at its (less generous) citizenship.

In this first stage of British migration policy, the governments' efforts focused on reducing primary migration from the Commonwealth. Once this goal had been achieved through the 1960s and 1970s migration reforms, the

[38] Joppke (n 20) 10. It is interesting to note that the Home Office, in displaying its duties, is formally exempted from the prohibition of racial discrimination. Elspeth Guild, 'European Developments. The EC Directive on Race Discrimination: Surprises, Possibilities and Limitations' (2000) 29 Industrial Law Journal 416; Terri Givens and Rhonda Evans Case, *Legislating Equality: The Politics of Antidiscrimination Policy in Europe* (OUP 2014).

[39] Harlow and Rawlings (n 7) 502.

[40] European Commission on Human Rights, *25 Cases of Citizens of the United Kingdom and Colonies v United Kingdom*, 4478/70, 4486/70, 4423/70, 4423/70, 4416/70, 4417/70, 4418/70 (10 October 1970). Andrew Drzemczewski, 'A "Non-Decision" of the Committee of Ministers under Article 32 (1) of the European Convention on Human Rights: The East African Asians Cases' (1978) 41 Modern Law Review 337, 338.

[41] Since the proceedings never reached a formal conclusion, the report was only available many years later. Drzemczewski (n 40).

[42] European Commission on Human Rights, *25 Cases of Citizens of the United Kingdom and Colonies v United Kingdom* (n 40), 205. British law would probably have also violated the Fourth Protocol of the ECHR (which enshrines the principle that "no one shall be deprived of the right to enter the territory of the State of which he is a national"), but the British government never ratified it.

[43] Drzemczewski (n 40) 341. The reference for the "non-decision" is the Committee of Ministers' Deputies, Resolution DH (77) 2, 21 October 1977.

UK government set up a new target: restricting secondary movement migration, also called family migration, in other words the immigration of spouses or family members who wanted to join their relatives in the UK. The next subsections will show how the British government pursued this goal and how the changed international context came in its way this time.

3.2 Marriage migration and the war on foreign husbands

Family migration was not of primary concern in the first stage of British migration policy. The legislation adopted during the 1960s and 1970s, while striving to reduce the entry of Commonwealth citizens and CUKC, provided a rather lenient regime for family reunification. The Immigration Act 1971, which laid the basis for the UK's migration framework, stated at Section 1(5):

> The rules shall be so framed that Commonwealth citizens settled in the United Kingdom at the coming into force of this Act and their wives and children are not, by virtue of anything in the rules, any less free to come into and go from the United Kingdom than if this Act had not been passed.

This provision is interesting for two reasons. First, the 1971 Act, while dismantling almost all non-patrial Commonwealth citizens' rights to move, granted those already settled in the UK a statutory right to be joined by their family, confirming that family migration was not seen as a problem.

Secondly, the 1971 Act talks about "wives," not about spouses, and this was not a lapse. The norm did not grant migrant women settled in the UK a right to be joined by their husbands: the legislator feared that this could have been used by male foreigners abroad to circumvent migration controls and entry to the UK via marriages of convenience. In the words of the Minister of State, Charles Waddington: "It would be absurd if, having tightened up the work-permit system to prevent young men coming here and going on to the labour market, we were to allow these same young men to come here by using marriage as a device."[44] It seems that British policymakers were indulgent toward secondary movements as long as they did not entail bringing male foreigners to the UK. Sham marriages, or marriages of convenience, became a particular and persistent concern of British policymakers and influenced all policies in this field.

[44] Quoted in House of Commons, 1986, ii. 108, cited in Joppke (n 20) 118.

The first provision that openly tackled marriage migration was the so-called husband ban, enacted by the Labour government in 1969, which prevented the entry of all male Commonwealth citizens via marriage migration, with few exceptions.[45] The ban was lifted five years later, in 1974, by the new Labour government which acknowledged the indefensibility of such blatant gender discrimination. At the same time, however, the Home Office amended the Immigration Rules to enable immigration officers to refuse entry clearance to foreign partners whose relationship was suspected to be non-genuine. In particular, foreign husbands were asked questions such as whether they intended to live with their wives in the UK in order to test if they concluded marriage solely for migration purposes or not. These tests however were not considered sufficient by the conservatives, and their leader Margaret Thatcher made the "war on foreign husbands" one of the main points of her electoral campaign in the 1970s.[46] As soon as Thatcher took office as Prime Minister in 1979, her government reintroduced the "husband ban."

At first, Thatcher's ban operated by requiring that the female sponsor had to be either born in the UK or have a parent born in the UK. This provision was effective in cutting off most applications, but its discriminatory character exposed it, again, to many criticisms. Therefore, in 1983, the government introduced new Immigration Rules targeting, this time, the detection of marriages of convenience. These new Rules shifted the burden of proof from the immigration officer to the husband abroad who now had to demonstrate that the marriage was genuine and that its "primary purpose" was not migration.[47] The "primary purpose" test was very difficult to overcome and it represented the main obstacle to family reunions.[48] British women protested and lobbied against the new rules and obtained their husbands' partial exemption from the test.[49] However, this again fueled the claims of discrimination.

Again, migrant supporters resorted to the Council of Europe to challenge the government migration law. In the case of *Abdulaziz, Cabales and Balkandali*,

[45] Helena Wray, 'An Ideal Husband? Marriages of Convenience, Moral Gate-Keeping and Immigration to the United Kingdom' in Elspeth Guild and Paul Minderhoud (eds), *The First Decade of EU Migration and Asylum Law* (Martinus Nijhoff Publishers 2011) 354.

[46] Layton-Henry" (n 28) 304. Joppke (n 20) 120.

[47] Statement of Change of the Immigration Rules, HC 251, para 57(a)

[48] Joppke reports data published by the House of Commons in 1986, according to which, in 1982, before the Rules amendment, the 82 percent of foreign husbands' rejections were justified under objective grounds (like the wife's citizenship); after the amendment, in 1984, the 87 percent of the husband rejections were motivated on primary purpose grounds. See Joppke (n 20) 125.

[49] Patrial women's husbands were only subjected to the primary purpose test. Layton-Henry (n 28) 288.

three non-British women applied to the European Court of Human Rights claiming that the British legislation violated their rights to family life and to non-discrimination by impeding their husbands from joining them in the UK.[50] As in the *East African Asians* case, the JCWI and other groups supporting migrants organized the litigation.[51] The proceedings concluded with a partial victory for the applicants. The European Court of Human Rights (ECtHR) found that British immigration rules did not violate the right to family life: the duty to respect family life does not oblige the UK to admit a non-citizen partner within its territory; moreover, the Court noticed that the three women could enjoy family life in their husbands' countries of origin.[52] However, the Court did find the British rules discriminatory on the grounds of sex because they treated applications differently depending on whether the sponsor was a man or a woman. Compelled by the ruling, the British government reformed the law again. However, instead of granting family reunification rights to women, it decided to "level down" the protection:[53] it removed Section 1(5) of the Immigration Act 1971 and thus eliminated the only family right provided by British law to men.[54] Now, men and women were equally deprived of their rights to family reunification.

The regulation of secondary migration remained firmly restrictive throughout the Conservative governments of the 1980s and 1990s. The primary purpose rule still dominated the procedure for family reunification, putting a cap on marriage migration and creating the so-called immigration widows.[55] NGOs reported that when cases of rejection based on the primary purpose rule were challenged in court, judges struggled with its interpretation, leading to the creation of a contradictory jurisprudence.[56] Still, with this rule, the UK managed to keep secondary movements under control, reconfirming itself, in this respect too, as the zero-immigration country.

[50] *Abdulaziz, Cabales and Balkandali* (1985) ECtHR, Application nos 9214/80, 9473/81, and 9474/81. The right to family life is protected under art 8 of the ECHR.

[51] Harlow and Rawlings (n 7) 503. The case originated by the grassroots movement called "Immigration Widows Campaign," which was based in the Islington Law Centre. More in Section 4 of this chapter.

[52] *Abdulaziz, Cabales and Balkandali* (n 50) para 68.

[53] Deborah Brake, 'When Equality Leaves Everyone Worse Off: The Problem of Leveling Down in Equality Law' (2004) 46 William and Mary Law Review 513.

[54] The Immigration Act 1988 removed s 1(5) of Immigration Act 1971; Joppke (n 20) 114. Harlow and Rawlings (n 7) 504, report the JCWI's account of the time where they noted how, despite the change in the law, the actual situation remained the same: the refusal rates for women spouses remained unchanged while the one for men spouses increased. Despite the ECtHR's condemnation, migration controls in the UK continue to discriminate on the grounds of gender.

[55] Wray (n 45) 357.

[56] David Pannick, 'The Primary Purpose Rule: A Rule with No Purpose' (Young JUSTICE 1993) 8.

3.3 The New Labour's government: A policy shift?

After eighteen years of continuous Conservative government, Tony Blair's "New Labour" party won the general election in 1997, marking the beginning of a new phase for British migration policy. With an "unprecedented policy reversal,"[57] the Labour government actively engaged in policy reforms to attract migrants to Britain by raising the number of work permits issued every year. A positive attitude toward immigration was also demonstrated during the negotiations for the 2004 EU enlargement: the UK was among the few Member States that did not apply any restriction to the new Union citizens coming from eastern European countries, who immediately enjoyed free movement rights in the UK.[58] As Figure 3.2 shows, New Labour's migration policies had a big effect and led to an exceptional increase in the number of migrants coming to the UK.

The motivation behind New Labour's migration policy probably lay in a strong economy and a high demand for workers.[59] The City of London became the symbol of the UK's economic transformation: during the 1990s, it became the cosmopolitan financial capital that we know today, generating a huge demand for high-skilled international labor. Accordingly, the type of migration that the UK experienced also changed; "a sort of " superclass" of international migrants emerged: highly skilled, highly paid economic jetsetters who are able to choose between a set of benefit packages offered by governments instead of companies."[60] It seemed that for once, market economy and employer lobbying prevailed over Britain's long-standing anti-migration stance.

Remarkably, New Labour's change of route was limited to "desired migration," and the government maintained a restrictive attitude toward "unwanted migrants." It introduced legislation against irregular migrants, ("bogus") asylum seekers, and, again, sham marriages.[61] Regarding the latter, on the one

[57] Randall Hansen, 'Paradigm and Policy Shifts: British Immigration Policy, 1997–2011' in James Hollifield, Philip Martin, and Pia M Orrenius (eds), *Controlling Immigration, a Global Perspective* (3rd edn, Stanford University Press 2014) 119.

[58] According to the reconstruction made by *The Guardian*, this was mainly due to a miscalculation. The Home Office, in 2003, produced a report saying that the UK will receive between 5,000 and 13,000 migrants from Eastern EU countries per year, while the Office for National Statistic estimated that between 2004 and 2012, the net inflow of migrants from the new members was 423,000. Nicholas Watt and Patrick Wintour, 'How immigration came to haunt Labour: the inside story', The Guardian (24 March 2015). <https://www.theguardian.com/news/2015/mar/24/how-immigration-came-to-haunt-labour-inside-story> accessed 18 March 2025.

[59] Layton-Henry (n 28) 330.

[60] Randall Hansen, 'Commentary' in Wayne A Cornelius and others (eds) *Controlling Immigration: A Global Perspective* (2nd edn, Stanford University Press 2003) 338, 339.

[61] Gaby Hinsliff and Martin Bright, 'Labour Fuels War on Asylum' *The Guardian* (6 February 2005) <https://www.theguardian.com/politics/2005/feb/06/immigration.immigrationandpublicservices> accessed 17 December 2024.

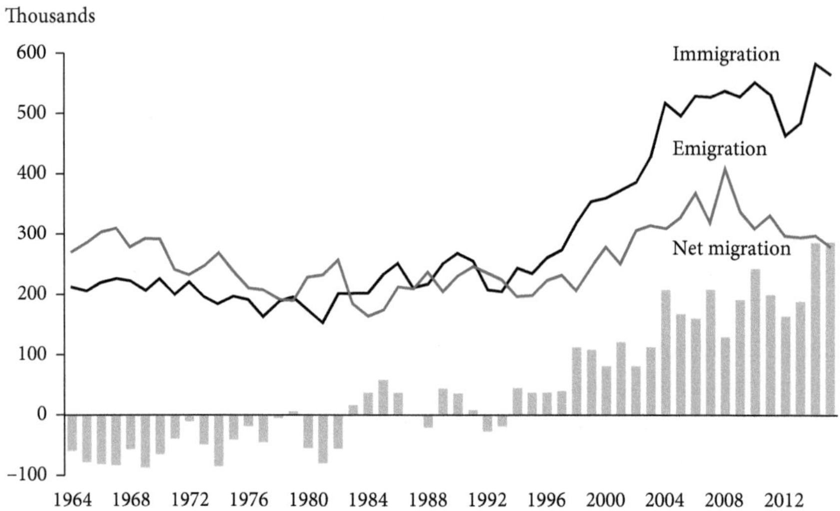

Figure 3.2 International migration in the UK, 1964–2015.
Source: Oliver Hawkins, "Migration Statistics" (House of Commons Library 2017) Number SN06077, 11.

hand, the government maintained its electoral promise to abolish the primary purpose rule because it was too arbitrary.[62] On the other, it issued a new law stating that a TCN who wanted to marry in the UK needed a special authorization ("certificate of approval") issued by the Home Department, proving that they were entitled to stay in the UK.[63]

Arguably, the most critical reform adopted by New Labour was the Human Rights Act of 1998 (HRA). Its declared intent was to "bring rights home" by making the rights of the ECHR directly enforceable before British courts, in view of building a human rights culture in the UK.[64] The HRA had far-reaching consequences on the British constitutional system, particularly because it empowered the judiciary.[65] Under the HRA, courts can review the acts of public authorities and declare them unlawful if they breach human rights; judges must also interpret British law in a way that is compatible with the HRA,[66] and when this is not possible, higher courts can issue a "declaration of

[62] Labour Party Manifesto 1997 <http://www.labour-party.org.uk/manifestos/1997/1997-labour-manifesto.shtml> accessed 18 March 2025.
[63] Immigration Regulations 2005 (SI 2005/15) and Asylum Immigration (Treatment of Claimants) Act 2004. Wray (n 45) 356.
[64] The Human Rights Act: The DCA and Home Office Reviews, p 43.
[65] England and Wales already had their Bill of Rights of 1689, but this is not binding on the entire UK and provides a very limited list of rights.
[66] HRA s 3.

incompatibility."[67] By these means, the HRA contributed to an ongoing process of constitutional reform, leading judges to play a more important role vis-à-vis the executive.

Since most of the litigation in the migration field takes the form of a challenge to an administrative act of the Home Office (eg a deportation order), this constitutional change bears important consequences for migrants. An important example of the HRA's impact concerns the above-mentioned rule that required TCNs to show a "certificate of approval" to marry in the UK. With civil society support,[68] three couples brought a judicial challenge to the law, raising the claim that the certificate breached their human rights protected by the HRA. The couples won the case before the High Court which issued a declaration of incompatibility.[69] Eventually, the litigation led politicians to reconsider the norm, which was repealed.[70]

3.4 Conclusion: Exposing the Home Office to judicial review

Migration dominated the UK political debate from the second half of the twentieth century. From 1962 to 1997, British people grew concerned about the number of migrants arriving in the UK but the government, by implementing very restrictive policies, managed to keep migration inflows at a minimum. This earned the UK the reputation of being a "deviant case": while most European countries professed restrictive approaches toward immigration but continued to experience large-scale inflows, the UK translated its restrictive promises into fact.[71] Joppke argued that this was thanks to "the Home Office absolutism in immigration policy."[72] The executive was very effective in delivering migration policies because it had no institutional constraints: British courts were docile, and individual rights were not protected from lawmakers' interference. Sterett noted that "Britain is one of the most centralized and least rights-oriented

[67] ibid s 4. Higher courts are the High Court, the Court of Appeal, and the Supreme Court. The declaration of incompatibility does not affect the validity of the law though. The doctrine of Parliamentary sovereignty and its exclusive power of making the law is maintained.

[68] The Joint Council for the Welfare of Immigrants intervened in all the stages of the proceedings, and the Aire Centre intervened before the Court of Appeal and the House of Lords.

[69] High Court, *Baiai and others v Secretary of State for the Home Department* [2006] EWHC 823 (Admin).

[70] Another example of how the HRA was used to defend migrants' rights is discussed in Parnesh Sharma, *The Human Rights Act and the Assault on Liberty: Rights and Asylum in the UK* (Nottingham University Press 2011).

[71] Gary P Freeman, 'Britain, the Deviant Case' in Cornelius, Martin, and Hollifield (eds) (n 28) 297.

[72] Joppke (n 20) 137. See also Hansen, *Citizenship and Immigration in Postwar Britain* (n 23) 25.

states in Europe.... It has no established way of shaping majoritarian choice to account for any minority concerns."[73]

Against this backdrop, the "progressive enlargement of British judges' constitutional role" assumes great importance.[74] This constitutional process started about fifty years ago and affected the separation of powers between the judiciary, on the one hand, and the executive and the legislative on the other. Constitutional lawyers trace the origin of this constitutional change to three different episodes.[75] First, the tradition of constitutional review, coming from the United States and continental Europe, exerted its influence on the UK legal culture. Then, the accession to the European Community provided British judges with a power that they never had before: they could scrutinize UK law vis-à-vis a superior source, EU law, and set aside the conflicting national legislation; this was a constitutional revolution for a country based on parliamentary sovereignty. And last, as said in the previous section, the strengthening of individual rights' protection came via the introduction of the Human Rights Act. This new legal setting "rejuvenated the judges"[76] who were previously supine in front of Parliament and the executive.[77]

The strengthening of the judiciary vis-à-vis other powers holds important consequences for the field of migration. Migration legal actions generally consist of an individual challenging the validity of an executive's act before a judge, through appeal or judicial review;[78] indeed, in the UK, most judicial review cases occur in the migration field.[79] Moreover, because many migration decisions have important repercussions on migrants' human rights, the HRA is a

[73] Susan Sterett, 'Caring about Individual Cases: Immigration Lawyering in Britain' in Austin Sarat and Stuart A Scheingold (eds), *Cause Lawyering: Political Commitments and Professional Responsibilities* (OUP 1998) 294.

[74] Anthony King, *The British Constitution* (OUP 2010) 115.

[75] ibid chapter 5; Roger Masterman and I Leigh (eds), *The United Kingdom's Statutory Bill of Rights: Constitutional and Comparative Perspectives* (OUP 2013) 183.

[76] Lord Neuberger's opening address to the PLP annual Judicial Review Trends and Forecasts conference, on 17 October 2017. <http://www.publiclawproject.org.uk/resources/265/the-role-of-the-judges-in-a-post-referendum-world> accessed 18 March 2025.

[77] King (n 74) 119.

[78] In the British system, appeals and judicial reviews are different legal actions decided by different bodies. The judicial appeals of an immigration decision are decided by the first-tier Tribunal and second-tier Upper Tribunal (Immigration and Asylum Chamber) and concern the facts and the merits of the case. Instead, judicial reviews are more complex and longer proceedings, under the competence of Administrative courts and (to a lesser extent) of the Upper Tribunal; these reviews concern errors of law.

[79] Susan Sterett, 'Judicial Review in Britain' (1994) 26 Comparative Political Studies 421, 435; Robert Thomas and Joe Tomlinson, 'A Design Problem for Judicial Review: What We Know and What We Need to Know about Immigration Judicial Reviews' (*UK Constitutional Law Association*, 16 March 2017) <https://ukconstitutionallaw.org/2017/03/16/robert-thomas-and-joe-tomlinson-a-design-problem-for-judicial-review-what-we-know-and-what-we-need-to-know-about-immigration-judicial-reviews/> accessed 17 December 2024.

fundamental tool for scrutinizing the Home Office. Finally, and importantly for this chapter, judicial empowerment is a necessary precondition for legal mobilization: British judges' changed disposition toward the executive created new opportunities for legal mobilization, both at the national and at the EU level. Unfortunately, it seems that this trend was reversed by the 2010–15 Coalition government which adopted reforms in 2013 and 2014 that severely restricted migrants' access to justice (see Section 7).

The next section will focus on how the EU impacted UK migration law. As said in the Introduction, this chapter focuses specifically on litigation for the rights of TCNs who are family members of Union citizens. The next section provides an overview of the relationship between UK migration law and EU law in the field of marriage migration and explains the EU laws that were relied upon for legal mobilization.

4. The impact of EU free movement rights on the UK's legal opportunity structure

> *The [EEC] Treaty does not touch any of the matters which concern solely the mainland of England and the people in it. These are still governed by English law. They are not affected by the Treaty. But when we come to matters with a European element, the Treaty is like an incoming tide. It flows into the estuaries and up the river. It cannot be held back. . . .*[80]

In 1988, Prime Minister Margaret Thatcher began her famous "Bruges" speech by congratulating the conference's chairman for courage in inviting her to speak about the European Economic Community (EEC): "it must seem rather like inviting Genghis Khan to speak on the virtues of peaceful coexistence!"[81] The speech is emblematic of Thatcher and the Conservative party's hostile attitude toward European integration, an attitude that later became known as Euroscepticism.[82] The UK joined the EEC in 1973, and several frictions and crises have punctuated its forty-two years of membership.[83] Looking back, it is

[80] Lord Denning in *HP Bulmer Ltd & Anor v. J. Bollinger SA & Ors* [1974] EWCA Civ 14 at 418.

[81] Margaret Thatcher, Speech to the College of Europe ("The Bruges Speech"), 20 September 1988, College of Europe Archive, <https://www.margaretthatcher.org/document/107332> accessed 18 March 2025.

[82] Simon Usherwood and Nick Startin, 'Euroscepticism as a Persistent Phenomenon' (2013) 51 Journal of Common Market Studies 1.

[83] Just two years after its accession, the UK issued the first referendum on its membership: the United Kingdom European Communities membership referendum held on 5 June 1975.

easy to recognize the warning signs of the UK's eventual decision to leave the EU in 2016.

In her study, Darian-Smith uses the debates surrounding the construction of the Channel Tunnel connecting England to France to depict British attitudes toward the EU. She notes that British people look at the EU through the lens of their colonial past: "England finds itself taking on the role of colonized, subject to the politico-economic power of the EU."[84] The European abolition of internal border controls was seen through a colonial lens too: now people from the Commonwealth and undocumented migrants could reach the UK more easily.[85] Remarkably, Darian-Smith's analysis resonates with the arguments put forward seventeen years later by the Leave campaign in the Brexit referendum, where the rhetoric of "taking back control" and the quest for fully governing the UK's borders and migration were at the forefront. Migration and EU membership have always been somehow linked in British public debate.

Britain's concerns over migration shaped its path with regard to European integration. Over the years, the UK negotiated several exemptions from EU migration laws in order to minimize the EU's influence over national policy. The Protocols on the UK's possibility to opt in and opt out of various EU measures are the clearest example of this attitude.[86] First, the UK obtained an opt-out facility: the possibility of being exempted from the Schengen Agreement and the related rules about the abolition of internal border checks. Then, through another Protocol, the UK stipulated an opt-in clause that modulates its participation in the Area of Freedom, Security, and Justice. As noted in the Introduction, the UK, in principle, is not bound by any measure pertinent to that Area, which includes the European migration and asylum policy; when, and if, the UK government wanted to participate in a specific measure, it can opt in.

Yet the UK could not escape the impact of EU citizenship and free movement law on its legal order. These are part of EU primary law and the UK could not opt out from them; it was as equally bound as any other Member State. These norms have an indirect impact on British migration policy because they regulate the entry and residence of EU migrants and their TCN family members, as we shall see in the next subsection. This turned out to be problematic,

[84] Eve Darian-Smith, *Bridging Divides: The Channel Tunnel and English Legal Identity in the New Europe* (University of California Press 1999) 4.

[85] This is a widespread perception, although the UK is not part of the Schengen Agreement which abolished border checks between EU Member States.

[86] See Treaty of Amsterdam, Protocol integrating the Schengen acquis into the framework of the European Union and Protocol (No 21) on the Position of the United Kingdom and Ireland in Respect of the Area of Freedom, Security and Justice, Annex to the TFEU.

particularly because EU law consistently proved to be more liberal than British migration law.

4.1 The *Surinder Singh* route and reverse discrimination

EU law recognizes free movement rights of both EU citizens and their family members, regardless of their nationality. EU citizens and their families can travel and reside without restriction in the territory of all the Member States for up to three months.[87] After that period, subject to the Union citizen being "economically active" or "self-sufficient" and being covered by health insurance, they have an indefinite right to reside in the host Member State and must be treated equally to national citizens.[88] Limitations and conditions apply, especially in cases where Union citizens are considered a threat to national security, public order, or public health, or in case they do not work and become an "unreasonable burden on the public finances of the host Member State."[89] However, these limitations have been interpreted narrowly by the ECJ, which was the first promoter of the idea that "Union citizenship is the fundamental status of Member States' nationals."[90]

TCN family members enjoy free movement rights because this guarantees the effective enjoyment of rights by Union citizens. These citizens would be deterred from moving to another Member State if their family members could not join them abroad. In *O. and B.*, the ECJ specified that TCN family members do not have autonomous rights but rather "derived" rights because they are "consequential to and dependent on [those] of the Union citizen."[91] Accordingly, TCN family members enjoy the same freedom and benefits granted to Union citizens but, at the same time, their status and the legitimacy of their stay depend entirely on that of their Union citizen family member.

The free movement rights recognized to Union citizens and their families are fairly generous and have created some unexpected situations. In the UK, the disparity between British immigration law and EU law led to what became

[87] Art 21 of the TFEU, further detailed and expanded in the Citizenship Directive 2004/38/EC of the European Parliament and of the Council of 29 April 2004 on the right of citizens of the Union and their family members to move and reside freely within the territory of the Member States.

[88] Art 18 of the TFEU and art 24 of the Citizenship Directive 2004/38.

[89] *Baumbast and R* (n 3) para 90.

[90] Case C-184/99 *Rudy Grzelczyk v Centre public d'aide sociale d'Ottignies-Louvain-la-Neuve* (2001) CJEU, ECLI:EU:C:2001:458 [31].

[91] Case C-456/12 *O & B* (2014) CJEU, ECLI:EU:C:2014:135 [36].

Table 3.1 Requirements for family reunification before Brexit: the requirements for a UK citizen sponsor are shown on the left, and those for an EU mobile citizen are on the right.

Requirements for a TCN family member of a UK citizen	Requirements for a TCN family member of an EU migrant
Pay the visa fee (£3,500)	Proof of relationship
Show a minimum income (at least £18,600 a year without children)	The EU migrant is a worker or has sufficient resources and health insurance.
Spouse: Minimum age (18) and proof that the relationship is genuine and subsisting	
Give information on previous applications	
Pay the healthcare surcharge	
Have a good knowledge of English (score 81 or 82)	

Note: These requirements are laid down in the British Immigration Rules and are often subject to change. These were the requirements in force when I conducted the investigation in the UK, but a recent reform has increased the minimum income to £29,000 (Statement of Changes HC 590, Minimum Income Requirement, 19 March 2024). See also ILPA information sheet, "Family Migration: Sponsoring a Partner under the Immigration Rules and the Minimum Income Requirement" 31 March 2017. <https://ilpa.org.uk/information-sheet-family-migration-sponsoring-a-partner-under-the-immigration-rules-and-the-minimum-income-requirement/> accessed 17 December 2024.

known as "reverse discrimination": the family members of EU migrants in the UK are better protected than those of British nationals in their own country.[92] To obtain a family visa, a TCN family member of a UK citizen needs to give proof of a "minimum income," have a good knowledge of English, pay a very high application fee, etc. These and other requirements do not apply to EU migrants and their TCN family members (see Table 3.1).

In this respect, the case of *Surinder Singh,* referred to the ECJ in 1990, set the tone of the following years-long discussions.[93] The case concerned a couple, a British and an Indian citizen, who moved to Germany to work and returned to the UK two years later. British authorities refused to grant Mr Singh a residency permit, and he filed an appeal invoking the free movement rights that he acquired as the spouse of an EU citizen in Germany. In its ruling, the ECJ held that a British citizen, who returns to the UK after exercising free movement

[92] Stefano Montaldo, 'Freedom of Movement, Social Integration and Naturalization: Testing Reverse Discrimination in the Recent Case Law of the Court of Justice' (2018) 2018 3 European Papers—A Journal on Law and Integration 2499; Fabio Spitaleri, *Le discriminazioni alla rovescia nel diritto dell'Unione europea* (Aracne 2010). Reverse discrimination has been openly acknowledged even in the case law of the ECJ, see Case C-127/08 *Metock* (2008) CJEU, ECLI:EU:C:2008:449 [76].

[93] Case C-370/90 *Surinder Singh* (1992) CJEU, ECLI:EU:C:1992:296.

rights in Germany, retains free movement rights for her and her family. The idea is that a TCN spouse must enjoy "[a]t least the same rights of entry and residence as would be granted to him or her under Community law, if his or her spouse chose to enter and reside in another Member State."[94] Here the ECJ adopted a functionalist type of reasoning: TCN rights are instrumental to ensuring free movement because EU citizens would be deterred from moving abroad in the first place if they knew that they would face problems upon return to their home Member State.

With the *Surinder Singh* decision, the ECJ extended the scope of the protection of EU free movement law to cover the situation of Union citizens who return to their home Member States with their (TCN) family members. The case had widespread consequences in the UK. The generous interpretation that the ECJ gave to Union citizenship and free movement norms acted as a catalyst, making people whose residence rights were denied under British law demand residence rights under EU law instead.[95]

Although British lawmakers diligently incorporated EU free movement law into British law, studies show that the rights of Union citizens and their family members were not fully protected in the UK.[96] Shaw, Miller, and Fletcher noted that there was a "friction between UK Immigration Law and EU Free Movement Law" which affected particularly the area of the rights of TCN family members of EU citizens.[97] This area is characterized by a high rate of refusal of residence applications by the Home Office and a high level of litigation.[98] It seems that, more than being a problem of transposition of EU law, there is an issue over its restrictive interpretation by the Home Office. The reluctance of British authorities is a key factor to understanding the legal mobilization analyzed in the following sections. Indeed, many of the people whose

[94] *Surinder Singh* (n 93) para 23.

[95] Helena Wray, Eleonore Kofman, and Agnes Simic, 'Subversive Citizens: Using EU Free Movement Law to Bypass the UK's Rules on Marriage Migration' (2021) 47 Journal of Ethnic and Migration Studies 447.

[96] The UK transposed the Citizenship Directive 2004/38 with the adoption of the Immigration (European Economic Area) Regulations 2006, SI 2006 No 1003. Amended by the Immigration (European Economic Area) (Amendment) Regulations 2009, SI 2009 No 1113. The Immigration (European Economic Area) (Amendment) Regulations 2011, SI 2011 No 1247. The Immigration (European Economic Area) (Amendment) Regulations 2012, SI 2012 No 1547; The Immigration (European Economic Area) (Amendment) (No 2) Regulations 2012, SI 2012 No 2560

[97] Jo Shaw, Nina Miller, and Maria Fletcher, *Getting to Grips with EU Citizenship: Understanding the Friction Between UK Immigration Law and EU Free Movement Law* (Edinburgh Law School Citizenship Studies 2013).

[98] ibid 23. "[T]he UK authorities routinely take longer than they are permitted to decide upon applications by TCN family members, have erred in the manner in which they have applied the rules relating to the evidencing of family relationships, and have been less than careful in their management of documentation and correspondence."

application for family reunification was refused turned to courts and claimed free movement rights.

4.2 The Legal Opportunity Structure of the British mobilization for family migration

From 1962 to 1997, migration policy in the UK was characterized by the "zero-immigration" target: successive UK governments set up a very restrictive system of migration controls with little recognition of migrant rights. This anti-migration stance was endorsed by both the Conservative and Labour parties, leaving migrants and their supporters without political representation and with few grounds to challenge the Home Office judicially.

If the political arena seemed closed to pro-migrant movements, the legal arena was not open either. Indeed, the UK has been labeled an "inhospitable environment" for legal mobilization.[99] As mentioned earlier, civil society actors brought cases before the ECHR Commission but these yielded little or no result. Moreover, the UK docile judicial system offered little opportunities to challenge the executive decisions or, even worse, the legitimacy of British migration law. Finally, access to courts in the UK is severely impaired by the high costs of litigation.

To be sure, in the UK litigation cost is partially mitigated by the fact that legal aid is a long-standing tradition in the British context.[100] Also, charities and NGOs often intervene in proceedings as third parties, whereby they have the possibility of being heard without bearing the costs of litigation. These third-party interventions are analogous to *amicus curiae* in the USA and have become more common in recent years: they are an excellent way for a case to reach public attention at a relatively low cost.[101]

[99] Vanhala (n 10) 529. Beyond litigation costs, Vanhala bases her evaluation on the fact that the UK is characterized by "a traditional distaste for enshrined rights, a legal culture privileging parliamentary sovereignty and the comparatively slow nature of new social movement development when considered in light of many other European nations." To this, she adds the "conservative" nature of the English judiciary. Each of these factors are the object of analysis in this chapter, which points out how the advent of EU rights and culture affected and opened up the LOS of the UK.

[100] Harlow and Rawlings (n 7) 243. To access legal aid, a person must pass a means test and a merits test: only people with relatively low income and with reasonable prospects of success will receive the benefit.

[101] To obtain permission to intervene, third parties need to convince the court that their intervention will make a relevant contribution to the case, will not negatively affect the parties, and will be non-partisan. Indeed, sometimes, the interest of the intervener might conflict with that of a party, leading the latter to oppose a permission for an intervention. See Rule 54.17 and Rule 52.11 of the Civil Procedure Rules. See also Public Law Project, "Third-party intervention—A practical guide", PLP Guides for Practitioners, 2008.

Another opening in the legal opportunity structure emerged when the Thatcher era came to an end. New legal tools became available to defend migrant rights. The most important were the HRA, incorporating the ECHR into British law, and Union citizenship and free movement rights, as interpreted by the ECJ's case law. As a result, the traditionally lenient British judiciary was gradually becoming more powerful, thanks to the new review powers granted by the HRA and to the country's accession to the EEC. This change in the British constitutional framework opened new and important windows of opportunities for legal mobilization, which were seized by migrant rights supporters to enhance scrutiny over the activity of the Home Office.

The following sections show how individuals, migrant supporter groups, and lawyers saw in EU free movement law and the preliminary reference procedure an opportunity not only to obtain a residence permit but also to challenge and transform UK migration law, to make it less restrictive or to circumvent its application.

5. Who mobilizes EU free movement law in the UK?

Before leaving the EU, British courts have referred a striking number of preliminary references to the ECJ regarding the rights of TCN family members of EU citizens. If we take a court-centric approach, we would expect that, first, British judges are especially inclined to refer and, second, these references come prominently from first-instance courts, in line with the intra-court competition theory. However, the UK case does not confirm any of these expectations. In fact, British courts can be generally defined as reticent to refer;[102] moreover, most of its migration references originated from second-instance courts.

To explain the UK's exceptional number of migration references we must look beyond courts and judges. These do not operate in a vacuum: to refer, judges need a case where a migrant's lawyer asks to review a Home Office's act vis-à-vis EU law standards. To understand the high number of references we thus need a shift in standpoint[103] and need to focus on who supports migrants' lawsuits and provides them with expertise in EU law.

The UK offers an incredibly fertile terrain for legal NGOs and Eurolawyers. They are the real game-changers who, despite the UK's "inhospitable

[102] Broberg and Fenger (n 17) 500.
[103] Vanhala (n 10) 526.

environment for legal mobilization,"[104] managed to mobilize EU law with a purpose.

In this section, I describe the groups and the professionals who support migrants in court to defend and strengthen their rights as well as to enhance the scrutiny over the Home Office's activities. I divided the actors into three categories: the first is that of (publicly funded) legal advisory centers, the second is composed of charities (NGOs) with a legal focus, and the third of lawyers with expertise in EU and migration law. A clarification may be necessary: in the British system, a lawyer can be either a solicitor or a barrister; the first is in charge of establishing first contact with clients, interacting with them, and preparing the documents for the case in courts. Barristers are specialized lawyers who usually intervene in complex cases and have the specific task of representing the client in court, following solicitors' instructions.

Below I provide a list of associations and groups that act in court in support of migrants, with the disclaimer that this is not exhaustive. I have identified these actors because they were active in or linked to cases that have been referred to the ECJ, but chances are that many other actors have been as active but are less visible or have been less successful in reaching the ECJ. Still, having a list is useful to give an idea of the rich and lively scene of migrant support groups operating in London and of the UK's well-established tradition of legal mobilization. In my view, this stands in contrast with Joppke's observation that there has been no dissent against the anti-migration policy in the UK: dissent took the form of grassroots organizations, charities, and social movements; they may have been less active within the British Parliament or in party politics but they made their voice heard in the streets and, particularly relevant to this chapter, in court.

5.1 Legal Advisory Centres

The UK has traditionally been very concerned with the problem of access to court and has a long-standing tradition of legal aid.[105] The field of migration is no exception: the Immigration Act 1971 provided for the grant of "financial support for organizations helping persons with rights of appeal";[106] this was

[104] ibid 524.

[105] First introduced with the Legal Aid Act of 1949.

[106] S 23 of the Immigration Act 1971. "The Secretary of State may with the consent of the support for Treasury make grants to any voluntary organisation which organisations provides advice or assistance for, or other services for the welfare helping persons with rights of, persons who have rights of appeal under this Part of this of appeal."

realized through the creation of an ad-hoc institution, the United Kingdom Immigrants Advisory Service (UKIAS), in charge of providing free legal advice to migrants. In the same years, during the 1970s, legal aid reached its maximum expansion, enabling lawyers to represent the more disadvantaged groups in society, among which are migrants. These circumstances led to the creation of many legal advisory centers across the UK, either managed by UKIAS or sponsored by local councils; these centers have on their staff migration lawyers who work as solicitors under legal aid schemes. The UKIAS was split into two different organizations in 1993: one called the "Immigration Advisory Service" and the other called "Refugee and Migrant Justice." These centers sponsored and supported many litigation proceedings in the field of migration and refugee law, until the day when cuts to the legal aid budget forced them to close (see Section 7).

Another important part of the British civil work/associations' history is the Islington Law Centre; it was established in the 1970s and is based in north-east London. The Islington local council provided the Law Centre with some funds and grants which were used to employ staff, mainly community workers and solicitors. Don Flynn, who worked at the Centre for eleven years, told me that in the 1970s that was the hub for many associations active in the neighborhood: trade unions, environmental organizations, and "all sorts of community activists."[107]

> There was a team of lawyers at the heart of the Law Centre. But then, in addition, there were people like me, who were getting out of the office and going to the local housing estates, or wherever, in order to see what the problem was, what people were experiencing, and then seeking to find a solution.[108]

When Don Flynn started working at the Islington Law Centre, his work dealt mainly with public-sector housing. Flynn proposed addressing also the migrants' situation and the Centre offered him a two-day intensive training course on basic immigration law: "In those days, after two days of immersion in immigration law you were amongst the leading experts on the issue."[109] As soon as the Centre advertised that they were working on immigration, a long queue of people formed in front of its door: immigration was clearly a common grievance in the community. In the Centre, Flynn discovered his passion for the

[107] Don Flynn, Interview of 14 December 2016, London.
[108] Don Flynn, Interview of 14 December 2016, London.
[109] Don Flynn, Interview of 14 December 2016, London.

field of migration, to which he has dedicated four decades of work. He started to work at the Centre as a community worker in 1977, then worked for the Joint Council for the Welfare of Immigrants, and finally, in 2006, he established his own NGO, the Migrants' Rights Network.[110]

5.2 Charities working in the field of migrants' rights

The Joint Council for the Welfare of Immigrants

During the 1960s, another important institution for migrant rights emerged: the Joint Council for the Welfare of Immigrants (JCWI). It was founded in September 1967 following a meeting of more than 200 representatives of different ethnic minorities in a Southall cinema.[111] The aim was to create an apolitical organization capable of bringing immigrant groups together that had previously been divided by different political views. Southall is a neighborhood in London also known as Little India, due to its large immigrant community from South-East Asia. The first leader of JCWI was a representative of the Indian Workers' Association of Southall, Vishnu Sharma.[112] The JCWI's work consists of a combination of case work, strategic litigation, policy campaigns, and training for migration lawyers. It also monitors the government's (and the Home Office's) activities and it does not receive government funding to preserve its independence. Most likely, this is the reason why it is "perennially overworked and underfunded."[113]

The JCWI remains still today one of the leading national, independent legal charities specialized in British immigration law. Don Flynn worked many years for the Council, and so described its work in strategic litigation:

> That was literally at the level of saying—look, we are looking for a case that has got these features in it. If you have got anybody coming to visit your centre who has got these features in it, please let us know because we think there is a basis to challenge the way in which the government has chosen to interpret this aspect of law.[114]

110 <http://www.migrantsrights.org.uk/> accessed 17 December 2024.

111 Matthew Hilton, *A Historical Guide to NGOs in Britain: Charities, Civil Society and the Voluntary Sector Since 1945* (Palgrave Macmillan 2012) 158.

112 <http://www.iwasouthall.org.uk/> accessed 17 December 2024.

113 Harlow and Rawlings (n 7) 521.

114 Don Flynn, Interview of 14 December 2016, London.

The JCWI acted as a solicitor in the case of *Akrich*;[115] it brought several cases before the ECtHR, among them the well-known "*East African Asians* case",[116] discussed in Section 3.

The AIRE Centre

The Advice for Individual Rights in Europe (AIRE) Centre is a British charity with a European focus. Despite being very well known in Europe for bringing hundreds of cases before national and international courts, the AIRE Centre is a surprisingly small charity with limited resources, which, at the time of my research, counted only eight lawyers among its staff. The AIRE Centre was set up by Nuala Mole "specifically to assist individuals to obtain the rights they are guaranteed by international agreements but that they have not been accorded by their national authorities."[117] The Centre achieves this goal through different activities: by conducting or intervening in litigation both at the national and international level (before the ECtHR especially), by supporting and advising lawyers and organizations working in their same field, and by providing legal advice to individuals and legal training to judges and lawyers throughout Europe.

The AIRE Centre is based in London, and from its office monitors the activity of the European courts. It produces a monthly bulletin that summarizes legal decisions from the ECtHR in several European languages (eg Albanian, Serbian, Romanian) to increase awareness of European rights. Moreover, it conducts a "case watch" on British courts: people advise the Centre if an interesting case is brought so that it can decide whether to intervene in the proceedings or not.[118] In the UK, because of limited resources and high litigation costs, the AIRE Centre normally acts as a third-party intervener, with few exceptions. To fund its activities, the AIRE Centre relies in part on legal aid (which is not sufficient to meet its outgoings) and on private donors.

To give an idea, the AIRE centre intervened or acted as a solicitor in the cases of *Rahman and Others*; *Alarape and Tijani*; *NA*; *MA and Others*; *N.S. and M.E. and Others*; *SM*; and *Bajratari*.[119]

[115] Case C-109/01 *Akrich* (2003) CJEU, ECLI:EU:C:2003:491 [24].

[116] European Commission on Human Rights, *25 Cases of Citizens of the United Kingdom and Colonies v United Kingdom*, (n 40).

[117] Catharina Harby, 'The Experience of the AIRE Centre in Litigating before the European Court of Human Rights' in Tullio Treves (ed), *Civil Society, International Courts and Compliance Bodies* (2005) 41.

[118] Adrian Berry, Interview of 23 November 2016, London.

[119] Case C-83/11 *Rahman and Others* (2012) CJEU, ECLI:EU:C:2012:519; Case C-529/11 *Alarape and Tijani* (n 3); Case C-115/15 *NA* (2016) CJEU, ECLI:EU:C:2016:487; Case C-648/11 *MA and Others* (2013) CJEU, ECLI:EU:C:2013:367; Joined cases C-411/10 and C-493/10 *N.S. and M.E. and*

Public Law Project

The Public Law Project (PLP) was founded in 1990 with the object of aiding people who have little or no access to public law remedies. The PLP states three main aims on its website: "to increase the accountability of public decision makers; to enhance the quality of public decision making; and to improve access to justice." In its view, judicial review is intrinsically linked to the public interest: it is not only finalized to obtain a just redress for the litigant but it is also a means to enhance the accountability of the public administration and to increase the standard of its decisions. The charity is based in London and relies on a small number of staff (among them solicitors) who undertake case work, training, campaigns, and research.

PLP's lawyers acted as solicitors in the cases of *ZZ*, C-300/11 and *Tolley*, C-430/15.[120]

5.3 Migration Practitioners

Immigration Law Practitioners' Association (ILPA)

The initial lack of expertise in the migration field was addressed with the creation of ILPA. This is a network of immigration practitioners and legal academics, which has its own official journal, the Journal of Immigration, Asylum and Nationality Law, and a website.[121] ILPA offers training to its members and regularly publishes information material on the most recent law reforms. Although ILPA generally does not directly participate in litigation for migrants' rights, its members do. Also, the ILPA's advisory service offer expertise and support to NGOs such as JCWI.

When the EU came to play a bigger role in the field of migration, a subcommittee in the ILPA decided to focus on EU law; members of charities, like Don Flynn and Nuala Mole of AIRE, were also part of the sub-committee, together with EU law professors such as Elspeth Guild, who became chair of the sub-committee, and non-British migration experts, like Kees Groenendijk (whom we will meet again in Chapter 4). The presence of international experts

Others (2011) CJEU, ECLI:EU:C:2011:865; Case C-129/18 *SM* (2019) CJEU, ECLI:EU:C:2019:248; Case C-93/18 *Bajratari* (2019) CJEU, ECLI:EU:C:2019:809.

[120] Case C-430/15 *Tolley* (1 February 2017) CJEU, ECLI:EU:C:2017:74; Case C-300/11 *ZZ* (4 June 2013) CJEU, ECLI:EU:C:2013:363.

[121] ILPA website: <http://www.ilpa.org.uk/> accessed 17 December 2024.

testifies to the sub-committee's goal of building a transnational network of EU law migration experts.

Barristers specialized in EU law

As we saw, charities and legal advisory centers often rely on their staff lawyers to bring cases and represent people before domestic and international courts. However, these lawyers usually act as solicitors, and when their cases arrive at courts, especially before the highest jurisdictions, they rely on barristers to advocate for their clients in court. In London, there are barristers who are known for their specialization in the migration field and for their committment to migrant rights, who always represent migrants and never the government. This is also evident from the migration references that arrive before the ECJ from the UK, where the migrants are often represented by the same barristers whose names appear repeatedly. Someone might argue that this conflicts with the UK "cab rank rule," according to which barristers should be impartial and accept whatever case is proposed to them. For instance, if the Secretary of State of the Home Office asks these migration barristers to represent the Department, they must accept the mandate. The "cab rank" rule was originally conceived to guarantee that even a person charged with the most ignominious crimes has access to judicial representation by a barrister, but this is also a way for the government to test the loyalty of barristers.[122] However, in practice, things work differently, as my interviewees told me: barristers, if they wish, can simply refuse to represent the Home Office by saying they are too busy and no consequences follow.[123]

London has a high concentration of courts and tribunals and, next to these, illustrious law firms. This environment increases competition among practitioners and even among charities and NGOs, on the one hand, and on the other, it facilitates the exchange of information and the prolificacy of litigation. As barrister Adrian Berry told me:

> What is true about free movement litigation is that we are quite involved, we are not just waiting in that kind of reactive way for clients to be in need our assistance, we are actually trying to find points to develop the law.[124]

[122] Interview with Elspeth Guild, London, 16 November 2016.
[123] This was confirmed in the interviews with Simon Cox and Adrian Berry, both barristers.
[124] Interview with Adrian Berry, London, 23 November 2016.

The procedure followed in the UK for the submission of preliminary references confirms barristers' proactive role. In British courts it is common practice that, first, the parties agree on the questions and the statement of facts,[125] and then the court, eventually amending the text proposed, orders the reference.

Competition affects barristers' work, even when they work for public interest organizations. They are very conscious of publicity: if their case arrives at an international court they will gain in terms of reputation and career, or the organization represented can attract the attention of possible donors. However, the search for publicity might negatively impact the cases too: it might create a conflict between the interest of the individual party (who normally prefers a swift trial with the best possible individual outcome) and the barrister or the NGO's goal that might do better from a longer trial with broader collective impact and an international outlook. Also, internal competition can lead lawyers and members of civil society to avoid sharing information on the cases, threatening cooperation and mutual learning.

6. Stretching the boundaries of EU free movement law: Three cases of legal mobilization in the field of marriage migration

This section takes three preliminary references to exemplify how civil society actors and Eurolawyers managed to mobilize EU free movement law before the ECJ. The cases concern the rights of TCN family members of Union citizens and deal with instances where EU free movement law was invoked by "static" UK citizens, the so-called purely internal situations. In the three cases of *Akrich*, *Zhu and Chen*, and *McCarthy*, a Union citizen and her TCN relative tried to fall under the protection of EU free movement law because this offered better protection than UK law and gives the applicants a chance to avoid deportation.

Out of the twenty-four cases referred by British courts, I could trace the presence of collective actors in nine. In three other cases, I could detect the presence of Eurolawyers for migrant rights, without the case having necessarily a political goal; *Zhu and Chen* is one of these. This is quite a high number if we consider that in many cases, the presence of civil society cannot be detected and offers further evidence of the UK's fertile terrain for legal mobilization in the free movement field.

[125] At times, discussion upon the text of a reference does not proceed smoothly. Simon Cox told me that, for instance, in the cases of *McCarthy* (Case C-434/09 *McCarthy* (2011) CJEU, EU:C:2011:277) and in that of *ZZ* (n 120), the back and forth with the barristers representing the Home Office lasted months.

6.1 *Akrich*

In 1997, Mrs Helina Akrich visited the JCWI's immigration legal advice service, and there she met Don Flynn. She is a British national married to a Moroccan national, and she asked Flynn for help as her husband was undocumented and risked deportation. The husband, Mr Hacene Akrich, had a complicated immigration history: he entered the UK in 1989 and lived there discontinuously for eight years, most of the time undocumented. He was deported from the UK in 1991, returned in 1992, and was deported again a few months later. Mr Akrich managed to enter the UK illegally once again and, in 1996, he married a British citizen, Helina Jazdzewska, now Mrs Akrich. According to UK Immigration Rules, despite being the spouse of a British citizen Mr Akrich did not have the right to a residence permit because he had received (more than one) deportation order.[126]

Don Flynn told me that he knew many couples in a similar situation to Mrs and Mr Akrich. He gave them all the same advice: they should move to an EU Member State for at least six months, work there, and obtain a resident permit in virtue of their EU rights to free movement. From a foreign Member State, they can apply again for leave to enter the UK but this time on the basis of the *Surinder Singh* rule: as spouses of British nationals who claimed their free movements rights and then returned to the UK. Mr and Mrs Akrich decided to follow Flynn's suggestion: they spent six months in Ireland, and Mr Akrich then applied again from there for a UK residence permit but this time relying on his newly acquired free movement rights.

Flynn's advice basically comprises "reverse discrimination" implemented: the treatment of British nationals is worse under British rules than for EU migrants, therefore the Akrich couple tried to fall within the protection of the EU's free movement rules. Flynn helped Mrs and Mrs Akrich to prepare the documents necessary to stay in Ireland legally and then, after some months, he assisted Mr Akrich in filing his application for leave to enter the UK as a family member of a Union citizen.

However, something in Mr Akrich's application went wrong. He applied at the British embassy in Dublin, and when the couple was interviewed about their original decision to move to Ireland, Mrs Akrich replied, maybe with too much honesty: "we had heard about EU rights, staying six months and then going back to the UK."[127] The Home Office rejected their application on the

[126] Immigration Rules 320 and 321 and *Akrich* (n 115).
[127] ibid para 36.

basis that Mrs Akrich had not genuinely exercised her Union citizen's rights but had moved to Ireland deliberately to evade the application of British immigration law.[128] Remarkably, EU law does not require that EU rights should be exercised *genuinely* or should not be used to *evade* British law; these are principles that, instead, come from the UK's family migration law (think of the primary purpose rule). The Home Office's interpretation of EU law appears deeply informed by the logic of British immigration rules.

Mr Akrich appealed against the Home Office rejection, with Flynn acting as solicitor. The proceedings focused on the issue of whether the Home Office could refuse a British citizen and her partner a residence permit solely on the basis of their intentions: they had moved to another Member State to evade British law. Upon request of Mr Akrich's lawyers, the court decided to submit a preliminary reference to the ECJ to shed light on the issue.

According to Flynn, the legal issue behind the reference was "boringly mundane": intentions have never been relevant to decide whether EU citizens and their families enjoy the right to freedom of movement. Indeed, the ECJ dismissed the Secretary of State's argument very quickly. However, probably in response to the UK government's submission, Advocate General Geelhoed decided to raise a couple of new issues in his Opinion. First of these was whether the TCN spouse needed to be legally present on the territory of the first Member State in order to enjoy free movement rights in the Union citizen's home Member State; the next was whether EU law should also require that the Union citizen and the TCN had not concluded a marriage of convenience.[129] Since the Advocate General's opinion is published only after the hearing, the parties did not have any chance to reply to these newly emerged issues. The ECJ accepted the view of the Advocate General and restated the need to avoid marriages of convenience and to verify whether Mr Akrich was residing in Ireland legally.[130] This interpretation introduced new limits on free movement law and shaped the rights of Union citizens and their TCN spouses. According to Flynn, it was an attempt by the Advocate General and the ECJ to show that they were taking the UK government's concerns seriously.

[128] ibid (n 115) para 37.

[129] Opinion of Advocate General Geelhoed, *Akrich* (n 115), 27 February 2003, paras 7 and 10. In the Advocate's General Opinion, and to a certain extent also in the ECJ decision, it seems implicit that Mr Akrich was also undocumented in Ireland. From my interview with Don Flynn, instead, it was clear that Mr Akrich entered Ireland with a visa obtained in virtue of his being a spouse of a Union citizen worker and was therefore legally resident.

[130] *Akrich* (n 115) para 61.

Impact of the *Akrich* ruling

In *Akrich*, the ECJ introduced a more restrictive interpretation of free movement rights: to enjoy free movement rights in a Member State, TCN family members need to show that their prior residence in another Member State was lawful.

At the individual level, this was completely irrelevant: the Akrich couple was legally resident in Ireland, and nobody doubted the authenticity of their marriage. Eventually, Mr Akrich managed to obtain a residence permit as the spouse of an EU citizen and he entered the UK legally.

But if we look at the broader impact of the case, the *Akrich* decision undoubtedly represented a step back for migrant rights: the new condition that the ECJ introduced made the enjoyment of free movement rights by TCN family members more difficult. Moreover, the ECJ judgment was published during a period when the UK government was very concerned with EU law being used to circumvent UK immigration law; obviously, the Akrich couple's strategic use of EU law was badly received by the Home Office. Just one month after the publication of the *Akrich* judgment, the UK government proposed a law reform that was later adopted as the Asylum Immigration Act 2004.[131] The Act, among other things, aimed at tackling sham marriages and it provided that in order to get married in the UK, a TCN needs the consent of the Home Office (in the form of a "Certificate of Approval").[132] The intent was to grant the right to marry only to those who were already legally residing in the UK (more on this in Section 6.3).

Wray argued that the real target of the introduction of the Certificate of Approval scheme was the "widespread abuse of the right to remain acquired by the [TCN] spouses of [EU] nationals;" although the UK government justified the law reform with an alleged general increase in the number of sham marriages, "the legislation seems disproportionate to the proven extent of the problem."[133] Pilgram noted how the Home Office itself confirmed Wray's intuition: "the government defended this measure as necessary, inter alia, to mitigate the ample possibilities to, and the actual prevalence of, abuse of EC law."[134]

Eventually, the ECJ overturned its conclusions in *Akrich* with the judgment rendered in *Metock* in 2008, a case that originated from Ireland.[135] The Court

[131] Asylum Immigration (Treatment of Claimants) Act 2004.
[132] Explanatory Notes of the Asylum Immigration Act 2004, at 4.
[133] Wray (n 45) 364 and 367.
[134] Lisa Pilgram, 'Tackling "Sham Marriages": The Rationale, Impact and Limitations of the Home Office's "Certificate of Approval" Scheme' (2009) 23 Journal of Immigration Asylum and Nationality Law 24, 27.
[135] *Metock* (n 92).

held that a Member State's requirement of a prior lawful residence would seriously obstruct the exercise of the freedom of movement granted to EU citizens and their TCN family members by the EU Treaties and, therefore, it is prohibited.

6.2 *Zhu and Chen*

The *Zhu and Chen* case is a great example of how experienced Eurolawyers can transform "purely internal situations" into cases of free movement law to expand migrant rights. Mrs Chen and Mr Zhu were a couple of Chinese nationality who decided to raise their second child, Catherine, in the UK. With this aim, Mrs Chen first traveled to Belfast in Northern Ireland to give birth so that her daughter could obtain Irish nationality by virtue of the *ius soli* principle provided by Irish law and applied extraterritorially to the entire island of Ireland.[136] Mrs Chen and new-born Catherine moved to Cardiff, where they asked for a permit to reside in the UK. Their request was based on the fact that Catherine is an Irish national and an EU citizen and therefore she enjoys residence rights in the UK. Mrs Chen, for her part, claimed a derivative right to reside as Catherine's mother.[137]

The Secretary of State rejected their application. It held that Catherine, in her brief life, never moved from a Member State to another: she was born in the UK (Northern Ireland) and she had lived there since birth; therefore, neither Catherine nor her mother were entitled to EU free movement rights, and theirs was an "attempted abuse."[138] Nevertheless, Mrs Chen appealed the decision in court and her lawyers successfully convinced the first-instance judge (Immigration Appeal Authority) to refer a question to the ECJ,[139] allowing the Court to clarify whether the UK practice was lawful under EU law.

[136] S 6(1) of the Irish Nationality and Citizenship Act of 1956 provided that any baby born on the island of Ireland is entitled to acquire Irish nationality. The *ius soli* principle was instead removed from British law with the British Nationality Act of 1981, hence Mrs Chen's daughter did not acquire British nationality.

[137] Under art 1 of Directive 90/364, nationals of Member States and their family members enjoy residence rights in another Member State provided that they are covered by sickness insurance and have sufficient resources during their period of residence. However, not all family members qualify for such residence rights, but only those who are "dependent relatives in the ascending line of the holder of the right of residence and his or her spouse." See Council Directive 90/364/EEC of 28 June 1990 on the right of residence (repealed by the Citizenship Directive 2004/38).

[138] Joshua Rozenberg, 'EU Backing for Chinese Mother's Right to Live in Britain' *The Daily Telegraph* (19 October 2004) <https://www.telegraph.co.uk/news/uknews/1474555/EU-backing-for-Chinese-mothers-right-to-live-in-Britain.html> accessed 17 December 2024.

[139] Interview with Adrian Berry, London, 23 November 2016.

The strategic nature of the *Zhu and Chen* case was apparent also for the ECJ, which observed:

> It is common ground that Mrs Chen took up residence in the island of Ireland in order to enable the child she was expecting to acquire Irish nationality and, consequently, to enable her to acquire the right to reside, should the occasion arise, with her child in the United Kingdom.[140]

It went largely unnoticed that the *Zhu and Chen* case did not start as an attempt to circumvent the British legislation (as the UK government claimed)[141] but rather the Chinese one-child policy law.[142] In fact, when pregnant, Mrs Chen moved to England because the Chinese government was still enforcing a very strict law for birth control, which forbade couples to have more than one child. The key to understanding *Zhu and Chen*'s tortuous story is knowing one of the exceptions recognized by Chinese law: couples can have a second child only if the baby is not of Chinese nationality and does not reside in China. This explains why the couple embarked on a European adventure to give Catherine not only an Irish passport but also a UK residence permit.

The strategy behind Mr Zhu and Mrs Chen's case was designed, once again, by two London-based migration lawyers, barristers Ramby De Mello and Adrian Berry. They had been contacted by the commercial law firm that was assisting Mrs Chen in Cardiff because of their long experience in litigating EU citizenship rights.[143] The lawyers knew that to get around Chinese law, the main obstacle was to obtain a residence permit outside China for Mrs Chen and her daughter. In fact, once Catherine had acquired Irish nationality, she would have been entitled to reside in Ireland, but her mother would not. And there was the idea of framing their situation in terms of EU free movement rights: Catherine holds the status of Union citizen, with the attached rights to move and reside in any of the EU Member States, and Mrs Chen, being her mother, could enjoy derived residence rights as a Union citizen's family member.

Notably, when the *Zhu and Chen* case was referred, the ECJ had not developed its jurisprudence on the derived rights of TCN family members of

[140] Case C-200/02 *Zhu and Chen* (2004) CJEU, ECLI:EU:C:2004:639 [9].

[141] ibid para 34.

[142] Dimitry Kochenov and Justin Lindeboom, 'Breaking Chinese Law—Making European One' in Fernanda Nicola and Bill Davies (eds), *EU Law Stories* (CUP 2017).

[143] Kochenov and Lindeboom (n 142) 228. This was confirmed during my interview with Adrian Berry, held in London in November 2016.

Union citizens, because decisions like *Baumbast* and *Zambrano* were yet to come.[144] This makes the lawyers' strategy particularly visionary because they claimed that the EU Treaties' provisions are directly binding on the UK government. Their argument was based on two considerations: first, Article 18 EC (now Article 21 TFEU) gives Catherine a directly enforceable right to move and reside in any Member State, even though she had never lived in a Member State different from the one where she was born (the UK). Second, they argued that Mrs Chen was also covered by EU free movement law as she is the mother of an EU citizen and a mother is, in a way, *dependent* on her daughter. In fact, Directive 90/364 granted derivative residence rights to relatives in the ascending line only if they are "dependent" on the mobile Union citizen.[145] The barristers proposed a broad interpretation of such requirement: Mrs Chen is *dependent* on her eight-month-old daughter in terms of her migration status.[146]

It took two years for the ECJ to decide the case, and in the meantime, the judgment in *Baumbast* was delivered. This was a lucky coincidence for *Zhu and Chen*, as the Court relied greatly on the principles established there by reasserting the binding force of EU citizenship rights enshrined in the Treaties. Despite having never exercised her freedom of movement, Catherine was declared to be entitled to a right to reside in the UK. Thus, the ECJ rejected the UK government's view that Mrs Chen was trying "improperly to exploit the provisions of Community law."[147] Regarding Mrs Chen's permit, the ECJ did not agree with the lawyers' view of the mother being dependent on her eight-month-old daughter.[148] Still, the Court adopted a functional interpretation: Catherine was completely dependent on her mother, so deporting Mrs Chen "would deprive the child's right of residence of any useful effect." For the sake of Catherine's right, her mother and carer should be allowed to live in the UK.

The *Zhu and Chen* case became famous for expanding free movement rights, and it is ascribed to the line of cases by which the ECJ has constructed the constitutional foundation of Union citizenship.[149] However, it is worth noting that

[144] While the case of *Zambrano* (Case C-34/09 *Ruiz Zambrano* (2011) CJEU, ECLI:EU:C:2011:124) (which is a landmark judgment in the field of the derived rights of TCN parents of Union citizen children) will be issued several years later, the case of *Baumbast* had been referred by a British Court in 1999, and the ECJ issued its decision in September 2002, few months after the referral in *Zhu and Chen* case. See *Baumbast and R* (n 3).

[145] See art 2(2) of the now repealed Council Directive 90/364/EEC of 28 June 1990.

[146] Kochenov and Lindeboom (n 142) 221. Kochenov and Lindeboom's chapter referred to paras 23 and 25 of the first-instance judge's decision.

[147] *Zhu and Chen* (n 140) para 34.

[148] ibid para 44.

[149] Michael Dougan, 'The Constitutional Dimension to the Case Law on Union Citizenship' (2006) 2006 Inter Alia: University of Durham Student Law Journal 77.

the economic situation of Mr Zhu and Mrs Chen set them aside from most TCN migrants. Mr Zhu is a businessman; he works as the director and majority shareholder of a thriving Chinese company. Interestingly, he could have obtained residence rights through one of the foreign investor schemes that the UK offers (so-called golden visa).[150] EU citizenship law was probably not the only chance to obtain a permit for Mrs Chen and her family; however, it was probably the cheapest solution available, and it eventually succeeded.

The impact of the *Zhu and Chen* decision

While according to EU law scholars the *Zhu and Chen* judgment "helped shape European law, moving the Union forward,"[151] the British media described it in a very different way. They portrayed it as a defeat for the Home Office and an advancement of the position of TCNs who abuse EU free movement law and the Irish *ius soli* rule. The case was depicted in this way by the media in both the UK and Ireland, and it led to a double backlash. First, at the judicial level, the first-instance judge who referred to the ECJ was considered responsible for the Home Office debacle, and the President of the Immigration Upper Tribunal issued a circular stating that, from that moment on, first-instance judges should abstain from referring to the ECJ. Even if the circular was allegedly in breach of the EU norms regulating the preliminary mechanism procedure,[152] it remained available on the Upper Tribunal's website for years. De facto, after this case, first-instance judges have never referred again on TCN family members of EU citizens.

But the *Zhu and Chen* case had its strongest (negative) impact transnationally. The case received media attention in Ireland where it was brought as an example of "baby tourism" or of how migrants exploit the Irish *ius soli* principle.[153] *Zhu and Chen* supplemented and reinforced the commonplace about TCN pregnant women flying to Ireland and giving birth on Irish soil for the sole reason of obtaining rights to residency in the UK. The case triggered a political debate about whether it was still appropriate to maintain the *ius soli* rules, and even before the ECJ ruled on the case, the Irish lawmakers held a referendum on the issue. Ultimately, a large majority of Irish citizens expressed

[150] European Commission, 'Investor Citizenship and Residence Schemes in the European Union, COM(2019) 12 Final' (2019) COM(2019) 12 final.

[151] Kochenov and Lindeboom (n 142) 201.

[152] ILPA filed a complaint to the EU Commission to urge an infringement case, but with no result.

[153] Rozenberg (n 138); Clare Dyer, 'Ruling Exposes Immigration Loophole' *The Guardian* (20 October 2004) <https://www.theguardian.com/uk/2004/oct/20/eu.immigrationandpublicservices> accessed 17 December 2024; Rainer Baubock and others (eds), *Acquisition and Loss of Nationality|Volume 2: Country Analyses: Policies and Trends in 15 European Countries* (Amsterdam University Press 2010) 293.

a preference for repealing the *ius soli* principle, and the Irish Citizenship Law was amended accordingly.[154]

Although *Zhu and Chen* clearly is a strategic litigation case (in the sense that the parties strategically sought a reference to the ECJ to promote their interpretation of EU free movement law), can we define it as a legal mobilization case? According to the definition adopted in Chapter 1, a litigation amounts to a legal mobilization when it features two elements: it pursues a social, political, or collective aim, and it features the presence of collective actors. Although *Zhu and Chen* had an important impact on the interpretation of EU law, the litigation was mainly pursued for the private interest of the parties in the case. Also, the only "collective actor" of the case is the barrister Adrian Berry, who is committed to the cause of free movement but who was also simply doing his job by serving his clients' best interests. In conclusion, *Zhu and Chen* is an interesting case to show the high level of legal sophistication and political impact of free movement cases, but it does not strictly amount to legal mobilization.

6.3 *McCarthy*

We have seen in the *Akrich* case how the restrictive UK policy on marriage migration can induce British citizens to invoke their European free movement rights within their home country. The case described below, *McCarthy*, has many things in common with *Akrich*. Both cases started with a British woman asking for a permit for her undocumented TCN husband; since UK Immigration Rules give their husbands no right to a residence permit, they asked for help from a legal advice centre, which set up an EU litigation strategy and brought their case to the ECJ. However, Mrs McCarthy's judicial history did not end as positively as Mrs Akrich's.

Mr George McCarthy, Mrs McCarthy's spouse, is a Jamaican citizen who entered the UK with a visitor permit in 2002; that same year, he met Mrs McCarthy and they decided to get married.[155] When his visitor permit was about to expire, Mr McCarthy asked for leave to remain as the spouse of a British citizen but his request was refused under the UK's Immigration Rules; at the time of the proceedings, he was living in the UK without a permit. The

[154] This is the "Twenty-Seventh Amendment of the Constitution of Ireland Referendum," held on 11 June 2004. In the debate before the referendum, the *Zhu and Chen* case was explicitly mentioned as an example of people abusing the *ius soli* in Ireland.

[155] *McCarthy* (n 125).

couple, who wanted to live together, asked for help from the Immigration Advisory Service (IAS), a charity providing representation and advice in immigration and asylum law.[156] The solicitors said that British law offered scarce or null opportunities for making Mr McCarthy's situation legal, however they noticed that Mrs McCarthy held dual citizenship: she was, by birth, a citizen of the UK and Ireland, like many Britons of Irish descent.[157] Such dual citizenship, in the solicitors' view, could offer the couple a chance to reside legally in the UK because Mrs McCarthy could obtain an EU residence permit based on her being an Irish citizen living in the UK. In fact, under Article 16 of the Citizenship Directive, "Union citizens who have resided legally for a continuous period of five years in the host Member State shall have the right of permanent residence there."[158] Once Mrs McCarthy obtained the permit, Mr McCarthy could apply for a residence permit as the spouse of a Union citizen migrant.

Once again, the lawyers were mounting a strategy grounded on the fact that in the field of marriage migration, EU migrants are better placed than UK citizens for obtaining UK residency rights. And it seems that, during those years, relying on the Citizenship Directive was a common strategy used by dual nationals to obtain a permit for their TCN family members.

"That was a weird case," Simon Cox, the barrister representing Mrs McCarthy, told me.[159] During the administrative stage, the Home Office refused Mrs McCarthy's application for permanent residence because she was not a "qualified person" under EU law: she was not a worker, self-employed, or a self-sufficient Union citizen, but she lived on benefits and, therefore, she did not have the right to reside under Article 7 of the Citizenship Directive.[160] It seems that the Home Office was mainly concerned with Mrs McCarthy's economic situation and did not consider her British nationality an obstacle to the enjoyment of free movement rights.

[156] IAS was the leading charity in this field, and one of the two organizations into which the UKIAS split in 1993, the second being the Refugee and Migrant Justice. See Section 5 of this chapter and <https://web.archive.org/web/20101216152533/http://iasuk.org/about-us.aspx> accessed 12 March 2025.

[157] According to the 2011 British census, there were 35,596 people living in England and Wales who held British and Irish passports. In 2021, UK-Irish passports saw a sixfold increase for UK-born residents, which is likely a Brexit effect. Data is available on the UK national statistics' website: <https://www.ons.gov.uk/> accessed 19 March 2025.

[158] Directive 2004/38 at art 16(1).

[159] Interview with Simon Cox, 18 November 2016.

[160] Art 7 of the Citizenship Directive 2004/38. An account of the British case law on the 'qualified persons' is provided by Paul Minderhoud, 'Directive 2004/38 and Access to Social Assistance Benefits' in Elspeth Guild and others (eds), *The Reconceptualization of European Union Citizenship* (Brill Nijhoff 2014) 83.

Instead, when Mrs McCarthy challenged the Home Office's rejection in court, the Tribunal decided to dismiss her appeal on a different ground. The judges saw a problem in the fact that she was a British national who had resided in the UK her entire life as a citizen, and not by virtue of her free movement rights.[161] This same argument was then upheld by the Court of Appeal, where Lord Justice Pill stated that "a United Kingdom citizen resident in the United Kingdom cannot, by virtue of also having Irish nationality, claim a permit which may be granted by virtue of the Directive."[162] In the judges' view, Mrs McCarthy did not qualify for an EU permanent residence permit because despite having resided legally in the UK for more than five years, she did so by virtue of her being a British citizen and without exercising her free movement rights.

Interestingly, the judges brought forward this interpretation on their own initiative, without the Home Office asking for it.[163] Simon Cox told me that the Home Office would not have supported such an interpretation: "The policy of the Home Office at that time was to treat dual citizens as they were just Irish, they didn't want to treat dual nationals worse because they are also British."[164] In fact, throughout the proceedings, the Home Office insisted on stating that the problem was not Mrs McCarthy's British passport but the fact that she had never been economically active or self-sufficient, as the Citizenship Directive requires.

After having lost the first two stages of the proceedings, Mrs McCarthy's lawyers saw in the ECJ their last chance to win the case. While the Court of Appeal considered it unnecessary to consult the Court,[165] eventually Mrs McCarthy's barristers convinced the House of Lords to ask for a reference, by arguing that under the *CILFIT* doctrine,[166] the court of last instance must refer.[167] However, it took several weeks for the two parties to reach an agreement about the questions to refer. Eventually, one question reflected the argument brought forward by the Court of Appeal, and the other the Secretary of State's position; both focus on the personal scope of the Citizenship Directive: was an Irish-UK

[161] Para 25 of the Tribunal decision reported in the judgment of the Court of Appeal at 29.

[162] *McCarthy v Secretary of State for the Home Department* (2008) England and Wales Court of Appeal, Case C5/2007/2454 [3], 32.

[163] ibid 29. This was confirmed by Simon Cox during the interview.

[164] Interview with Simon Cox, 18 November 2016, London.

[165] *McCarthy* (n 163) 32.

[166] Court of Justice of the European Union, Case C-283/81 *Srl CILFIT and Lanificio di Gavardo SpA v Ministry of Health* (6 October 1982) CJEU, ECLI:EU:C:1982:335.

[167] The order of referral was issued during the pretrial phase, ie during the hearing concerning the leave for appeal before the House of Lords. *McCarthy* (n 125) was one of the last requests for preliminary reference issued by the House of Lords, which, shortly after (October 2009), has been replaced by the newly instituted UK Supreme Court.

citizen a "beneficiary" within the meaning of Article 3 of the Citizenship Directive, notwithstanding that she or he has always lived in the UK? And, under the Citizenship Directive, did a person reside legally in the UK even if she or he is economically inactive?

The answer of the EU judges was not positive for Mrs McCarthy and other dual nationals in the UK. Relying on a "literal, teleological and contextual" interpretation,[168] the ECJ stated that:

> [I]n so far as the Union citizen concerned has never exercised his right of free movement and has always resided in a Member State of which he is a national, that citizen is not covered by the concept of "beneficiary" for the purposes of Article 3(1) of Directive 2004/38, so that that directive is not applicable to him.[169]

In so doing, the ECJ restricted the personal scope of the Citizenship Directive, which, from the case of *McCarthy* on, no longer applied to dual nationals who have always lived in one of the two countries of which they possess nationality. The Court also excluded the application of Article 21 TFEU (Union citizens' freedom of movement) since the administrative decision at stake (the rejection of her permanent residence status) did not deprive Mrs McCarthy of her right to live in the UK or in another Member State.[170] Furthermore, the ECJ noted that dual nationals' family members, like Mr McCarthy, do not enjoy free movement rights in the UK either since these "are not autonomous rights of those family members, but derived rights, acquired through their status as members of the beneficiary's family."[171] This clarification has not been requested, and this suggests that the ECJ judges had in mind that the request for an EU permit was strategic to obtain a permit for her husband. Simon Cox noted that "[p]robably, the CJEU had enough of EU law being used for non-EU citizens and thought that they have gone far enough in intruding in Member States' migration policy." Also, in his opinion, Mrs McCarthy "didn't fit [the CJEU's] image about what EU law is about: she had not moved, worked. If she was a bit more 'economic' probably the result would have been different."[172]

[168] *McCarthy* (n 125).

[169] ibid.

[170] *McCarthy* (n 168) para 49. For a commentary on the interpretation of art 21 TFEU in the *McCarthy* case, see Koen Lenaerts, 'The Court's Outer and Inner Selves: Exploring the External and Internal Legitimacy of the European Court of Justice' in Maurice Adams and others (eds), *Judging Europe's Judges: The Legitimacy of the Case Law of the European Court of Justice* (A&C Black 2014) 41.

[171] *McCarthy* (n 125) para 42.

[172] Interview with Simon Cox, 18 November 2016, London.

This somehow echoes scholars' comments of the decision; Elsuwege noted how "[i]ndividual circumstances rather than a systematic and predictable interpretation of the EU Treaty rules seem to guide the Court's rulings."[173]

The impact of the *McCarthy* decision

The *McCarthy* judgment was received with skepticism by EU law scholars[174] and with disappointment by migration lawyers in the UK. These questioned whether it was appropriate to seek a reference to the ECJ in such a weak case.[175] The preliminary ruling, with its European-wide effect, did not only affect the losing party in the case, Mrs McCarthy and her husband, but also shrank the rights of TCN family members of dual nationals. The British government adopted a specific amendment to the EEA Regulation to "make it clear that a person will not be regarded as an EEA national where they are also a United Kingdom national."[176] The ECJ's decision in *McCarthy* closed one of the main channels that TCN spouses were using for obtaining a residence permit in the UK.

However, a recent development in the ECJ's case law partly vindicated dual citizens and their spouses residing in the UK. The case of *Lounes*, also from a British court (High Court), allowed the ECJ to review its interpretation.[177] Mr Lounes is the husband of a Spanish national who, after many years of life in the UK, acquired British citizenship. The referring court asked whether, upon having been naturalized British, she ceased to be covered by Directive 2004/38 in the UK, or whether she must still be considered a beneficiary of free movement and Union citizenship rights for her and her husband. The ECJ this time read the issue differently and stated that although she lost the rights conferred by the Citizenship Directive, she still holds her Treaty rights (Article 21 TFEU). In particular, since she had exercised her free movement rights in the past, and she had integrated into life in the UK to the point of becoming a citizen, her husband is entitled to a derived right to reside in the UK with her.[178] The Court therefore indirectly recognized that Article 21 TFEU implies

[173] Peter Van Elsuwege, 'Court of Justice of the European Union European Union Citizenship and the Purely Internal Rule Revisited. Decision of 5 May 2011, Case C-434/09 Shirley McCarthy v. Secretary of State for the Home Department' (2011) 7 European Constitutional Law Review 308, 324.

[174] "The distinction drawn by the Court between McCarthy and Garcia Avello is also, with great respect, utterly unconvincing." According to Elspeth Guild, Steve Peers, and Jonathan Tomkin, *The EU Citizenship Directive: A Commentary* (OUP 2014) 49.

[175] This was confirmed in my interviews with solicitors who are members of ILPA network.

[176] Amendment of the Immigration (European Economic Area) Regulations 2012, no 1547/2012 of 19 June 2012.

[177] Case C-165/16 *Lounes* (2017) CJEU, ECLI:EU:C:2017:862.

[178] In the ECJ's words: "Directive 2004/38 must be interpreted as meaning that, in a situation in which a Union citizen (i) has exercised his freedom of movement by moving to and residing in a Member State other than that of which he is a national, under Article 7(1) or Article 16(1) of that

a right to family life, which cannot be denied to the Union citizen only because she acquired the host Member State's citizenship.[179]

Admittedly, this sort of contradictory jurisprudence seems to make the rationale behind the attribution of Union citizenship rights more obscure, rather than clarifying it. However, *Lounes* undoubtedly represents a step forward for dual nationals and their family members in the UK, and in the post-Brexit scenario, it became a useful decision to rely upon for the many Union citizen migrants who naturalize British and have a TCN partner.

7. The Home Office's reaction

On the one hand, the UK case study is a great example of EU law used with skill and creativity to expand migrant rights. On the other, it is also a story of "justice contained."[180] Next to the vibrant scene of migrant NGOs and Eurolawyers that feed cases and supply resources for legal mobilization, there was a government and a Home Office determined to fight fiercely to avoid any expansion of migrant rights. It is not rare, in the UK, to see the government appealing a case until the last stage, even if this entails spending public money in costly litigation. The government has relied on the preliminary reference mechanism too to put forward its interpretation of EU law that, generally, goes in the direction of narrowing down EU rights.[181] According to a lawyer I interviewed, the Home Office does not do this often though, because it see the CJEU as a "liberal Court."[182]

Besides litigation, one of the UK government's main strategies to counteract pro-migrant litigation was to limit access to court. The 2010–15 Coalition government introduced two important reforms in this sense: the first was to abolish migrants' rights to appeal in court, with the only exception of asylum

directive, (ii) has then acquired the nationality of that Member State, while also retaining his nationality of origin, and (iii) several years later, has married a third country national with whom he continues to reside in that Member State, that third-country national does not have a derived right of residence in the Member State in question on the basis of Directive 2004/38. The third-country national is however eligible for a derived right of residence under Article 21(1) TFEU." *Lounes* (n 177) para 62.

[179] *Lounes* (n 177) para 60; Vincent Réveillère, 'Family Rights for Naturalized EU Citizens: "Lounes"' (2018) 55 Common Market Law Review 1855, 1863.

[180] Lisa J Conant, *Justice Contained: Law and Politics in the European Union* (Cornell University Press 2002).

[181] For instance, this happened in the case of *Tolley* (n 20) on social security, where the counterpart was represented by solicitors from PLP. This information was obtained through an interview with members of PLP, acting as solicitors of Mrs Tolley in the case.

[182] Interview with Adrian Berry, 23 November 2016, London.

and human rights cases, substituting it with administrative review;[183] the second was the legal aid reform (LASPO) of 2012, whereby it removed financial support for many areas of civil and administrative law, including housing, family law, welfare benefits, and migration.[184] Migrants became eligible for legal aid only if their case concerns international protection, human trafficking, domestic violence, and personal liberty; otherwise, they need to apply for "exceptional funding," but the chances of success are slim.[185]

The legal aid reform had a huge impact, both for migrants and UK nationals; according to official data, there was a drop of 70 percent in the number of cases that received legal aid, and only 5 percent of the applications for exceptional funding were accepted.[186] While the government's declared aim was to reduce the number of immigration cases, the LASPO also had tremendous repercussions on the activity of law centers and legal charities working for migrants' rights, leading many of them to close. An eminent example is the Immigration Advisory Service (IAS).[187] This service was the UK's largest NGO providing representation and advice in immigration and asylum law; IAS represented in court, among others, the *McCarthy* case and the *NS* case, one of the leading cases in the field of asylum.[188] Charities such as this had a direct impact on the development of EU immigration and asylum law, and they no longer exist.

Besides shutting down opportunities for legal mobilization, the British government fought the ECJ's influence politically. They were concerned about the ECJ's influence over the Member States' policy and tried to limit the Court's powers. In 1996, during an intergovernmental conference, the John Major government proposed to introduce a complaint mechanism for Member States

[183] The government first abolished the right to appeal for family visitors with the Crime and Courts Act 2013, s 52. Then the 2014 Appeals and Immigration Act cut most of the appeal rights, leaving only three possible grounds for appeal: human rights, asylum rejection, and asylum revocation (probably because of European standards requiring an adequate remedy for such cases). The impact of these reforms is huge, especially because administrative review is by no means comparable with having the case reviewed by a judge. For more detail: Robert Thomas, 'Immigration and Access to Justice: A Critical Analysis of Recent Restrictions' in Ellie Palmer and others (eds), *Access to Justice: Beyond the Policies and Politics of Austerity* (Hart Publishing 2016) 123.

[184] Legal Aid, Sentencing and Punishment of Offenders Act 2012, entered into force on 1 April 2013.

[185] Rowena Moffatt and Carita Thomas, 'And Then They Came for Judicial Review: Proposals for Further Reform' (2014) 28 Journal of Immigration, Asylum and Nationality Law 237.

[186] See the official report by the National Audit Office, Implementing Legal Aid Reforms. <https://www.nao.org.uk/wp-content/uploads/2014/11/Implementing-reforms-to-civil-legal-aid1.pdf> accessed 17 December 2024.

[187] Owen Bowcott and legal affairs correspondent, 'Tens of Thousands Lose Support as Immigration Advisory Service Closes' *The Guardian* (11 July 2011) <https://www.theguardian.com/law/2011/jul/11/immigration-advisory-service-closes-blames-government> accessed 17 December 2024; 'Legal Aid Cuts Leave Migrants and Asylum Seekers Vulnerable' *The Guardian* (15 July 2011) <http://www.theguardian.com/law/2011/jul/15/legal-aid-cuts-migrants> accessed 17 December 2024.

[188] Joined cases C-411/10 and C-493/10 *NS and ME and Others* (n 119).

whereby they could ask to review the ECJ's decisions in order "to make the [then] ECJ more politically accountable and to limit the cost of ECJ decisions."[189] Alter defined this British proposal as "the most serious [challenge] to date because it went beyond rhetoric to articulate and specify an anti-ECJ policy."[190] More recently, former Prime Minister David Cameron proposed, during the negotiation that preceded the Brexit vote, to "control migration from the European Union" by "addressing ECJ judgments that have widened the scope of free movement in a way that has made it more difficult to tackle this kind of abuse."[191] In Cameron's view, the ECJ and its case law were responsible for the alleged migration problem affecting the UK; the Court enabled Union citizens and their TCN family members to "abuse" free movement provisions.

Eventually, Brexit settled this political struggle. It deprived UK citizens and EU migrants of their free movement rights, and many TCN family members lost their right to reside in the UK. Brexit has important implications for the respect of the rule of law too and we will not know for some time whether the "European culture of rights" has penetrated deeply enough in the British legal system to survive in the post-EU era.

8. Conclusion

> *Our sovereignty has been taken away by the European Court of Justice ... No longer is European law an incoming tide flowing up the estuaries of England. It is now like a tidal wave bringing down our sea walls and flowing inland over our fields and houses—to the dismay of all.*[192]

This chapter deals with the legal mobilization for migrants' rights before the ECJ in the UK. The chapter started with a simple observation: British courts have referred a large number of questions to the ECJ on the same issue: the rights of TCNs who are family members of EU citizens. The chapter analyzes UK migration within a historical perspective, assessing the role of litigation for

[189] Alter and Vargas (n 12) 467; Mark A Pollack, *The Engines of European Integration: Delegation, Agency, and Agenda Setting in the EU* (OUP 2003) 180.

[190] Karen Alter, 'Who Are the "Masters of the Treaty"? European Governments and the European Court of Justice' (1998) 52 International Organization 121, 140.

[191] Letter of Prime Minister David Cameron to Donald Tusk, 10 November 2015. <http://news.bbc.co.uk/2/shared/bsp/hi/pdfs/10_11_15_donaldtuskletter.pdf> accessed 18 December 2024.

[192] Lord Denning, 1990, cited by Karen Alter, *Establishing the Supremacy of European Law: The Making of an International Rule of Law in Europe* (OUP 2002) 56.

migrant rights within the UK's broader political context, and assessing how opportunities for legal mobilization evolved in the last decades.

Scholars do not have a univocal account of the legal opportunity structure in the UK. As we said in Section 2, depending on the field analyzed, the UK seems to be closed or open to EU legal mobilization. In the migration and free movement domains, migrant supporters have successfully promoted in court the use of the preliminary reference procedure to expand the right of TCN migrants. In this chapter, I identified three elements that point to an opening of opportunities for legal mobilization by migrants' rights supporters. The first is the British political context. The high salience of migration issues in the UK and the very polarized debates about them led the anti-immigration stance to establish itself firmly in the government, leaving no room for political opposition representing migrants' interests. This might have convinced minority groups to turn to the courts, since no other political venue was available.[193] Moreover, the government's fierce anti-immigration stance also means that migrants in the UK had to face hostile laws and environments; they often need to rely on European or international norms to safeguard their rights.

The second element is the evolution of the judicial role in the UK. Political scientists and constitutional scholars pointed out that in the past, the UK lacked strong scrutiny over the executive action. This is also in regard to the Home Office, which is responsible for enforcing migration policy. In the 1960s, a gradual process of constitutional reform started, culminating in a British "rights revolution": the UK accession to the EEC and the adoption of the HRA deeply changed the position of the judicial power vis-à-vis the executive. Judicial scrutiny over acts of public authority increased in quantity and quality, and judges became more inclined to scrutinize the Home Office activity under EU and ECHR standards. Unfortunately, the recent restrictions introduced on migrants' rights to appeal risk reversing this trend and posing a real threat to British rule of law.[194]

The third element is the capacity of groups to organize and mobilize EU law for migrants' rights. Although Joppke has noted that the "unitary British state did not provide any point of entry for immigrant-friendly dissent," I showed how groups like JCWI have been present in the UK public life since the 1960s. These groups mobilized migrant rights several times before either domestic, international, or EU courts; this has been possible because they often have in-house lawyers, rely on an experienced group of EU law barristers loyal to the migrant's cause, and receive (less and less) financial support from legal aid.

[193] Section 3.
[194] Thomas (n 183).

To be sure, the intensity and efficacy of the legal mobilization efforts have increased substantially over time: the first cases challenging marriage migration before the Human Rights Committee of the Council of Europe were a failure, while more recent legal mobilization was more effective. However, this success attracted the hostility of the government, which intervened to close opportunities for legal mobilization.

The impact of the legal mobilization is difficult to assess in the UK case. As shown, the ECJ's decisions were often disappointing for migrants' rights supporters, and at times, even detrimental to their cause (see *Akrich* and *McCarthy*, but also *Zhu and Chen* for its impact on Ireland). However, many cases that were referred from the UK, not analyzed in detail in this chapter, led to an important expansion of EU citizens' and TCN migrants' rights. Some of these UK-referred cases, like *Baumbast*, *Carpenter*, or *Alarape and Tijiani*,[195] are foundational citizenship cases, whereby the ECJ has emancipated EU citizenship from its "market roots."[196]

More importantly, the outcome of legal mobilization does not necessarily coincide with the outcome of the single proceedings. It should be measured with at least two different sets of considerations: whether the individual migrant benefited from the proceedings, and whether the Home Office will adjust its actions in the future according to the possibility of incurring another legal challenge. This is what legal mobilization scholars call the "perception of the threat of litigation,"[197] according to which courts are not only rulemakers and sanction-providers but they have the capacity to generate messages for the broader community. As King noted: "ministers, civil servants and other public officials no longer simply act and then wait to see whether their actions will be reviewed. They act knowing that their actions may be reviewed. Whenever they act, they thus need to take the possibility of judicial review into consideration."[198] Under this view, the litigation threat can be more effective in bringing about social change and in shaping public authorities' attitudes than a single judicial victory; however, to that effect, immigrants must be granted full access to courts, and Brexit along with the British government's reforms may cast a long shadow on future legal mobilization in the UK.

[195] *Baumbast and R* (n 3); Case C-60/00 *Carpenter* (11 July 2002) CJEU, ECLI:EU:C:2002:434; *Alarape and Tijani* (n 3).

[196] Eleanor Spaventa, 'Earned Citizenship: Understanding Union Citizenship through its Scope' in Dimitry Kochenov, *EU Citizenship and Federalism: The Role of Rights* (CUP 2017) 207.

[197] Charles Epp, 'Implementing the Rights Revolution: Repeat Players and the Interpreting of Diffuse Legal Messages' (2008) 71 Law and Contemporary Problems 41, 47; Michael McCann, *Rights at Work: Pay Equity Reform and the Politics of Legal Mobilization* (University of Chicago Press 1994) 280.

[198] King (n 74) 126.

4

The Netherlands

Mobilizing EU Justice for a Different Form of Integration

"You need to have the right case, at the right time, with the right judge."[1]

1. Why the Netherlands?

From an overview of the Court of Justice's case law database, it emerges immediately that the Netherlands has a special relationship with the Family Reunification Directive 2003/86.[2] From October 3, 2005, when the Family Reunification Directive entered into force, to December 2022, the European Court of Justice (ECJ) has received twenty-four requests for preliminary rulings concerning its interpretation, eleven of which came from Dutch courts. To be sure, the Netherlands is among the Member States that refer the most, together with Germany and Italy.[3] This is especially true in the migration field, where a fifth of all preliminary references came from Dutch courts.[4] However, Dutch references about the Family Reunification Directive significantly outnumber those of any other Member State, including Italy and Germany. So far, most Member States have never requested a preliminary ruling on the Family Reunification Directive (see Figure 4.1). This raises the question of whether, behind these Dutch cases, there was legal mobilization.

After a closer look at the data and the preliminary references made over time (Figure 4.2), it is clear that the Dutch case differs from the Italian one. While the Italian references were more numerous and very concentrated within a

[1] Interview with lawyer Gerben Dijkman, 13 December 2017, Utrecht.

[2] Council Directive 2003/86/EC of 22 September 2003 on the right to family reunification.

[3] Morten Broberg and Niels Fenger, 'Variations in Member States' Preliminary References to the Court of Justice—Are Structural Factors (Part of) the Explanation?' (2013) 19 European Law Journal 488, 492.

[4] More in Chapter 1 of the book. I have gathered these data by relying on CURIA, the CJEU's official online database of case law. I have cross-checked my data with the 'Quarterly Overview of CJEU judgments and pending cases' issued by the Centre for Migration Law of the Nijmegen University: <https://www.ru.nl/law/cmr/documentation/cmr-newsletters/> accessed 17 December 2024.

Legal Mobilization for Migrant Rights. Virginia Passalacqua, Oxford University Press.
 DOI: 10.1093/9780198943006.003.0004

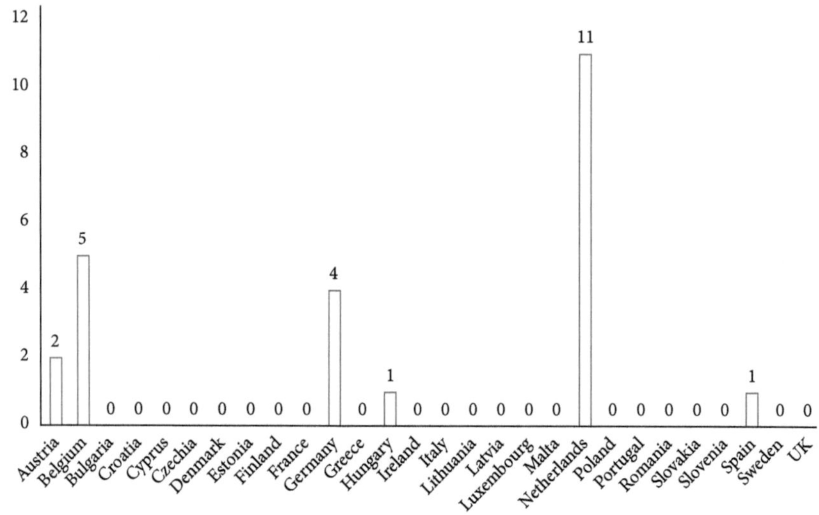

Figure 4.1 Requests for preliminary rulings concerning the Family Reunification Directive up to December 2022.

period of time, the Dutch references were more diluted and constant. This suggests a different use of the Directive, which was not mobilized with a single goal in mind.

The second reason I chose the Netherlands as a case study, in line with the case selection strategy, is that many of the references submitted to the ECJ regard a controversial issue that was (and still is) at the center of Dutch political debates. Many of the Dutch references on the Family Reunification Directive focus on the legitimacy of the so-called civic integration requirements.[5] In 2005 and 2006, Dutch lawmakers adopted two laws that reformed the migrants' integration strategy;[6] these laws made third-country nationals' (TCNs) admission and permanence in the Netherlands conditional upon the passing of a test on the Dutch language and society. In so doing, these reforms significantly curtailed the right to family reunification, with migrants abroad required to take the test before entering the Netherlands. The laws were met with strong opposition by migrant rights supporters, a fact that corroborated

[5] These are Case C-155/11 PPU *Imran* (2011) CJEU, ECLI:EU:C:2011:387; Case C-153/14 *K and A* (2015) CJEU, ECLI:EU:C:2015:453; Case C-257/17 *C and A* (2018) CJEU, EU:C:2018:876; Case C-484/17 *K* (2018) CJEU, ECLI:EU:C:2018:878.

[6] 2005 Act on the Civic Integration from abroad (*Wet Inburgering Buitenland*) and the 2006 amendment on the 1998 Civic Integration Act (*Wet Inburgering*). See Section 3 for further comments on these reforms.

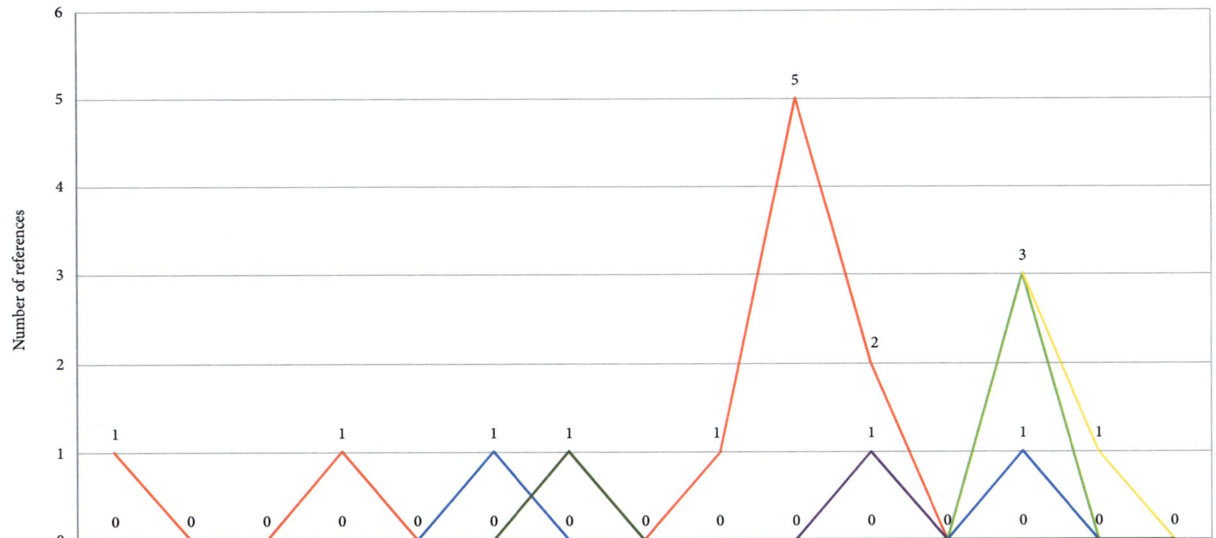

	2008	2009	2010	2011	2012	2013	2014	2015	2016	2017	2018	2019	2020	2021	2022
Austria	0	0	0	0	0	1	0	0	0	0	0	0	1	0	0
Belgium	0	0	0	0	0	0	0	0	0	0	1	0	3	1	0
Germany	0	0	0	0	0	0	1	0	0	0	0	0	3	0	0
Hungary	0	0	0	0	0	0	0	0	0	0	1	0	0	0	0
Netherlands	1	0	0	1	0	0	1	0	1	5	2	0	0	0	0
Spain	0	0	0	0	0	0	1	0	0	0	0	0	0	0	0

Figure 4.2 Preliminary references on the Family Reunification Directive per country across time (until 2022).

my idea that the many Dutch references could be the signal that a legal mobilization took place.

The references in the Netherlands cannot be explained only by the conflict between the Family Reunification Directive and the national integration policy. The Netherlands is by no means the only country that limits the right to family reunification by imposing integration requirements: Germany, Austria, France, Denmark, and Latvia have similar provisions.[7] These countries, however, did not produce a similar number of references (Figure 4.1).[8] How can we explain the higher number of Dutch references? What conditions particular to the Netherlands' subjective and structural factors enabled these references? Did civil society play any role in this?

The chapter identifies structural and subjective factors conducive to EU legal mobilization. As in the UK, in the Netherlands direct effect and the preliminary reference procedure empowered judges who traditionally have limited powers to review the legitimacy of national laws. In this empowerment, a crucial role was played by a successful alliance between academics and civil society which was essential to perceive the opportunities offered by EU law and to persuade lower instance judges to participate in the enforcement of migrant rights.

Many of the Dutch preliminary references on the Family Reunification Directive are the result of legal mobilization, but not all. Academics, lawyers, and organizations for migrants' rights decided to rely on the ECJ to challenge the Dutch "civic integration test" that hampers the right to family reunification in the Netherlands. But beyond these legal mobilization cases, other references submitted *ex officio* exploited the potential of the Family Reunification Directive and the preliminary reference procedure to advance migrant rights. Dutch courts, and especially the *Raad Van State* (Council of State), have proven remarkably aware of EU rights and took on themselves the task of defending the correct enforcement and application of the Family Reunification Directive. Dutch courts have not always been as receptive but this was the result of structural changes in the judiciary, as this chapter will explain.

[7] Henri Labayle and Yves Pascouau, 'Study on the "Conformity Checking of the Transposition by Member States of 10 EC Directives in the Sector of Asylum and Immigration" Done for DG JLS of the European Commission End 2007' Contract JLS/B4/2006/03 102 <http://odysseus-network.eu/wp-content/uploads/2015/03/2003-86-Family-reunification-Synthesis-.pdf> accessed 17 December 2024.

[8] Until May 2018, the ECJ received eight references for a preliminary ruling concerning specifically the issue of integration measures or conditions, five of which are from the Netherlands: *Imran* (n 5); Case C-138/13 *Dogan* (2014) CJEU, ECLI:EU:C:2014:2066; Case C-579/13 *P and S* (4 June 2015) CJEU, ECLI:EU:C:2015:369; *K and A* (n 5); Case C-561/14 *Genc* (2016) CJEU, ECLI:EU:C:2016:247; Case C-123/17 *Yön* (2018) CJEU, ECLI:EU:C:2018:632; *C and A* (n 5); *K* (n 5).

The following sections set the scene for the analysis of the Dutch case by explaining the political and historical background of immigration in the Netherlands. Section 2 covers the period from the 1950s to 2005, when the law on civic integration requirements, the target of the legal mobilization, was adopted. Section 4 explains the particular meaning of the Family Reunification Directive in the Dutch context, the negotiation that led to its adoption, and its impact in the Dutch legal context. The second part of this chapter is devoted to the analysis of the concrete dynamic of the mobilization. After having presented the actors behind the mobilization (Section 5), and the structural factors in the Dutch judiciary and procedure that either constrained or facilitated the mobilization (Section 6), I will describe two cases (*Imran* and *K and A*) where the Family Reunification Directive was first mobilized against the civic integration test (Section 7). In the last section, I draw some conclusions on the conditions that made the backfire possible.

2. Integration of migrants in the Netherlands: The journey to multiculturalism and back

After the Second World War, the Netherlands underwent a process that transformed it from an emigration to an immigration country. Like the UK and other Western European states, the first consistent influx of migrants arrived in the second half of the twentieth century. Some of them came from its former colonies: mainly people from Indonesia and Suriname who decided to leave their countries because of the uncertain future or the unstable political situation resulting from their country's declaration of independence from the Netherlands (which was 1945 and 1975, respectively). Another consistent influx of immigrants arrived in the Netherlands in the 1970s. These were attracted by the advanced Dutch industrial economy, in the context of what has been called "*postindustrial* migration";[9] this was the case of people coming from Italy, Spain, Morocco, and Turkey.[10] The arrival of Turkish immigrants was facilitated by a labor agreement concluded between the Turkish and the Dutch governments, the goal of which was to remedy the unemployment of the

[9] Douglas S Massey, 'Why Does Immigration Occur? A Theoretical Synthesis' in Charles Hirschman, Philip Kasinitz, and Josh De Wind (eds), *The Handbook of International Migration: The American Experience* (Russell Sage Foundation 1999) 35.

[10] Kees Groenendijk and Eric Heijs, 'Immigration, Immigrants and Nationality Law in the Netherlands, 1945–98' in Randall Hansen and P Weil (eds), *Towards a European Nationality, Citizenship, Immigration and Nationality Law in the EU* (Palgrave 2001) 144.

former and to fill the labor gap in the latter state.[11] Finally, a third wave of immigrants came to the Netherlands to seek asylum, during the 1980s and 1990s.[12] These immigrant influxes have contributed to turning the Netherlands into the nation that we know today, with the second biggest Turkish community in Europe, its Middle Eastern groceries and Chinatowns, and the reputation of being a country capable of accommodating a highly diverse population.

The Netherlands learned how to accommodate diversity long before the twentieth-century migration flows. Since its foundation 200 years ago, Dutch society has always been composed of different political, religious, and social groups, stuck together thanks to a strong consensus culture; that is why "tolerance was more or less a practical necessity in a divided and fragmented society."[13] Emblematic, in this regard, is the twentieth-century Dutch phenomenon of "pillarization": religious and class divisions were structured into four main groups (pillars)—Catholics, Protestants, Liberals, and Socialists. All Dutch social life was organized around these four pillars. Although the Netherlands was officially "depillarized" in the 1960s, divisions and fragmentations remained but simply developed along different lines.[14] In the 1970s, when the immigrant population grew in number, its ethnic and socioeconomic diversity opened a new important cleavage in Dutch society, which is of concern for Dutch policymakers still today.

To address this new cleavage in Dutch society, policymakers put forward two different strategies. First, in the 1980s, the Netherlands embraced a multicultural approach, developing a progressive minority policy; then, at the end of the 1990s and beginning of 2000s, policymakers revised their previous commitments and adopted a more assimilationist approach toward minorities, distancing themselves from multiculturalist ideals. To be sure, this way of classifying the different stages of Dutch integration policy may seem too simplistic and the two different approaches to integration are not as radically divergent as mainstream accounts tend to represent: the Netherlands has never been a fully-fledged supporter of multiculturalism nor has it become its fiercest opponent.[15] However, this division into periods is useful for understanding the political shift that occurred in the early 2000s, which is also the backdrop of

[11] Liza Mügge, *Beyond Dutch Borders: Transnational Politics among Colonial Migrants, Guest Workers and the Second Generation* (Amsterdam University Press 2010) 42.

[12] Groenendijk and Heijs (n 10) 144.

[13] Wim Voermans, 'A 200-Year-Old Constitution: Relic or Enigma?' in Giuseppe Franco Ferrari, Reijer Passchier, and Wim Voermans (eds), *The Dutch Constitution beyond 200 Years: Tradition and Innovation in a Multilevel Legal Order* (Eleven International Publishing 2018) 14.

[14] ibid 15.

[15] Maarten P Vink, 'Dutch "Multiculturalism" Beyond the Pillarisation Myth.' (2007) 5 Political Studies Review 337.

the legal mobilization studied in this chapter. In the following subsection, I will further describe the evolution of Dutch integration policies.

2.1 The Netherlands as a model of a multicultural society

In the 1980s, as mentioned, Dutch policymakers decided to embrace a progressive stance toward ethnic minorities and integration. This choice was propelled by the publication of an influential report by the Scientific Council for Government Policy (*WRR*) in 1979.[16] The report warned the government about the fact that contrary to its expectations, many immigrants arriving in the Netherlands were there to stay: many of them, even if initially considered as a temporary labor force, or guest workers, would not return to their countries of origin. Moreover, the report shed light on the disadvantaged conditions in which these ethnic minorities were living; because of "a cumulation of adverse socio-economic and cultural factors," they were relegated "at the bottom of the social ladder."[17] The report had a huge influence on the government, which changed its stance on ethnic minorities. It released a policy document (the *minderhedennota*) that enshrined its new goals: reducing the gap between ethnic minorities and the "indigenous population" and creating a more just society that gives equal opportunities to all.[18] The resulting policy on minorities (*minderhedenbeleid*) provided for different measures aimed at promoting the participation and emancipation of minorities in society, also by requiring that the receiving community made an effort to accommodate diversity.

An important measure that reduced disparity in the legal status was to open up access to citizenship for people with a migration background. The government achieved this by amending the requirement for naturalization and by liberalizing Dutch naturalization policies.[19] The resulting 1985 Dutch Nationality

[16] ibid 340. See also Ricky Van Oers, Betty De Hart, and Kees Groenendijk, 'The Netherlands' in Rainer Baubock and others (eds), *Policies and Trends in 15 European States*, vol 2 (Amsterdam University Press 2006) 402. The WRR report is available online: WRR—The Netherlands Scientific Council for Government Policy, 'Ethnic Minorities' (1979) 17 <https://english.wrr.nl/publications/reports/1979/05/09/ethnic-minorities> accessed 17 December 2024.

[17] ibid 9.

[18] Van Oers, De Hart, and Groenendijk, 'The Netherlands' (n 16) 12. Ricky Van Oers, *Deserving Citizenship: Citizenship Tests in Germany, the Netherlands and the United Kingdom* (Martinus Nijhoff Publishers 2013) 43.

[19] To be precise, the liberalization process that affected Dutch naturalization policies started in 1953, breaking with the past. Dutch naturalization policies had assumed a restrictive character during the First World War, when the idea of citizenship as belonging to the nation state was predominant; naturalization was granted to those who served the Dutch nation (eg those who participated in the Resistance during the war) or to those who could demonstrate an emotional tie to the Netherlands. Van Oers, De Hart, and Groenendijk, 'The Netherlands' (n 16) 394.

Act,[20] adopted under the influence of the *minderhedenbeleid*, facilitated naturalization procedures for first-generation immigrants, gave second generations the possibility to opt for Dutch citizenship at eighteen years, and confirmed the automatic acquisition of Dutch citizenship at birth for third-generation immigrants.[21] Interestingly, the new naturalization procedure for immigrants contained a precursor of the language and integration requirement. During an interview with a state official, the applicants had to demonstrate their ability to speak Dutch and their knowledge of Dutch society;[22] however, since at that time naturalization was seen as only one step in the process to achieve integration, applicants were expected to have a level of spoken Dutch sufficient for communicating with Dutch nationals, and written Dutch was not even tested.[23] Thanks to these reforms, the number of people belonging to ethnic minorities who acquired Dutch citizenship through naturalization increased significantly.

Coherently with multicultural ideas, the Dutch government took the view that minority integration does not mean renouncing one's cultural tradition and identity. That is why the government decided that not only minorities' cultural expression should not be repressed but it should be incentivized on equal terms to that of the majority. Many Islamic and Hindu schools opened in the following years, along with non-Christian places of worship.[24]

To increase minorities' political participation, the government acted on two fronts. On the one hand, it granted the right to vote in local elections to non-citizen residents. On the other, it introduced a system for minorities' consultation that relied on ethnic organizations as intermediaries. However, "[m]inority organizations needed to be supported to provide the government with clearly identifiable and, hopefully, representative discussion partners."[25] To this end, the government allocated public funds to support ethnic minority organizations and created consultative bodies where these groups and the government could discuss integration policies.[26] These ethnic organizations

[20] *Rijkswet op het Nederlanderschap*, replacing the 1982 Act on nationality. The Act was adopted in 1984 but entered into force on 1 January 1985.

[21] This is called "double *jus soli*," a norm first introduced in 1953, that was under review at that time. Groenendijk and Heijs (n 10) 145.

[22] The knowledge of Dutch language and society first appeared as a requirement for naturalization in a circular of 1977 (*Hoofdafdeling Privaatrecht afdeling Nationaliteit en Burgerlijke Staat*, 10 March 1977, Staatscourant 27 April 1977, no 81, p 4); the circular was the first instrument to formalize the requirements for obtaining Dutch citizenship. This was an important step in the process that transformed Dutch citizenship from a state's concession into an individual right. Van Oers, De Hart, and Groenendijk, 'The Netherlands' (n 16) 398.

[23] Van Oers, *Deserving Citizenship* (n 18) 44.

[24] Vink (n 15) 341.

[25] ibid 345.

[26] ibid 342.

proved to be very active in the political arena. Not only did they participate in consultations but they also set up political campaigns and strategic litigation, as the second part of this chapter will show.

2.2 The Netherlands' rejection of multiculturalism

Mainstream accounts hold that the Dutch multicultural view of society began to crumble in the 1990s and early 2000s. Public opinion began to show some anxieties regarding immigrants' integration, propelled by the common account that "integration of immigrants in Dutch society had failed."[27] The multicultural approach adopted by Dutch policymakers in the 1980s was openly challenged and supplanted by an ideal of "active citizenship",[28] that immigrants should become responsible for themselves and for finding their place in society. Of course, this did not happen overnight, but it was the result of a slow change in language, attitudes, and public opinion, reflected in politicians' public statements.

Some key facts and public figures are usually mentioned in the literature to describe the change in the political climate of those years. These are the publication of the influential essay "*Het multiculturele drama*" ("The multicultural drama") by a Social-Democrat politician who openly questioned multicultural ideals;[29] the 9/11 terrorist attack which increased islamophobia throughout the Western world; the assassination of filmmaker Theo van Gogh in 2004 at the hand of an extremist Muslim man who was outraged by van Gogh's movie on Islam;[30] and the rise of xenophobic politicians like Pim Fortuyn, leader of the Pim Fortuyn List, who focused his electoral campaign on the failure of integration, accusing Muslim minorities of being backward and not respecting women's and gay rights.[31] Fortuyn was murdered a few days before the 2002 Dutch legislative elections, an event that probably boosted his popularity since his party enjoyed a surprisingly good result, subsequent to his death. These

[27] Van Oers, De Hart, and Groenendijk, 'The Netherlands' (n 16) 403.

[28] ibid 403.

[29] The book is *Het multiculturele drama* by Paul Scheffer (NRC 2000). The author "warned that an alienated foreign population undermines the social cohesion of Dutch society and called for a new policy based on shared language and norms." In Li'av Orgad, *The Cultural Defense of Nations: A Liberal Theory of Majority Rights* (OUP 2015) 103.

[30] 'Controversial Filmmaker Shot Dead' *The Independent* (2 November 2004) <http://www.independent.co.uk/news/world/europe/controversial-filmmaker-shot-dead-18345.html> accessed 17 December 2024.

[31] Virginie Guiraudon, Karen Phalet, and Jessika Ter Wal, 'Monitoring Ethnic Minorities in the Netherlands' (2005) 57 International Social Science Journal 75, 85.

tragic political murders are further proof of the heated climate surrounding Dutch integration policies at that time.

These renowned episodes should be taken as symptoms rather than the cause of multiculturalism's decline. But then, why did Dutch public opinion and policymakers depart from their multicultural commitments? Some scholars argue that to begin with, the Netherlands has never been as multiculturalist as mainstream accounts had depicted. The term multiculturalism was understood and used in its descriptive sense, and Dutch society never truly committed to the normative component of the concept.[32] A different explanation is provided by Besselink, who noted that politicians from across the whole political spectrum started seeing multiculturalism as a veil that was hiding serious economic, social, and cultural problems in Dutch society.[33] Because of a sort of "multicultural taboo," it became impossible to openly address issues like immigrant children's bad performance in school, or Muslim women's segregation, which were of legitimate concern to the Dutch population.

It is hard to tell whether such social clashes between the Muslim minority and the Dutch autochthones were real or a perception made up by the same politicians and media which campaigned for a more assimilationist type of society. Guiraudon noted that "[w]hile monitors showed an improvement of the situation of ethnic minorities, especially with respect to education and employment throughout the 1990s, this was ignored by elected politicians and the media, which increasingly spoke of the failure of the integration of minorities."[34] An official parliamentary report issued in 2004 was received in the same way; although it concluded that the status of integration in Dutch society was fairly good, it was intentionally disregarded by most politicians.[35] Thus it is hard to assess whether multiculturalism failed or whether politicians wanted to depict it as a failure. In any case, between the 1990s and the 2000s, the general attitude toward migration and minorities drastically changed, leading to a new cycle of political reforms.

[32] Vink (n 15) 344.

[33] Leonard FM Besselink, 'Integration and Immigration: The Vicissitudes of Dutch "Inburgering"' in Elspeth Guild, Kees Groenendijk, and Sergio Carrera (eds), *Illiberal Liberal States: Immigration, Citizenship, and Integration in the EU* (Ashgate 2009) 242.

[34] Guiraudon, Phalet, and Wal (n 31) 85.

[35] The report, commissioned by the Parliament this time, titled 'Building Bridges' (*Bruggen Bouwen*, TK 28689, no 8-9, 19 January 2004). The report concluded that integration was successful for most migrants in the Netherlands, despite the many faults in the integration policies and in its application. The politicians accurately cherry-picked the information contained in the report and delivered to the public a message of failure of integration and of the necessity to introduce more stringent civic requirements for immigrants. See Besselink (n 28) 250. Also Van Oers (n 18) 52.

The crisis of multiculturalist ideals led the government to backtrack and change previous progressive reforms. For instance, in 1992, after a decade-long discussion and campaigns (especially by Turkish ethnic organizations),[36] migrants had finally obtained the possibility to be naturalized as Dutch without renouncing their previous nationality. This led to a steady rise in the number of naturalizations that were received in two opposed ways: left-wing parties welcomed this as a sign of increased integration, while right-wing parties saw this as evidence that citizenship risked losing its meaning. "The idea had emerged that naturalization had become 'too easy', and that immigrants had been treated too liberally or had even been 'pampered', without having to face any obligations."[37] The latter view ultimately prevailed, and in 1997, the center-right government opted again for intolerance toward dual nationality and re-introduced the condition that foreigners renounce their previous nationality if they wished to become Dutch. The view that citizenship was a reward, which would be granted only after the successful completion of an integration path, gained terrain.

While the old view held that the state should be responsible for integration, and naturalization was a step to further it and should be encouraged, the new policies adopted a very different approach.[38] At the beginning of the 2000s, policymakers introduced the idea that immigrants are individually responsible for their integration. The state should only set the conditions that immigrants have to fulfill to be considered integrated. Only if successful do they gain admittance, secure a residence permit, and acquire citizenship. In line with this view, the then Minister of Alien Affairs and Integration in the Balkenende II government, Rita Verdonk, defined the acquisition of Dutch nationality as "the first prize."[39]

In those years, the ideal of a multicultural society, where people holding different nationalities, identities, and beliefs could be considered equally Dutch, was crumbling. Little by little, a more assimilationist view of society prevailed. We will see in detail in the next section how this new idea of society and belonging prompted legal reforms in the field of migration law, leading to the introduction of the notorious civic integration requirements.

[36] Groenendijk and Heijs (n 10) 159.

[37] Ricky Van Oers, Betty De Hart, and Kees Groenendijk, 'Report on The Netherlands' (Robert Schuman Centre for Advanced Studies 2013) RSCAS/EUDO-CIT-CR 2013/1 12.

[38] Ricky Van Oers, 'Justifying Citizenship Tests in the Netherlands and the UK' in Guild, Groenendijk, and Carrera (eds) (n 33) 123.

[39] Declaration made by the Former Minister of Alien Affairs and Integration Verdonk (VVD), reported Van Oers, De Hart, and Groenendijk, 'The Netherlands' (n 16) 403.

3. The legal mobilization's target: The New Integration Policy

We have seen in the previous section the downward trend of Dutch multiculturalism: after a peak in the 1980s, it reached a low point in the 2000s. In these years, integration policies gained momentum, and heated discussions on how integration should be handled were taking place both at the national and the European level. This political climate constitutes the backdrop to the restrictive law reforms on integration that I discuss in this section that were adopted with two main acts (the 2005 Act of Civic Integration from Abroad and the 2006 Civic Integration Act). Section 4 will focus on instruments offered by EU law to fight against such reforms: the Family Reunification Directive and its significance for the Dutch immigration and integration policies.

The Netherlands navigated through this difficult period of redefinition of what it meant to be Dutch with the Balkenende II governments, which ruled from 2003 to 2007 with the support of two right-wing parties: the CDA (Cristian Democrats) and the VVD (People's Party for Freedom and Democracy). This followed the short-lived Balkenende I government, stemming from the turbulent 2002 elections which saw the rise of Pim Fortuyn's party (despite Fortuyn's assassination) and then its swift decline due to a lack of leadership. To keep pace with the political preferences expressed by the Dutch electorate in 2002, during the 2003 electoral campaign, all political parties shifted right, promising a more restrictive model of integration.[40] This new integration model was embodied in the *inburgering* policy (literally from *burger*, citizen, the "becoming citizen" policy). The idea was that an immigrant has to *inburger*, by learning Dutch culture and society before having access to any right of residence or social support.[41]

Although all leaders during the electoral campaign had promised an *inburgering* policy, the Balkenende II government had the task of enacting it. The government started by reallocating the competencies for integration policies: before the election, the ministry in charge was that of social policies, while now these policies were moved under the competence of the newly established Alien Affairs and Integration ministry, led by Rita Verdonk (VVD). In the view of some commentators, this change already implied a transformation in how integration policies were conceived: from a social policy aimed at

[40] Bonjour and Vink noted how, toward the end of the century, there was "a significant shift in preferences of all political parties towards the restrictive end of the policy spectrum . . . particularly in the field of migration and integration policies." Saskia Bonjour and Maarten Peter Vink, 'When Europeanization Backfires: The Normalization of European Migration Politics' (2013) 48 Acta Politica 389, 402.

[41] Besselink (n 33) 243.

inclusion, they were now closely linked to immigration and border control.[42] Accordingly, the *inburgering* policy was enforced not through incentives but rather through a system of sanctions whereby people who failed the civic integration tests faced high fines and could lose their residence permits. The next subsections explain in more detail the two main acts that realized the *inburgering* policy.

3.1 The Act on Civic Integration from Abroad (*Wet Inburgering Buitenland*)

The flagship of the new Dutch integration policy is the 2005 Act of Civic Integration from Abroad (entered into force in March 2006). This was based on an unprecedented idea that in order to be admitted, aspiring immigrants need to demonstrate their commitment to integration by passing an exam before setting foot in the Netherlands. Not all migrants have to take the test but only those who fulfill two conditions: they come from a country where a visa requirement exists and they wish to live in the Netherlands for a long period.[43] Therefore, for instance, Japanese citizens would be exempted from taking the exam because they do not need a visa to enter the Netherlands, thanks to bilateral agreements; Indian seasonal workers would be equally exempted because their residence would be temporary.

The exam consists of a computer test divided into two parts: one assessing the person's knowledge of Dutch society, and the second concerning her/his skills in the Dutch language (level A1-minus, later raised to A1).[44] The cost of taking the exam was 350 euros plus the cost of the material to prepare for the test (initially 60 euros then increased to 110 euros) and the money for the journey to the closest Dutch embassy or consulate where the exam is held.[45] All these are considerable expenses, especially for people coming from countries subject to visa requirements, which are mainly in the so-called Global South.

The effect of *Wet Inburgering Buitenland* was rather abrupt. Immediately after its introduction, the number of applications for a residence visa in the

[42] ibid 246; Kees Groenendijk, 'Pre-Departure Integration Strategies in the European Union: Integration or Immigration Policy?' (2011) 13 European Journal of Migration and Law 1.

[43] Besselink (n 33) 246.

[44] Official information are reported on the page of the Immigration and Naturalization Service: <https://ind.nl/en/Pages/basic-civic-integration-examination-abroad.aspx> accessed 17 December 2024.

[45] These costs were later reduced thanks to the legal mobilization we analyze. See Regulation of the State Secretary for Security and Justice of 19 February 2016, number 736437, amending the Aliens Regulations 2000 (142nd amendment).

Netherlands drastically dropped from 29,000 applications in 2004 to 14,500 in 2006.[46] In the government's view, this was probably a positive result because when they saw that most of the people taking the exam had passed it, they decided to raise the pass/fail threshold. Moreover, the civic integration test from abroad was only the first step on the *inburgering* path of the migrants: after three years of residence in the Netherlands, they were expected to pass a second exam, as the next subsection will show. Although the Netherlands was the first country to require such a pre-entry test also for family members, it was promptly followed by other countries, such as Germany and France.[47]

3.2 The Civic Integration Act (*Wet Inburgering*)

While the Act of Integration from Abroad deals with people still to be admitted in the Netherlands, the Civic Integration Act was addressed to migrants already in the country. A first version of the Act was first introduced in 1998 but it consisted of enrolling immigrants into an integration program and in language and society courses with an optional test at the end, with no fines or sanctions in the case of failure. However, after the political turmoil of the new century, and the 2002 elections, the ruling political parties considered the law no longer fit for purpose. In line with the new *inburgering* policy, the main novelty contained in the 2006 amendment of the Civic Integration Act was the introduction of a compulsory civic integration test, the passing of which was conditional to obtaining social rights and a permanent residence permit.

By looking at who is subjected to the *inburgering* test, we can understand something about the rationale underpinning this policy. Initially, the proposal of Minister Rita Verdonk envisioned the test for all migrants applying for long-term residence as well as selected Dutch citizens. However bizarre it may sound to examine citizens' level of civic integration, the idea was clearly that some citizens were less Dutch than others. The government envisioned the test only for those Dutch citizens born outside of the "European part of the Netherlands," for example people who were naturalized, rather than Netherlands born, and citizens who were born in Dutch Caribbean territories.[48] The proposal was

[46] Besselink (n 33) 246.

[47] Germany and France provided for the test in 2007, the UK in 2010, and Austria in 2011. Yves Pascouau, 'Measures and Rules Developed in the EU Member States Regarding Integration of Third Country Nationals—Comparative Report' (European Policy Centre 2016) 37.

[48] Besselink (n 33) 248.

met with skepticism in Parliament, and the government eventually had to amend it.

The second version of the Act narrowed the group of citizens subjected to the test: only Dutch citizens who were naturalized before 1993 (ie before the integration test became a requirement for naturalization) and who either lived on social benefits, or acquired their citizenship through their children (this is a circumstance that applies in particular to Muslim women), or were employed in religious office (most probably the government was thinking of Imams) were subjected to the test.[49] This barely hidden targeting of Muslim Dutch was stopped by the Advisory Division of the *Raad Van State*, the Dutch Council of State, the last instance administrative court that can act as advisor to the government during lawmaking. Upon the government's request, the *Raad Van State* issued several opinions on the new proposed law, pointing out that imposing the test on certain categories of citizens was discriminatory and violated several international treaties.[50] The *Raad Van State*'s opinions compelled the government to definitively drop the idea of subjecting Dutch citizens to *inburgering*; eventually, the test applied only to non-citizens who asked for long-term residence in the Netherlands or who were employed in religious offices.

The Civic Integration Act entered into force in January 2007. Eventually, its final version provided that all TCN migrants, including those already in the country, who are older than sixteen and younger than sixty-five, have to pass a civic integration test after five years of residence (three and a half years if they had already passed the civic integration test from abroad). The test assesses migrants' civic knowledge and their language proficiency; the level of Dutch required (A2) is higher than that for the civic integration test from abroad, but the cost of the two tests was similar (270 euros).[51] Concerning knowledge about Dutch society, the test has been criticized for featuring questions such as "What do you do if you see two men kissing?" which seems to put Muslim applicants in a difficult position.[52] In instances where applicants do not take or do not pass the test, they face a series of sanctions that range from a fine by the

[49] ibid 250.

[50] Raad Van State, Advice of 29 June 2006, Kamerstukken II 2005/06, 30 308, no 4; Advice of 3 August 2006, Kamerstukken II 2005/06, 30 308, no 106; Advice of 2 November 2006 (no W03.06.0433/I). Van Oers (n 18) 55; Besselink (n 33) 248; Guus Extra and Massimiliano Spotti, 'Testing Regimes for Newcomers to the Netherlands' in Guus Extra, Massimiliano Spotti, and Piet Van Avermaet (eds), *Language Testing, Migration and Citizenship* (Continuum 2009).

[51] Besselink (n 33) 248.

[52] Brandon Hartley 'Taking the Integration Test: How Do You Deal with a Noisy Party next Door?' *Dutch News*, 22 January 2016, <https://www.dutchnews.nl/2016/01/integrating-in-the-netherlands-inburgering-test/> accessed 20 March 2025.

municipality (which could reach 1,000 euros for repeat applicants) to a cut to their social benefit or even the refusal of their long-term residence permit request.[53] The sanction depends on migrants' situation and on the municipality's evaluation of their chances of passing the test.

4. The Family Reunification Directive and its impact on the Netherlands

As the first part of this chapter shows, Dutch judges have submitted more preliminary references about the Family Reunification Directive than any other EU Member State's judiciary. This hints at the presence of legal mobilization or, at least, the special significance of the Directive in the Dutch context. To understand this, the next subsections explore the local meaning of the EU Family Reunification Directive, investigating what was the position and the role of the Dutch government during the negotiations for its adoption, how the Directive was transposed in the Netherlands, and finally, what its impact has been on the Dutch migration legal framework.

4.1 The negotiations

The Family Reunification Directive's purpose is "to determine the conditions for the exercise of the right to family reunification by third-country nationals residing lawfully in the territory of the Member States."[54] Its first proposal was presented by the EU Commission on December 1, 1999, and this was followed by three years of complex negotiations in the Council, rendered more difficult by the fact that at that time, unanimity voting was still required in EU migration lawmaking.[55] The Member States finally reached unanimous agreement within the Council in February 2003, and the Directive was adopted in September of that year.[56]

[53] See art 31 of the *Wet Inburgering* law, and art 21(1)k of the Vreemdelingenwet 2000 (Dutch Alien Law); also Besselink (n 33) 248; Labayle and Pascouau (n 7) 66. The Dutch law also allows the applicants to take a loan to pay for their civic integration courses and exams; however, if they fail, the government can ask them to repay the loan, which can amount to several thousand euros. See the recent Case C-158/23 *Keren* (2025) CJEU, ECLI:EU:C:2025:52, where the ECJ found several inconsistencies between this practice and EU law.

[54] Art 1 of the Family Reunification Directive.

[55] Georgia Papagianni, *Institutional and Policy Dynamics of EU Migration Law* (Martinus Nijhoff 2006) 159; Sergio Carrera, *In Search of the Perfect Citizen? The Intersection between Integration, Immigration, and Nationality in the EU* (Martinus Nijhoff 2009) 154.

[56] ibid 154.

The Netherlands was one of the most active governments during the negotiations as it wanted to make sure that the final text would "fit Dutch policies as closely as possible."[57] As explained in the previous section, important immigration reforms were underway in the Netherlands at that time. Three subsequent governments participated in the negotiations (Kok II, Balkenende I, and Balkenende II), and they shared a positive attitude toward the idea of harmonizing the area of family reunification, as long as this did not interfere with their policy agenda. A particularly decisive role was played by the Balkenende I government: even though this government remained in power only for a few months this coincided with the decisive phase of the negotiations, and its Interior Minister seized the opportunity to shaping the family reunification regime in a way to make it compatible with its planned *inburgering* tests. The Dutch government strategy consisted first of ensuring that the Directive set a standard of protection for TCN migrants' family rights that was not much higher compared to Dutch family reunification law. Second, the government promoted the idea of a pre-departure integration test among other Member States (the "Dutch model" of integration) and sponsored the introduction of specific integration clauses in the Directive, as we shall see.[58]

The compromise reached between the Commission and the Council resulted in a Directive characterized by the tension between two diverging objectives: granting migrants the right to family reunification and leaving Member States the possibility to set limits on the exercise of such a right. To protect family unity and help TCN migrants to integrate in the Member States,[59] the Directive provides that Member States shall admit family members of TCNs under certain circumstances.[60] This obligation on the Member States translates into an individual enforceable right of the migrant, as the ECJ had the opportunity to clarify in its first ruling on the Directive:

> Article 4(1) of the Directive imposes precise positive obligations, with corresponding clearly defined individual rights on the Member States since it

[57] Bonjour and Vink (n 40) 394–95.

[58] Kees Groenendijk and Tieneke Strik, 'Family Reunification in Germany, Netherlands and the EU since 2000: Reciprocal Influence and the Role of National and EU Actors' in Stephan Beichel-Benedetti and Costanze Janda (eds), *Hohenheim Horizons, Festschrift für Klaus Barwig* (Nomos 2018) 372; Bonjour and Vink (n 40) 396.

[59] The preamble of the Family Reunification Directive, at para 4, states: "Family reunification is a necessary way of making family life possible. It helps to create sociocultural stability facilitating the integration of third country nationals in the Member State, which also serves to promote economic and social cohesion, a fundamental Community objective stated in the Treaty."

[60] Art 1 of the Directive states: "The purpose of this Directive is to determine the conditions for the exercise of the right to family reunification by third country nationals residing lawfully in the territory of the Member States."

> requires them, in the cases determined by the Directive, to authorize family reunification of certain members of the sponsor's family, without being left a margin of appreciation.[61]

Interestingly, in this judgment, the ECJ has set a higher standard of protection for the right to family unity than the one granted under the European Convention on Human Rights (ECHR) framework. In fact, according to the European Court of Human Right's (ECtHR) case law, although family life is a fundamental right (Article 8 ECHR), "[w]here immigration is concerned, Article 8 cannot be considered to impose on a State a general obligation to respect the choice by married couples of the country of their matrimonial residence and to authorize family reunion in its territory."[62] Even if ECtHR case law offers protection against expulsion because it implies that states cannot divide families already united in their territory, the case law is of limited use when it comes to admissions: states are not obliged to admit non-citizen family members to reunite the family.[63] On the contrary, the ECJ stated that when the sponsor and the migrants meet the Directive's requirements, Member States have a positive obligation to admit family members, with no further discretion.[64]

That said, it is important to note that the EU Family Reunification Directive does not lean overly toward the side of the migrant either. The Directive leaves some discretion to Member States in the establishment of residence and income requirements that the sponsors and the applicants need to fulfill. For instance, Member States may require the applicant to show that the sponsor has stable and regular resources, a "normal" accommodation according to the

[61] Judgment of the Court, *Parliament v Council*, Case C-540/03, 27 June 2006, para 60. The ECJ's first judgment on the Directive was issued in the context of an annulment action brought by the European Parliament.

[62] *Sen v The Netherlands* (2001) European Court of Human Rights, App No 31465/96 36.

[63] We saw in Chapter 3, for instance, that in the Court's view family unity can be achieved also by moving the family in the partner's country of origin. See the case of *Abdulaziz, Cabales and Balkandali* (1985) ECtHR, App nos 9214/80, 9473/81, 9474/81.

[64] The ECJ itself notes that the EU standards are higher than the ECtHR's, see paras 59 and 60 of the judgment in *Parliament v Council* (n 61). Groenendijk explained the difference between the ECHR and the EU standards very clearly: "The ECtHR, in its case law on Article 8 ECHR, always starts from the principle of state sovereignty in immigration matters. Article 8 sets certain limits on the exercise of that sovereignty. Generally, however, the Court in Strasbourg allows the states a certain margin of appreciation. Under the Directive, the reasoning is exactly the reverse. The Directive grants a right to family reunification in a specific Member State. Member States may, under certain circumstances (e.g. the grounds mentioned in Article 16), restrict that fundamental right. Restrictions, however, have to be interpreted restrictively." Kees Groenendijk, 'Family Reunification as a Right under Community Law' (2006) 8 European Journal of Migration and Law 215, 219.

national or regional standards, and sickness insurance for the family (Article 7(1)).[65]

During the negotiations for the establishment of these requirements, the Netherlands played a decisive role. Two of these requirements have been introduced upon proposal by the Dutch government; one is the spouse's minimum age before reunion: while most of the Member States agreed that eighteen years was sufficient, the Netherlands obtained that Member States can push this minimum up to twenty-one years.[66] The second provision, as anticipated, regards integration: in the Dutch Parliament, the discussion on the introduction of the pre-entry integration test had already started[67] and in view of its adoption, the government supported the proposal of the Danish government by introducing in the Directive the possibility to ask family members to comply with "integration measures" (Article 7(2)).[68] Initially opposed by states like France and Belgium, these were discussed again in the Council meetings that followed and then were finally adopted in February 2003.[69]

Remarkably, the meaning of such "integration measures" was unclear. The Dutch government thought of them as one of the requirements for the applicant to be admitted, therefore they were seen as similar to the integration conditions under discussion at the national level. However, the preamble of the Directive—which reflects the Tampere milestones[70]—commits to a different model of integration, one that promotes family unity as a means to enhance integration and social cohesion:

> Family reunification is a necessary way of making family life possible. It helps to create sociocultural stability facilitating the integration of third country nationals in the Member State, which also serves to promote economic and social cohesion, a fundamental Community objective stated in the Treaty.[71]

[65] Art 7(1) of the Family Reunification Directive.

[66] Art 4 of the Directive.

[67] After the elections of 2002, the Balkenende I government proposed the *inburgering* reform of the integration field, and one of its proposals consisted in the introduction of the civic integration test from abroad (see Section 3.1). "In December 2002, a motion by a CDA MP in favour of a pre-admission integration test for family migrants was adopted in the Second Chamber of the Dutch Parliament with the support of all major political parties. The Dutch delegation used this motion as an argument in the negotiations in Brussels." In Groenendijk and Strik (n 58) 371.

[68] See Carrera, *In Search of the Perfect Citizen?* (n 55) 170.

[69] ibid 170–71.

[70] Tampere European Council, Presidency Conclusions, SN 200/99, 15–16 October 1999. See also Sergio Carrera, '"Integration" as a Process of Inclusion for Migrants? The Case of Long-Term Residents in the EU' (CEPS 2005) No 219/March 2005 <https://www.ceps.eu/ceps-publications/integration-process-inclusion-migrants-case-long-term-residents-eu/> accessed 20 March 2025.

[71] Family Reunification Directive, para 4 (n 2).

There is a conflict, then, between two models of integration. In the Dutch government's view, integration is a precondition that TCNs should fulfill to gain admittance. Instead, in the Tampere's conclusions and in the Commission's original legislative proposal, the integration of migrants is the goal, to be achieved by admitting their family members. These two conflicting views on integration were a source of disagreement among Member States during the negotiations, and even if the governments eventually agreed on what is today Article 7(2), these divergent views and legal uncertainty left room for the legal mobilization that we will analyze in the next sections.[72]

4.2 The transposition

The Dutch government transposed the directive without much trouble, thanks particularly to the negotiating work it had done before its adoption.[73] The civic integration test did not incur any obstacle, especially because Article 7(2) of the Directive allows Member States to introduce "integration measures" for family members (which the Dutch government conveniently translated as "integration condition").[74] Thus, the government could proceed with its integration reform and adopt, in 2005, the Act on Civic Integration from Abroad.[75] As explained, the condition of passing the civic integration test from abroad to be admitted as a family member in the Netherlands was considered by the government one of the "integration measures" that the Directive allows. The government claimed that the aim of the *inburgering* policy was precisely to increase the chances that migrants are successfully integrated into Dutch society by making sure that they studied the Dutch language and society before their arrival. However, it is of note that should the migrant not pass the test, family reunification is automatically denied.

This may give the impression that the Family Reunification Directive did not introduce clear standards for protecting migrant rights to family reunion, or, at least, that Member States could easily avoid their application. However, as we shall see, the Directive provides for limitations to States' discretion, and its first impact arrived five years after its adoption, thanks to the EU Commission. In its 2008 report on the implementation of the Directive, the Commission

[72] Groenendijk (n 64) 224.
[73] Groenendijk and Strik (n 58) 357.
[74] More on this in Section 7.
[75] Art 7(2): Member States may require third country nationals to comply with integration measures, in accordance with national law.

pointed out the discrepancies between the Dutch integration requirements and the Directive's integration measures:

> The objective of such measures is to facilitate the integration of family members. Their admissibility under the Directive depends on whether they serve this purpose and whether they respect the principle of proportionality. Their admissibility can be questioned on the basis of the accessibility of such courses or tests, how they are designed and/or organized (test materials, fees, venue, etc.), whether such measures or their impact serve purposes other than integration (e.g. high fees excluding low-income families).[76]

Reading between the lines, the Commission's evaluation echoed some of the same concerns expressed by migrant supporters, who also questioned the Dutch test's legitimacy. In their view, because of its high fees and high pass/fail threshold, the Dutch pre-entry test serves to discriminate against and exclude migrants coming from low-income countries, rather than to integrate them.[77] Because of their scarce material resources and limited educational skills, migrants from poor countries are more likely to fail the test.

The Commission report eventually did not convince the Dutch government to amend its policy. However, by presenting doubts about its compatibility with EU law standards, the Commission attracted attention to the possibility that Dutch law could be challenged through EU law remedies. In effect, a few months later, the first preliminary reference request on the Family Reunification Directive was submitted by the *Raad Van State*, in the case of *Chakroun*.[78] Mrs Chakroun's application for family reunification was refused because her husband, the sponsor, had a lower income than that required by Dutch law in cases where couples formed after the sponsor arrived in the Netherlands. The referring Court questioned this income requirement's legitimacy: the Directive provides only that the sponsor should have a stable and regular income, sufficient to maintain the family without social assistance.[79]

[76] Report from the Commission to the European Parliament and the Council on the Application of Directive 2003/86/EC on the Right to Family Reunification, COM(2008) 610 final, Brussels, 8.10.2008.

[77] Human Rights Watch, 'The Netherlands: Discrimination in the Name of Integration. Migrants' Rights under the Integration Abroad Act' (*Human Rights Watch*, 13 May 2008) <https://www.hrw.org/report/2008/05/13/netherlands-discrimination-name-integration/migrants-rights-under-integration> accessed 20 March 2025.

[78] Case C-578/08 *Chakroun* (2010) CJEU, ECLI:EU:C:2010:117.

[79] Art 7(1)(c) of the Family Reunification Directive only requires that the sponsor has "stable and regular resources which are sufficient to maintain himself/herself and the members of his/her family, without recourse to the social assistance system of the Member State concerned."

The ECJ found Dutch law in conflict with the Directive because it draws a distinction based on when the family is formed that does not exist in the Directive, and it asks for an income higher than what is considered sufficient. Since the Directive "imposes precise positive obligations, with corresponding clearly defined individual rights, on the Member States," their eventual margin of appreciation "must not be used by them in a manner which would undermine the objective of the Directive, which is to promote family reunification."[80] By setting an income level higher than that prescribed by the Directive for couples who formed after the sponsor's migration, Dutch law hampers the Directive's objective and is illegitimate.

The *Chakroun* case was important because it contributed to revealing the potential of the Family Reunification Directive for defending migrants' rights. We will see in the second part of this chapter how the Directive was then used as an instrument to challenge the *inburgering* policy. The next section focuses on the actors who understood the Directive's potential and who decided to mobilize it against the integration conditions. It is argued that the constraining effect that the Directive came to have in the Dutch context, rather than being a result of the ECJ's autonomous role was the result of a legal mobilization effort undertaken by a group of civil society actors that supports migrants' rights in the Netherlands.

4.3 A directive that backfires

The impact of the Family Reunification Directive on the Netherlands' migration policy has been studied by political and legal scholars. According to Groenendijk, "all those involved in the negotiations on the new Directive underestimated the far-reaching effects the Directive will have on the national immigration law and practices of the Member States."[81] Kees Groenendik is today Emeritus Professor of Sociology of Law at the University of Nijmegen and he is one of the leading experts of EU migration law and policy. He was personally involved in the Directive's negotiations and foresaw the obstacles that the Directive would have represented for the restrictive Dutch migration policy.[82]

[80] *Chakroun* (n 78) para 43.
[81] Groenendijk (n 64) 220.
[82] During the negotiations, he represented five Dutch NGOs in the Standing Committee of Experts on international immigration, refugee, and criminal law, Groenendijk (n 64) 221.

Similarly, Bonjour and Vink emphasized the constraining effect of the Directive in the Dutch context. They claimed that although the Dutch government initially supported the adoption of the Directive, "Europeanization backfired": "The Directive came to have an unexpected constraining effect, first as a result of the Court's jurisprudence, and second because the preferences of Dutch politicians have shifted ever further beyond what the Directive will allow."[83] The authors explain how after 2002, Dutch politicians' policy preferences shifted toward the right because national elections marked a surge of support for far-right and xenophobic parties.[84] However, they did not explore further the reason behind the ECJ's generous reading of the Directive; in their view, the Court upheld a right-based interpretation of the Directive and departed from Member States' preferences simply because it is an autonomous actor that "acts in a way that may not reflect the wishes of (all) member states."[85] While the important role of the ECJ case law is acknowledged, we still know little about the processes that led to the Directive having a different effect within Dutch law than initially expected. What some scholars have called the Directive's "backfiring" is the result of the migrant supporters' efforts to mobilize the Family Reunification Directive before the ECJ to challenge the legitimacy of the *inburgering* policy.

Legal mobilization scholars are traditionally skeptical about the idea that courts are fully autonomous actors. As Epp noted: "Even liberal judges armed with control of their dockets and an entrenched bill of rights, however, cannot make rights-supportive law unless they have rights cases to decide, and the process of mobilizing cases rests on far more than judicial fiat."[86] In other words, no court can issue high-impact judgments unless it has the right cases before it; even if the ECJ was fully autonomous, it could not develop its case law without the preliminary reference requests that it received on the Family Reunification Directive. Only by investigating who has mobilized this Directive before national courts, how, and why, can we fully understand why it came to play such a constraining role in the Dutch context.

[83] Bonjour and Vink (n 40) 404.

[84] Section 3 of this chapter.

[85] The two authors mention Marks' theory of multilevel government, which sees the ECJ as an autonomous supranational actor of European integration, Bonjour and Vink (n 40) 401.

[86] Charles Epp, *The Rights Revolution: Lawyers, Activists, and Supreme Courts in Comparative Perspective* (University of Chicago Press 1998) 15.

5. Who mobilizes EU migration law in the Netherlands? Actors, organizations, and platforms

This section provides an overview of the main actors that use and mobilize EU migration law. As in the UK, in the Netherlands it seems that there are two opposing factions: on the one hand, there is the government, with its Ministry of Justice and Security and its Immigration and Naturalization Service (*Immigratie-en Naturalisatiedienst* (*IND*)); on the other hand, there are individuals, organizations, and private practitioners who defend the rights and the interests of the migrants. Below is a schematic overview of the actors and organizations that we will see in action in Section 7.

5.1 On the government's side

Immigratie-en Naturalisatiedienst (*IND*). When it comes to immigration, the most important public authority in the Netherlands is the *IND*, the Immigration and Naturalization Service. Under the Ministry of Justice and Security, it is in charge of assessing all individual applications for admission, residence, and naturalization based on Dutch law. Its decisions can be challenged by the applicants first, via an administrative procedure, and then judicially. In court, the *IND* relies either on private lawyers, based in The Hague (*landsadvocaten*), or on their legal staff.

Journaal Vreeemdelingenrecht: This is the second most important Dutch migration law journal. It was founded to keep *IND* staff informed of recent changes in immigration law; therefore it has mainly represented the view of the government and the *IND* (while the *Asiel & Migrantenrecht* tends to represent the point of view of migrants and private practitioners, as we shall see below). However, it seems that recently the *Journaal Vreeemdelingenrecht* became more independent, thanks to a change in its board.[87]

5.2 Pro-immigrant Organizations

Inspraak Orgaan Turken (*IOT*).[88] This is the main organization representing the interests of the Turkish minority in the Netherlands. Despite being a small

[87] Interview with Groenendijk, 20 February 2018, Nijmegen.
[88] Official website: <https://www.iot.nl/> accessed 17 December 2024.

organization, it counts on the support of a large and active community.[89] The *IOT* was created in the 1980s, during the multicultural years, prompted by a Dutch minority policy that provided incentives for migrants' participation in society. As one of the eight ethnic groups taking part in the "National Minorities Consultation," it was involved in regular talks with the government (at least three times a year) and was publicly funded.[90] Since its creation, the *IOT* has been very active in defending the interests of Turkish immigrants in the Netherlands by using a range of techniques like campaigns, lobbying, and litigation strategies.[91] Since it primarily defends the rights of the Turkish minority, it has made large use of the EU–Turkey Association Agreements and its so-called standstill clause, a rule of non-regression that proved crucial to preserve the Turks' rights from the passing of gradually more restrictive migration and integration policies.[92] However, the *IOT* was also ready to rely on the Family Reunification and the Long-Term Residence Directives in cases where their mobilization was useful for defending Turkish migrants' rights, as we shall see. Among the most important mobilizations in which the *IOT* took part are that against the loss of social security benefits in case migrants return to Turkey (2000–14), the campaign against the increase in residence permit fees (2002–14), and the mobilization against the civic integration tests (2006–11) that will be addressed in this chapter.[93] In 2013, the government decided to amend its consultation policy with minorities and withdrew its financial support to ethnic minority groups, *IOT* included. Therefore, since 2014, the *IOT* has become a membership-based association, funded by its members and conducting smaller-scale activities.

[89] The organization has a "klein bureau en grote achterban" (small desk and a large support). See CA Groenendijk, M Rondhuis, and MHA Strik, 'Klagen Bij de Europese Commissie. Effecten van Tien Jaar Juridische Belangenbehartiging Door Het Inspraakorgaan Turken in Nederland' (2015) 6 Asiel & Migrantenrecht 22, 27.

[90] Vink (n 15) 341–42. This policy was introduced in 1997 with the 1997 Law on the Consultation of Minority Policy (Wet Overleg Minderhedenbeleid).

[91] Groenendijk and Heijs (n 10) 159.

[92] Agreement Establishing an Association between the European Economic Community and Turkey, signed in Ankara, 12 September 1963, OJ L 361/29, 13 December 1977. For the legal status of Turkish nationals, the Additional Protocol to the Agreement, signed on 23 November 1970, is especially important, OJ L 293, 29 December 1972, pp 3–56.

[93] A description of the IOT's complaints before the EU Commission is provided by Groenendijk, Rondhuis, and Strik (n 89). Other accounts of IOT legal mobilization can be found in Alexander Hoogenboom, 'Moving Forward by Standing Still? First Admission of Turkish Workers: Comment on Commission v Netherlands (Administrative Fees)' (2014) 35 European Law Review 707; Narin Tezcan-Idriz, 'Dutch Courts Safeguarding Rights under the EEC-Turkey Association Law. Case Note on District Court Rotterdam Judgments of 12 August 2010, and District Court Roermond Judgment of 15 October 2010' (2011) 13 European Journal of Migration and Law 219; Jos Hoevenaars, 'A People's Court? A Bottom-Up Approach to Litigation Before the European Court of Justice' (Radboud University 2018) 178.

Vluchtelingen Werk Nederland (Dutch Refugees Council). This is an organization founded more than thirty years ago in support of refugees and asylum seekers.[94] The organization is independent of the government, even if it is publicly subsidized, and it counts on the work of some professionals and a large number of volunteers. They have local offices spread across the whole Dutch territory, whereby they provide legal and social support to refugees and asylum seekers. The Dutch Refugee Council is also interested and involved in strategic litigation. In 2012, a member of the Council staff, Sadhia Rafi, created the *Commissie Strategisch Procederen* (Strategic Litigation Committee), where she was joined by four academics and four lawyers.[95] The Committee has a specific aim, that of supporting preliminary references to the ECJ; it also gives free legal advice to lawyers whose cases found a way to Luxembourg.

5.3 Migration academics

In the Netherlands, academia is traditionally very engaged in political debates, campaigns, and litigation, especially in the migration field. A leading example is Kees Groenendijk who is one of the leading experts on EU migration and asylum law and has been involved in dozens of strategic litigation cases by advising either the immigration lawyers or the organizations supporting migrants, like the *IOT*.[96] Groenendijk is only one of the Dutch academics involved in strategic litigation; there are also the migration lawyers from Vrije Universiteit Amsterdam, including Thomas Spijkerboer who was involved in litigation for gay rights before the ECJ, and Marcelle Reneman who is in charge of the Migration Legal Clinic (more on this below). Academics contribute to legal mobilization also by providing and spreading knowledge on EU law. For instance, after the adoption of the Family Reunification and the Long-Term Resident Directives, Gronenedijk and his colleague Elspeth Guild set up courses and seminars on the new EU laws for the Dutch Judges' Academy, because "if they don't know the directive, they're not going to take it seriously."[97]

[94] Official website: <https://www.vluchtelingenwerk.nl/nl/over-ons> accessed 17 December 2024.

[95] Interview with Sadhia Rafi, 14 December 2017, Amsterdam. Also here: "Strategisch procederen," 27 February 2014, <https://www.advocatenblad.nl/2014/02/27/strategisch-procederen/> accessed 17 December 2024.

[96] As attested in his article on strategic litigation for Turkish citizens' rights. Groenendijk, Rondhuis, and Strik (n 89).

[97] Interview with Professor Kees Groenendjik, 20 February 2018, Nijmegen.

VU Migration Law Clinic. This is a law clinic based at the Vrij University (Amsterdam) where students under the supervision of migration law professors work together on cases pending before the ECJ. The clinic has a law blog where they publish their legal analyses online so that they can be read by lawyers, academics, and, hopefully, judges.[98] Sometimes the students work directly with the lawyers of the cases, conducting legal research for the litigation before the ECJ. The clinic had the first proof of its impact during the hearing in the case of *A&S*:[99] for the first time, during the oral hearings, the ECJ asked the lawyer some questions on the VU Migration Law Clinic's opinion that was attached to the lawyer's submission. This shows not only that the ECJ judges read the submission but also that they found the document relevant to the case. Given the inadmissibility of *amicus curiae* briefs before the ECJ in the context of preliminary reference proceedings, this is a relevant step further for public interest groups' access to the ECJ.

5.4 Migration lawyers

The Netherlands, like the UK and Italy, has a very committed migration bar that sides with migrants and is willing to challenge the government. One of the most important organizations of migration lawyers is the *Werkgroep Rechtsbijstand in Vreemdelingenzaken* (Legal Aid Working Group on Immigration (*WRV*)). The group was founded in the 1970s by "young and left-wing lawyers" who became interested in the issue of refugees when the first asylum seekers arrived in the Netherlands.[100] At that time, the *WRV* was composed of around twenty committed members who successfully engaged in political lobbying of Parliament to improve the situation of migrants and asylum seekers. Today, the *WRV* is part of a bigger membership association of migration lawyers (*Stichting Migratierecht*), with 500 members, among them practitioners, legal advisers, researchers, and other experts.[101] Its main mission is to make migration law and decisions available to legal practitioners, to train them, and to provide legal assistance. It publishes one of the two Dutch migration legal journals, *Asiel & Migrantenrecht*.

[98] The official Migration Law Clinic website: <https://migrationlawclinic.org/> accessed 17 December 2024.

[99] Case C-550/16 *A and S* (2018) CJEU, ECLI:EU:C:2018:248.

[100] Quirijn Visscher, 'De Politieke Wortels van de WRV' (2009) 9/10 Migrantenrecht 459, 260.

[101] Official website: <https://www.stichtingmigratierecht.nl/over-ons> accessed 17 December 2024.

6. Structural factors: Access to judicial review and judicial receptivity in the Netherlands

Because the preliminary reference procedure starts in the context of national proceedings, it is important to understand whether the Netherlands offers opportunities for legal mobilization, in other words, what are the structural factors at the national level that enable or constrain legal mobilization (Chapter 1). First, such structural factors consist in the rules that regulate access to courts and litigants' possibility to challenge the legitimacy of national laws in court; they also include Dutch judges'receptiveness to civil society's claims and if they are willing and able to make reference to the ECJ. The following subsection will thus explore access to judicial review in the Netherlands while the second subsection analyzes Dutch judges' propensity to submit a reference to the ECJ.

6.1 Migrants' access to judicial review in the Netherlands

Most migration cases consist in a challenge to the validity of an administrative decision issued by a public authority. The cases analyzed in this chapter are no exception since they involve the appeal against decisions by the *IND* denying family reunification. In the Netherlands, regardless of the content of the administrative act in question, a person should first file an administrative appeal against the decision and only subsequently ask for judicial review on the ground that the act is contrary to national, EU, or international norms. Although the Dutch constitution prohibits judicial review of legislation,[102] a litigant might still challenge the legitimacy of Dutch law vis-à-vis EU or international standards; in fact, if these norms are directly applicable (ie they are self-executing international norms or EU norms having direct effect), they enjoy primacy over national laws, and Dutch judges must enforce them.[103]

This makes the Netherlands an interesting case for legal mobilization via preliminary reference. Historically the Netherlands was a country with weak judicial review and thus we would expect a low level of EU litigation, in line with Wind's theory positing that countries with weak judicial review culture generate less preliminary references.[104] Instead, EU and international norms

[102] Art 120 of the Dutch Constitution explicitly forbids judges from reviewing the legitimacy of laws.
[103] Barbara Oomen, *Rights for Others: The Slow Home-Coming of Human Rights in the Netherlands* (CUP 2013) ch 2.
[104] Marlene Wind, 'The Nordics, the EU and the Reluctance towards Supranational Judicial Review' (2010) 48 Journal of Common Market Studies 1039.

are often invoked to review the legitimacy of Dutch laws, primarily because they are the only valid legal basis for judicial review of national legislation.[105] As De Witte and Claes noted, they are "more effectively enforceable than the constitution."[106]

The judicial review proceedings consist of a first stage before District courts (first-instance court), having immigration-specialized chambers that are composed of one or three judges. If the District court's decision is appealed, this leads to a second stage before the *Raad Van State* (Council of State), the highest administrative court (see Figure 4.3).[107]

Although migrants have the right to ask for judicial review, the lack of means might dissuade them from starting a case, given the high court fees and the cost of legal representation. To counteract this, the Dutch constitution establishes a system of legal aid that covers the cost of legal representation, which is required in the judicial stage of the review.[108] Instead, during the administrative phase of the proceedings, migrants are often assisted by the Dutch Refugee Council, thanks to the volunteers and paralegal staff present in their local offices. As for the court fee, people with an income below a certain level can ask for a fee reduction. In sum, migrants' access to judicial review in the Netherlands is fairly well supported.

6.2 Dutch judges and the preliminary reference mechanism: Is the "gentlemen's agreement" myth or reality?

As mentioned earlier, the Netherlands is one of the EU Member States that refers more cases to the ECJ than other States. Most of its preliminary references come from last-instance courts: the Dutch Supreme Courts (*Hoge Raad*) and the Dutch Council of State (*Raad van State*).[109] In the migration field, the

[105] Monica Claes and Bruno De Witte, 'Report on the Netherlands' in Anne-Marie Slaughter, Alec Stone Sweet, and JHH Weiler (eds), *The European Court and National Courts—Doctrine and Jurisprudence: Legal Change in its Social Context* (Hart 1997) 173.

[106] ibid 174.

[107] This is the case especially for judicial review proceedings against an IND's decision, but not all the appeals filed by migrants are dealt by the immigration and asylum chambers and by the Raad Van State. Depending on the issue raised by the immigrants, if it relates to other fields like labor law, social security, or fundamental rights, the cases can fall under the competence of the Centrale Raad van Beroep (Central Appeals Tribunal) and the Hoge Raad (Supreme Court).

[108] Arts 17 and 18 of the Dutch Constitution.

[109] According to Krommerdijk, about a third of Dutch referrals come from lower courts. Jasper Krommendijk, 'De Lagere Rechter Aan Banden. Is Er Nog Ruimte Voor de Lagere Rechter Om Te Verwijzen Naar Het HvJ?' [2018] Sociaal-Economische Wetgeving 183; Jasper Krommendijk, *National Courts and Preliminary References to the Court of Justice* (Edward Elgar Publishing 2021) 27.

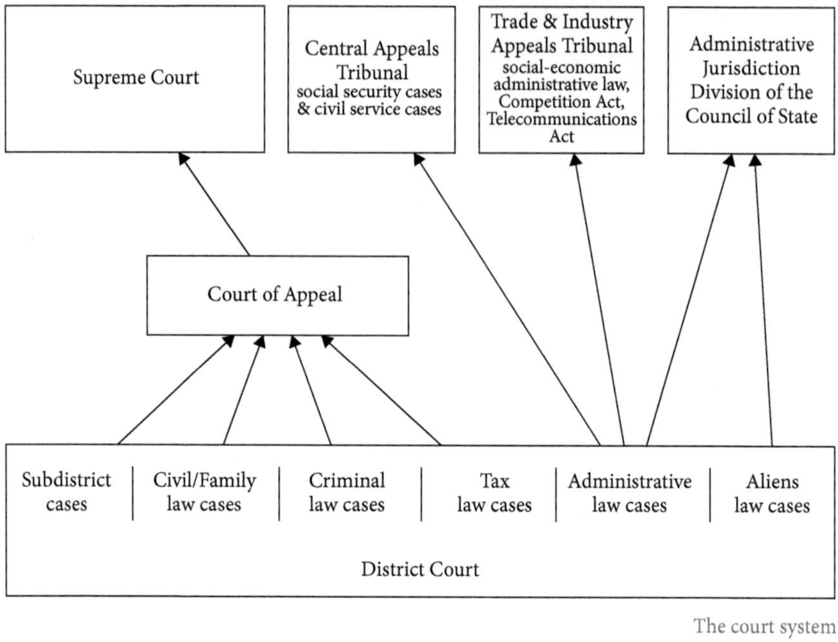

Figure 4.3 The Judiciary System in the Netherlands.
Source: The official website of the Netherlands judiciary system (<http://www.rechtspraak.nl>accessed 23 March 2025).

positive attitude of the *Raad Van State* toward EU law and preliminary references is relatively new. Indeed, an important event for the Dutch judicial system was the so-called European turn of the *Raad Van State*. Apparently, until 2008, experts and lower courts were generally unsatisfied toward the *Raad Van State*'s way of interpreting EU migration law.[110] Similar concerns were also raised internally by the *Raad Van State*'s advisory division,[111] which warned judicial colleagues of the possibility of losing jurisdiction on immigration law.[112] In response to these criticisms, the *Raad Van State* took a "European turn". Acknowledging the growing importance of EU law, they decided to strengthen

[110] Groenendijk, during his farewell lecture held in April 2008, showed some interviews he conducted with Dutch immigration judges who complained about the fact that the Raad Van State was interpreting EU law as it was Dutch law, without giving it an independent meaning.

[111] Raad Van State has two divisions having two different roles: one is the advisor of the Government on legislation, and the second is the judicial division, ie the last-instance administrative court. Since it works very close to the government, the Raad Van State has been accused in the past of not being completely independent from the government; however, the two careers for the judicial staff and for the advisors to the government are kept separate.

[112] Interview with Kees Groenendijk, 20 February 2018, Nijmegen.

the *Raad Van State*'s expertise in the field by selecting judges with a background in EU law (eg Kamiel Mortelmans, former EU law professor at Utrecht University; other judges are former Dutch agents before the Court of Justice of the EU).[113] As part of this new trend, the *Raad Van State* started referring more cases to the ECJ and initiated new internal practices aimed at improving the quality of Dutch referrals to the Court. For instance, an internal committee was established in the *Raad Van State*, where the state counsellors who are experts in EU law sit; when other counsellors want to submit a reference, they should first consult with this committee.[114] This renewed attention to EU law and to the preliminary mechanism created a fertile terrain for preliminary references and legal mobilization before the ECJ.

The different attitude of Dutch higher and lower courts toward preliminary references has attracted scholarly attention, and Dutch academics advanced different hypotheses about why this is the case, looking critically at this practice.[115] Groenendijk wrote an influential article on this issue, stating that there was talk about the existance of a "gentlemen's agreement" between the migration chambers of the District courts and the *Raad Van State*: lower courts would abstain from referring, leaving to the highest court the choice on whether to refer or not. Despite the lack of official documents proving the existence of such an agreement, other authors began referring to it and questioned its legitimacy.[116] Indeed, the issue is important: if such an agreement existed, it would make it more difficult for individual litigants to reach the ECJ since they would have to wait until proceedings reaches the last stage; moreover, Article 267 TFEU establishes that any court or tribunal may ask for a preliminary ruling from the ECJ, and the Dutch practice can entail a violation of this provision.

A judge from the *Raad Van State* told me that the "gentlemen's agreement" is more a myth than reality.[117] In this judge's opinion, District courts "have lots of cases, they have a tough job, very often they are sitting alone", therefore they simply have less incentive and resources to make a preliminary reference.

[113] Jasper Krommendijk, 'The Preliminary Reference Dance between the CJEU and Dutch Courts in the Field of Migration' (2018) 10 European Journal of Legal Studies 101, 138.

[114] Interview with Raad Van State Judge, 22 February 2018, The Hague.

[115] Krommendijk, 'The Preliminary Reference Dance between the CJEU and Dutch Courts in the Field of Migration' (n 113).

[116] Kees Groenendijk 'Waarom rechters niet naar Luxemburg gaan: politieke structuur of rechtscultuur?' in R Baas and others (eds) *Rechtspleging en rechtsbescherming. Liber amicorum voor prof. dr. Leny E. de Groot-van Leeuwen* (Kluwer 2015) 187. Krommendijk, 'De Lagere Rechter Aan Banden' (n 109); Jasper Krommendijk, 'The Highest Dutch Courts and the Preliminary Ruling Procedure: Critically Obedient Interlocutors of the Court of Justice' (2019) 0 European Law Journal.

[117] Interview with Raad Van State Judge, 22 February 2018, The Hague.

Another practical barrier to lower judges' references is the fact that before the entry into force of the Lisbon Treaty, they did not have the power to submit references on matters related to the Area of Freedom, Security and Justice (AFSJ), and therefore not on migration. Data confirm that this was an important barrier. After the Lisbon Treaty entered into force in 2009, there was a rise in the number of requests for preliminary rulings by lower courts, and this is still a current trend.

Through my interviews I discovered the existence of a new practice among Dutch judges.[118] Before submitting a preliminary reference, District court judges circulate the text of the questions they want to ask to their colleagues of other District courts and of the *Raad Van State*, asking for comments and feedback. This was originally an informal practice, done via email, but then the Utrecht District Court issued an official order asking for advice from its colleagues before making the reference.[119] Even if this practice could eventually increase the quality of preliminary reference requests, it can also expose judges to criticisms and pressure by other colleagues and especially by the higher court. For instance, according to Alter's theory of competition between courts,[120] this practice may represent a problem for lower judges who want to bypass the *Raad Van State*'s judicial interpretation.

We can conclude that despite its limitations, the Dutch judicial system offers fertile ground for legal mobilization through EU law. Its judges are open to refer and are also making significant efforts to increase the quality of Dutch preliminary references. Lower courts have historically been less prone to refer, but as we shall see in the next section, civil society actors managed to overcome their reluctance.

7. The legal mobilization before the ECJ on the civic integration test

The previous sections have outlined the legal and political background of the preliminary references on the civic integration test. This section will describe the background of two legal mobilization cases (*Imran* and *K and A*), showing that academics, pro-migrants organizations, and lawyers played an important

[118] Interview with Raad Van State Judge, 22 February 2018, The Hague. Interview with Groenendijk, 20 February 2018, Nijmegen.

[119] This was in the national proceedings that gave rise to the preliminary ruling in Case C-680/17 *Vethanayagam and Others* (2019) CJEU, ECLI:EU:C:2019:627.

[120] Karen Alter, 'The European Court's Political Power' (1996) 19 West European Politics 458, 467.

role in the litigation. I have decided to focus on these two cases because they pioneered a new way to challenge the *inburgering* policy, and their example was later followed by other preliminary references (discussed in the next section). Importantly, the legal mobilization was not limited to the ECJ: other cases against the two *inburgering* laws were brought (and ended) before national courts,[121] and the Dutch Refugee Council and the *IOT* filed complaints to the Commission to prompt an infringement procedure.[122] These examples of legal mobilizations go beyond the scope of this book but are intertwined with the preliminary references analyzed, and I will discuss them in the conclusion of this chapter.

7.1 *Imran*

The *Imran* case shows how sometimes you can make an impact just by asking for a preliminary reference, without even getting to the ruling. The case was dropped before the ECJ could issue its judgment but nevertheless, it had relevant impact on the integration policy and the legal mobilization strategies of two Member States, the Netherlands and Germany.[123]

The idea of this preliminary reference emerged during a lecture on family reunification that Professor Groenendijk gave to the Dutch Refugee Council's (hereinafter, DRC) staff. Somebody raised the fact that refugees and migrants in the Netherlands do not enjoy a right to family reunification in practice because of the Act on Civic Integration from Abroad. The norm introduced a civic integration test that was too expensive, both in terms of registration fee and preparation material. Moreover, the preparation material was not available in all languages and therefore many applicants were not able to read it. In particular, migrants from the poorest countries were placed in a very difficult situation. They often have to undertake very long journeys (even to other countries) to reach the closest Dutch consulate or embassy where they can take the test, and they have few material and educational resources, which makes their chances of passing the test very low. Having listened to these complaints, Groenendijk told the DRC staff that they could use EU law more proactively and that they should try to challenge the Act before the ECJ: if they found a good case, he could help them in bringing the litigation

[121] This is the case of litigation by Turkish migrants against the policy, Tezcan-Idriz (n 93).
[122] Groenendijk and Strik (n 58) 377.
[123] *Imran* (n 5).

to Luxembourg.[124] The DRC took this suggestion seriously, and a few months later, they got back to Professor Groenendijk with a potentially very strong test case: *Imran*.

The *Imran* case started in spring 2009, when the DRC's local office in Vianen (a small city close to Utrecht) decided to assist Mr Safi in filing his family reunification request. Mr Safi is an Afghan citizen who had been residing in the Netherlands since 2000. After a long time apart from her he wanted to reunite with his wife, Mrs Bibi Mohammad Imran, and their eight children, who in the meantime were living in Pakistan. It took several years to Mr Safi to meet all the conditions required by EU and Dutch law for filing a family reunification request. He first had to obtain a residence permit,[125] then a sufficient income (he was working at three jobs simultaneously) and an appropriate house to accommodate his big family. However, the Act of Civic Integration from Abroad imposed a further condition: the family members should pass the civic integration test. Unfortunately for the Safi family, Mrs Imran, who travelled all the way to Delhi with their eight children to take the test, did not pass it and her visa application was rejected. Ironically, the children obtained the visa instead and joined their father on August 5, 2009.

Three features make the *Imran* case a compelling example of how the civic integration test was an obstacle to the right to family reunification: (i) The failure to pass the civic integration test was the only reason why Mrs Imran could not reunite with her husband; (ii) Dutch authorities applied the civic integration requirement in a very restrictive manner: they did not grant Mrs Imran the medical exemption she asked for, and they did not take into account the fact that she could not access the material to prepare for the test (as it was not available in her language); (iii) Mrs Imran's visa rejection had a terrible impact on the well-being of the whole family, including her children. In fact, the eight siblings had been catapulted into a new foreign state, far away from their mother, having to live with a father that they barely knew (they had lived apart for the last nine years) and who was extremely busy with his three jobs, all of which he needed to maintain in order to have sufficient income necessary to complete his wife's reunification process.[126] In sum, the Imran family was in a difficult and absurd situation that was completely ignored by Dutch authorities, which based their decision solely on Mrs Imran's failure to pass the test.

[124] Interviews with Kees Groenendijk, on 8 August 2016 and 20 February 2018, both in Nijmegen.

[125] Mr Safi entered the Netherlands as an asylum seeker. Despite his asylum application being rejected, he obtained another residence permit thanks to a regularization policy.

[126] These circumstances are in part described in the facts of the case, in part they were told to me by the lawyer: Interview with Gerben Dijkman, 13 December 2017, Utrecht.

With the help of the DRC, Mrs Imran filed an administrative complaint against the visa rejection from Afghanistan, and when this was also refused, the DRC decided to appeal in court. To represent Mrs Imran in the proceedings, the DRC contacted Gerben Dijkman, an immigration lawyer based in Utrecht with whom they often collaborate. The DRC put Dijkman and Groenendijk in contact; Groenendijk offered his assistance with the case and the lawyer enthusiastically accepted. Interestingly, when I asked Dijkman whether *Imran* was a test case, he answered that officially it was not but that Groenendijk was probably waiting for a "good case to test his arguments," and that *Imran* fit this bill but was "too good, in the end."[127]

Since the very start, the goal was to bring the *Imran* case before the ECJ. During the proceedings before the Zwolle-Lelystad District Court, the first-instance court, Groenendijk drafted an advisory opinion for the lawyer, where among other things he argued that Article 7(2) of the Family Reunification Directive has been incorrectly transposed into Dutch legislation:

> The provision only permits the person concerned to participate in integration measures. The word "integration conditions" in that provision is a manifest translation error. The other language versions refer to "integration measures" (integration measures, mésures d'integration, Integrationsmassnahmen).[128]

Moreover, the Dutch lawmaker did not transpose Article 5 of the Directive, stating that Member States must duly take into account the best interest of the child when examining applications for family reunification. Finally, Groenendijk argued that the requirement to pass the civic integration test from abroad is contrary to the principle of proportionality: the test imposes high costs and sacrifices on the applicants, but there is no evidence that, once the test is passed, the chances of integration have increased.[129] In sum, the Dutch integration policy hinders the *effet utile* of the Directive, that is to promote family reunification and not to make it more difficult.

Dijkman, for his part, had to convince the Zwolle District Court to make a reference. This was not an easy task because, as explained in the previous

[127] Interview with Gerben Dijkman, 13 December 2017, Utrecht.

[128] CA Notitie, Groenendijk in beroepsprocedure AWB 10/9716, (tussen) uitspraak VK Zwolle (ruk) 28 juli 2010, vel 1000798 (Note by Prof CA Groenendijk, 28 July 2010). The letter was subsequently published on MigratieWeb. Here is the original text in Dutch: "Art. 7(2) van richtlijn 2003/86 is onjuist omgezet in de Nederlandse wetgeving. De bepaling laat alleen toe te eisen dat de betrokkene deelneemt aan inburgeringsmaatregelen. Het word 'inburgeringsvoorwaarden' in die bepaling is een kennelijke vertaalfout. In de andere taalversies is sprake van 'inburgeringsmaatregelen' (integration measures, mésures d'integration, Integrationsmassnahmen)."

[129] ibid.

section, at that time, only the last-instance courts were submitting preliminary references.[130] Therefore, he elaborated an original strategy:

> I thought, I can do two things: I can copy-paste Professor Groenendijk's argument in my own pleading for a referral, and then the judges would think: "OK, this is what Mr Dijkman thinks, shall we take him seriously?" Or, I can just say explicitly: "here is a letter for you from Professor Groenendijk." Officially it shouldn't matter for the court who puts down the argument, but in practice it does matter. Groenendijk is recognised as an authority, even in Europe, on this specific Directive.[131]

Eventually, the lawyer's technique was successful: he submitted Groenendijk's letter as a separate document in the proceedings, and the District Court decided to submit a request for a preliminary reference to the Court of Justice, asking that it be dealt with under the urgent procedure.[132] The Zwolle-Lelystad District Court was the first Dutch lower court to ask for a preliminary reference in the AFSJ area. It may be appropriate to say that be it a myth or reality, the "gentlemen's agreement" was definitively breached.

The reference in *Imran* represented a hard test for the Act on the Civic Integration from Abroad, at least in the view of Groenendijk, the DRC, and Dijkman. But apparently, the lawyers representing the *IND* underestimated its potential impact. It was only when the case was referred to Luxembourg, and communicated to the Dutch government's agents, that it was realized how important a challenge *Imran* represented. In the words of a Dutch government agent at that time, "this was not the kind of cases where you want to have this law tested."[133] When the IND and the representatives of the Dutch Minister of the Interior realized that the Imran case would likely end with a defeat in Luxembourg, they decided to offer Mrs Imran a resident permit in order to end the proceedings and avoid the ECJ's ruling. On May 11, 2011, the Ministry informed the ECJ that it had declared Mrs Imran's objection well founded. On May 30, 2011, the Zwolle-Lelystad District Court also informed the ECJ of the changed situation, confirming that Mrs Imran had eventually obtained a temporary permit but asking for the continuation of the case since its interpretation was still relevant to decide on the award of damages. Despite this, the ECJ

[130] See what was said in the previous section on the Dutch lower courts' restraint from making preliminary references.
[131] Interview with Gerben Dijkman, 13 December 2017, Utrecht.
[132] Pursuant to art 104b of the Rules of Procedure of the Court of Justice.
[133] Interview with former Dutch agent, February 2018, The Hague.

issued an order of no need to adjudicate.[134] The *Imran* case therefore came to a premature end, and the Dutch government avoided a probable debacle in Luxembourg.

7.2 The impact of the EU Commission's opinion in Imran

At first glance, *Imran* was an individual victory and a collective defeat: the Safi family was finally reunited in the Netherlands, but the Dutch government managed to prevent its Act on Civic Integration from Abroad from being tested in Luxembourg. However, before the case was abruptly stopped, the EU Commission had already submitted its written observations, and these confirmed Groenendijk and Dijkman's arguments in full. What turned *Imran* into an significant case, interestingly, was revelation of the Commission's written observations. Below I will explain the Commission's argument and how it was effectively used by migrant supporters.

The Commission made a textual and teleological interpretation of the Directive. "First of all, it is not a question of conditions as referred to in Article 7(1) of which *proof* must be provided, but of "integration measures" that Member States may require the family member to comply with."[135] To support its claim further, the Commission compared the various language versions of the Directive (as Groenendijk did) and made an interpretation of it in view of its stated aims. In the Commission's view, the stated that the goal of the Directive is to promote family reunification, and this would enable migrants' successful integration. Therefore, the integration measures that the Member States may adopt should not constitute a limit to family reunification: "On the contrary, the integration measure must contribute to a successful family reunification.... It is therefore a positive measure and not an exclusion ground or an access condition."[136]

Under the ECJ rules in force at that time, the Commission's observations were not made public and are to be shared only among the parties in the

[134] Order in the Case of Case C-155/11 PPU *Bibi Mohammad Imran v Minister van Buitenlandse Zaken* (10 June 2011) CJEU.

[135] See Commission Observations, *Imran*, C-155/11, Sj.g(2011)540657, Brussel, 4 May 2011, para 21, translation by the author.

[136] ibid para 29. Also in pars 31: "Member States have the possibility to impose integration measures. However, they must be proportionate and must not function as a mechanism to impede the purpose of the directive, which is to promote family reunification. They cannot therefore lead to a refusal of family reunification." To support this argument, the Commission cited extensively the ECJ's judgments in the cases of *Parliament v Council* (n 61) and *Chakroun* (n 78), and relevant human rights norms contained in the Nice Charter and the ECHR that protect family life and the best interest of the child.

case. However, after the disappointing premature closure of the *Imran* case, Dijkman, Groenendijk, and the DRC went to utmost lengths to reveal the Commission's document as broadly as possible, even beyond national borders. The text was published on online platforms (such as *Migratierecht.net*), making it available for migration lawyers to use. Groenendijk, who had worked with migration lawyers and experts in Germany, forwarded the Commission's observations to colleagues there. The observations, originally available only in Dutch, were translated into German and circulated on German online resources for immigration lawyers.

Soon, the case of *Imran* manifested its impact in Germany, where an integration test similar to that of the Netherlands had been introduced.[137] German immigration lawyers were citing the Commission Observations in *Imran* in national proceedings, attaching the document to the files of the proceedings as an argument to challenge the validity of the German integration test. Moreover, the Commission Observations were used to convince German courts to make a reference to the ECJ. After a first attempt where the German government stopped the referral by granting a permit to the litigant,[138] a case finally reached the ECJ. This was the case of *Dogan*,[139] a case of a Turkish national whose application for family reunification was dismissed because she failed the pre-entry integration test. Although the referring court asked whether the integration test was compatible with both the Turkey Association Agreement and the Family Reunification Directive, the ECJ declared the integration test in violation of the standstill clause of the former instrument and did not answer the question about the Directive.[140]

Imran had a huge impact within the Netherlands. Immigration lawyers were aware of the EU Commission Observations and started using them before Dutch courts to challenge the validity of family reunification denials based solely on the failure to pass the civic integration test. The Dutch government became aware of this situation. The *IND* changed the way in which the Act on Civil Integration from Abroad was applied, granting more exemptions based on the health or the personal circumstances of the applicant (the so-called hardship clause, introduced in 2011 but still rarely used).[141] In sum, the integration conditions were informally softened but they were still very restrictive and represented a big obstacle for family reunification.

137 Pascouau (n 47) 37.
138 Case C-513/12 *Ayalti* (2013) CJEU, ECLI:EU:C:2013:210.
139 *Dogan* (n 8).
140 ibid para 40.
141 Art 3.71 para 2 of the Immigration Law, Vb 2000, entered into force since April 2001.

7.3 *K and A*

After having been very close to victory in *Imran*, Dijkman, the DRC, and Groenendijk were even more determined to obtain a preliminary ruling on the Act on Civil Integration from Abroad. The Commission Observations demonstrated that their arguments were correct but to make the Family Reunification Directive uniformly enforced, they needed a ECJ judgment.

This time, Dijkman and the DRC did not wait for the perfect case. *K* was the case of a woman who failed the integration test abroad for not very compelling reasons (she asked for an exemption on medical grounds and declared herself to be illiterate, but during a hearing, there emerged some documents that proved her wrong).[142] However, the team could rely on the Commission Observations in the case of *Imran*, and on a new ally, the Vrij University (VU) Migration Law Clinic. Dijkman, Groenendijk, the DRC, and the researchers from the clinic met regularly in Dijkman's office in Utrecht to discuss the best strategy for the case. While the lawyer and the professor focused on the EU law arguments of incompatibility with the Directive, the Migration Law Clinic conducted research regarding how the civic integration test abroad was applied in practice by the *IND*, gathering statistics and information on practical difficulties that applicants encounter during the process of taking the integration test.[143]

The case of *K* received a first positive ruling already in the first stage of the proceedings before the District Court of The Hague. The EU Commission Observations proved decisive, as Dijkman told me: "I sent the documents from the previous referral in *Imran*, the Commission's opinion, and I basically said 'Well, this is how you should do it.'"[144] The District Court could not ignore the Commission's statement and had two alternatives, either upholding the Commission's view or challenging it and asking for a new interpretation to the ECJ. It opted for the first and declared that the Directive precludes a Member State from denying family reunification exclusively on the ground that the applicant did not pass the integration test.[145]

[142] Interview with Gerben Dijkman, 13 December 2017, Utrecht.

[143] Migration Law Clinic, "De Wet Inburgering in Het Buitenland in EU-Rechtelijk Perspectief" (2014) <https://migrationlawclinic.files.wordpress.com/2014/08/expert-opinion-de-wet-inburgering-in-het-buitenland-in-eu-rechtelijk-perspectief.pdf> accessed 17 December 2024.

[144] Interview with Gerben Dijkman, 13 December 2017, Utrecht.

[145] We can see the reference to the Commission Observations also in the *K and A* judgment (n 5) para 40: "The Rechtbank's-Gravenhage [District Court of The Hague] considered it to be decisive in that regard that, in its written observations in the proceedings of the case giving rise to the order in Mohammad Imran (C-155/11 PPU, EU:C:2011:387) which were included in K's file before the Rechtbank's-Gravenhage [District Court of The Hague], the Commission took the view that Article 7(2) of the Directive 2003/86 precludes a Member State from refusing the spouse of a third country

The District Court decision in *K* constituted a very bad precedent for the *IND*. Considering this situation, for the *IND* it was better to have the case referred to the ECJ and have the opportunity to advocate for a different interpretation of the Directive. Therefore, *IND* lawyers filed an appeal before the *Raad Van State* and asked the Court to issue a request for preliminary reference. Although both parties showed their support for the request for a preliminary ruling, the *Raad Van State* decided to wait for another case to refer, hence it merged *K* with *A*. This is a regular practice for the *Raad Van State*: it always tries to submit more than one case at a time to the ECJ in order to avoid a situation such as had occurred in *Imran*; after having invested so much time on a case, it does not want the case subsequently to be dropped because the government suddenly decided to grant a permit to the applicant.[146]

Three years after the failed reference in the *Imran* case, on July 9, 2015, the ECJ pronounced on the compatibility of the pre-departure civic integration test with the Family Reunification Directive. First, it confirmed its interpretation in *Chakroun* that the Directive imposes specific obligations on Member States which must authorize the entry of the sponsor's family member, provided that all conditions are met.[147] However, among these conditions, laid down in Chapter IV of the Directive, there are also the integration measures of Article 7(2): Member States can subject the entry of the family member to compliance with certain integration measures because this would not *per se* undermine the Directive's aims.

At the outset, the ECJ seems to leave more discretion to Member States, in comparison to what was observed by the Commission in *Imran*. However, the Court then added some caveats. It stated that "since the authorisation of family reunification is the general rule," the integration measures should be interpreted strictly. Integration requirements must be proportionate and achieve their objective, to facilitate family members' integration, and they "must not go beyond what is necessary to attain them."[148] Moreover, the Court noted that the way in which the integration measures have been applied in Dutch law and in the referred cases is problematic because they are able systematically to prevent family reunification, the promotion of which is the main aim of the Directive. In fact, the applicants' individual circumstances were not taken into

national living lawfully in that Member State entry and residence exclusively on the ground that that spouse has not, outside the European Union, passed the civic integration examination provided for in the legislation of that Member State."

[146] Interview with Raad Van State Judge, 22 February 2018, The Hague.
[147] *K and A* (n 5) paras 45–49.
[148] Judgment in *K and A* paras 50–51.

account in order to decide whether to dispense them from taking the test.[149] In addition, the preparation and registration fees required for taking the integration test are so high that they are capable of making family reunification impossible or excessively difficult.[150]

The *K and A* judgment resulted in a compromise solution between the position of migrant supporters and the government. In principle, Member States can require family members to comply with integration measures prior to their admission, however the way in which these requirements have been designed in Dutch law is such that they might render the exercise of the right to family reunification impossible or excessively difficult, and therefore they are contrary to the Directive. Even if it was a compromise decision, *K and A* represented an important victory for supporters of migrants because it imposed a limit on States' discretion on the basis of the consideration of migrants' rights. The next section will show the judgment's impact on how the integration test is applied in the Netherlands and on how the issue of migrants' integration is dealt with in EU law.

8. The legal mobilization's impact on Dutch integration policy and on the EU conception of integration

In the cases of *Imran* and *K and A*, by overcoming lower courts' reticence and government's obstruction, supporters of migrants managed to mobilize the Family Reunification Directive before the ECJ to challenge the legitimacy of the *inburgering* policy. This led to what some scholars described as the Directive's "backfiring"[151], which is the unexpected restraining effect of this EU law instrument over the Dutch government policy preferences. Thanks to the mobilization, the ECJ was offered the opportunity to issue its interpretation on the meaning of "integration measures" (Article 7(2) of the Directive). This new judicial interpretation had practical implications on three different levels: (i) on how TCN's integration is conceived in general in the EU; (ii) on Dutch integration law and IND's practice; and (iii) on practitioners' understanding of the Directive. I will now explain these three outcomes, with the belief that according to migrant supporters, the mobilization has yielded positive and negative results.

[149] ibid para 63.
[150] Judgment in *K and A*, paras 64–70.
[151] Bonjour and Vink (n 40).

8.1 The mobilization's impact on the concept of integration

We saw that the Dutch policy on immigration experienced a significant shift in the beginning of the 2000s (Subsection 2.2). While earlier, lawmakers actively promoted integration through policies of social inclusion and equality, the government then decided to conceive integration as a condition for obtaining territorial admission, social inclusion, and an equal status. This new integration policy, revolving around the *inburgering* concept, was the target of the legal mobilization that culminated in the cases of *Imran* and *K and A*.

Interestingly, a few months before the reference in *K and A*, the *Centrale Raad Van Beroep* (Central Appeals Tribunal) had referred another case, *P and S*,[152] which also questioned the legitimacy of the civic integration test vis à vis EU law. However, *P and S* focused on the *Wet Inburgering* Act, the Dutch law that imposes a test on the TCN who already resides regularly in the Netherlands and who wants to acquire or to maintain a long-term residence status.[153] The reference was submitted *ex officio* by the judges, without the litigants asking for it. However, Professor Groenendijk helped the lawyer in the case, Jeremy Bierbach, to formulate his submissions, and the arguments put forward were in line with those of *K and A*.[154] The applicant and the lawyer challenged the legitimacy of the civic integration test as being in conflict with long-term resident migrant rights, in particular with their right to be treated equally to Dutch citizens.[155] Eventually, *P and S* and *K and A* were decided almost at the same time by the Second Chamber of the ECJ, which reached a similar conclusion.

As noted, these cases bear an importance that transcends Dutch borders and concerns the whole EU polity. In fact, *K and A* and *P and S* "obliged the Court, as hard cases, to define its standpoint on integration."[156] By asking for a definition of integration measures and conditions, migrant supporters were posing

[152] *P and S* (n 8). The question was referred on November 2013, while *K and A* was referred in April 2014.

[153] See Section 3.2, this is the test introduced for migrants who had already been admitted in the Netherlands. The government introduced the test as a condition to acquire long-term residence status, as permitted by art 5(2) of the Long-Term Residence Directive: "Member States may require third-country nationals to comply with integration conditions, in accordance with national law." However, when the *Wet Inburgering* Act was introduced in 2007, the government decided to impose the test also on migrants that already had long-term residence status, who in case of failure, would pay a high fee. This was the case of the applicants in *P and S*.

[154] Interview with Jeremy Bierbach, 14 December 2014, Amsterdam. Interview with Kees Groenendijk, 20 February 2018, Nijmegen.

[155] Art 11 of the Long-Term Residence Directive 2003/109.

[156] Daniel Thym, 'Towards a Contextual Conception of Social Integration in Eu Immigration Law. Comments on P & S and K & A' (2016) 18 European Journal of Migration and Law 89, 106.

more fundamental questions, such as what is the EU model of integration? Is this compatible with the Dutch assimilationist turn?

The ECJ's rulings fell short of the expectations that many migrant supporters had. The Court's Second Chamber, responsible for both the decisions in *K and A* and *P and S*, reversed the way in which integration was previously understood in the framework of EU migration policy. Until then, in line with the statements in the Tampere Conclusions,[157] recalled in the preambles and wording of the Family Reunification and Long-Term Resident Directives,[158] a consistent group of migration scholars had interpreted the EU approach to integration as based on incremental rights, quasi-equality between migrants and citizens, and active policies of social inclusion.[159] This scholarship would thus see the integration model to which the EU aspires to as being similar to that of a multicultural society, where differences are welcome and accepted, and where the emphasis is on rights and equality. Alternatively, other scholars argued that integration in the EU was characterized by a "cultural outlook," emphasizing the importance of migrants' assimilation to the culture of the majority.[160] Arguably, the rulings in *K and A* and *P and S* locate the EU closer to the latter point of view.[161]

The ECJ's view on integration was difficult to predict also because it is not fully in line with the position that the majority of Member States expressed during the Family Reunification Directive's negotiations. In fact, the Dutch delegation had openly advocated for the inclusion of the possibility to require integration conditions in the text of the Family Reunification Directive, but this proposal was met with skepticism by other Member States, that eventually agreed on the milder "measures." Arguably, the decision in *K and A* redefined the Family Reunification Directive in a way that was not initially foreseen by the Commission and the Council, and it validated the Dutch model of integration.[162] The ECJ confirmed its reasoning in its subsequent case law, stating the

157 Moritz Jesse, 'Integration Measures, Integration Exams, and Immigration Control: P and S and K and A' (2016) 53 Common Market Law Review 1065, 1080.

158 Scholars argued that the choice of the word "measures" instead of "conditions" could not be random. The difference between the two words exists also in the Long-Term Residence Directive 2003/109. Sarah Ganty, 'Les Tests d'intégration Civique Sous Le Contrôle de La Cour de Justice de l'Union Européenne: Un Exercice d'équilibriste Périlleux Entre Marge d'appréciation Des États Membres et Protection Des Ressortissants de Pays Tiers' [2016] Journal européen des droits de l'homme 32, 51.

159 Mark Bell, 'Civic Citizenship and Migrant Integration' (2007) 13 European Public Law 311, 329.

160 Thym (n 156) 90.

161 On the elusiveness of the notion of "social integration" in EU migration and mobility law, see the special issue: Francesco Costamagna and Stefano Montaldo, 'Social Integration in EU Law: Content, Limits and Functions of an Elusive Notion—Introduction' (2018) 3 European Papers 659.

162 For another critical view on how the ECJ's judicial lawmaking trumps the political view of the lawmaker to impose a different model of (economic) integration, see Martin Höpner and Armin Schäfer, 'A New Phase of European Integration: Organised Capitalisms in Post-Ricardian Europe' (2010) 33 West European Politics 344.

legitimacy of Dutch integration conditions in other instances, such as *C and A* and *K* (Subsection 8.3).[163]

8.2 Mobilization impact on Dutch integration law

On a more positive note, the *K and A* ruling confirmed the ECJ's rigorous commitment with respect to the right to family reunification. The Court confirmed the findings of *Parliament v Council* and *Chakroun*: family reunification is an individual right conferred by the EU upon TCN migrants residing legally in a Member State, and States are bound to respect it, with limited margin of appreciation. This means that Member States have limited discretion in the implementation of integration conditions and cannot make the exercise of the right to family reunification impossible or too difficult. Given how strict the Dutch norms on the civic integration test were, the ECJ decision entailed relevant amendments.

First, in light of *K and A*, the government adopted legal change to the Act implementing the Alien Law (*Vreemdelingencirculaire* 2000).[164] Immigration authorities cannot reject a family reunification application any longer solely because the applicant failed the test. The *IND* must consider the applicant's individual circumstances and apply the conditions required by national law in a way that respects the proportionality principle.[165] More concretely, the *IND* must consider whether applicants should be granted an exemption from taking the civic integration test because of their particular situations, such as the presence of minor children, specific health conditions, or the unsafe situation of the third country.[166] Another newly introduced exemption from taking the test applies in cases where the preparation material is not available in the language of the applicant. If, nevertheless, the *IND* decides to refuse the reunification request, the migrant can ask for a judicial review of the decision whereby judges must also make sure that the applicant did not qualify for one of the exemptions listed. This guarantees a judicial scrutiny over the *IND*'s decision.

[163] *C and A* (n 5); *K* (n 5).

[164] Art B.1/4.7 Vreemdelingencirculaire 2000 (B). <https://wetten.overheid.nl/BWBR0012289/2016-01-01?VergelijkMet = BWBR0012289%3Fg%3D2015-07-01> accessed 17 December 2024.

[165] Ganty (n 158) 39.

[166] ibid. "The IND does not reject the application for a provisional residence permit because of the integration requirement if there are special individual circumstances that lead to the foreign national being unable to pass the civic integration examination successfully. This can be a single circumstance or a combination of different circumstances" (author's translation).

Another positive impact that *K and A* had on migrants' situation regards the fees they are required to pay.[167] The Dutch government reduced the fees substantially (from 350 euros to 150 euros), as well as the cost of the preparation material for taking the integration test (from 110 euros to 60 euros).[168] Overall, even if an immigrant must still take the civic integration test from abroad, the conditions surrounding taking it have improved considerably.

8.3 Mobilization's impact on how the Directive is perceived

Lastly, the cases of *Imran* and *K and A* changed the way in which migration practitioners think about the Family Reunification Directive. Thanks to these first preliminary references, "lawyers and judges became acquainted with European Migration Law and its implications, and national courts started submitting requests for a preliminary ruling from the Court of Justice."[169] These judgments unveiled the untapped potential of the Directive as an instrument to protect family reunification from unlawful barriers set up by a government.

As a consequence, new preliminary references on the Family Reunification Directive arose from the Netherlands. Some of them where promoted by civil society actors (like the case of *A and S*, supported by the VU legal clinic), but others have been referred under the initiative of national judges alone, without the parties asking for it (like *C and A*, according to the text of the reference).[170] These references show that judges and practitioners are now more acquainted with the Family Reunification Directive and its implications than they had been earlier, and they are ready to rely on the preliminary reference mechanism to enforce it. However, if we take a more pessimistic view, we can also read the preliminary reference mechanism as a symptom of the reluctance of the *IND* to subscribe fully to the higher standards set by the Directive.

For instance, the cases of *C and A* and *K* regard the situation of TCN spouses who, after more than five years of residence as family members, asked for an autonomous residence permit.[171] They could not pass the civic integration test

[167] Jesse (n 157) 1083 and 1085.

[168] Regulation of the State Secretary for Security and Justice of 19 February 2016, number 736437, amending the Aliens Regulations 2000 (142 amendment).

[169] Groenendijk and Strik (n 58) 364.

[170] *A and S* (n 99); *C and A* (n 5). This is the case of two TCNs that are spouses of Dutch citizens, who see their permanent residence permits denied because they do not pass the integration test. The national court decision is: Raad Van State, Order for Reference in the case of C and A, 201600860/1/V2 and 201604637/1/V2, 10 May 2017.

[171] This is expressly provided by the Family Reunification Directive, at art 15: "1. Not later than after five years of residence, and provided that the family member has not been granted a residence permit for reasons other than family reunification, the spouse or unmarried partner and a child who has

required by Dutch law, and the *IND* withdrew their permits.[172] The ECJ restated that a decision to withdraw a permit of a family member cannot be based on the sole fact that the TCN did not pass the test, but that other circumstances should be taken into account, "such as the age, level of education, economic situation or health," which can exempt them from passing the test.[173] Arguably, these conclusions could be already implied from the *K and A* judgment and, in my view, are paradigmatic of the fact that the *IND* still applies a restrictive approach to these rights' enforcement. If preliminary references are still needed this may mean that the *IND* keeps interpreting the Directive in a way that is not fully consistent with the ECJ's judgments.

9. Conclusion

This chapter has examined the legal mobilization that underpinned some Dutch cases on the Family Reunification Directive and the civic integration test. While the Dutch government was initially in favor of the Directive and duly transposed it into national law in 2004, the situation changed after the first judgments of the ECJ, when the Court interpreted the Directive in a way that emphasized its potential as a pro-migrant rights instrument. The Court's judgments were crucial for clarifying the content of the new EU norms and fully fleshing out the implications that the introduction of a right to family reunification carried within the Directive. This chapter shows that the first important ECJ rulings on the Directive were the outcome of legal mobilization conducted by migrant supporters who foresaw the Directive's potential.

By looking at the ECJ case law through the lens of legal mobilization, the chapter argues that the conditions that have made the Family Reunification Directive backfire in the Netherlands are to be found in its positive structure of legal opportunities and in the work of migrant supporters. First, the Netherlands presents an open legal opportunity structure for legal mobilization thanks to its open-minded judiciary (especially since the 2008 "European turn" of the *Raad Van State*) and its positive rules on access to courts. Second, altruistic actors were capable of perceiving the Family Reunification Directive's

reached majority shall be entitled, upon application, if required, to an autonomous residence permit, independent of that of the sponsor. . . 4. The conditions relating to the granting and duration of the autonomous residence permit are established by national law."

[172] *K* (n 5); *C and A* (n 5).

[173] *C and A* (n 5) para 63; *K* (n 5) para 23.

potential and capitalizing on the opportunities offered by a mobilization before the ECJ. This was thanks to the help of academics such as Kees Groenendijk. Also crucial was the fact that academics were in contact with migrant supporter organizations, and these organizations decided to participate in the legal mobilization project. Finally, the availability of lawyers who believed in the migrants' cause and decided to invest their time and work in the mobilization effort was important. Altogether, these civil society actors played a crucial role in mobilizing the Directive, and they did so under the sole incentive of supporting the migrants' cause. In the words of Groenendijk: "I never got a penny for what I did. Just cute paintings from Mrs Imran's children."[174] These sociopolitical factors should be taken into account when trying to understand the roots and the direction that Europeanization takes. In fact, even the most autonomous Court, without migrant supporters mobilizing EU law, would remain silent.

As mentioned earlier, the cases of *Imran* and *K and A* were only a part of a broader litigation strategy set up to mobilize EU law against Dutch integration policy. In fact, migrant supporters mobilized the Directive also via other venues. For instance, the DRC filed two complaints before the Commission, denouncing as incorrect the Dutch transposition of the Directive.[175] The *IOT*, the organization of Turkish migrants in the Netherlands, organized a strategic litigation before Dutch national courts that obtained the exclusion of Turkish migrants from the obligation of taking the civic integration test, thanks to the application of the standstill clause of the Ankara Agreement.[176] The *IOT* also contested the high fees required in order to obtain a permit, a controversy that started within the framework of the Long-Term Residence Directive but which eventually also concerned the Family Reunification Directive.[177]

Even if we saw that national courts' judgments can bear important results in the mobilization, only a ruling by the ECJ can affect the interpretation of the Family Reunification Directive across the entire Union. Such judicial

[174] Interview with Kees Groenendijk, 20 February 2018, Nijmegen.

[175] Groenendijk and Strik (n 58) 378.

[176] See the judgments of the District Court Rotterdam of 12 August 2010, and District Court Roermond Judgment of 15 October 2010, described in the article of Tezcan-Idriz (n 74).

[177] See the Raad Van State's judgment on 9 October 2012, ECLI:NL:RVS 2012:BY0145, JV 2012/470: "Although the scope of application of Directives 2003/86 and 2003/109 is not the same, both Directives apply to third-country nationals, both aim to promote the integration of third-country nationals in Member States and both require Member States to introduce a system in which third-country nationals are entitled to a residence permit if they meet a number of procedural and material requirements. In addition, both directives have in common the fact that they do not contain provisions on fees and therefore leave discretion to the Member States in this respect. In view of these similarities between the Directives, it must be assumed that the considerations of the CJEU as presented in 1.4 are applicable mutatis mutandis in the context of Directive 2003/86."

interpretation had a catalyzing effect, and other preliminary requests followed on the application of the Directive in other fields: for people with subsidiary protection, for minors, for family members of national citizens, etc. These new cases, on the one hand reveal the potential that an indeterminate instrument such as a Directive bears, which can be used to expand migrants' rights in different fields. On the other, they also show how reluctant the *IND* was and still is to protect and respect migrants' rights to family reunification in full, as interpreted by the ECJ.

5

Greece

The Zero-Reference Case

1. Introduction: Reluctant judges or inactive parties?

Litigation before the European Court of Justice (ECJ) is increasingly important in the interpretation and enforcement of the rights of individuals in Europe, including migrants.[1] Having understood this, non-governmental organizations (NGOs) and migrant rights defenders are increasingly engaged in the mobilization of EU law through the preliminary reference procedure.

The previous chapters on Italy, the UK, and the Netherlands illustrate how legal mobilization efforts were behind spikes in migration-related references of cases from national courts to the ECJ. There, groups of migrant rights defenders decided to invoke EU law in court and ask for a preliminary reference to the Court of Justice to contest restrictive migration laws. These legal mobilization cases allow us to understand the conditions under which civil society actors decide to rely on EU justice. They also show the techniques that these actors use to increase the likelihood of having a case referred: they either convince national judges to refer cases or they shape judges' knowledge of EU law, for instance by organizing conferences, writing academic articles, and submitting expert opinions.

After analyzing "positive" cases of EU legal mobilization, this chapter turns to a "negative" case. Indeed, migration references predominantly come from the same few countries, while some Member States never or rarely mobilized the rights of migrants before the ECJ. How can we account for this absence? What factors hamper litigation before the ECJ?

Research on the lack of preliminary references has mainly focused on national judges, exploring the motives behind their choice to withhold references. Being national judges the gatekeepers to the ECJ, it is natural to think

[1] In this chapter, as in the rest of the book, the terms "migrant" and "migration" refer exclusively to citizens of a country that is not part of the EU, regardless of their status (eg refugees, long-term residents, etc).

Legal Mobilization for Migrant Rights. Virginia Passalacqua, Oxford University Press.
 DOI: 10.1093/9780198943006.003.0005

that the lack of references is due to their reluctance to engage in judicial cooperation. Golub argued that domestic politics can explain this reluctance, showing that British judges were affected by the Euro-pessimistic climate in the UK.[2] Wind focused on the national legal-political context too, arguing that in Nordic countries, national judges are less prone to refer due to their lack of familiarity with judicial review.[3] Glavina explored the lack of references in two new Member States, arguing that institutional factors such as time pressure and high workload can be important constraints.[4]

However, some of these works acknowledge that parties' lack of initiative may also contribute to the lack of references.[5] This is in line with legal mobilization studies, which posits that courts are mainly reactive institutions. Thus, rather than focusing exclusively on why judges do not refer, this chapter widens the lens and asks whether mobilizing actors have tried to persuade judges to refer cases to the ECJ and, if so, why these actors have failed before 2023.

The chapter leverages the findings from the case studies where EU legal mobilization was present to check if these cases can assist in elucidating a case in which EU legal mobilization is lacking. Our negative case is Greece, a country where, up until 2023, the EU rights of migrants have remained "unmobilized," in the sense that they have never been the object of a preliminary reference. This is especially puzzling given that Greece has been affected by extreme migration flows since 2008 and many legal NGOs operate there to support migrant rights.

This chapter investigates whether the absence of EU litigation can be explained by a lack of mobilizing actors—for example, actors who use the law to change the status quo—or by factors external to these actors that prevent them from effectively mobilizing the law. In the first instance, pro-migrant movements would be missing or lacking essential resources for legal mobilization. In the second, the "legal opportunity structure" for EU litigation would be a closed one, meaning for instance that there are obstacles in access to courts or national judges are unwilling to refer.

[2] Jonathan Golub, 'The Politics of Judicial Discretion: Rethinking the Interaction between National Courts and the European Court of Justice' (1996) 19 West European Politics 360, 377.

[3] Marlene Wind, 'The Nordics, the EU and the Reluctance towards Supranational Judicial Review' (2010) 48 Journal of Common Market Studies 1039, 1057.

[4] Monika Glavina, 'Reluctance to Participate in the Preliminary Ruling Procedure as a Challenge to EU Law: A Case Study on Slovenia and Croatia' in Clara Rauchegger and Anna Wallerman (eds), *The Eurosceptic Challenge: National Implementation and Interpretation of EU Law* (Hart Publishing 2019) 204; also Jasper Krommendijk, 'Why Do Lower Courts Refer in the Absence of a Legal Obligation? Irish Eagerness and Dutch Disinclination' (2019) 26(1) Maastricht Journal of European and Comparative Law 785.

[5] Glavina (n 4) 204.

While both mobilizing actors and an open legal opportunity structure feature in instances in which EU rights have been effectively mobilized, only cases of non-mobilization can shed light on whether (the absence of) these factors can account for the lack of litigation.

2. Factors explaining (the lack of) legal mobilization before the ECJ

As seen in the previous chapters, the literature on legal mobilization and social movements offers two valuable concepts to explain the (non-)emergence of legal mobilization.

2.1 Structural factors: The EU legal opportunity structure

The first is that of "legal opportunity structure" (LOS),[6] a concept derived from the analogous "political opportunity structure" developed in social movement theories. This comes from the observation that by providing incentives or disincentives to act, the political environment shapes the expectations of social movements for the success of collective actions, and consequently affects their decision to mobilize.[7] We still lack an agreed-upon definition of LOS and, as Vanhala critically noted, scholars tend to use it to indicate "[v]irtually anything that can be seen as having helped a movement mobilize or attain its goals."[8] Defining LOS in overly comprehensive terms risks undermining its analytical value, because it becomes too broad and vague, thus difficult to distinguish it from similar concepts. For the sake of conceptual clarity, I consider part of the LOS only factors *external* to the mobilizing actors.[9] These pertain to three

[6] Chris Hilson, 'New Social Movements: The Role of Legal Opportunity' (2002) 9 Journal of European Public Policy 238, 243; Ellen Ann Andersen, *Out of the Closets and into the Courts: Legal Opportunity Structure and Gay Rights Litigation* (University of Michigan Press 2006) 12; Gianluca De Fazio, 'Legal Opportunity Structure and Social Movement Strategy in Northern Ireland and Southern United States' (2012) 53 International Journal of Comparative Sociology 6.

[7] Sidney G Tarrow, *Power in Movement: Social Movements and Contentious Politics* (3rd edn, CUP 2011) 163.

[8] Lisa Vanhala, *Making Rights a Reality? Disability Rights Activists and Legal Mobilization* (CUP 2010) 20. For instance, Case and Givens define it as "the nature of the available legal stock, the rules governing access to the judiciary, and resources for legal advocacy." Rhonda Evans Case and Terri Givens, 'Re-Engineering Legal Opportunity Structures in the European Union? The Starting Line Group and the Politics of the Racial Equality Directive' (2010) 48 Journal of Common Market Studies 221, 224. Andersen defines the LOS broadly to include cultural and legal frames too: Andersen (n 6) 12.

[9] "Mobilizing actors" is a broad term to indicate groups that purposely mobilize the law (collective actors, social movements, NGOs etc).

main categories: the available law, judicial receptivity, and the rules on access to courts.[10]

Remarkably, calling these factors external does not mean that mobilizing actors are affected by them passively. On the contrary, as suggested in the literature, actors can affect structural factors and shape them.[11] Additionally, it is essential to bear in mind that opportunities for legal mobilization exist only to the extent that movements perceive them as such. As Tarrow warned: "there is no such thing as 'objective' opportunities—they must be perceived and attributed to become the source of mobilization."[12] An easy example here regards the legal stock: if a person is not aware of their rights, they will never invoke or mobilize them. Recent research on migrant rights litigation further showed that under the same LOS, divergent perceptions can explain why one actor mobilizes and another does not.[13]

These legal mobilization concepts need to be adapted to the specific migration and preliminary reference mechanism context. Indeed, the interaction between the national and the EU opportunity structure is complex and the outcome is not always in the direction of empowering citizens.[14] The preliminary reference procedure, despite being used to enforce EU rights, remains "a procedure from court to court" that sits between the national and the supranational level.[15] Litigants first need to gain access to national courts to then have their cases referred to the ECJ; this means that the national structure of opportunities, with its rules on access to court, heavily determines the EU LOS. Moreover, EU law is part of a multilevel system of rights and remedies where it represents only one legal strategy among many. The same claim may often be framed by using national, EU, or international law, and the choice of legal source determines the suitable remedy and court (national and constitutional court, ECJ, etc).

For these reasons, when identifying the factors that can explain the presence and the absence of legal mobilization before the ECJ, it is crucial to look at the

[10] More on this in chapter 1. In this sense, I largely adhere to De Fazio's definition that comprises "1) accessibility to courts; 2) availability of justiciable rights; 3) receptivity of the judiciary toward a social movement's claims." De Fazio (n 6) 6.

[11] Lisa Vanhala, 'Legal Opportunity Structures and the Paradox of Legal Mobilization by the Environmental Movement in the UK' (2012) 46 Law & Society Review 523, 528.

[12] Tarrow (n 7) 163.

[13] Kris van der Pas, 'All That Glitters Is Not Gold? Civil Society Organisations and the (Non-) Mobilisation of European Union Law' 62 Journal of Common Market Studies 2, 525.

[14] Dia Anagnostou, *Rights and Courts in Pursuit of Social Change: Legal Mobilisation in the Multi-Level European System* (Hart Publishing 2014) 20.

[15] Pierre Pescatore, *Court of Justice of the European Communities: References for Preliminary Rulings under Article 177 of the EEC Treaty and Cooperation between the Court and National Courts* (Office for Official Publications of the European Communities 1986) 33.

interplay between the national and the EU legal systems. Alter and Vargas have formulated four steps to explain when EU law can be successfully mobilized: 1) there needs to be a specific aspect of EU law from which collective actors can draw; 2) litigants must embrace EU law to advance their political claim; 3) a domestic court must support their claim; 4) litigants must follow up their legal victory politically.[16]

This was largely confirmed in the previous empirical chapters. Moreover, these chapters identified two factors as determining the open or closed nature of the EU LOS. The first regards the legal stock: the available EU law shall present, in the eyes of migrant rights defenders, a comparative advantage with respect to national law. The second concerns domestic courts: national judges shall prove to be willing and able to refer. In the latter lies one of the most interesting features of an open EU LOS: access to (the EU) court crucially depends on (national courts') judicial receptivity.[17]

Such specific judicial receptivity might depend on many different factors that the literature identified (eg "competition-between-courts dynamic,"[18] the judicial review culture,[19] attitudes toward the EU).[20] It is also important to note that judicial receptivity is not immune to the influence of mobilizing actors, as the previous chapters have shown. Through judicial training, conferences, and academic articles, migrant rights defenders can make a judge more prone to refer. An eminent example is Italy, where ASGI and *Magistratura Democratica* published articles and organized several public events to make judges aware of the conflict between Italian and EU law.

All this considered, one hypothesis (Hypothesis 1) for the lack of references is that Greece's structure of opportunities for EU legal mobilization is closed. This may be due to:

a) Legal stock: EU law does not offer a comparative advantage with respect to Greek law;
b) Judicial receptivity: Greek judges are unwilling or unable to refer;
c) There is no access to courts.

[16] Karen Alter and Jeannette Vargas, 'Explaining Variation in the Use of European Litigation Strategies: European Community Law and British Gender Equality Policy' (2000) 33 Comparative Political Studies 452.
[17] Virginia Passalacqua, 'Legal Mobilization Via Preliminary Reference: Insights from the Case of Migrant Rights' (2021) 58 Common Market Law Review 751, 770.
[18] Karen Alter, 'The European Court's Political Power' (1996) 19 West European Politics 458, 466.
[19] Wind (n 3).
[20] Golub (n 2).

2.2 Subjective factors: Actors, resources, and legal consciousness

As stated earlier, structural factors are only part of the explanation. An open LOS is not sufficient per se to explain the emergence of EU legal mobilization because EU legal opportunities can be seized only by actors that have the necessary resources.[21] While the LOS refers to factors that are *external* to the mobilizing actors, mobilization resources concern the factors *internal* to them,[22] and these shall be considered too as possible explanations for the lack of EU litigation.

Arguably, the most important resource for legal mobilization is the presence of a support structure.[23] In the case of migrant rights, this often consists of altruistic actors, actors who are not migrants but who mobilize on their behalf.[24] This is especially true for migrants who are newcomers to Europe and who can hardly have a clear understanding of the law, their rights, and even less of EU rights and procedures. For this reason, their mobilization crucially depends on the help provided by altruistic actors who supply fundamental information and know-how for the litigation.

In the specific preliminary reference context, mobilizing actors need to persuade a national judge to refer a case to the ECJ. To this end, they need to possess excellent knowledge of EU law, which is a critical resource to reach the ECJ.[25] In this respect, allies can be very important suppliers of Euro-expertise. One possible ally is Eurolawyers who are "part insiders of the EU legal field, part members of their local community—that facilitates their efforts to mobilize "compliance constituencies" and harness transnational law to broker contentious social change."[26] Another frequent ally is EU law academics, whose special expertise allows them to perceive openings in the EU LOS and to point out to mobilizing actors that a certain EU norm bears potential for the contestation of national law and practices. We have seen this in the chapter about the Netherlands, where academics such as Kees Groenendijk were crucial in

[21] Tanja A Börzel, 'Participation Through Law Enforcement. The Case of the European Union' (2006) 39 Comparative Political Studies 128, 129.

[22] Hilson (n 6) 260; Tarrow (n 7) 16.

[23] Charles Epp, *The Rights Revolution: Lawyers, Activists, and Supreme Courts in Comparative Perspective* (University of Chicago Press 1998) 3.

[24] Paul Statham, 'Political Opportunities for Altruism? The Role of State Policies in Influencing Claims-Making by British Antiracist and Pro-Migrant Movements' in Marco Giugni and Florence Passy, *Political Altruism? Solidarity Movements in International Perspective* (Rowman & Littlefield 2001) 133.

[25] This has been shown in previous Chapters 2 to 4 of this book, where the legal mobilization was often led or concretely supported by legal scholars.

[26] Tommaso Pavone, 'From Marx to Market: Lawyers, European Law, and the Contentious Transformation of the Port of Genoa' (2018) 53 Law & Society Review 5.

pointing to relevant EU laws and suggesting possible mobilization strategies. By shaping mobilizing actors' perceptions, legal experts can have a major influence on the decision to mobilize or not.

In the context of litigation, another mobilization resource is the money to pay for proceedings. Preliminary references are initiated within national proceedings, which means that actors need the money required to initiate and sustain legal action. In some national contexts, where litigation fees are particularly high, the availability of funds can determine actors' ability to access court and mobilize the law. Compared to other mobilization strategies such as political campaigning, legal mobilization is quite cheap, but we should not ignore the fact that the availability of money to litigants can be critical in the under-financed world of pro-migrant activism. We have seen that in the UK, the rise in litigation costs and the cut in public funding for legal aid significantly curtailed migrant supporters' ability to go to court.

Building on these considerations, I have formulated a second hypothesis that focuses on internal factors. According to this hypothesis (Hypothesis 2), the lack of EU legal mobilization can be explained by a lack of resources, which translates into:

a) Altruistic actors: There is a lack of migrant rights defendants in Greece;
b) Material and intellectual resources: There are migrant rights defendants in Greece, but they lack money, Euro-expertise, or expert allies.

Sections 4 and 5 will use empirical evidence to test these hypotheses, but first, the next section explains why Greece is a suitable case study.

3. Greece and its puzzling lack of references

I identified Greece as a case study for two main reasons. First, after looking at my database containing all migration references up to December 2022 (a total of 505), Greece stands out as one of the few EU countries that has never referred a preliminary question in the migration field to the ECJ.[27] This is quite striking because my database contains many types of reference regarding TCNs' rights, be they family members of Union citizens, refugees, long-term

[27] Under the term migration field, I include all the EU legislation that regulate the status of third-country nationals (TCN). These include norms on asylum seekers and refugees, association agreements with third countries, and norms on the rights of TCNs who are family members of EU citizens.

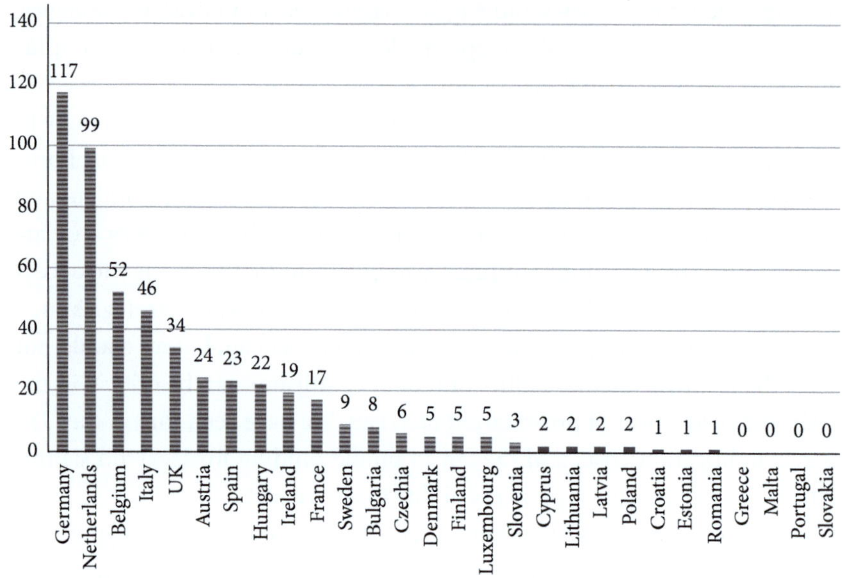

Figure 5.1 Preliminary references in the migration field per referring country until December 2022.

Source: author's original database based on Curia and NEMIS, NEAIS, and NEFIS newsletters. These newsletters contain up-to-date lists of migration, asylum, and free movement cases before the Court of Justice. They are published regularly on the website of the Migration Law Center of Radboud University: <https://www.ru.nl/en/center-for-migration-law/research/background-documentation> accessed 18 December 2024.

residents, or undocumented migrants.[28] What makes Greece particularly puzzling, however, is its sociopolitical context: Greece abounds with big and small organizations working for migrant rights, making it fertile terrain for legal mobilization.

As Figure 5.1 shows, until December 2022, four EU countries had never submitted a preliminary reference in the migration field: Greece, Malta, Portugal, and Slovakia. To be suitable case studies, the countries must have structural characteristics that do not automatically exclude the possibility of having references in the migration field. For instance, a country like Slovakia, with a small migrant population would not qualify.[29] Another important factor is that

[28] See Chapter 1 for more on this. My database is not limited to the Area of Freedom, Security and Justice; it includes free movement norms that address TCNs and Association Agreements between the EU and third countries.

[29] On this account, only Slovakia would be excluded, as its number of non-EU citizens per 1,000 inhabitants is clearly below the EU average (Eurostat, Migration and Migrant Population Statistics, 2024 <https://ec.europa.eu/eurostat/statistics-explained/index.php?title=Migration_and_migrant_

in general, new Member States have a lower number of references compared to old ones.[30] This seems particularly relevant for our sample because many countries with zero or few references are new Member States: Malta, Slovakia, Croatia, Estonia, Latvia, Lithuania, and Romania. Their status as new Member States is likely to be the explanation for the lack of references.

Greece is not a new Member State. It joined the EU in 1981, and since 2010 it has faced "extreme migratory pressure."[31] During that year, "the Greek external land and sea border accounted for 90% of all detection of irregular border crossing along all EU external land and sea borders."[32] Since then, Greece's pivotal importance for migration flows directed to Europe has grown, reaching its peak in 2015 and 2016 with the so-called refugee crisis.[33]

Another reason why one should expect legal mobilization via preliminary references in Greece is the important presence of altruistic actors working in the migration and asylum field, providing a "support structure" for legal mobilization.[34] When large numbers of asylum seekers started reaching Greece, local and international NGOs mobilized in their support to compensate for the Greek government's shortcomings. One of the basic needs of asylum seekers is to have legal assistance throughout the asylum procedure and for this reason, legal NGOs are abundant in Greece. This suggests that Hypothesis 2(a) of this chapter (lack of migrant rights defenders) does not hold for the Greek case. Our puzzle deepens.

A final aspect that points to Greece as a likely case for EU legal mobilization arose when the research for this study was already in train. In 2023, Greek courts submitted two migration references for the first time: in February, the Greek Council of State made its first reference to the ECJ in the asylum field,[35]

population_statistics#:~:text=Migrant%20population%3A%2027.3%20million%20non,compared%20to%20the%20previous%20year> accessed 18 December 2024).

[30] Morten Broberg and Niels Fenger, 'Variations in Member States' Preliminary References to the Court of Justice—Are Structural Factors (Part of) the Explanation?' (2013) 19 European Law Journal 488, 491.

[31] Paul McDonough and Evangelia (Lilian) Tsourdi, 'The "Other" Greek Crisis: Asylum and Eu Solidarity' (2012) 31 Refugee Survey Quarterly 67, 67.

[32] European Union Agency for Fundamental Rights (FRA), 'Coping with a Fundamental Rights Emergency—The Situation of Persons Crossing the Greek Land Border in an Irregular Manner' (2011) 4.

[33] Anna Triandafyllidou, 'Migration in Greece' in Kevin Featherstone and Dimitri A Sotiropoulos (eds), *The Oxford Handbook of Modern Greek Politics* (OUP 2020) 556.

[34] Epp (n 23).

[35] Greek Council of State, Case number 177/2023. The case concerned the listing of Turkey as a safe third country, although it stopped accepting the readmission of asylum seekers. It was recently decided by the ECJ: Case C-134.23 *Elliniko Symvoulio gia tous Prosfyges and Ypostirixi Prosfygon sto Aigaio [Greek Refugee Council and Refugee Support Aegean]* (4 October 2024) CJEU, ECLI:EU:C:2024:838.

and in August 2023, it was the turn of the Administrative Court of Thessaloniki, also on asylum procedures.[36] While these cases fall outside the scope of my investigation, which covers the period up to December 2022, they can be nevertheless useful for understanding why a migration reference had not been made earlier because they suggest that Greek courts may not be, or may no longer be, reluctant to refer.

The next sections will test the two hypotheses described in Section 2. To do this I have analyzed the Greek sociolegal and judicial framework by gathering data on national and international judicial activity. I have complemented this with ten interviews, one with a Greek judge and nine with migrant rights defenders, and several informal conversations with Greek academics and practitioners.

This study has two important limitations. The first regards access: except for apex courts, Greek courts' judgments are not publicly available. The second regards interviewing as a method: Lawyers and judges may understandably be reluctant to admit their responsibility for the lack of references, which is why I triangulated interviews with other types of data.[37]

4. Structural obstacles: The EU legal opportunity structure in Greece

This section examines whether structural factors can explain Greece's lack of migration references. Using legal mobilization language, this section asks whether the reason why Greece does not have migration references lies in its closed LOS.

When it comes to mobilization through preliminary references, three conditions make a LOS open. First, EU law should present significant advantages compared to Greek law, in the sense of being more protective of migrant rights. Second, domestic judges shall not be structurally reluctant to refer. Third, actors must have access to national courts. The following subsections will verify each of these conditions.

[36] Thessaloniki Administrative Court, Case Number 560/2023, registered at the CJEU as Case C-610/23 *Al Nasiria*, still pending.

[37] Mario L Small and Jenna M Cook, 'Using Interviews to Understand Why: Challenges and Strategies in the Study of Motivated Action' (2023) 52 Sociological Methods & Research 1591, 1606.

4.1 The comparative advantage of EU legislation

A crucial condition for the existence of preliminary references is that EU law is being litigated before national courts by actors who assert its lack of clarity, validity, or compatibility with the Member State's legal framework and practices. The latter is the most common case and "[i]t seems well founded to assume that Member States that persistently fail to fulfil their EU obligations are more likely to face legal challenges in their national courts than are Member States that do fulfil their obligations."[38]

The preliminary reference procedure is often used as a "citizens' infringement" to assess whether national acts are compatible with EU law.[39] Research on mobilization for migrant rights in Italy, the UK, and the Netherlands show that EU litigation was used to challenge restrictive policies in the field of migrant detention and family reunification which, according to migrant rights defenders, were incompatible with EU standards. For this reason, we shall expect non-compliance with EU law to be a good predictor of references to the ECJ, because it prompts litigants to invoke the respect of EU law in courts. We should also consider that migrant rights defendants would not mobilize any piece of EU law that is not complied with, but they would invoke only those EU norms that they consider more advantageous for the rights of migrants than national ones.

From these considerations, we can further specify Hypothesis 1(a) in these terms: Greek legislation aligns with EU migration law, or EU migration law is comparatively more restrictive and offers fewer protections for migrant rights than Greek law. Consequently, litigants and advocacy groups have no incentive to invoke Greek law in court.

Evidence suggests the opposite. During the last thirteen years, academics and NGOs have documented severe flaws in Greece's asylum and migration systems, considered to be below European standards.[40] Since 2009, Greece has been "under the spotlight because of its continuing inability to provide effective protection to asylum-seekers arriving at its shores," as provided by

[38] Broberg and Fenger (n 30) 489.

[39] Bruno De Witte, 'The Impact of Van Gend En Loos on Judicial Protection at European and National Level: Three Types of Preliminary Questions' in Antonio Tizzano and Sacha Prechal (eds), *50th Anniversary of the Judgment in Van Gend en Loos, 1963–2013* (Office des Publications de l'Union Européenne 2013).

[40] ECRE, 'Asylum in Greece: A Situation Beyond Judicial Control?' (2021) 9; McDonough and Tsourdi (n 31).

EU law.[41] The inconsistencies with EU law have been ascertained by the EU Commission too, which opened an infringement procedure in 2010.[42] Several judgments of the European Court of Human Rights (ECtHR) found the detention and living conditions of migrants in Greece degrading,[43] and the ECJ found its asylum reception system to have "systemic deficiencies," in one of the most famous strategic litigation cases ever brought, *N.S. and Others* of December 2011.[44] Notably, this case was referred by Irish and British courts and not by Greek courts. More recent references from Germany also report that refugees cannot be sent back to Greece because they would run "a serious risk of being subjected to inhuman or degrading treatment within the meaning of Article 4 of the Charter of Fundamental Rights of the European Union."[45]

In 2014, Greece's already deficient asylum system had to face one of the biggest people's exodus in European history, the so-called refugee crisis triggered by the Syrian war. From 2014 to 2016, more than 1 million of asylum seekers arrived in Greece to take the Balkan route and reach northern European countries (Figure 5.2). This massive transit came to a halt in March 2016, when the EU Member States and Turkey signed the controversial EU–Turkey Statement, under which Turkey agreed to take back all Syrian nationals who arrived in Greece via Turkey. Although civil society actors denounced the Statement as being contrary to EU law and human rights, the Greek government implemented it by introducing a fast-track procedure whereby all applications by people coming from Turkey would be considered inadmissible under the "safe third country" or "first country of asylum" concepts.[46] Interestingly, the subsequent decrease in arrivals did not lead to better reception conditions; instead,

[41] Anna Triandafyllidou, 'Migration in Greece' in Kevin Featherstone and Dimitri A. Sotiropoulos (eds), *The Oxford Handbook of Modern Greek Politics* (OUP 2020) 557.

[42] According to the paper by McDonough and Tsourdi, this was prompted by a coalition of NGOs that sent a notice to the Commission "alleging misapplication of 'the EU asylum acquis in relation to all aspects of the asylum procedure and the treatment of asylum seekers'." McDonough and Tsourdi (n 31) 73. It is worth noting that for a long time, the Commission has turned its face to the violations committed in Greece; see Marcella Cometti, 'La risposta della Commissione europea al "deterioramento" del diritto di asilo in Grecia: riflessioni sull'attenuato attivismo dell'Istituzione "guardiana dei Trattati"' [2022] Freedom Security and Justice 175.

[43] The first decision by the European Court of Human Rights was the case of *M.S.S. v Belgium and Greece*, Application no 30696/09.

[44] Joined cases C-411/10 and C-493/10 *NS and ME and Others* (3 March 2011) CJEU, ECLI:EU:C:2011:865.

[45] Pending Cases 753/22 *QY* and C-288/23 *El Baheer.*

[46] UNHCR, 'Legal Considerations on the Return of Asylum-Seekers and Refugees from Greece to Turkey as Part of the EU–Turkey Cooperation in Tackling the Migration Crisis under the Safe Third Country and First Country of Asylum Concept' (2016); Amnesty International, 'Greece: A Blue Print for Despair. Human Rights Impact of the EU–Turkey Deal' EUR 25/5664/2017.

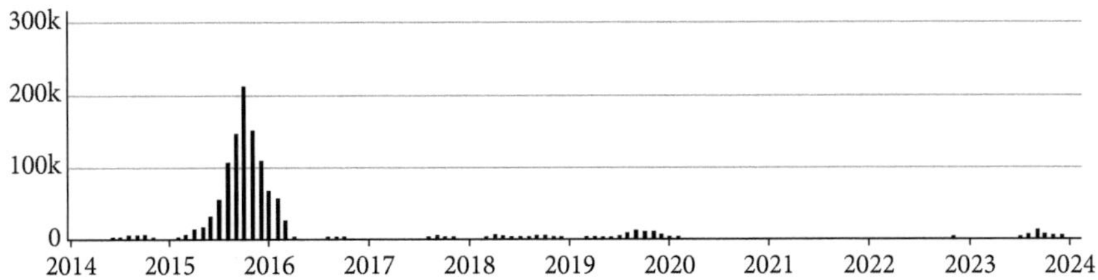

Figure 5.2 UNHCR data on monthly sea and land arrivals to Greece, 2014–2024.
Source: UNHCR operational data portal. <https://data2.unhcr.org/en/situations/mediterranean/location/5179#_ga=2.141817522.1659126773.1685179446-8305936.1685179446> accessed 18 December 2024.

reception centers continued to be overcrowded and NGOs denounced a worsening of health and safety conditions.[47]

From this brief analysis, we can say that EU law presents considerable advantages for migrant rights compared to Greek law. According to NGO reports, Greece fails to fulfill its EU-derived obligations in four main migration areas:

1. Access to asylum procedure (eg EU–Turkey statement and the concept of safe third countries);
2. Quality of the asylum procedure (eg no legal aid, no interview, no translator);
3. Treatment of vulnerable individuals;
4. Detention of undocumented migrants.

In line with the idea that the preliminary reference procedure can be used as the "infringement procedure" taken by the European citizen, these are also the areas where we should expect the emergence of EU legal mobilization.

4.2 Greek judges' supposed reluctance to make preliminary references

When asking why there are no migration references from Greece to the Court of Justice, the common answer is that Greek judges are reluctant to refer: "The low number of preliminary referrals by Greek courts could indicate a general reluctance to make use of the CJEU machinery."[48]

[47] Triandafyllidou (n 33) 558.
[48] ECRE (n 40) 12.

This conviction was corroborated by an important decision. As mentioned in the previous section, in 2016 the Member States concluded the EU–Turkey Statement whereby the Turkish government committed to readmitting to Turkish territory those Syrian nationals who arrived in Greece. Two pro-migrant lawyers tried to challenge the Statement in court by legally representing two Syrian nationals who risked being readmitted to Turkey and filed an appeal against the decision that declared their asylum request inadmissible. The case progressed to the last-instance administrative court, the Greek Council of State, where the lawyers asked to submit a preliminary reference regarding the definition of Turkey as a safe third country.[49] The Council ruled with a slim majority of thirteen to twelve that there is no reasonable doubt on the meaning of safe third country under EU law, thus there is no need to request a reference.[50] Among the many dissenting judges, two were vice presidents, a testament to the fracture of views that existed within the Council of State—and arguably to the fact that there were some doubts regarding the interpretation of the norm.

The Council of State's decision not to refer has led to speculation that the judges may be influenced by politico-strategic factors and are reluctant to refer sensitive questions to the ECJ.[51]

However, in the past, the Greek Council of State did not avoid references in delicate cases of potential constitutional clashes, and instead, it engaged in constructive dialogue with the ECJ.[52] Moreover, when discussing the political motives behind judgments, it is difficult to discern reality from speculation: even if individually interviewed, judges would hardly admit that their decisions are politico-strategic and thus not neutral.[53] And even admitting that the Council of State's decision not to refer was politically motivated, it seems far-fetched to think that for a decade, all Greek judges, from any court and tribunal, systematically refused to refer for politico-strategic reasons.

Although obtaining evidence regarding the political motivations behind references can be challenging, we possess data that allows us to assess whether

[49] The preliminary reference would have been on art 38 of the Asylum Procedure Directive 2013/32.

[50] Greek Council of State, Judgment of 22 September 2017, no 2347/2017 and no 2348/2017.

[51] ECRE (n 40) 12. And yet, in this respect, it is perhaps interesting to note that one of the dissenting vice presidents was Athanasios Rantos: Shortly after the judgment, he was promoted by the Greek government as President of the Council of State and then Advocate General at the ECJ. This may suggest his good reputation with the government despite the dissenting opinion.

[52] Panos Kapotas, 'Greek Council of State' (2014) 10 European Constitutional Law Review 162.

[53] This is evidenced by Krommendijk's study where he interviewed several national judges and found small evidence that their decision (not) to refer is motivated by politico-strategic reasons. Jasper Krommendijk, *National Courts and Preliminary References to the Court of Justice* (Edward Elgar Publishing 2021) 89.

Table 5.1 Total preliminary references from Greece until 2022.

Greek referring court	Number of references
Supreme Court	14
Council of State	64
Other Courts or Tribunals	120

Source: Court of Justice Annual Report 2022 - Statistics concerning the judicial activity of the Court of Justice, at 25.

Greek judges are reluctant to refer. Data on Greece's referral rate shows that Greece is among the Member States that refer the least, placing itself in twentieth position. However, with its 10 million inhabitants, Greece is also one of the smallest Member States and if we check by population size, the result changes quite dramatically.[54] Perhaps even more noteworthy, the Greek last-instance administrative court, the Council of State, exhibits a significantly higher inclination to refer compared to its civil and criminal law counterpart, the Greek Supreme Court. The latter has faced criticism from the ECtHR for its lack of reasoning behind its refusal to make references.[55] However, as the Supreme Court is not in charge of migration cases, its reluctance to refer bears no real implications for us here.

The data on Greek preliminary references is also useful to understand whether lower courts feel pressure not to refer. To be sure, as shown by Krommendijk, lower courts exhibit a "natural reluctance" to refer because references are difficult and time-consuming and judges want to solve disputes in their own court.[56] But in some national contexts, specific factors may further lead lower courts to withhold references; this was the case of the Netherlands, where a "gentlemen's agreement" between lower courts and the Dutch Council of State was deemed to be among the reasons why District Courts refrained from referring cases to the ECJ.[57]

Greece is a country with a civil law jurisdiction and a "bureaucratic-type judiciary," meaning that judges are highly independent from external political pressure since their selection and appointment procedures are determined by

[54] Broberg and Fenger (n 30) 492.

[55] *Georgiou v Greece*, ECtHR, Application no 57378/18, 14 March 2023.

[56] Krommendijk (n 53) 38.

[57] See Chapter 4 of this book. Kees Groenendijk, 'Waarom Rechters Niet Naar Luxemburg Gaan: Dialoog of Weerstand, Politieke Structuur of Rechtscultuur?' in Reyer Baas and others (eds), *Rechtspleging en rechtsbescherming. Liber amicorum voor prof. dr. Leny E. de Groot-van Leeuwen* (Kluwer 2015) 187.

judicial self-governing bodies.[58] One could argue that this makes the Greek judicial system very hierarchical, and lower courts do not dare to refer because this might harm their evaluation (made by senior judges) and thus judges' promotion. Evidence does not seem to support this hypothesis.

As Table 5.1 shows, Greek lower courts and tribunals are the main sources of preliminary references.[59] To understand whether submitting a preliminary reference was discouraged or seen as detrimental to a judge's career, I interviewed a Greek administrative judge who sent two preliminary references to the ECJ, once as a judge rapporteur and another as a member of the panel. The judge denied any pressure from higher courts not to refer or any detrimental impact on their career after the reference was made: "I did not have any problem, obviously. I mean there is no kind of pressure or anything." Still, they admitted that not every judge wants to receive the attention that comes with submitting a reference: "I mean, many judges don't want to attract so much attention to their work."[60]

The interview is in line with what has been found in surveys and in the literature, which is that some Greek lower-court judges might feel naturally intimidated by the task of making references. But this is not different from any other Member States and hardly explains the lack of references.[61]

Lastly, another influential theory to explain national judges' reluctance to refer is Wind's argument positing that courts in majoritarian democracies are less familiar with supranational judicial review and thus less prone to refer than courts in countries with constitutional democracies.[62]

This does not seem to apply to Greece, as judicial review is not alien nor new to the Greek judicial system. Although Greece does not have a constitutional court, it has a tradition of constitutional review that dates back to the nineteenth century, when the courts themselves "gradually and incrementally established the power of the judiciary to deny the application of unconstitutional statutes."[63] Then, in 1927, ordinary courts' power of constitutional review was

[58] Michael Ioannidis, 'The Judiciary' in Kevin Featherstone and Dimitri A Sotiropoulos (eds), *The Oxford Handbook of Modern Greek Politics* (OUP 2020) 127.

[59] One might find this obvious, as there are more lower courts than upper courts. However, only last-instance courts have the obligation to refer and in countries such as the Netherlands and Ireland, apex courts are responsible for most of the references.

[60] Interview with Greek judge, 4 May 2023.

[61] Krommendijk (n 53); John Coughlan, Jaroslav Opravil, and Wolfgang Heusel, 'Judicial Training in the European Union Member States' (European Parliament's Committee on Legal Affairs 2011) PE 453.198 EN.

[62] Wind (n 3).

[63] Ioannidis (n 58) 119.

enshrined in the Greek constitution.[64] Thus, "Greek courts generally follow a diffuse, incidental, and concrete system of review,"[65] meaning that ordinary courts, from the first to the last instance, are used to revise the legitimacy of the legislation by themselves, setting aside unconstitutional laws if necessary. To be sure, in the hierarchical Greek judicial system, the task of engaging in constitutional review is often left to the Council of State, which, for this reason, is considered "Greece's constitutional court par excellence"[66] and has displayed judicial activism in the recent past.[67]

In conclusion, data on Greek judges does not point to a general reluctance to refer. Given its size, Greece has referred an average amount of cases, of which almost half were referred by the Council of State, which also serves as the last-instance migration and asylum court. Regarding lower courts, their reference rate, judicial culture, and hierarchy suggest that these might feel some self-restraint, but probably not to the point of avoiding references.

4.3 No access to (higher) courts

In a book chapter on migrant detention, two Greek administrative judges offer an alternative explanation for non-referrals. The chapter explains that "Greek administrative judges regularly encounter problems of interpretation of EU law when reviewing detention decisions,"[68] however the Greek judicial remedies pose some "inherent constraints."[69]

Migrant detention is one of the areas where the Greek system exhibits some tension with EU law, as confirmed by the fact that the EU Commission sent two letters of formal notice against Greece for failing to comply with the Return Directive 2008/115.[70] The alleged infringements are many, ranging from the

[64] ibid.

[65] Julia Iliopoulos-Strangas and Stylianos-Ioannis G Koutnatzis, 'Greece: Constitutional Courts as Positive Legislators' in Allan R Brewer-Carías (ed), *Constitutional Courts as Positive Legislators: A Comparative Law Study* (CUP 2011) 544.

[66] ibid 546.

[67] Dia Anagnostou, 'Judicial Activism in the Name of the Nation: Reneging on the Integration of Immigrants in Greece' (2016) 43 Journal of Law and Society 596.

[68] Angeliki Papapanagiotou-Leza and Stergios Kofinis, 'Can the Return Directive Contribute to Protection for Rejected Asylum Seekers and Irregular Migrants in Detention? The Case of Greece' in Madalina Moraru, Galina Cornelisse, and Philippe De Bruycker (eds), *Law and Judicial Dialogue on the Return of Irregular Migrants from the European Union* (Hart Publishing 2020) 282.

[69] ibid.

[70] European Commission, INFR(2014)2231. The Commission issued first a letter of formal notice, mentioned by Papapanagiotou-Leza and Kofinis (n 68) 290. Then it sent a second letter on 29 September 2022.

maximum duration of detention, the reasons to detain migrants, and the definition of the phrase "illegal stay."[71]

So why Greek judges haven't made any references on the Return Directive? The inherent constraints mentioned by the two Greek judges consist of the procedural norms that regulate administrative detention and limit the ability of the judges to interact with the ECJ.[72] Two elements are critical in this respect: first, the decision of the first-instance court is not subject to appeal; second, the law requires that the decision is taken swiftly. Thus, "judges prefer to avoid the time and energy-consuming procedure of preliminary references and, instead, focus on the factual circumstances of the case."[73]

Access to appropriate judicial review is a problem in asylum determination procedures too, for two reasons. First, the asylum procedure in Greece has a four-layer structure, of which the first two are before administrative bodies (Figure 5.3).[74] This makes Greece different from most EU Member States, where courts are competent to review first-instance asylum decisions.[75] In Greece, only after the application is reviewed a second time can the asylum seeker appeal and go before an administrative court and, eventually, the Council of State.[76] It is disputed whether the first two bodies, being administrative, can be considered a "court or tribunal" for the purposes of Article 267 of the Treaty on the Functioning of the European Union (TFEU), but there are good reasons to think that at least the Independent Appeals Committee is a court or tribunal (it is independent, its decisions are subject to appeal before administrative courts, from 2017 to 2019 two of its members were administrative judges, and today all its members are).[77] The uncertainty around this issue may have discouraged members of the Committee from making a reference.

[71] ibid 288; Danai Angeli and Dia Anagnostou, 'A Shortfall of Rights and Justice: Judicial Review of Immigration Detention in Greece' (2022) 14 European Journal of Legal Studies 97, 104.

[72] Papapanagiotou-Leza and Kofinis (n 68) 297. The authors mention: "(i) the legislative requirement for a swift procedure and an immediate delivery of the judgment; (ii) the lack of appeals against this judgment; (iii) the requirement to provide only brief reasons for the judgment; and (iv) the lack of specific procedural rules for the objections against detention."

[73] ibid 299.

[74] The composition of the appeals authority has changed. This body was initially called Appeals Authority and was composed of three experts. A reform changed its name and its composition. For an overview, AIDA country reports at <https://asylumineurope.org/reports/country/greece/asylum-procedure/general/short-overview-asylum-procedure/> accessed 18 December 2024.

[75] EASO, *Border Procedures for Asylum Applications in EU + Countries*, 2020, 14 <https://euaa.europa.eu/sites/default/files/publications/Border-procedures-asylum-applications-2020.pdf> accessed 18 December 2024.

[76] Subsequent reforms changed the composition of these four layers, eg before the administrative court competent to review the committee's decision was the administrative appeal court, while now it is the first instance court.

[77] Paul Craig and Gráinne de Búrca, *EU Law: Text, Cases, and Materials* (6th edn, OUP 2015) 498.

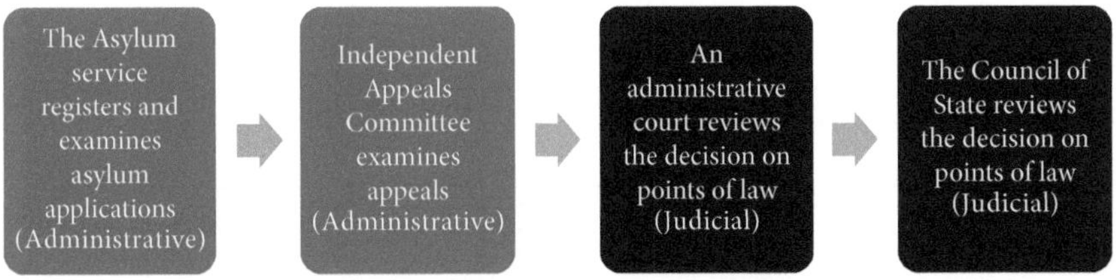

Figure 5.3 The structure of the Greek asylum procedure.

When discussing access to court, it is also important to consider that legal assistance to asylum seekers was not regularly provided in Greece. Although the EU Asylum Procedure Directive requires free legal assistance and representation at the appeals stages of the asylum procedure,[78] the Greek government struggled to set up a legal aid scheme for asylum seekers, which was introduced only in 2016 and started operating in September 2017, and even then not without problems.[79] As we shall see, NGOs partially filled the gap left by the state (also thanks to funding from the EU Commission) but this free legal representation covers only the second administrative stage of the procedure, leaving the judicial parts out. Asylum seekers who want to bring their case before the administrative courts, and eventually the Council of State, must apply for legal aid under standard Greek law provisions, which in itself is a complex procedure and requires legal assistance.[80]

A final practical obstacle was brought to my attention by an NGO member and lawyer; in the experience of the organization, after receiving the second negative decision on the asylum application, "the great majority of our clients leave. So, we don't have a hearing in the end."[81] The problem is that more than a year can pass between the moment when the appeal is filed and the hearing before the administrative court.

> So, in the meantime, people are leaving illegally. They go to Germany. . . Either they leave or they reapply for asylum. So, they would rather consider a

[78] Art 20 of the Asylum Procedure Directive 2013/32.

[79] AIDA, Country Report: Greece 2021, 71.

[80] Interview with an RSA member. Also the AIDA (n 89) 47, mentions that there are legal and practical problems: "These range from strict and complex procedural rules for judicial review, requiring applications to be well-substantiated, written in Greek and registered by a lawyer; to the Court's delays from 10 days of up to 4 months in deciding on suspensive effect, thereby leaving applicants at risk of deportation; to limited access to free legal assistance."

[81] Interview with HIAS member, 15 May 2023.

Table 5.2 Asylum applications in Greece.

Number of application	2013	2014	2015	2016	2017	2018	2019	2020	2021	2022
1st application	7,860	7,585	11,370	49,875	56,940	64,975	74,910	37,860	22,660	29,125
Subsequent application	NA	NA	1,098	1,238	1,708	1,984	2,369	2,711	5,695	8,245

Source: Authors' elaboration of Eurostat data and AIDA National country report—Greece.

Note: AIDA reports are published every year on the ECRE website. They provide data on asylum subsequent applications for the years 2015–2020 which are not available on Eurostat.

> subsequent application, which is a different story. But it's understandable when, for instance, they are rejected on the safe third country basis. They would go for a subsequent application because Greece has this informal policy, super informal, that if you've been here for more than a year, they will examine the merits of your application... So, either they leave or they pull out of the judicial procedure because they want to reapply for asylum. And yes, it's nine out of ten.[82]

For an applicant receiving a rejection or an inadmissibility decision, it is easier to file a new application rather than go through complex and costly judicial review proceedings. Data on asylum applications confirms this, showing an exceptionally high number of subsequent applications, as displayed in Table 5.2. Remarkably, data also shows that the number of subsequent applications has grown exponentially in the last years, raising the question of whether this is a more recent phenomenon and thus unable to explain the lack of references between 2008 and 2020.

This subsection has thus far outlined several obstacles regarding access to courts that hamper migrants' ability to reach Greek higher courts. However, it is important to recall two procedures provided by the Greek legal system which can be described as a road to the Council of State. The first is the "pilot trial", a procedure introduced in 2010 that allows courts to refer their case to the Council of State "when an issue of general interest with effects on a larger number of people is at stake."[83] The procedure can be activated upon request of one of the parties in the proceedings or *ex officio* by a lower court.

[82] . Interview with HIAS member, 15 May 2023. This practice was confirmed also in the interview with Metadrasi member, 3 August 2023.

[83] Art 1 of Greek Law 3900/2010, 'Rationalization of procedures and expedited administrative trial', entered into force on January 1, 2011. Ioannidis (n 58) 120.

The second procedure is the annulment action provided for by Article 95 of the Greek Constitution. This enables litigants to petition directly before the Council of State to annul "enforceable acts of the administrative authorities for excess of power or violation of the law."[84] The norm also applies to "executive organs' omissions despite their obligation to act."[85] This procedure has great potential for challenging administration acts and omissions, and indeed it has been used by political parties and NGOs in the migration field in the past.[86] Its potential to trigger preliminary references is further proven by the fact that one of the 2023 references was issued in a case brought to the Council of State via petition. And yet, before then, it had never been used to ask for preliminary references in the migration field.

5. Internal factors: The presence of altruistic actors with relevant resources

The previous section has concluded that even if there are structural obstacles to the emergence of migration references, the Greek LOS is not closed. While Greek judges are not generally reluctant to submit preliminary references, there are significant obstacles to access to court that make legal mobilization before the ECJ harder.

This section turns to the actors of the mobilization to test the second hypothesis of this study, which posits that the absence of EU legal mobilization is due to a lack of altruistic actors or resources.

Many groups promote migrant rights in Greece. From online reports and conversations with Greek academics, I could identify eight leading organizations that regularly provide legal support to migrants:

- The Greek Refugee Council (GCR)
- Refugee Support Aegean (RSA)
- United Nations High Commissioner for Refugees—Greece (UNHCR)
- Hebrew Immigrant Aid Society—Greece (HIAS)
- Metadrasi
- European Council on Refugees and Exiles (ECRE)
- Greek Helsinki Monitor
- The Hellenic Action for Human Rights

[84] Iliopoulos-Strangas and Koutnatzis (n 65) 554.
[85] ibid 554.
[86] Anagnostou (n 67) 601.

Three of these organizations, UNHCR, GCR, and Metadrasi, have played a crucial role during the so-called refugee crisis. From 2015 to 2017, GCR and Metadrasi provided free legal assistance to thousands of asylum applicants arriving on the Greek islands within the framework of a program partially funded by the European Commission and coordinated by UNHCR.[87] The program ran until September 2017 and was a way to compensate for the Greek state's inability to provide free legal aid to all the applicants during the appeals stage of the asylum application, as required by EU law.[88]

HIAS is an international NGO that operates in different countries to promote asylum seekers' and refugees' rights. Its office in Greece mainly deals with litigation for migrant rights. RSA is a rather new organization active since 2017; its focus on European legal strategies (both EU and ECHR-derived) makes it an excellent candidate for EU legal mobilization.

Remarkably, RSA and GCR are the two organizations that obtained a preliminary reference by the Council of State in 2023.[89] They are thus an excellent interviewee to ask why this did not occur earlier?

ECRE is a bit different from the other organizations because it is mainly a European network of legal-focused pro-migrant organizations. It is a reference point for migration lawyers and activists.

Differently from the other organizations, the Greek Helsinki Monitor and the Hellenic Action for Human Rights are two Greek NGOs that do not focus exclusively on migrant and refugee rights. They work in the field of minorities and civil rights, which led them to represent many migration and asylum cases before domestic and international courts.

This overview presents a wealth of organizations working for migrant rights in Greece. However, while the presence of migrant rights defenders is essential for legal mobilization to happen, it might not be sufficient. To mobilize EU law and convince national judges to refer, altruistic actors need specific resources.

From the outset, it is important to note that migrant rights defenders in Greece have often operated in crisis mode. While the government was trying to build an asylum system quickly,[90] NGOs such as RSA and Metadrasi were filling the gaps left by the state, helping the unprecedented number of people reaching Greece's borders and islands, often in situations of overcrowding and

[87] AIDA (n 89) 48.

[88] But also after the program ended, the Greek legal aid program remained unable to cover all the demands. From AIDA Country Report Greece 2018, at 16: "Out of a total of 15,355 appeals lodged in 2018, only 3,351 (21.8%) asylum seekers benefited from the state-funded legal aid scheme."

[89] *Elliniko Symvoulio gia tous Prosfyges and Ypostirixi Prosfygon sto Aigaio [Greek Refugee Council and Refugee Support Aegean]* (n 35).

[90] McDonough and Tsourdi (n 31) 89.

underfunding. Since 2019, migration NGOs experienced further difficulties in carrying out their work because of growing hostility toward them; the UN Special Rapporteur for Human Rights Defenders noted that "[d]efenders active in this area, including lawyers and journalists, have been facing criminalization, intimidation, harassment and smear campaigns."[91]

To understand Greek actors' perceptions, strategies, and resources, I relied on interviews with members of the core legal team of the organizations listed above, in a total of nine interviews. This was not possible in the case of Metadrasi,[92] so I interviewed one of its former lawyers. All the people that I interviewed were Greek and spoke good English. The interviews were conducted via video call, except for two interviews conducted by phone. The interviews concerned two main topics: 1) whether they have ever asked for a preliminary reference, and 2) their connections to EU legal experts and academia. During the interviews, a third issue emerged: their preference for the ECtHR. I will address each of these issues in order.

5.1 Altruistic actors' perceptions of the preliminary reference procedure

Lawyers and NGO members were eager to share the vast experience and knowledge acquired by defending migrant rights in Greece. However, they had little to say about preliminary references. Most of them have never tried to obtain a preliminary reference from Greek courts and some of them never considered this option. When I asked why, they gave me different reasons. Some confirmed that there are difficulties in accessing Greek courts, but they also added that they didn't come across an issue that they wanted to submit via preliminary reference. In addition, Greek judges would not refer anyway. Some of them said that they would rather go to the ECtHR.

For instance, RSA is one of the organizations that engages more with EU legal strategies.[93] Together with GCR, it brought to the Council of State the

[91] Special Rapporteur on the situation of human rights defenders, Mary Lawlor, 'Report on the Visit to Greece' (2023) A/HRC/52/29/Add.1 para 65.

[92] I sent several emails to current and former senior lawyers of the organization but I never got a reply.

[93] RSA did so beyond preliminary references: They filed complaints to the EU Commission regarding the definition of Turkey as a safe third country (RSA, 'Greece arbitrarily deems Turkey a "safe third country" in flagrant violation of rights', 1 March 2022 <https://rsaegean.org/en/turkey-safe-third-country/> accessed 18 December 2024) and regarding the incorrect transposition of the Asylum Procedure Directive and Reception Condition Directive in the Greek legal system (RSA, 'Asylum seekers in Greece lodge complaint on infringement of Asylum Directives', 16 June 2021 <https://rsaegean.org/

case that led to the first migration reference in 2023 regarding Turkey being a safe third country.[94] However, it noted that:

> with the exception of a safe third country, we wouldn't necessarily have done this for other types of cases . . . We haven't necessarily done this in other areas to the extent that we may not have found an issue that needs to be clarified, at least on the specific issues that we're sort of working on. But very often we will have arguments that relate to the directives. So, to disapply domestic provisions, because they're not in line with the directive directly invoking provisions of the directive. Also, for Greek judges, that's not necessarily the easiest thing to sort of engage with. But indeed, I wouldn't say that we have systematically incorporated references in our litigation.[95]

The other applicant in the case that led to the 2023 migration reference is the GCR. It is "the first and oldest Greek NGO which provides legal assistance to persons in need of international protection"[96] and the organization that engaged the most with the preliminary reference procedure. During the interview, the GCR member mentioned two attempts to obtain a reference, one in 2014 and another in 2022.[97] The 2014 attempt concerned detention, which is decided by first-instance administrative judges, against whose decision there is no remedy. According to the interviewee, "it was maybe too much for the first-instance court to send something to Luxembourg."[98] More generally, the GCR member believes that there is a general reluctance to refer by Greek courts and in particular by the Greek Council of State, allegedly because migration "is too close to politically sensitive issues such as borders and national security", or because the judges "don't really feel that they need to do that; they feel . . . capable of replying" to a question regarding the interpretation of EU law.[99]

One episode corroborated Greek migrant rights defenders' perception that Greek courts are reluctant to refer. We must go back to the years of the refugee

en/asylum-seekers-in-greece-lodge-complaint-on-infringement-of-asylum-directives/> accessed 18 December 2024).

[94] *Elliniko Symvoulio gia tous Prosfyges and Ypostirixi Prosfygon sto Aigaio [Greek Refugee Council and Refugee Support Aegean]* (n 35).

[95] Interview with RSA member, 4 May 2023.

[96] Interview with GCR member, 31 May 2023.

[97] The other one was GCR's intervention in a case before the Council of State which gave rise to decision 1398/2022. The text of the judgment does not mention the preliminary reference request.

[98] Interview with GCR member, 31 May 2023.

[99] Interview with GCR member, 31 May 2023.

crisis, more specifically to 2017, when the Council of State delivered its (in)famous decision not to refer regarding the legitimacy of the EU–Turkey Deal. At that time, the Greek Asylum Service was declaring all the asylum applications submitted by Syrian nationals inadmissible, in compliance with the Deal.[100] Metadrasi and GCR were in charge of providing legal aid to asylum seekers on the islands,[101] so they started appealing these rejections. According to a former Metadrasi lawyer, they inserted the request to make a preliminary reference to the ECJ into each appeal: "We had . . . three standard paragraphs in the end that we were putting in our memos."[102] This was confirmed by another lawyer formerly working for GCR on Samos: "It was almost a template argument that we used in our submissions as GCR."[103]

Perhaps unsurprisingly, all these template requests for preliminary reference were ignored by the Asylum Appeals Committees. However, two of the Syrian cases were further appealed and brought to the Council of State; here the Syrian applicants were represented by two of the best-known Greek migration lawyers (Giota Massouridou and Marianna Tzeferakou) who reiterated the request to have the case referred to the ECJ, probably in a more articulate way.[104] This time, the Council of State did not ignore their request but, by a slim majority, refused it, nevertheless.

The Council of State's decision was eagerly awaited by all migrant rights defenders in Greece, including legal aid lawyers on the Greek islands. When the news of dismissal arrived on the islands, it left a lasting impression on the possibility of reaching the ECJ:

> We had this feeling that . . . it's not an open road; in general, that what we were asking for in most of the cases was rejected. . . I think this was especially after the first Syrian cases when they were rejected by the Council of State. So, I think that after this . . . all of us were very disappointed.[105]
>
> I remember we were all on the islands expecting to see how these cases would be decided, to see how we continue litigation on the islands. And when the decisions came out in September 2017, I remember that we said: "OK, if

[100] Mariana Gkliati, 'The Application of the EU–Turkey Agreement: A Critical Analysis of the Decisions of the Greek Appeals Committees' (2017) 10 European Journal of Legal Studies 80, 86.

[101] AIDA (n 89) 48. This was part of a program sponsored by the EU Commission and UNHCR.

[102] Interview with Metadrasi former member, 3 August 2023.

[103] Interview with Senior Legal Officer at ECRE, 19 September 2023.

[104] This is the same case I mentioned in subsection 4.2 of this chapter, Greek Council of State, cases no 2347/2017 and no 2348/2017 (n 50). I tried to contact both lawyers several times but I haven't managed to secure an interview.

[105] Interview with Metadrasi former member, 3 August 2023.

> this is the response of this Council of State, we'll continue our litigation to protect people individually at least." I remember this was the feeling at the time.[106]

It is relevant to point out that when talking about preliminary references, almost all the interviewees mentioned the 2017 Council of State's decision. In the NGOs' account, this decision was a critical juncture. It shaped their perception of Greek courts, strengthening their conviction that these courts are reluctant to refer migration cases:

> The discussion at that time in 2017 confirmed this fear that, because migration is such a political issue, judges are careful. And reluctant... we knew migration is a very political area and we knew this can affect judicial action. And we felt that this was confirmed by those decisions.[107]

When I asked a GCR member why they thought that the Council of State changed its position and decided to refer in 2023, they replied that this has to do with political considerations too. First, the legal issue at stake was different as it was no longer about the definition of a safe third country but whether Turkey should be removed from the list of safe third countries because it does not allow readmissions. Second, the factual situation was different as there is a considerable number of Syrians in limbo because they cannot be readmitted. Third, the Council of State realized that the EU–Turkey Statement was not a solution for Greece, so the judges should no longer shield the Statement from judicial review:

> In my understanding, back in 2016, there was the idea that the EU–Turkey statement could be a solution to the refugee crisis in Europe. Now, we don't have the same understanding after seven years of applications. I mean, it's well known that despite the EU–Turkey statements, the number of applicants that have been indeed readmitted to Turkey is really low. . . [T]he refugee issue is not so critical for the time being in Greece. . . . [I]t's [because] we have a very low number of arrivals, which has to do also with pushbacks—but that's another story. You know, it's not on the peak of the political agenda. So, I think that the Council, the judges, were not feeling so much the stress that they have to deal with a very hot political issue.[108]

[106] Interview with Senior Legal Officer at ECRE, 19 September 2023.
[107] Interview with Senior Legal Officer at ECRE, 19 September 2023.
[108] Interview with GCR member, 31 May 2023.

These interviews give the general feeling that civil society actors see Greek courts as too sensitive to political considerations and thus willing to shield Greek law from supranational judicial scrutiny.

Lastly, it is useful to compare these interviews with the view of the administrative court judge who sent a preliminary reference request on asylum in August 2023. The court referred *ex officio*: "the lawyer never proposed to actually refer the case to the CJEU. She had no idea that we were going to do that. She didn't even think of saying that there is some problem, some conflict with EU law at that point."[109]

I then asked the judge whether, in Greece, lawyers tend to submit legal memos which can be used as a basis for preliminary reference requests, and this was the answer:

> No, it can be the case before the Council of State. I'm not so sure about that... Normally in our cases we don't get that... Many of the applicants come with legal aid, so lawyers are definitely not specialized. They're just random lawyers who have no idea what they're talking about and they make a lot of mistakes, too. So, it's far, far from actually being able to draft a preliminary reference. They have much bigger problems with their appeals. And even specialized lawyers from NGOs usually have a huge backlog, a huge workload. So, they cannot really spend that kind of energy doing that. They sometimes get somebody to draft a good legal argument and that is repeated over and over and over again. But it rarely is really a question of referring something to the CJEU.[110]

To sum up, we can say that Greek civil society actors have only sporadically tried to mobilize before the ECJ. One reason lies in migrant right defenders' perception that Greek judges are reluctant to refer, in a way similar to what was found by van der Pas in the Netherlands.[111] Here in Greece, such conviction seems linked to the belief that judges follow politico-strategic considerations that affect their willingness to refer cases to the ECJ and their receptiveness to migrant supporters' requests. The perception of a closed legal opportunity structure was strengthened by the 2017 decision of the Council of State, which left a lasting impression on lawyers and activists. However, this is not all the story, as the next subsections will show.

[109] Interview with Greek Judge, 4 May 2023.
[110] Interview with Greek Judge, 4 May 2023.
[111] van der Pas (n 13) 13.

5.2 The lack of EU legal expertise

Migrant rights defenders often rely on scant financial resources. They have little funding, small legal teams, and face unfriendly or hostile government policies. Despite all this, from small offices with one or two lawyers they manage to mobilize and reach the Court of Justice. This is largely thanks to their non-material resources, among which the availability of EU legal expertise occupies a special place. This expertise can be in-house, such as provided by Eurolawyers among their staff, but often it is provided for free by external allies, such as EU law academics.

EU legal expertise is valuable not only for enhancing litigants' understanding of EU law and "ghostwriting" preliminary questions.[112] EU legal expertise is also indispensable to reveal openings in the EU LOS and raise altruistic actors' legal knowledge. For instance, when the Greek lawmaker decided that migrants could be detained on public security grounds pending removal, EU legal experts would understand that this offers an opportunity for contestation via the Return Directive, which does not allow administrative detention for reasons of public security.[113]

In Greece, there are only three law schools and, at the time of writing, none offers a course in EU migration law. When I asked migrant rights defenders in Greece whether they ever received help from legal scholars or EU law experts, they replied in the negative. The GCR member told me:

> In the drafting? Not really, because it's in Greek. . . . no, we don't have the support of academics from Greece, because . . . there are not a lot of people that are dealing with such issues in Greece. . . We do have contacts with the Greek academia. However, the Greek academia . . . are not really involved in issues of EU law on asylum. They are more [interested in] discussing . . . more geopolitical issues. So, things that have to do with integration and the understanding of the refugee phenomenon or things like that; but not as such, the interpretation of Article 38 on safe third countr[ies] . . . .[114]

[112] Tommaso Pavone, *The Ghostwriters: Lawyers and the Politics behind the Judicial Construction of Europe* (CUP 2022).

[113] Under the Directive, there are only two valid grounds for migrant detention: risk of absconding or hampering the removal procedure. Art 15 of Directive 2008/115/EC of the European Parliament and of the Council of 16 December 2008 on common standards and procedures in Member States for returning illegally staying third-country nationals, OJ L 348, 24 December 2008.

[114] Interview with GCR member, 31 May 2023.

HIAS confirmed this:

> [I]t's not that we have been approached by people to collaborate. I don't think anybody has done this... Because we don't have law clinics in Greece. It's not really a thing either. So, I would say that we have collaborated more with foreign academics than Greeks.[115]

During the refugee crisis, time constraints and resources might have played a role in the NGOs' capacity to think strategically and collaborate with academics. In the words of a Metadrasi lawyer providing legal aid on one of the Greek islands during the most difficult years between 2016 and 2017:

> I think that the general problem in Greece is that ... everything was so massive, so many cases. So, you didn't have the time ... to spend a lot of time to examine the case from different angles and aspects. You were supposed to do everything, to react very quickly. And especially in the border procedure, one day, the applicant was there and the other one, after the rejection, he disappeared. You didn't know where they went. So, maybe this also responds to your question why we didn't have ... a collaboration with academia, because we didn't have the time to, we didn't have the luxury.[116]

I recent years ECRE has tried to cover this gap and it provides expert opinions to Greek organizations. According to the member I interviewed, the NGOs working in Greece have a very good knowledge of EU law and procedures but financial constraints might impact their ability to get training: Greek lawyers "work under bad conditions" with little access to training and travel to undertake networking and exchanges, as is normal in other countries.[117]

5.3 The preference for an alternative venue: The ECtHR

Through the interviews I could detect a last reason for altruistic actors' lack of engagement with the ECJ: their preference for the ECtHR. When I asked the Greek Helsinki Monitor whether it has ever tried to persuade a Greek judge

[115] Interview with HIAS member, 15 May 2023.
[116] Interview with Metadrasi member, 3 August 2023.
[117] Interview with ECRE member, 19 September 2023.

to refer, my interviewee replied that they never did, because it was difficult to reach Greek courts, but they immediately added: "By the way, I'm not even sure that, if we reached somewhere, we would have gone there. Because we have the case law of the European Court [of Human Rights]." The members of the NGO "don't find the need to make a referral to the Court of Justice."[118] Another experienced migration lawyer told me that while they represented more than 5,000 applicants before the ECtHR, they asked for a reference from Greek judges only three or four times as they are less familiar with the procedure.[119]

While it is common to have lawyers specialized in applications before the ECtHR, and thus less familiar with other courts, in Greece this seems to be a general attitude. Other interviewees told me that they see the ECtHR as a "more reachable" court.[120]

The interview with a staff member of the Greek office of UNHCR confirmed this. They explained to me that, although in Europe their "judicial engagement" strategy involves intervening before both European courts, in Greece they mainly focus on the ECtHR. This is because, in Greece, the ECtHR is perceived as the main jurisdiction for human rights violations, including violations in the asylum and reception systems.[121] Moreover, the general lack of preliminary references from Greece prevented the UNHCR from filing online submissions to the ECJ as they take on in cases referred from other countries.[122]

The predilection for the ECtHR resonates with Greece's history of litigation for migrants and minorities before the that Court. Although compared to other countries such as the UK, Greece "lacks a tradition of public interest litigation,"[123] it has a long tradition of litigating before the ECtHR, including for migrant rights. According to Anagnostou, "[i]n Greece, from 2008–2009 onwards, a group of lawyers with a progressive and/or leftist orientation began

[118] Interview with a member of the Greek Helsinki Monitor, 3 February 2024.

[119] Interview with independent lawyer, 2 February 2023.

[120] Interview with HIAS member, 18 September 2023.

[121] Interview with UNHCR staff member, 12 April 2023.

[122] Contrary to the ECtHR, the ECJ does not allow amicus curiae or third-party interventions from persons who were not a party in the national proceedings *a quo*. For this reason, the UNHCR publishes online its third-party submissions, where everybody (including ECJ judges) can read them: <https://www.unhcr.org/publications/unhcr-interventions-court-justice-eu> accessed 18 December 2024. Jasper Krommendijk and Kris van der Pas, 'To Intervene or Not to Intervene: Intervention before the Court of Justice of the European Union in Environmental and Migration Law' (2022) 26 The International Journal of Human Rights 1394; Virginia Passalacqua, 'Who Mobilizes the Court? Migrant Rights Defenders Before the Court of Justice of the EU' (2022) 15 Law and Development Review 381; Ilaria Anrò, 'L'amicus Curiae Presso La Corte Di Giustizia Dell'Unione Europea: Qualche Riflessione per l'apertura Delle Porte Del Kirchberg' [2023] Rivista del Contenzioso Europeo 62.

[123] Evangelia Psychogiopoulou, 'European Courts and the Rights of Migrants and Asylum Seekers in Greece' in Dia Anagnostou (ed), *Rights and Courts in Pursuit of Social Change: Legal Mobilisation in the Multi-Level European System* (Bloomsbury Publishing 2014).

to systematically bring migrant-related complaints before domestic courts and in the Strasbourg Court to challenge restrictive immigration detention practices and highly deficient asylum procedures."[124] Interestingly, in this case, the lack of access to courts and judicial remedies helps lawyers as they easily pass the "exhaustion of remedy" condition.[125]

The ECtHR and the ECJ are not equivalent nor alternative courts; they have different mandates and jurisdictions. When it comes to asylum, however, there is a lot of overlap between the two because the EU asylum legislation is to a great extent derived from international and human rights law. Thus, looking at the number of ECtHR asylum judgments issued in proceedings against Greece can be revealing. While until 2023, Greece lacked asylum preliminary references to the ECJ, there were plentiful Greek cases that went before the ECtHR. According to the DICTA database on asylum judgments issued by the ECtHR, among the EU countries, Greece is second only to France (see Figure 5.4) in cases that came before it.[126] It is worth noting that, according to the data available, many of the ECtHR cases against Greece pre-date the so-called refugee crisis and the 2017 Council of State's decision not to refer (Figure 5.5);[127] this excludes the fact that collective actors went to Strasbourg in reaction to Greek courts' reluctance to refer, but it is a pre-existing legal strategy.

Why do Greek migrant rights defenders seem to prefer Strasbourg over Luxembourg? Arguably, the ECtHR takes longer to issue a judgment (up to ten years), and, depending on the issue, it applies equal or lower standards than the ECJ.[128] Also in terms of the effectiveness of its judgments, the ECtHR lacks the systemic impact of preliminary rulings, which are binding on all the Member States' courts.[129] While it is true that the same violation

[124] Dia Anagnostou, *The European Convention of Human Rights Regime: Reform of Immigration and Minority Policies from Afar* (Routledge 2022) 115.

[125] Anagnostou (n 124) 83.

[126] DICTA: Digital Case Tool on Asylum <https://www.dicta.eu/fmi/webd/dicta?homeurl = https://www.dicta.eu> accessed 18 December 2024.

[127] However the DICTA database has important limitations: it lists judgments, not pending cases, thus it lacks many applications filed in the last years which still await a decision.

[128] For instance, this is the case of detention of asylum seekers: Victor Davio, 'Detention in the Hungarian Transit Zones: A Case of Higher Fundamental Rights Protection by EU Law Vis-à-Vis the ECHR' (2022) 3 European Law Review 393–409; in general on the relationship between EU and ECHR standards: Gráinne De Búrca, 'The Evolution of EU Human Rights Law' in Paul Craig and Gráinne de Búrca (eds), *The Evolution of EU Law* (OUP 2021) 495.

[129] In the words of a legal NGO that has recently brought two applications to the ECtHR against illegal push backs: "Given the ECtHR's structural and procedural limitations, a positive decision in these two cases would be limited to the facts of these individual cases and bring partial redress only for the named Applicants. The proceedings are therefore insufficient to condemn the systematic nature of the crimes being committed, which the Legal Centre Lesvos has previously demonstrated amount to Crimes Against Humanity." Legal Center Lesvos, statement published on Facebook on 22 December 2021 <https://www.facebook.com/LesvosLegal/posts/4951351631570177> accessed 18 December 2024.

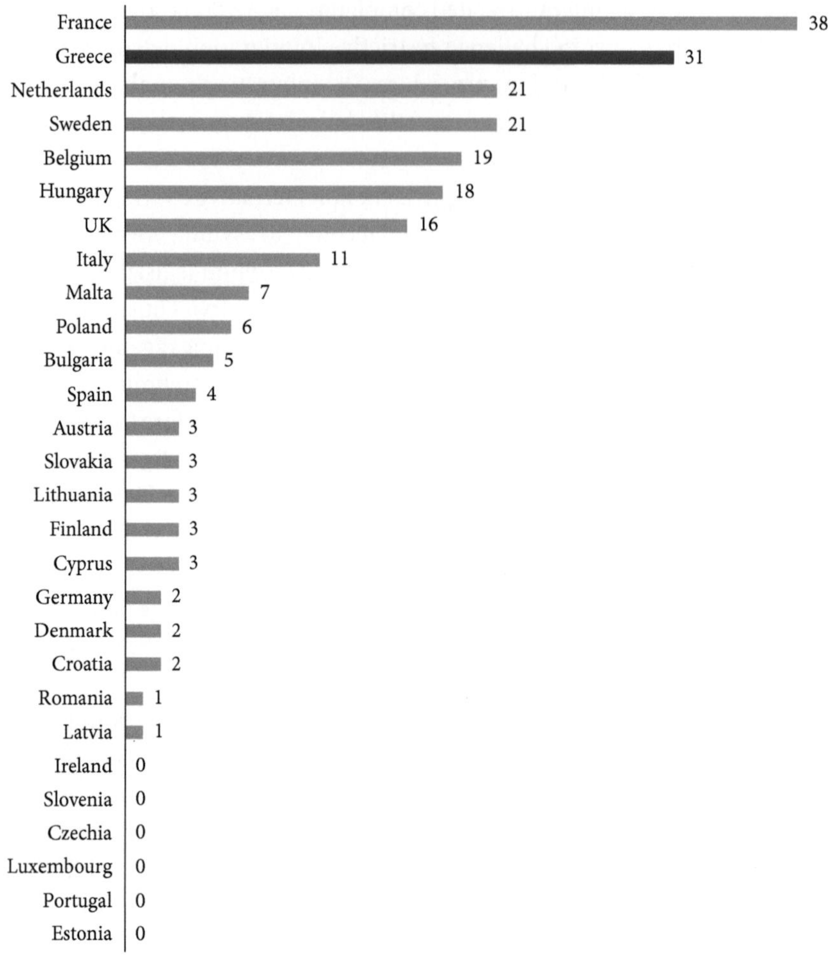

Figure 5.4 Judgments decided by the ECtHR in the field of asylum and refugees from 1989 to 2023.
Source: DICTA database elaborated by the author.

can be sanctioned before different courts and through different remedies,[130] it is also important to notice that some claims can be brought only before the ECJ. For instance, the ECtHR cannot rule on the legitimacy of actions and

[130] Nikolas Feith Tan and Thomas Gammeltoft-Hansen, 'A Topographical Approach to Accountability for Human Rights Violations in Migration Control' (2020) 21 German Law Journal 335; Annick Pijnenburg and Kris van der Pas, 'Strategic Litigation against European Migration Control Policies: The Legal Battleground of the Central Mediterranean Migration Route' (2022) 24 European Journal of Migration and Law 401.

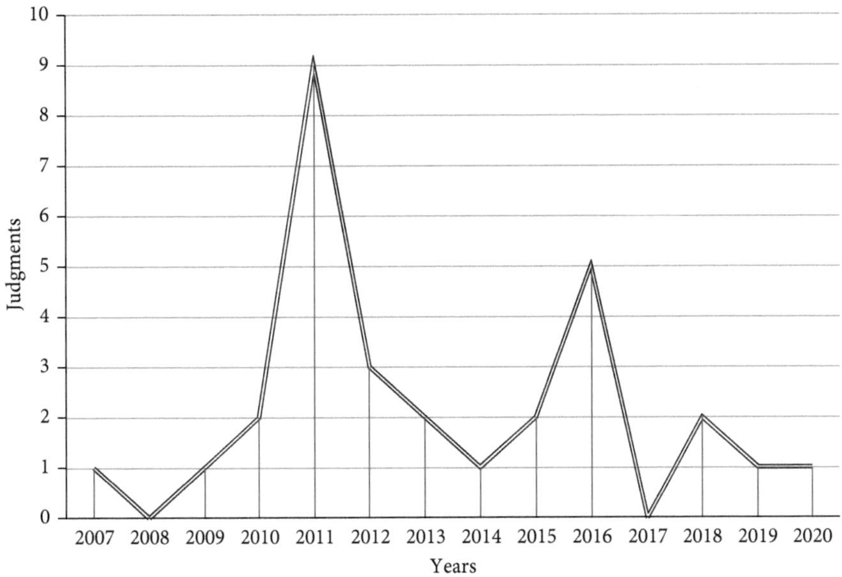

Figure 5.5 Asylum judgments delivered by the ECtHR in cases brought against Greece.
Source: DICTA Database elaborated by the author.

laws of the EU as this is not part of the European Convention on Human Rights.[131]

Many of the ECtHR applications have been brought by the lawyers and NGOs that I interviewed, and they offer two important insights. First, the ECtHR is better equipped to address human rights violations with no remedies before domestic courts, contrary to the ECJ. An eminent example is the case of illegal and violent pushbacks of migrants by sea: the Greek authorities failed to investigate this practice, leading NGOs to bring "an avalanche" of applications to the ECtHR.[132] A second factor is the excellent reputation of the ECtHR in Greek legal culture. In the words of an ECRE member:

[131] But EU Member States remain liable before the ECtHR for acts performed under EU law. Johan Callewaert, 'Convention Control Over the Application of Union Law by National Judges: The Case for a Wholistic Approach to Fundamental Rights' (2023) 8 European Papers—A Journal on Law and Integration 331.

[132] Interview with a member of the Greek Helsinki Monitor, 3 February 2024. The ECtHR has communicated thirty-two of these applications to the Greek government, thus we expect the judgments soon. More details can be found on the webpage of Racist Crime Watch, "200+ παράνομες επαναπροωθήσεις περίπου 10000 αλλοδαπών ερευνούν Εισαγγελία Αρείου Πάγου και Συνήγορος Πολίτη μετά από προσφυγές του ΕΠΣΕ" at <https://racistcrimeswatch.wordpress.com/2021/07/21/1-1211/> accessed 18 December 2024.

> I remember even as a child hearing about the European Court of Human Rights in the news more than the CJEU. And hearing about this ability for a person to go there and remedy their own personal injustice, and the financial compensation that the Court could grant in the judgment... Still now it's like this, the Court is this almost mythical being that will save you when Greece fails you. And this is a very common mentality in Greece; that the Greek state constantly failed Greek people in many ways.[133]

This is a manifestation of what Tilly calls the "limited repertoire of collective actions":[134] Greek migration lawyers and NGOs' preference for the ECtHR over the ECJ is not always motivated by strategic considerations but is rather engrained in the way in which they have been fighting for migrant and minority rights for years. Greek lawyers are used to a specific type of international litigation, which has the advantage of familiarity, and they have only recently started experimenting with different forms of actions.

6. Conclusion: Lack of access, lack of experts, and the Strasbourg predilection

This chapter investigated Greece's persistent absence of EU legal mobilization for migrant rights. Despite being subject to large migration flows since 2008, Greece's legal framework and reception system consistently fall short of EU standards. While EU law and the preliminary reference procedure offer avenues for challenging national migration policies and strengthening migrant rights, these opportunities remain largely theoretical, failing to materialize in practice. Why? Is this inertia attributable to structural impediments, such as issues with judges and norms, or subjective factors involving lawyers and pro-migrant movements? By analyzing the legal and social context, the chapter uncovers notable barriers to accessing courts in Greece. Paradoxically, even when some avenues existed stakeholders rarely capitalized on them, missing opportunities to initiate preliminary references.

The chapter tested two hypotheses. The first refers to the EU LOS: have the Greek legal framework and judicial reluctance to refer hampered the ability of movements to mobilize in court and reach the ECJ? Data suggests that, in

[133] Interview with Senior Legal Officer at ECRE, 19 September 2023.

[134] Charles Tilly, 'Speaking Your Mind Without Elections, Surveys, or Social Movements' (1983) 47 Public Opinion Quarterly 461, 463. I am grateful to William Jones for this suggestion.

general, Greek (administrative) judges are not structurally reluctant to refer. However, particularly in the detention and asylum fields, there are significant obstacles to access to courts that can make it difficult for groups to reach apex courts. Still, procedures do exist, such as Article 95 of the Greek Constitution, which can be used to reach the Council of State; this was used in 2023 when two migration NGOs finally obtained a preliminary reference. Overall, we cannot consider the EU LOS completely closed in Greece, and thus, this hypothesis is confirmed only partially.

The second hypothesis refers to internal factors and posits that movements do not have the necessary resources to mobilize. Relying on interviews, the chapter traces how actors perceive the EU LOS, which is essential for mobilization to happen.

What emerges is that until recently, Greek migrant rights defenders have not relied systematically on the preliminary reference procedure to contest national law and practices. They either did not detect situations where EU law could be usefully mobilized before the ECJ or they thought that, in any case, Greek judges would be reluctant to refer. This can be due to the lack of collaboration with EU legal experts and academics who, in other countries, have been crucial promoters of preliminary references. According to the interviewees, the Greek civil society field lacks stable collaborations between EU law academics, Eurolawyers, and activists, which in other countries constitute a fertile ground for the mobilization of cases before the ECJ. Finally, the interviews revealed a predilection of Greek migrant rights defenders for the Strasbourg court, where cases are often brought. Greek NGOs have a long tradition of litigating before the ECtHR, while the ECJ remained a relatively unfamiliar court. Overall, the second hypothesis is confirmed: the lack of mobilizing actors' initiative to seek preliminary references is part of the explanation.

This chapter contributes to the fields of legal mobilization, strategic litigation, and preliminary references in three ways. First, it addresses a gap in the literature by examining a case of non-mobilization, an aspect often overlooked but critical for identifying factors that we take for granted in positive cases, such as access to courts. Second, the study goes beyond looking at judges alone and encompasses lawyers and NGOs in its analysis, providing a more comprehensive understanding of the barriers to legal mobilization. Third, the findings highlight the importance of considering actors' perceptions, legal consciousness, and traditional repertoires of action. In contrast to other Member States, Greek migrant defenders lack contacts with EU legal experts who could guide them in utilizing EU legal strategies effectively. Consequently, actors remain unaware of the opportunities presented by the preliminary reference procedure, preferring instead to mobilize before the ECtHR. This insight underscores the need for greater awareness and capacity-building initiatives to leverage EU legal mechanisms effectively in Greece's migrant rights advocacy efforts.

Recent events point to possible changes. As mentioned, in 2023, Greek courts finally made two references in the asylum field. One was made *ex officio* by a first-instance court, while the other was the result of a strategic effort by two Greek NGOs, GCR and RSA. The ECJ judgment in this second case was recently published and supports the view of the NGOs.[135] This judgment may result in an important shift as it shows Greek civil society actors that EU litigation can bring about positive changes for refugees and migrants. As Miller showed for Denmark, positive judgments by the ECJ have the potential to shape national courts and civil society's strategies, exposing the power of using EU law to challenge the status quo.[136] In the case of Greece, we still do not know how the ECJ will respond to the second preliminary reference, but already this first favorable judgment might show civil society actors the potential of EU litigation and that Greek courts are not reluctant to refer, after all, thus changing their perceptions on judicial receptivity.

[135] *Elliniko Symvoulio gia tous Prosfyges and Ypostirixi Prosfygon sto Aigaio [Greek Refugee Council and Refugee Support Aegean]* (n 35); Refugee Support Aegean and Greek Refugee Council, 'CJEU Ruling on the Concept of "Safe Third Country"' <https://rsaegean.org/en/cjeu-ruling-on-the-concept-of-safe-third-country/> accessed 16 October 2024.

[136] Jeffrey Miller, 'Explaining Paradigm Shifts in Danish Anti-Discrimination Law' (2019) 26 Maastricht Journal of European and Comparative Law 540, 542.

6

Conclusion

Opportunities and Barriers to the Mobilization of EU Migration Law

The actors and the stories described in this book provide an image of mobilization through EU law which is quite different from what we have come to know in recent years. This book's protagonists are far from the "unsung heroes"[1] of the early days of European judicial integration, who orchestrated cases to advance the European project or liberalize the Member States' economy. They are also quite distant from the "gentlemen-politicians of law" who, by strengthening the EU legal order, were promoting their own careers,[2] or from the "architect[s] of regional economic integration" that used EU law to foster the free market economy.[3] To be sure, the actors behind the migration references are also relatively different from the trade unions and non-governmental organizations (NGOs) active in fields such as gender equality or environmental policy,[4] that could count on transnational networks, popular support, and access to EU institutions and policymakers. We can say that the "conflict constellations"[5] and power dynamics that characterize migration litigation set it apart from other fields. Most of the migrant supporters described in this book sustain litigation under a tight budget or even dip into their own savings, they have to navigate a politically hostile environment and fight against public institutions and administration to defend the rights of others.[6]

[1] Amedeo Arena, 'The "Unsung Heroes" of Costa v Enel: Enabling "Supremacy by Judicial Fiat" ' *EUI Webinar, The Court in the Archives* (2021) <https://www.iris.unina.it/handle/11588/873314> accessed 23 March 2024.

[2] Antoine Vauchez, 'The Transnational Politics of Judicialization. Van Gend En Loos and the Making of EU Polity' (2010) 16 European Law Journal 1, 9.

[3] Tommaso Pavone, 'From Marx to Market: Lawyers, European Law, and the Contentious Transformation of the Port of Genoa' (2018) 53 Law & Society Review.

[4] Rachel A Cichowski, *The European Court and Civil Society: Litigation, Mobilization and Governance* (CUP 2007) 66.

[5] Andreas Hofmann, 'The Legal Mobilisation of EU Market Freedoms: Strategic Action or Random Noise?' (2024) 0 West European Politics 1, 3.

[6] Seyla Benhabib, *The Rights of Others: Aliens, Residents, and Citizens* (CUP 2004); Mario Savino, *Le Libertà Degli Altri. La Regolazione Amministrativa Dei Flussi Migratori* (Giuffrè Editore 2012);

Legal Mobilization for Migrant Rights. Virginia Passalacqua, Oxford University Press.
 DOI: 10.1093/9780198943006.003.0006

In part, this is because migration is a hard case for legal mobilization. Political opportunities for positive changes in the migration field are virtually closed, and in recent years the general attitude towards migrants has been worsening in Europe. Pro-migrant groups and activists are often the targets of political attacks by right-wing governments in power or, worse, their activities are rendered more difficult by strict laws and the criminalization of acts of solidarity with migrants.[7] Tellingly, in all the countries studied in this book, pro-migrant rights defenders had to operate in a political environment hostile to migrants and their defenders (Table 6.1).

But the current European tendency to adopt stricter migration policies does not only make the political climate more hostile, it is also often the very reason why pro-migrant groups decide to mobilize before the courts. They respond to calls for help from individuals whose rights are under attack. Think of Don Flynn, one of the protagonists in the chapter on the UK, who told me: "Mrs Akrich walked into the Law Centre asking for help because her husband was about to be deported."[8] Historically, human rights and courts have been among the most important allies of migrants to resist illiberal restrictive policies.[9] As Chapters 2, 3, and 4 of this book show, a pejorative change in national rules and policies can prompt actors to resort to national courts and the European Court of Justice (ECJ). In Italy, the trigger of the legal mobilization was the new crimmigration policy introducing severe criminal sanctions against migrants who resided in Italy without a regular permit. In the UK, the causes for legal action are to be found more spread over time; they consisted of a series of laws and practices that rendered family reunification more complicated, affecting both EU migrants and British citizens married to third-country national (TCN) persons. In the Netherlands, the then government introduced a new civic integration test that had a detrimental effect on the chances of entering the country and enjoying the right to family reunification because the test operated as a filter for migrants who applied for a visa from abroad. In these three countries, different episodes of EU legal mobilization followed in reaction to these pejorative changes to the national laws. Migrant supporters

Thomas Gammeltoft-Hansen and others (eds) *The Rights of Others: Essays in Honour of Jens Vedsted-Hansen* (DJØF Forlag 2013).

[7] PICUM, 'Cases of Criminalisation of Migration and Solidarity in the EU in 2023' (2024) <https://picum.org/wp-content/uploads/2024/04/Cases-of-criminalisation-of-migration-and-solidarity-in-the-EU-in-2023.pdf> accessed 23 March 2025.

[8] Interview with Don Flynn, 14 December 2016, London.

[9] Christian Joppke, 'Why Liberal States Accept Unwanted Immigration' (1998) 50 World Politics 266; Susan Sterett, 'Legal Mobilization and Juridification: Migration as a Central Case' (2016) 38 Law & Policy 273.

Table 6.1 Subjective and structural factors that affect the possibilities of having legal mobilization for migrant rights before the ECJ.

	ITALY	THE UK	THE NETHERLANDS	GREECE
SUBJECTIVE FACTORS				
• Altruistic actors	Association of judges + Practitioner association	Migration NGOs + Eurolawyers	Academics + Migration NGOs	National and international asylum NGOs
• Perception of opportunities in EU litigation	Yes, thanks to academic experts of migration and EU law	Yes, thanks to lawyers specialized in EU law and migration	Yes, thanks to academic expert of migration and EU law	No
• Financial Resources for the litigation	None, pro bono work	Legal aid, pro bono work, and NGO staff	Legal aid, pro bono work and NGO staff	NGO staff
STRUCTURAL FACTORS				
• Political environment	Hostile	Hostile	Hostile	Hostile
• EU law offers advantages compared to national law	More protection of the rights of undocumented migrants	More protection of family reunion	More protection of family reunion	More protection of the right to access asylum procedures, more protection of migrants in detention and vulnerable migrants etc
• Access to national courts	Granted	Granted with problems (high litigation cost)	Granted	Obstacles in accessing higher courts
• Courts are willing and able to refer	Yes	Lower courts may be discouraged from referring	Lower courts may be discouraged from referring	Mixed attitude

mobilized to resist these policies, protect migrant rights, and challenge the newly introduced laws before the ECJ.

The described dynamic offers two insights that advance our understanding of how EU legal mobilization emerges. First, the scheme usually proposed by the literature posits that a premise for the mobilization is an expansion or a new opening in the EU legal opportunity structure (LOS), such as a positive change in the available EU legal stock or procedures.[10] But the case studies add another scenario: a *negative* change in the *national* legal stock can also prompt actors to go to the ECJ to resist change. This invites us to make more complex the terms of the analysis. Legal mobilization can come as the consequence of a change in the LOS, which can either consist of a positive change at the EU level or, conversely, of a negative change in the national legal framework. We can say that both scenarios generate a situation where an EU norm comes to offer a higher level of protection than national laws. In this sense, the existence of an opening in the EU LOS should be assessed as something relative to national law: it might derive from a new, more protective, legislation adopted at the EU level or from a new pejorative practice or rule adopted at the Member State level.

The second insight concerns the relationship between political opportunities and legal action. This has long been the object of study of legal mobilization scholars, who reached opposite conclusions. On the one hand, scholars note that marginalized groups who operate in "unfavorable domestic political settings" may be more likely to disengage from international courts "when the odds are against them."[11] Conversely, other scholars have noted that being in a situation of political disadvantage can push actors to rely on courts because "the very lack of political opportunities may induce the adoption of a legal strategy, with litigation displacing efforts to reach concessions by policymakers."[12] These diverging views leave us with an open question: does an unfavorable political structure incentivize or discourage marginalized movements from using (international) litigation?

The findings in this book partially confirm the political disadvantage argument, according to which a negative political environment can prompt actors to rely on law and courts. The fact that most of the legal mobilization cases have emerged in the context of a hostile political climate towards migrants seems to indicate that, among migrant rights supporters, the will to enact legal resistance prevails over resignation and mistrust in the courts. This finding, however, needs to be weighed against the fact that the pro-migrant mobilization studied in this book is largely carried out by altruistic actors and not by the

[10] Karen Alter and Jeannette Vargas, 'Explaining Variation in the Use of European Litigation Strategies: European Community Law and British Gender Equality Policy' (2000) 33 Comparative Political Studies 452, 456; Venera Protopapa, 'Shaping Equality for Migrants. Legal Mobilisation in Italy and the Race Equality Directive' (2019) 1 Journal européen des droits de l'homme 3.

[11] Lisa Harms, 'Claiming Religious Freedom at the European Court of Human Rights: Socio-Legal Field Effects on Legal Mobilization' (2021) 46 Law & Social Inquiry 1206, 1209.

[12] Stefan Thierse and Sanja Badanjak, *Opposition in the EU Multi-Level Polity: Legal Mobilization against the Data Retention Directive* (Palgrave Pivot 2021) 49; Chris Hilson, 'New Social Movements: The Role of Legal Opportunity' (2002) 9 Journal of European Public Policy 238, 250.

migrants themselves: non-migrant activists and lawyers may ponder legal and political opportunities differently from the marginalized group itself and may have more trust in the judicial system.

The book shows that environments hostile to migrants and minorities do not automatically exclude the possibility of mobilizing cases from national courts to the ECJ, thus configuring EU litigation as a form of resistance through court. Another example of this, that goes beyond the case studies of this book, is Hungary. The Hungarian government is famous for its illiberal policies towards asylum seekers, in open disregard for international and EU norms, and for its persecution of movements acting in solidarity with migrants.[13] To make EU legal mobilization even more difficult, in recent years the Fidesz government has seriously undermined the independence of Hungarian courts to the point that judges risk losing their jobs if they submit preliminary references to the ECJ of which the government does not approve, such as in the asylum field.[14] And yet, the Hungarian Helsinki Committee, an NGO, has managed to obtain several preliminary references to the ECJ to highlight the incompatibility of Hungarian laws with EU asylum law.[15] The organization faces many difficulties, including some national courts being adamantly unwilling to refer, but also thanks to in-house international staff it invested in training in EU law and international law, and it systematically asks for preliminary references to be submitted. In an interview, one of the Hungarian Helsinki Committee's senior lawyers told me that while it is not easy for them to obtain references, "it's impossible to influence the legislation" otherwise; one of the only strategies left to asylum seekers' rights defenders is to go to court and invoke EU law, and if the court refuses to disapply national law, they always ask the judge to submit a preliminary reference.[16] The Hungarian Helsinki Committee obtained many successes before the ECJ, and even if these haven't always been matched by coherent political reforms,[17] this confirms that even extremely hostile and

[13] Reuters, 'Hungary Passes Anti-Immigrant "Stop Soros" Laws' *The Guardian* (20 June 2018) <https://www.theguardian.com/world/2018/jun/20/hungary-passes-anti-immigrant-stop-soros-laws> accessed 6 October 2024; Case C-821/19 *Commission v Hungary* (16 November 2021) CJEU, ECLI:EU:C:2021:930.

[14] Eszter Zalan, 'Hungarian Judge Claims She Was Pushed out for Political Reasons' *EUobserver* (6 July 2021) <https://euobserver.com/rule-of-law/arfcdab903> accessed 6 October 2024.

[15] Just to name a few: Case C-364/11 *El Kott* (19 December 2012) CJEU, ECLI:EU:C:2012:826; Case C-556/17 *Torubarov* (29 July 2019) CJEU, ECLI:EU:C:2019:626; Case C-406/18 *PG* (19 March 2020) CJEU, ECLI:EU:C:2020:216; Case C-564/18 *LH v Bevándorlási és Menekültügyi Hivatal (Tompa)* (19 March 2020) CJEU, ECLI:EU:C:2020:218; Joined Cases C-924/19 PPU and C-925/19 PPU *FMS and Others* (14 May 2020) CJEU, ECLI:EU:C:2020:367.

[16] Interview with Gruša Matevžič, Senior legal officer at the Hungarian Helsinki Committee, 8 June 2022, online.

[17] Gruša Matevžič and Katalin Juhász, 'Implementing Judgments in the Field of Asylum and Migration on Odd Days' (2022).

repressive regimes do not automatically exclude the possibility of conducting EU legal mobilization for migrant rights.

Another insight, this time from the case studies, is that most migrant supporters were not confronted with the choice of whether to adopt a political strategy or a legal one. Because of their professional background or the specific focus of their organization, if they faced an injustice, they were naturally inclined to reflect on how the law could be used to remedy it. Using Israël's words, most of the organizations of migrant supporters we saw in action in the case studies are "built directly on a legal frame that shapes the way in which a social problem is raised and addressed politically."[18] Their embeddedness in legal frames means that the law is their primary lens to understand society and their main tool to influence politics. In other words, the law is their preferred political strategy because it is their only one.

The prominence of legal strategies also derives from the high level of judicialization that characterizes the migration field. Often the problems that migrants face are framed in legal terms and naturally require legal assistance: if migrants face a negative administrative or judicial decision, they immediately turn to lawyers or legal organizations to ask for help. Some of these organizations not only try to solve the individual's problem but mount a litigation strategy that can challenge the entire policy. The law occupies a central role in migrants' lives and, as a consequence, in pro-migrant activism too. This is not the case for other fields, such as environmental protection, where the relationship between activists and lawyers can follow different dynamics.[19] The high level of judicialization sets the migration field apart from other areas of activism and gives a unique role to lawyers and legal experts.

Another reason why migration is considered a hard case for legal mobilization is because of the structural scarcity of resources for litigation. Wealthy clients or affluent funders are rare in the migration field (even if they do exist)[20] and this means that litigation is often financially sustained thanks to legal aid, pro bono work, and free time provided by altruistic actors. This is further complicated by the fact that legal aid is often insufficient and usually does not cover the travel expenses to Luxembourg. In this respect, the negative case

[18] Liora Israël, 'Rights on the Left? Social Movements, Law and Lawyers after 1968 in France' in Dia Anagnostou, *Rights and Courts in Pursuit of Social Change: Legal Mobilisation in the Multi- Level European System* (Hart Publishing 2014) 94.

[19] Lisa Vanhala, 'Is Legal Mobilization for the Birds? Legal Opportunity Structures and Environmental Nongovernmental Organizations in the United Kingdom, France, Finland, and Italy' (2018) 51 Comparative Political Studies 380, 19.

[20] One example is the case of *Zhu and Chen*, reported in Chapter 3 of this book.

study of Greece offers some insights. The legal aid system for asylum applicants in Greece is structurally deficient and NGOs had to step in to provide basic legal support to the many asylum seekers arriving on the islands during the years from 2015 to 2020. The huge number of cases dealt with and the scarce resources have probably negatively impacted the work of lawyers and public decision-makers. Partial evidence is the paragraph copied and pasted into the end of each asylum application requesting a preliminary reference, which reasonably had lower chances of convincing the asylum committee to refer than an ad hoc and individually reasoned request would do.

The case of Greece, contrasted with the other positive cases, highlights how the presence of a support structure is not enough to ensure a referral.[21] Not all migrant supporters are the same, and there are huge variations between pro-migrant organizations in different EU Member States, which helps understand the uneven mobilization of EU migration law. In Greece, there is an impressive array of national and international organizations that operate specifically in support of migrant rights, both governmental and non-governmental. Some of these organizations possess enough resources to have an in-house team of lawyers specialized in migration and asylum law; moreover, the volume of work and the reach of these organizations increased during the so-called refugee crisis when they enlarged their funding and staff. However, despite the availability of more actors and resources, for a long time none of these organizations focused on litigation before the ECJ, even if EU law offered greater protection than Greek law. Some of these organizations never perceived the opportunities that EU litigation offered, others considered Greek courts unwilling to refer, and others preferred bringing claims before the European Court of Human Rights, in part because of their training as human rights lawyers which makes them see this Court as more natural and familiar, and in part because of obstacles to access to the higher jurisdiction in Greece.[22] In general, EU legal experts, such as Eurolawyers and EU law professors, were rarely involved in the litigation strategies, contrary to the positive cases analyzed in other countries. This is an important warning that even if migration and asylum laws have been heavily harmonized and are now decided mostly at the EU level, the process of Europeanization of legal practice and legal strategies can proceed more slowly and it may take years for movements and NGOs to build trust and incorporate new EU legal techniques.

[21] Charles R Epp, *The Rights Revolution: Lawyers, Activists, and Supreme Courts in Comparative Perspective* (1st edn, University of Chicago Press 1998).

[22] More on this in Chapter 5.

The example of Greece confirms that one of the most important factors to explain the emergence of EU legal mobilization for migrant rights is not financial resources or the political environment, which are roughly constant in all the case studies. Rather, legal mobilization is highly dependent on altruistic actors' availability of specific EU legal skills and their capacity to see opportunities in EU justice.[23] In the positive case studies, lawyers and pro-migrant groups did not just provide free time and work, they were also those who perceived the potential of EU litigation and capitalized on it. Here, we can see a defining trait of legal mobilization before the ECJ: EU legal experts, law professors, and Eurolawyers are central motors in the activation of EU justice. The mobilization of EU legal knowledge is a precondition for the mobilization before national courts and the ECJ. These actors are often those who come up with the idea of mobilizing before the ECJ, they can see the opportunities that EU law offers, and they explain it to other actors such as legal aid lawyers or NGOs for migrant rights. In this way, following Merry's influential conceptualization, they can be fully considered "translators": "people in the middle" that vernacularize transnational sources by adapting them to local institutions and meanings and "who translate the discourses and practices from the arena of international law and legal institutions to specific situations of suffering and violation."[24] In the context explored in this book, this process of vernacularization consists of framing migrants' local grievances in EU law terms by presenting them as problematic because they violate EU law and standards.

Importantly, the vernacularization of EU law has national courts as one of its main targets. Indeed, the initiation of the preliminary reference procedure remains in the hands of domestic courts, thus in order to reach the ECJ pro-migrant groups need to convince national judges to refer. This is a necessary step to transform the preliminary reference procedure into a tool for the decentralized enforcement of EU law and into the infringement procedure of the individual.[25] A successful technique that altruistic actors use to convince

[23] Antoine Vauchez, 'The Map and the Territory: Re-Assessing EU Law's Embeddedness in European Societies' (2020) 27 Maastricht Journal of European and Comparative Law 133, 136.

[24] Sally Engle Merry, 'Transnational Human Rights and Local Activism: Mapping the Middle' (2006) 108 American Anthropologist 38, 39.

[25] Bruno De Witte, 'The Impact of Van Gend En Loos on Judicial Protection at European and National Level: Three Types of Preliminary Questions' in Antonio Tizzano and Sacha Prechal (eds), *50th Anniversary of the Judgment in Van Gend en Loos, 1963-2013* (Office des Publications de l'Union Européenne 2013) 95; Mark A Pollack, *The Engines of European Integration: Delegation, Agency, and Agenda Setting in the EU* (OUP 2003) 123; Roberto Adam, 'Il Rinvio Pregiudiziale Tra Tutela Dei Diritti Soggettivi e Controllo Delle Inadempienze Statali' (2023) 1 Il Diritto dell'Unione Europea 8; Morten Broberg, 'Preliminary References as a Means for Enforcing EU Law' in András Jakab and Dimitry Kochenov (eds), *The Enforcement of EU Law and Values: Ensuring Member States' Compliance* (OUP 2017).

domestic judges to refer is to expose them to EU law knowledge and migrant-friendly interpretations of the law. And such endeavor often does not start in the courtroom but beforehand, with small-scale campaigns aimed at explaining why national law is contrary to EU law. At this stage, the migrant cause benefits enormously from allies belonging to the same epistemic community of national judges, such as legal academics, judicial professional associations, and legal educational institutions. In the eyes of the judges, these members of their legal community have the authority to state what the most reliable interpretation of the law is and whether national law is incompatible with EU law. These legal experts contribute to giving domestic judges the impression that enforcing EU law vis-à-vis conflicting national norms is the appropriate "legal praxis," as "shared values enhance the collective determination of judicial players and their ability to stand up against powerful political actors."[26] To amplify the role of these allies and make sure that their voice reaches judges and lawyers, migrant supporters disseminate their ideas through various channels, such as reports, articles in specialized journals, conferences, mailing lists, and case documents. This is crucial to create the conditions leading national judges to refer. It is also a very prolific strategy because migrant supporters' arguments can be picked up not only by the single court adjudicating the litigated case but also by other judges who become convinced that there is a problem and use their powers to refer cases.

Perhaps the best example of this dynamic that this book offers is the Italian case study where law professors, members of a pro-migrant network, published an article on the incompatibilities of Italian law with EU law in which they suggested the text for a preliminary reference. The article was widely discussed in blogs and conferences and circulated in the mailing list of a progressive judges' association.[27] The wide dissemination of legal arguments and ideas was central to explaining the scale of the Italian mobilization, where almost twenty courts decided to refer; it would be impossible for one organization to initiate legal actions before so many courts at the same time. The Netherlands case study also offers a good example of how the epistemic community can be leveraged, yet with fewer people involved in the mobilization: the lawyer representing the migrant in the case submitted a written expert opinion by an influential EU and migration law professor to the national court, in which it was suggested to that court to refer. The Dutch court accepted the advice.[28]

[26] Ezequiel A González-Ocantos, *Shifting Legal Visions: Judicial Change and Human Rights Trials in Latin America* (CUP 2016) 37.

[27] More on this in Chapter 2.

[28] More on this in Chapter 4.

What has been outlined until now have largely been subjective factors, in other words characteristics or techniques of the pro-migrant movements that influenced the emergence of EU litigation. The book also identified some structural factors that can play a huge role in facilitating or hampering the legal mobilization. Probably the best, yet negative, example of this is Greece. The Greek judicial system contains important obstacles to the access to higher courts for migrants and their defenders. The most evident is the procedure for reviewing the lawfulness of migrants' detention, which structurally limits the possibility of obtaining a reference. The decision on whether to confirm detention must be adopted by the Greek courts as quickly as possible, typically within a couple of days, and this procedure does not provide for the possibility of filing an appeal, so it is automatically definitive. This does not give Greek lower courts enough time to study the case thoroughly and to make a reference; in addition, detention cases cannot be adjudicated by higher courts such as appeal courts or the Council of State, which have more experience. The Greek asylum determination procedure presents problems too: this develops in four stages of which the first two are before administrative or quasi-judicial bodies, and it is uncertain whether they have the power to refer cases to the ECJ. Only a few asylum cases are appealed up until the third stage, which the Court of Appeal decides. These difficulties in reaching higher courts may negatively impact the chances of having a case referred to the ECJ.

The findings of the book contribute to putting into perspective the widely shared belief that the preliminary reference mechanism cannot be used strategically because national courts are "naturally reluctant" to refer.[29] It is true that in many instances, an attempt by civil society actors to reach the ECJ can be frustrated by national courts' unwillingness to refer. However, the book shows that pro-migrant actors can resort to different techniques to overcome this obstacle and convince judges to refer, including skillful legal practice, dissemination of EU legal knowledge, and venue shopping (strategically choosing a court that is more prone to refer). Judges are not a monolithic entity that thinks alike and does not move from its own positions, and there are significant differences from one court to another. Moreover, as recently shown in the literature that focuses on national courts' attitudes towards the preliminary reference, judges listen to what the parties ask and to their interests in the case.[30]

[29] Jasper Krommendijk, *National Courts and Preliminary References to the Court of Justice* (Edward Elgar Publishing 2021) 38.

[30] Karin Leijon and Monika Glavina, 'Why Passive? Exploring National Judges' Motives for Not Requesting Preliminary Rulings' (2022) 29 Maastricht Journal of European and Comparative Law 263, 273; Monika Glavina, 'Reluctance to Participate in the Preliminary Ruling Procedure as a Challenge to EU Law: A Case Study on Slovenia and Croatia' in Clara Rauchegger and Anna Wallerman (eds), *The Eurosceptic Challenge: National Implementation and Interpretation of EU Law* (Hart Publishing 2019) 209.

Even the allegedly more conservative courts, under different circumstances or when subjected to persuasive legal arguments, can decide to make a reference.

This book provides a lens through which to evaluate the conditions under which migration preliminary references arise and are relied upon to shape law and politics. The combination of the structural and subjective factors identified gives us a better understanding of the reasons behind the variation in EU legal mobilization across the Member States, pointing out important differences both at the actors' level and at the level of the national legal and procedural context. Mobilizing EU justice requires investing in EU technical expertise, leveraging key allies, and shaping the opportunity structure to make national judges prone to refer. Contrary to early accounts of litigation for gender equality, the field of migration does not offer many positive insights to support the idea that EU law could empower minorities. Migrants are the subject and the beneficiaries of the EU litigation but are rarely in control of the legal strategies and the direction of their cases. Rather, migrant rights supporters, especially if equipped with EU legal expertise, are entrusted with new legal arguments and venues, which they use to capitalize on the opportunities offered on migrants' behalf. These altruistic actors, who fight every day for the rights of others, are the single most important factor in enforcing EU migration law vis-à-vis non-compliant Member States.

ANNEX 1

Table of preliminary references per country and EU legal basis (1981–2022)

One unit corresponds to one preliminary reference, including inadmissible or withdrawn references. If two references are joined, they count as two (eg Joined cases C-411/10 and C-493/10). Multiple cases submitted as one reference count as one (eg *K and A*, Case C-153/14). Sources: CURIA website and Radboud University's Centre for Migration Law Newsletters (NEAIS, NEMIS, and NEFIS, available at <https://cmr.jur.ru.nl/> accessed 24 March 2025). I have excluded references that did not deal with third-country nationals (eg dealing with EU migrants instead). Often a single reference addresses more than one EU norm; in that case, I counted it under the main one. Some references may be missing, as the CURIA database is not complete.

	EU–Turkey Agreement	TCN family member of Union citizens	Return Directive	Qualification I and II	Dublin II and III	Family Reunification Directive	Asylum Procedures I and II	Schengen Borders Code	Long-Term Residence Directive	Reception conditions I and II	Single Permit	Visa Code	Passport Regulation	Transit through Switzerland	Researchers and Students Directive	Social Security for TCN Regulation	Border Traffic Regulation	Facilitation Directive	Mutual Recognition of Expulsion Decision	Port state control	Trafficking victims	Morocco–EEC Agreement	Tunisia–EEC Agreement	Algeria–EEC Agreement	Total
Austria	5	2	1	5	5	2	1	1	2	0	0	0	0	0	0	0	0	0	0	0	0	0	0	0	24
Belgium	0	8	13	9	1	5	5	0	2	2	0	1	0	0	0	0	0	0	0	0	0	5	0	1	52
Bulgaria	0	0	2	5	1	0	0	0	0	0	0	0	0	0	0	0	0	0	0	0	0	0	0	0	8
Croatia	0	0	0	0	1	0	0	0	0	0	0	0	0	0	0	0	0	0	0	0	0	0	0	0	1
Cyprus	0	0	1	0	0	0	0	1	0	0	0	0	0	0	0	0	0	0	0	0	0	0	0	0	2
Czechia	0	0	2	1	1	0	1	0	0	1	0	0	0	0	0	0	0	0	0	0	0	0	0	0	6
Denmark	4	1	0	0	0	0	0	0	0	0	0	0	0	0	0	0	0	0	0	0	0	0	0	0	5
Estonia	0	0	1	0	0	0	0	0	0	0	0	0	0	0	0	0	0	0	0	0	0	0	0	0	1
Finland	0	2	1	0	1	0	0	0	1	0	0	0	0	0	0	0	0	0	0	0	0	0	0	0	5
France	0	0	6	1	1	0	0	5	1	1	0	0	0	0	0	0	0	0	0	0	0	0	0	2	17
Germany	45	6	7	17	7	4	16	4	2	0	0	2	1	1	2	1	0	0	0	0	0	0	2	0	117
Greece	0	0	0	0	0	0	0	0	0	0	0	0	0	0	0	0	0	0	0	0	0	0	0	0	0
Hungary	0	2	1	5	1	1	8	0	2	0	0	0	0	0	0	1	1	0	0	0	0	0	0	0	22
Ireland	0	7	0	4	3	0	3	0	0	2	0	0	0	0	0	0	0	0	0	0	0	0	0	0	19
Italy	0	0	23	0	7	0	2	0	7	2	3	0	0	0	0	0	0	1	0	1	0	0	0	0	46
Lithuania	0	0	0	1	0	0	1	0	0	0	0	0	0	0	0	0	0	0	0	0	0	0	0	0	2
Latvia	0	0	0	0	0	0	0	2	0	0	0	0	0	0	0	0	0	0	0	0	0	0	0	0	2
Luxembourg	0	3	0	0	0	0	2	0	0	0	0	0	0	0	0	0	0	0	0	0	0	0	0	0	5
Malta	0	0	0	0	0	0	0	0	0	0	0	0	0	0	0	0	0	0	0	0	0	0	0	0	0
Netherlands	18	10	9	12	14	11	5	4	4	2	0	4	0	0	0	2	0	0	0	0	1	2	0	1	99
Poland	0	0	0	0	0	0	0	1	0	0	0	1	0	0	0	0	0	0	0	0	0	0	0	0	2
Portugal	0	0	0	0	0	0	0	0	0	0	0	0	0	0	0	0	0	0	0	0	0	0	0	0	0
Romania	0	1	0	0	0	0	0	0	0	0	0	0	0	0	0	0	0	0	0	0	0	0	0	0	1
Slovakia	0	0	0	0	0	0	0	0	0	0	0	0	0	0	0	0	0	0	0	0	0	0	0	0	0
Slovenia	0	0	0	0	2	0	1	0	0	0	0	0	0	0	0	0	0	0	0	0	0	0	0	0	3
Spain	1	4	3	0	0	1	1	2	9	1	0	0	0	0	0	0	0	0	1	0	0	0	0	0	23
Sweden	0	2	1	0	4	0	1	1	0	0	0	0	0	0	0	0	0	0	0	0	0	0	0	0	9
UK	4	24	0	3	2	0	0	0	0	0	0	0	0	0	0	0	0	0	0	0	0	1	0	0	34
Total:	77	72	71	63	51	24	47	21	30	11	3	8	1	1	2	4	1	1	1	1	1	8	2	4	505

ANNEX 2

List of preliminary references per country and EU migration norm (1981–2022)

1. EU–Turkey Agreement

Agreement establishing an Association between the European Community and Turkey, signed at Ankara, 12 September 1963 and related protocols, known as the "Ankara Agreement"

NAME	CJEU CASE NUMBER	DATE OF DECISION	COUNTRY	INTERVENING MEMBER STATE
DEMIREL	C-12/86	30 September 1987	Germany	DE, FR, EL, UK
SEVINCE	C-192/89	20 September 1990	Netherlands	DE, NL
KUS	C-237/91	16 December 1992	Germany	DE
EROGLU	C-355/93	5 October 1994	Germany	DE
AHMET BOZKURT	C-434/93	6 June 1995	Netherlands	NL, DE, EL, UK
TAFLAN-MET AND OTHERS	C-277/94	10 September 1996	Netherlands	NL, DE, EL, ES, FR,
RECEP TETIK	C-171/95	23 January 1997	Germany	DE, FR, UK,
SELMA KADIMAN	C-351/95	17 April 1997	Germany	FR, NL
SULEYMAN EKER	C-386/95	29 May 1997	Germany	DE, EL, FR, AU
KOL	C-285/95	5 June 1997	Germany	DE, ES, FR, UK
ERTANIR	C-98/96	30 September 1997	Germany	DE
GÜNAYDIN	C-36/97	30 September 1997	Germany	DE, EL, FR
HAYDAR AKMAN	C-210/97	19 November 1998	Germany	DE, EL
BIRDEN	C-1/97	26 November 1998	Germany	DE, EL, FR
SEMA SÜRÜL	C-262/96	4 May 1999	Germany	DE, FR, AT, UK
NAZLI	C-340/97	10 February 2000	Germany	DE, FR
KOCAK AND ÖRS	C-102/98	14 March 2000	Germany	DE, FR

NAME	CJEU CASE NUMBER	DATE OF DECISION	COUNTRY	INTERVENING MEMBER STATE
ERGAT	C-329/97	16 March 2000	Germany	DE, FR
SAVAS	C-37/98	11 May 2000	UK	UK, DE, EL, FR, IT
EYÜP	C-65/98	22 June 2000	Austria	DE, AU, UK
BICAKCI	C-89/00	19 September 2000	Germany	N/A
BÜLENT KURZ, NÉ YÜCE	C-188/00	19 November 2002	Germany	DE
BIRLIKTE	C-171/01	8 May 2003	Austria	AU
ABATAY AND OTHERS + NADI SAHIN	Joined cases C-317/01 and C-369/01	21 October 2003	Germany	DE, FR, NL
ÖZTÜRK	C-373/02	28 April 2004	Austria	AT, DE
ENGIN AYAZ	C-275/02	30 September 2004	Germany	DE
CETINKAYA	C-467/02	11 November 2004	Germany	DE, PO
DÖRR AND ÜNAL	C-136/03	2 June 2005	Austria	AU, DE
AYDINLI	C-373/03	7 July 2005	Germany	DE
ERGÜL DOGAN	C-383/03	7 July 2005	Austria	AU, DE
GÜROL	C-374/03	7 July 2005	Germany	DE, AU
SEDEF	C-230/03	10 January 2006	Germany	DE
ERGUN TORUN	C-502/04	16 February 2006	Germany	DE, SK
GÜZELI	C-4/05	26 October 2006	Germany	DE, SK
DERIN	C-325/05	18 July 2007	Germany	DE, IT, UK
TUM AND DARI	C-16/05	20 September 2007	UK	UK, NL, SL
MURAT POLAT	C-349/06	4 October 2007	Germany	DE, IT, NL, PL, UK
EZGI PAYIR, BURHAN AKYUZ, BIROL OZTURK	C-294/06	24 January 2008	UK	UK, DE, IT, NL
KAHVECI	C- 152/08	25 July 2008	Spain	N/A
ER	C-453/07	25 September 2008	Germany	DE
ALTUN	C-337/07	18 December 2008	Germany	DE, EL
SOYSAL AND SAVATLI	C-228/06	19 February 2009	Germany	DE, DK, EL, SL
SAHIN	C-242/06	17 September 2009	Netherlands	NL, DE, CY, IT, UK

NAME	CJEU CASE NUMBER	DATE OF DECISION	COUNTRY	INTERVENING MEMBER STATE
ÜMIT BEKLEYEN	C-462/08	21 January 2010	Germany	DK, NL
GENC	C-14/09	04 February 2010	Germany	DE, DK
F. TOPRAK AND I. OGUZ	Joined cases C-300/09 and C-301/09	9 December 2010	Netherlands	NL, DK, DE
METIN BOZKURT	C-303/08	22 December 2010	Germany	DE, DK, IT
H. AKDAS AND OTHERS	C-485/07	26 May 2011	Netherlands	NL, UK
FATMA PEHLIVAN	C-484/07	16 June 2011	Netherlands	NL, DE, IT
TURAL OGUZ + AIRE	C-186/10	21 July 2011	UK	UK
BARIS UNAL	C-187/10	29 September 2011	Netherlands	NL
ZIEBELL	C-371/08	8 December 2011	Germany	DE, DK, EE, EL, UK
TAYFUN KAHVECI + OSMAN INAN	Joined cases C-9/10 + C-7/10	29 March 2012	Netherlands	NL, PL
NATTHAYA DÜLGER	C- 451/11	19 July 2012	Germany	DE, IT, AT
GÜLBAHCE	C-268/11	8 November 2012	Germany	DE
DEMIRKAN	C 221/11	24 September 2013	Germany	DE, CZ, DK, EE, EL, FR, NL, SK, UK,
DEMIR	C -225/12	7 November 2013	Netherlands	NL, DE, IT
DOGAN	C-138/13	10 July 2014	Germany	DE, NL, AU, DK.
ESSENT	C-91/13	11 September 2014	Netherlands	NL, DK
DEMIRCI AND OTHERS	C-171/13	14 January 2015	Netherlands	NL
CANER GENC	C-561/14	12 April 2016	Denmark	DK, AT
SIDIKA UCAR AND RECEP KILIC	Joined cases C-508/15 and C-509/15	21 December 2016	Germany	DE
FURKAN TEKDEMIR	C-652/15	29 March 2017	Germany	DE, AT
YÖN	C-123/17	7 August 2018	Germany	DE
M. ÇOBAN	C-677/17	15 May 2019	Netherlands	NL

NAME	CJEU CASE NUMBER	DATE OF DECISION	COUNTRY	INTERVENING MEMBER STATE
A	C-89/18	10 July 2019	Denmark	DK
A, B, P	C-70/18	03 October 2019	Netherlands	NL, DK, IE, UK
SOLAK	C-258/18	13 February 2020	Netherlands	NL
GR	C-720/19	21 October 2020	Germany	AT
BY AND OTHERS	C-194/20	3 June 2021	Germany	DK, NL, PL
B	C-379/20	2 September 2021	Denmark	DK
X	C-279/21	22 December 2022	Denmark	DK
S, E, C	C-402/21	9 February 2023	Netherlands	NL, DK, DE
MEISLEV	C-375/23	4 July 2024	Denmark	DK

2. Third-country national family members of Union citizens

Articles 18–21 TFEU; Council Directive 73/148/EEC of 21 May 1973 on the abolition of restrictions on movement and residence within the Community for nationals of Member States with regard to establishment and the provision of services, Regulation 1612/68 of the Council of 15 October 1968 on freedom of movement for workers within the Community; Regulation 492/2011 of the European Parliament and of the Council of 5 April 2011 on freedom of movement for workers within the Union; Directive 2004/38/EC of the European Parliament and of the Council of 29 April 2004 on the right of citizens of the Union and their family members to move and reside freely within the territory of the Member States

NAME	CJEU CASE NUMBER	DATE OF DECISION	COUNTRY	INTERVENING MEMBER STATE
LEVIN	C-53/81	23 March 1982	Netherlands	NL, DK, FR
MORSON AND JHANJAN	Joined cases C-35/82 and C-36/82	27 October 1982	Netherlands	NL, UK.
DIATTA	C-267/83	13 February 1985	Germany	NL, UK, DE,
SURINDER SINGH	C-370/90	7 July 1992	UK	UK
LAND NORDRHEIN-WESTFALEN V KARI UECKER AND VERA JACQUET V LAND NORDRHEIN-WESTFALEN	Joined cases C-64/96 and C-65/96	5 June 1997	Germany	DE, FR

NAME	CJEU CASE NUMBER	DATE OF DECISION	COUNTRY	INTERVENING MEMBER STATE
KABA I	356/98	11 April 2000	UK	UK
CARPENTER	C-60/00	11 July 2002	UK	UK
MRAX V BELGIAN STATE	C- 459/99	25 July 2002	Belgium	BE, AT
BAUMBAST	C-413/99	17 September 2002	UK	UK, DE
NANI GIVANE AND OTHERS	257/00	9 January 2003	UK	UK, DE
KABA II	466/00	6 March 2003	UK	UK
AKRICH	C-109/01	23 September 2003	UK	UK, EL
ZHU AND CHEN	C-200/02	19 October 2004	UK	IE, UK
MATTERN AND CIKOTIC	C-10/05	20 March 2006	Luxembourg	DE, UK
JIA	C-1/05	9 January 2007	Sweden	SE, BE NL, SK, UK
EIND	C-291/05	11 December 2007	Netherlands	NL, CZ, DK, DE, EL, UK
METOCK	C-127/08	25 July 2008	Ireland	IE, DK, DE, EL, CY, MT, NL, AT, FI, UK.
DENIZ SAHIN	C-551/07	19 December 2008	Austria	N/A
IBRAHIM	C-310/08	23 February 2010	UK	UK, DK, IE, IT
ZAMBRANO	C-34/09	8 March 2011	Belgium	BE, DK, DE, IE, EL, NL, AT, PL
SHIRLEY MCCARTHY	C-434/09	5 May 2011	UK	UK, DK, EE, IE, NL
DERECI AND OTHERS	C-256/11	15 November 2011	Austria	AU, DK, DE, IE, EL, NL, PL, UK
TOMASZ ZIOLKOWSKI AND BARBARA SZEJA AND OTHERS	Joined cases C-424/10 & C-425/10	21 December 2011	Germany	DE, IE, EL, UK
RAHMAN + AIRE	C-83/11	5 September 2012	UK	UK, BE, DK, DE, IT, NL, PL
LUCJA CZOP AND MARGITA PUNAKOVA	Joined cases C-147/11 and C-148/11	6 September 2012	UK	UK, PL
IIDA	C-40/11	8 November 2012	Germany	DE, BE, CZ, DK, IT, NL, PL, UK
O. AND S.	Joined cases C-356 and 357/11	6 December 2012	Finland	NL, FI, DK, DE, IT, PL.

NAME	CJEU CASE NUMBER	DATE OF DECISION	COUNTRY	INTERVENING MEMBER STATE
YMERAGA AND OTHERS	C-87/12	8 May 2013	Luxembourg	LB, BE, CZ, DK, DE, PL
ALARAPE AND TIJANI + AIRE	C-529/11	8 May 2013	UK	UK, DK
ZZ	C-300/11	4 June 2013	UK	UK, FR, CZ, IT, SK
HADJ AHMED	C-45/12	13 June 2013	Belgium	BE, CZ
ALOKPA AND MOUDOULOU	C-86/12	10 October 2013	Luxembourg	LB, BE, CZ, DE, EL, LI, NL, PL
FLORA MAY REYES	C-423/12	16 January 2014	Sweden	SE, CZ, NL, UK
ONUEKWERE	C-378/12	16 January 2014	UK	UK, CZ, DE, IE, IT, PL
O. & B.	C-456/12	12 March 2014	Netherlands	NL, BE, CZ, DK, DE, EE, PL, UK
S. & G.	C-457/12	12 March 2014	Netherlands	NL, BE, CZ, DK, DE, EE, PL, UK
MCCARTHY AND MCCARTHY RODRIGUEZ	C-202/13	18 December 2014	UK	UK, EL, ES, PL, SK
OGIERIAKHI	C-244/13	10 July 2014	Ireland	IE, EL, PL.
KULDIP SINGH + IMMIGRANT COUNCIL OF IRELAND	C-218/14	26 July 2015	Ireland	IE, DK, EL, ES, PL, UK
NA + AIRE	C-115/15	30 June 2016	UK	UK, DK, NL, PL
RENDÓN MARÍN	C-165/14	13 September 2016	Spain	ES, DK, EL, FR, IT, NL, PL, UK
CS	C-304/14	13 September 2016	UK	UK, FR, DK, PL
CHAVEZ VILCHEZ	C-133/15	10 May 2017	Netherlands	NL, BE, DK, FR, LI, PL, UK, NW
LOUNES	C-165/16	14 November 2017	UK	UK, ES, PL
K. AND H.F.	Joined cases C-366/16 and 331/16	2 May 2018	Belgium + Netherlands	NL, BE, EL, FR, UK
COMAN	C-673/16	5 June 2018	Romania	RO, LV, HU, NL, PL
BANGER	C-89/17	12 July 2018	UK	UK, ES, AT, PL
DEHA ALTINER AND RAVN	C-230/17	27 June 2018	Denmark	DK, BE, IE, (NW)
DIALLO	C-246/17	27 June 2018	Belgium	BE, PL
SM + *AIRE* + CCLC	C -129/18	26 March 2019	UK	UK, BE, CZ, DE, NL, PL

NAME	CJEU CASE NUMBER	DATE OF DECISION	COUNTRY	INTERVENING MEMBER STATE
CHENCHOOLIAH	C- 94/18	10 September 2019	Ireland	IE, DK, NL, AT
BAJRATARI + AIRE	C-93/18	02 October 2019	UK	UK, CZ, DK, NL, AU
MAHMOOD	C-169/18	10 January 2019	Ireland	IE, DE, UK
SUBDELEGACIÓN DEL GOBIERNO EN CIUDAD REAL	C-836/18	27 February 2020	Spain	ES, DK, DE, NL
RYAN AIR	C-754/18	18 June 2020	Hungary	HU, CZ, EL
SUBDELEGACIÓN DEL GOBIERNO EN TOLEDO	Joined C-451/19 and C-532/19	5 May 2022	Spain	ES
ORDRE DES BARREAUX FRANCOPHONES ET GERMANOPHONE AND OTHERS V CONSEIL DES MINISTRES	C-718/19	22 June 2022	Belgium	BE, ES, PO, DK
X	C-930/19	2 September 2021	Belgium	BE
VI V COMMISSIONERS FOR HER MAJESTY'S REVENUE AND CUSTOMS	C-247/20	10 March 2022	UK	0
X	C-459/20	22 June 2023	Netherlands	NL, DK, DE
E.K. V STSCR	C-624/20	7 September 2022	Netherlands	NL, DK, DE
Srs, AA	C-22/21	15 September 2022	Ireland	IE, CZ, DK, NL, NO
M.D.	C-528/21	27 April 2023	Hungary	HU, CZ
Z.K. & M.S.	C-248/22	10 March 2023	Ireland	IE, CZ, DK, NL, NO
PREUVE DU LIEN DE DÉPENDANCE	C-607/21	Pending	Belgium	N/A

3. Return Directive

Directive 2008/115 of the European Parliament and of the Council of 16 December 2008 on common standards and procedures in Member States for returning illegally staying third-country nationals

NAME	CJEU CASE NUMBER	DATE OF DECISION	COUNTRY	INTERVENING MEMBER STATE
KADZOEV	C-357/09 PPU	30 November 2009	Bulgaria	BU, LI
ASAD ABDALLAH	C-144/11	8 September 2011	Italy	N/A
ASSANE SAMB	C-43/11	6 July 2011	Italy	N/A
DEMBA NGAGNE	C-140/11	29 June 2011	Italy	N/A
ELENA VERMISHEVA	C-187/11	6 July 2011	Italy	N/A
IBRAHIM MUSIC	C-156/11	21 June 2011	Italy	N/A
JOHN AUSTINE	C-63/11	21 June 2011	Italy	N/A
LUCKY EMEGOR	C-50/11	21 June 2011	Italy	N/A
MOHAMED ALI CHERNI	C-113/11	26 May 2011	Italy	N/A
MOHAMED MRAD,	C-60/11	21 June 2011	Italy	N/A
PATRICK CONTEH	C-169/11	7 July 2011	Italy	N/A
SURVIVAL GODWIN	C-94/11	21 June 2011	Italy	N/A
YEBOAH KWADWO	C-120/11	13 July 2011	Italy	N/A
EL DRIDI	C-61/11 PPU	28 April 2011	Italy	IT
ACHUGHBABIAN	C-329/11	6 December 2011	France	FR, DK, DE, EE
XIAOMIE ZHU AND OTHERS	C-51/12	6 February 2013	Italy	N/A
BEREGOVOI ION	C-52/12	6 February 2013	Italy	N/A
SUN HAI FENG	C-53/12	6 February 2013	Italy	N/A
YANG LIUNG HONG	C-54/12	6 February 2013	Italy	N/A
AHMED ETTAGHI	C-73/12	4 July 2012	Italy	N/A
TAM	C-74/12	4 July 2012	Italy	N/A
MAJALI ABDEL	C-75/12	4 July 2012	Italy	N/A
SAGOR	C-430/11	6 December 2012	Italy	IT, DE, NL
MBAYE	C-522/11	21 March 2013	Italy	N/A
ARSLAN	C-534/11	30 May 2013	Czechia	CZ, DE, FR, SK, CH
M. G.,N. R.	C-383/13 PPU	10 September 2013	Netherlands	NL, PL
GJOKO FILEV, ADNAN OSMANI	C- 297/12	19 September 2013	Germany	DE, CZ

NAME	CJEU CASE NUMBER	DATE OF DECISION	COUNTRY	INTERVENING MEMBER STATE
MAHDI	C-146/14 PPU	5 June 2014	Bulgaria	BU
DA SILVA	C-189/13	3 July 2014	France	FR
PHAM	C-474/13	17 July 2014	Germany	DE, NL
BERO AND BOUZALMATE	C-473/13 and C-514/13	17 July 2014	Germany	DE, NL, SE, CH
SOPHIE MUKARUBEGA	C-166/13	5 September 2014	France	FR, EL, NL
KHALED BOUDJLIDA	C-249/13	11 December 2014	France	FR, NL
MOUSSA ABDIDA	C-562/13	18 December 2014	Belgium	BE, FR, UK
SAMIR ZAIZOUNE	C-38/14	23 April 2015	Spain	ES, PL
Z.ZH AND I.O.	C-554/13	11 June 2015	Netherlands	NL, BE, CZ, EL, FR, PL
CELAJ	C-290/14	1 October 2015	Italy	IT, CZ, DE, EL, NO, CH
ABDELHAFID BENSADA BENALLAL	C-161/15	17 March 2016	Belgium	BE, FR
MASOUD MEHRABIPARI	C-390/14	5 June 2015	Cyprus	N/A
SÉLINA AFFUM	C-47/15	7 June 2016	France	FR, CZ, CH, HU, EL
OURHAMI	C-225/16	26 July 2017	Netherlands	NL, DK
NIANGA	C-199/16	11 August 2017	Belgium	N/A
E.	C-240/17	16 January 2018	Finland	FI, BE, DE, ES, PL, CH
K.A. AND OTHERS	C-82/16	8 May 2018	Belgium	BE, EL
GNANDI	C-181/16	19 June 2018	Belgium	BE, CZ, DE, FR, NL
AA	C-526/18	23 October 2018	Sweden	N/A
ARIB AND OTHERS	C- 444/17	19 March 2019	France	FR, DE
WM	C-18/19	2 July 2020	Germany	DE, SE
JZ	C-806/18	17 September 2020	Netherlands	NL, CZ, DE
B.	C-233/19	30 September 2020	Belgium	BE, CZ, NL
L.M.	C-402/19	30 September 2020	Belgium	BE, NL
MO	C-568/19	8 October 2020	Spain	ES
TQ	C-441/19	14 January 2021	Netherlands	NL, BE
BZ	C-546/19	3 June 2021	Germany	DE, NL

NAME	CJEU CASE NUMBER	DATE OF DECISION	COUNTRY	INTERVENING MEMBER STATE
M.	C-673/19	24 February 2021	Netherlands	NL, EE, PL
M.A.	C-112/20	11 March 2021	Belgium	BE
VT	C-641/20	5 May 2021	Belgium	N/A
UN	C-409/20	3 March 2022	Spain	ES
K	C-519/20	10 March 2022	Germany	DE, NL
I.L.	C-241/21	6 October 2022	Estonia	EE, ES
Up	C-825/21	20 October 2022	Belgium	BE
STAATSSECRETARIS VAN JUSTITIE EN VEILIGHEID (EXAMEN D'OFFICE DE LA RÉTENTION)	Joined cases C-704/20 and C-39/21	8 November 2022	Netherlands	NL
X	C-69/21	22 November 2022	Netherlands	NL
PL	C-56/22	8 September 2022	Belgium	
A.L.	C-629/22	26 April 2023	Sweden	N/A
XXX AND XXX	Joined Cases C-711/21 and C-712/21	22 June 2023	Belgium	BE, NL
AA	C-663/21	6 July 2023	Austria	AU, BE, CZ, DE, NL
CD	C-257/22	9 November 2023	Czech Republic	CZ
BANDUNDU	C-203/23	16 November 2023	Belgium	N/A
CHANGU	C-352/23	Pending	Bulgaria	
AL HOCEIMA	C-636/23	Pending	Belgium	
ZHANG	C-669/23	Pending	Netherlands	

4. Qualifications I and II

Council Directive 2004/83/EC of 29 April 2004 on minimum standards for the qualification and status of third-country nationals or stateless persons as refugees or as persons who otherwise need international protection and the content of the protection granted; Directive 2011/95/EU of the European Parliament and of the Council of 13 December 2011 on standards for the qualification of third-country nationals or stateless persons as beneficiaries of international protection, for a uniform status for refugees or for persons eligible for subsidiary protection, and for the content of the protection granted

NAME	CJEU CASE NUMBER	DATE OF DECISION	COUNTRY	INTERVENING MEMBER STATE
ELGAFAJI	C-465/07	17 February 2009	Netherlands	NL, BE, EL, FR, IT, FI, SE, UK
ABDULLA, KAMIL HASAN, MOSA RASHI, JAMAL	Joined cases C-175/08 C-176/08 C-178/08 C-179/08	2 March 2010	Germany	DE, IT, CY, UK
BOLBOL	C-31/09	17 June 2010	Hungary	HU, BE, DE, FR, UK
B. & D.	C- 57/09 and 101/09	9 November 2010	Germany	DE, NL, SE, UK, FR
Y AND Z	C-71/11	5 September 2012	Germany	DE, FR, NL
M.M.	C-277/11	22 November 2012	Ireland	IE, CZ, DE, HU, NL, PL, SE
EL KOTT AND OTHERS + UNHCR	C-364/11	19 December 2012	Hungary	HU, BE, DE, FR, RO, UK
X, Y AND Z + UNHCR	Joined cases C-199/12 + C-200/12 + 201/12	7 November 2013	Netherlands	
DIAKITÉ	C-285/12	30 January 2014	Belgium	BE, DE, FR, UK
H.N.	C- -604/12	8 May 2014	Ireland	IE, BE, DE, IT
QURBANI	C-481/13	17 July 2014	Germany	DE, NL, AU
A, B, C + UNHCR	Joined cases C-148/13, 149/13, 150/ 13.	02 December 2014	Netherlands	NL, DE, CZ, BE, EL, FR
M'BODJ	C-542/13	18 December 2014	Belgium	BE, DE, EL, FR, UK
SHEPHERD	C-472/13	26 February 2015	Germany	DE, EL, NL, UK
H.T.	C-373/13	24 June 2015	Germany	DE, EL, IT
ALO & OSSO	Joined cases C-443/14 and C-444/ 14	1 March 2016	Germany	DE, EL
M	C-560/14	9 February 2017	Ireland	IE, CZ, FR
LOUNANI	C-573/14	31 January 2017	Belgium	BE, EL, ES, FR, IT, HU, PL, UK
F	C-473/16	25 January 2018	Hungary	HU, FR, NL

NAME	CJEU CASE NUMBER	DATE OF DECISION	COUNTRY	INTERVENING MEMBER STATE
MP	C-353/16	24 April 2018	UK	UK
ALHETO	C-585/16	25 July 2018	Bulgaria	CZ, HU
AHMED	C-369/17	13 September 2018	Hungary	HU, CZ, FR, NL
AHMEDBEKOVA	C-652/16	4 October 2018	Bulgaria	CZ, EL, HU, UK
FATHI	C-56/17	4 October 2018	Bulgaria	HU, PL, UK
AYUBI	C-713/17	21 November 2018	Austria	AU
M, X, X	Joined cases C-391/16 and C-77/17 C-78/17	14 May 2019	Czech Republic and Belgium	CZ, BE, DE, FR, HU, NL, UK
BILALI	C-720/17	23 May 2019	Austria	AU, HU, NL, PL, UK
E.Z.	C-238/19	19 November 2020	Germany	DE
O.E.	C-255/19	20 January 2021	UK	UK, FR, HU
X.T.	C-507/19	13 January 2021	Germany	DE, BE, FR
S.E.	C-768/19	9 September 2021	Germany	DE, HU
CF, DN	C-901/19	10 June 2021	Germany	DE, FR, NL
L.W.	C-91/20	9 November 2021	Germany	DE, BE, PL
N.B. & A.B.	C-349/20	3 March 2022	UK	UK, DE
X.X.X.X.	C-483/20	22 February 2022	Belgium	BE, IT
G.M.	C-159/21	22 September 2022	Hungary	HU, CZ, NL
P.I.	C-280/21	12 January 2023	Lithuania	LI
E. & F.	C-456/21	26 October 2021	Netherlands	N/A
W.S.	C-621/21	16 January 2024	Bulgaria	DE, FR
K, L	C-646/21	11 June 2024	Netherlands	NL, CZ, EL, ES, FR, HU,
A.A.	C-663/21	6 July 2023	Austria	AU, BE, CZ, DE, NL
X	C-756/21	29 June 2023	Ireland	IE, DE, NL
X.X.X.	C-8/22	6 July 2023	Belgium	BE, NL
X. & Y.	C-125/22	9 September 2023	Netherlands	NL, BE, DE, FR

NAME	CJEU CASE NUMBER	DATE OF DECISION	COUNTRY	INTERVENING MEMBER STATE
S. & A.	C-151/22	21 September 2023	Netherlands	NL, DE
J.F.	C-222/22	29 February 2024	Austria	AU, DE
OFPRA	C-294/22	5 October 2023	France	FR, BE
X.X.X.	C-374/22	23 November 2023	Belgium	BE
M.A.	C-402/22	6 July 2023	Netherlands	NL, HU
SN, LN	C-563/22	13 June 2024	Bulgaria	BU
X.X.X.	C-614/22	23 November 2023	Belgium	BE
BUNDESAMT FÜR FREMDENWESEN UND ASYL AND OTHERS	Joined Cases C-608/22, C-609/22	4 October 2024	Austria	AU, BE, ES, FR
KRASILIVA	C-753/23	Pending	Czech Republic	N/A

5. Dublin II and III

Council Regulation 343/2003 of 18 February 2003 establishing the criteria and mechanisms for determining the Member State responsible for examining an asylum application lodged in one of the Member States by a third-country national; Regulation 604/2013 of the European Parliament and of the Council of 26 June 2013 establishing the criteria and mechanisms for determining the Member State responsible for examining an application for international protection lodged in one of the Member States by a third-country national or a stateless person

NAME	CJEU CASE NUMBER	DATE OF DECISION	COUNTRY	INTERVENING MEMBER STATE
PETROSIAN	C-19/08	29 January 2009	Sweden	CZ, EL, HU, NL, AU, PL, FI, NO
N. S. + M.E. AND OTHERS	Joined cases C-411/10 and C-493/10	21 December 2011	UK + Ireland	IE, UK, BE, CZ, DE, EL, FR, IT, NL, AU, PL, SL, FI, CH
KASTRATI	C-620/10	3 May 2012	Sweden	DE, EL, IT, UK, NL
K.	C-245/11	6 November 2012	Austria	AU, CZ, FR, IT, HU, PL, UK
HALAF	C-528/11	30 May 2013	Bulgaria	DE, IT, NL, UK, CH
MA, BT, DA + AIRE	C-648/11	2 September 2013	UK	UK, BE, CZ, EL, HU, NL, SE, CH

NAME	CJEU CASE NUMBER	DATE OF DECISION	COUNTRY	INTERVENING MEMBER STATE
PUID	C-4/11	14 November 2013	Germany	DE, BE, IE, EL, FR, IT, PL, UK, CH
ABDULLAHI	C-394/12	10 December 2013	Austria	AU, EL, FR, IT, HU, UK, CH
MIRZA	C-695/15 PPU	17 March 2016	Hungary	HU, DE, NL
GHEZELBASH	C-63/15	7 June 2016	Netherlands	NL, CZ, EL, FR, SE
KARIM	C-155/15	7 June 2016	Sweden	SE, CZ, EL, FR, NL, CH
C. K. AND OTHERS	C-578/16 PPU	16 February 2017	Slovenia	SL, IT, UK
AL CHODOR AND OTHERS	C-528/15	15 March 2017	Czech Republic	CZ, EL, UK,
AHMED	C-36/17	5 April 2017	Germany	N/A
A.S.,	C-490/16	26 July 2017	Slovenia	SL, EL, FR, IT, HU, AU, UK, CH
JAFARI	C-646/16	26 July 2017	Austria	AU, EL, FR, IT, HU, UK, CH
MENGESTEAB,	C-670/16	26 July 2017	Germany	DE, HU, UK
KHIR AMAYRY	C-60/16	13 September 2017	Sweden	SE, BE, DE, NL, PL, UK, SW
MAJID SHIRI	C-201/16	25 October 2017	Austria	AU, CZ, UK, CH,
AZIZ HASAN	C-360/16	25 January 2018	Germany	PL, CH
ADIL HASSAN	C-647/16	31 May 2018	France	FR, HU
X	C-213/17	5 July 2018	Netherlands	NL, DE, HU
X AND X	Joined Cases C-47/17 and C-48/17	13 November 2018	Netherlands	NL, DE, HU, UK, CH
M.A. AND OTHERS	C-661/17	23 January 2019	Ireland	IE, DE, NL, UK
JAWO	C-163/17	19 March 2019	Germany	DE, IT, BE, HU, NL, UK, CH
H. AND R.	Joined Cases C-582/17 and C-583/17	2 April 2019	Netherlands	NL, DE, FI, UK, CH
I.N.	C-897/19 PPU	2 April 2020	Croatia	CR, IE, EL, IC, NO,
H.A.	C-194/19	15 April 2021	Belgium	BE, NL
I. & S.	C-19/21	1 August 2022	Netherlands	NL, BE, EL, FR, CH
RO	C-720/20	1 August 2022	Germany	DE, BE, IT, NL, PL
C. & B.	Joined Cases C-704/20 and C-39/21	8 November 2022	Netherlands	NL

NAME	CJEU CASE NUMBER	DATE OF DECISION	COUNTRY	INTERVENING MEMBER STATE
MINISTERO DELL'INTERNO	Joined Cases C-228/21, C-254/21, C-297/21, C-315/21, C-328/21	30 November 2023	Italy	IT, DE, FR, NL
I.A.	C-231/21	31 March 2022	Austria	AU, DE
MA, PB, LE	Joined Cases C-245/21 and C-248/21	22 September 2022	Germany	DE, CH
A B	C-262/21	2 August 2021	Finland	FI, SE
B, F, K	Joined Cases C-323/21, C-324/21, C-325/21	12 January 2023	Netherlands	NL, FR, IT, CH
S., N. & S.	C-338/21	30 March 2023	Netherlands	NL, DE
E.N.	C-556/21	30 March 2023	Netherlands	NL, DE
E., S.	C-568/21 E. & S. 2	21 September 2023	Netherlands	NL, AU
L.G.	C-745/21	16 February 2023	Netherlands	NL
BU	C-80/22	7 May 2024	Italy	N/A
OV	C-217/22	7 May 2024	Italy	N/A
AHY	C-359/22	18 April 2024	Ireland	IE, EL
X	C-392/22	29 February 2024	Netherlands	NL, BE, CZ, DE, IT, AU, PL

6. Family Reunification Directive

Council Directive 2003/86/EC of 22 September 2003 on the right to family reunification

NAME	CJEU CASE NUMBER	DATE OF DECISION	COUNTRY	INTERVENING MEMBER STATE
CHAKROUN	C-578/08	4 March 2010	Netherlands	EL, NL
IMRAN	C-155/11 PPU	10 June 2011	Netherlands	N/A
MARJAN NOORZIA	C-338/13	17 July 2014	Austria	AU, EL
K & A	C-153/14	9 July 2015	Netherlands	NL, DE, AU
ORUCHE	C-527/14	2 September 2015	Germany	
MIMOUN KHACHAB	C-558/14	21 April 2016	Spain	ES, HU, DE, NL, FR.
A&S	C-550/16	12 April 2018	Netherlands	NL, PL

NAME	CJEU CASE NUMBER	DATE OF DECISION	COUNTRY	INTERVENING MEMBER STATE
C AND A	C-257/17	7 November 2018	Netherlands	NL, AU
K. AND B.	C-380/17	7 November 2018	Netherlands	NL
K	C-484/17	7 November 2018	Netherlands	NL
E.	C-635/17	13 March 2019	Netherlands	NL
Y.Z., Z.Z. AND Y.Y.	C-557/17	14 March 2019	Netherlands	NL, PL
X	C-706/18	20 November 2019	Belgium	BE, PO
G.S. AND V.G.	Joined cases C-381/18 and C-382/18	12 December 2019	Netherlands	NL, DE, PO
T.B.	C-519/18	12 December 2019	Hungary	HU, NL
B.M.M. AND OTHERS	Joined cases C-133/19 C-136/19 and C-137/19	16 July 2020	Belgium	BE, DE, AU, PL
BUNDESREPUBLIK DEUTSCHLAND V SW	Joined Cases C-273/20 and C-355/20	1 August 2022	Germany	NL
BUNDESREPUBLIK DEUTSCHLAND V XC	C-279/20	1 August 2022	Germany	DE, IT
C.R. AND OTHERS	C-560/20	20 January 2024	Austria	AU, NL
X	C-230/21	17 November 2022	Belgium	BE
AFRIN	C-1/23 PPU	18 April 2023	Belgium	BE, FR, DE, ES, NL
SAGRARIO	C-63/23	Pending	Spain	

7. Asylum Procedures I and II

Council Directive 2005/85/EC of 1 December 2005 on minimum standards on procedures in Member States for granting and withdrawing refugee status; Directive 2013/32/EU of the European Parliament and of the Council of 26 June 2013 on common procedures for granting and withdrawing international protection

NAME	CJEU CASE NUMBER	DATE OF DECISION	COUNTRY	INTERVENING MEMBER STATE
DIOUF	C-69/10	28 July 2011	Luxembourg	LU, DE, EL, NL
H.I.D. AND B.A.	C-175/11	31 January 2013	Ireland	IE, EL
TALL + FEDASIL	C-239/14	17 December 2015	Belgium	BE, HU
DANQUA	C-429/15	20 October 2016	Ireland	IE
SACKO	C-348/16	26 July 2017	Italy	IT, BE, CZ, FR, HU, PL,
MAGAMODOV	C-430/17	19 September 2017	Germany	N/A
A	C-404/17	25 July 2018	Sweden	SE, UK
X	C-175/17	26 September 2018	Netherlands	NL, BE, PL
X AND Y	C-180/17	26 October 2018	Netherlands	NL, BE, EE, PL
ADDIS	C-517/17	16 July 2020	Germany	DE, BE, CZ, FR, HU, NL
E.G.	C- 662/17	18 October 2018	Slovenia	SL, NL
D. AND I.	C-586/17	15 November 2018	Netherlands	N/A
IBRAHIM BASHAR AND OTHERS -	Joined cases C-297/17, C-318/17, C-319/17 and C-438/17	19 March 2019	Germany	DE, BE, FR, HU, IT, NL, PL, UK
TORUBAROV	C-556/17	29 July 2019	Hungary	HU, SK
HAMED AND OMAR	Joined Cases C-540/17 and C-541/17	13 November 2019	Germany	DE, BE, CZ, FR, HU, NL
FR	C-422/18 PPU	27 September 2018	Italy	N/A
C.J.S.	C-269/18 PPU	5 July 2018	Netherlands	N/A
PG	C-406/18	19 March 2020	Hungary	HU, DE
LH	C-564/18	19 March 2020	Hungary	HU, DE, FR
FMS AND OTHERS	Joined Cases C-924/19 PPU and C-925/19 PPU	14 May 2020	Hungary	HU
EY	C-40/19	5 June 2020	Hungary	N/A
KD	Case C-67/19	29 June 2020	Hungary	
TN	C-210/19	26 June 2020	Hungary	
M.S.	C-616/19	10 December 2020	Ireland	IE
JP	C-651/19	9 September 2020	Belgium	BE, FR

NAME	CJEU CASE NUMBER	DATE OF DECISION	COUNTRY	INTERVENING MEMBER STATE
THC	C-755/19	11 February 2021	Belgium	N/A
LH	C-921/19	10 June 2021	Netherlands	NL
LR	C-8/20	20 May 2021	Germany	DE
BUNDESAMT	C-18/20	9 September 2021	Austria	AU, CZ, DE, FR, HU, NL
E. M. T.	C-20/20	16 October 2020	Belgium	N/A
VL	C-36/20 PPU	25 June 2020	Spain	ES
XXXX	C-483/20	22 February 2022	Belgium	BE, IT
RO	C-720/20	1 August 2022	Germany	DE, BE, IT, NL, PL
A E.A.	C-153/21	30 November 2022	Luxembourg	BE, DE, LU, NL
GM	C-159/21	22 September 2022	Hungary	HU, CZ, NL
X	C-756/21	29 June 2023	Ireland	IE, DE, NL
SI, TL, ND, VH, YT, HN	C-497/21	22 September 2022	Germany	DE
BU	C-564/21	1 December 2022	Germany	DE, HU
M.A. V VALSTYBĖS SIENOS APSAUGOS TARNYBA	C-72/22	30 June 2022	Lithuania	LI
A.A.	C-216/22	8 February 2024	Germany	DE, AU
HAMM	C-352/22	18 June 2024	Germany	DE, IT
JB, SB, FB	C-364/22	25 May 2023	Germany	DE, PL
S.N. & L.N.	C-563/22	13 June 2024	Belgium	BU
Q.Y.	C-753/22	18 June 2024	Germany	DE, BE, CZ, IE, EL, FR, IT, LU, NL, AU
CV	C-406/22	4 October 2024	Czech Republic	CZ, DE, NL

8. Schengen Borders Code

Regulation 562/2006 of the European Parliament and of the Council of 15 March 2006 establishing a Community Code on the rules governing the movement of persons across borders; Regulation 2016/399 of the European Parliament and of the Council of 9 March 2016 on a Union Code on the rules governing the movement of persons across borders

NAME	CJEU CASE NUMBER	DATE OF DECISION	COUNTRY	INTERVENING MEMBER STATE
GARCIA & CABRERA	Joined cases C-261/08 + C-348/08	22 October 2009	Spain	ES, IT, AU
MELKI & ABDELI	Joined cases C-188/10 + C-189/10	22 June 2010	France	FR, BE, CZ, DE, GR, NL, PL, SK
ANAFE	C-606/10	14 June 2012	France	FR, BE
ADIL	C-278/12 PPU	19 July 2012	Netherlands	NL, CZ, DE, FR
JAOO	C-88/12	14 September 2012	Netherlands	N/A
ZAKARIA	C-23/12	17 January 2013	Latvia	LV
AIR BALTIC CORPORATION	C-575/12	4 September 2014	Latvia	LV, IT, FI, CH
A	C-9/16	21 June 2017	Germany	DE, CZ, CH, GR
EL DAKKAK	C-17/16	4 May 2017	France	FR, GR
TOURING TOURS AND TRAVEL	Joined Cases C-412/17 and C-474/17	13 December 2018	Germany	DE
E.P.	C-380/18	12 December 2019	Netherlands	NL, BE, DE, CH
J AND OTHERS	C-341/18	5 Feburary 2020	Netherlands	NL, DE, GR
D.Z. VS BLUE AIR	C-584/18	30 April 2020	Cyprus	CY, DE, NL
MIGRATIONSVERKET	C-193/19	4 March 2021	Sweden	SW, NL, PL
FU	C-554/19	4 June 2020	Germany	DE, CZ, PL
KONSUL RZECZYPOSPOLITEJ POLSKIEJ	C-949/19	10 March 2021	Poland	PL, CZ, DE
NW	C-368/20	26 April 2022	Austria	AU, DK, DE, FR, SW
ADDE—ASSOCIATION AVOCATS POUR LA DÉFENSE DES DROITS DES ÉTRANGERS	C-143/22	21 September 2023	France	FR, PL

9. Long-term Residents

Council Directive 2003/109/EC of 25 November 2003 concerning the status of third-country nationals who are long-term residents

NAME	CJEU CASE NUMBER	DATE OF DECISION	COUNTRY	INTERVENING MEMBER STATE
SERVET KAMBERAJ	C-571/10	24 April 2012	Italy	FR, BE, IT
MANGAT SINGH	C-502/10	18 October 2012	Netherlands	NL, BE
MLAMALI	C-257/13	14 November 2013	France	N/A
SHAMIM TAHIR	C-469/13	17 July 2014	Italy	IT, FR, DE, NL, PL
TÜMER	C-311/13	5 November 2014	Netherlands	NL
VAN HAUTHEM	C-176/14	16 March 2015	Belgium	N/A
P & S	C-579/13	4 June 2015	Netherlands	NL, PO
CGIL-INCA	C-309/14	2 September 2015	Italy	IT, FR, PL
LOPEZ PASTUZANO	C- 636/16	7 December 2017	Spain	ES
X	C-302/18	3 October 2019	Belgium	BE, CZ, FR, IT, AU, DE
W.T.	C-448/19	11 June 2020	Spain	ES
PO	C-531/19	29 July 2020	Spain	N/A
RQ	C-533/19	24 July 2020	Spain	N/A
SR	C- 534/19	24 July 2020	Spain	N/A
DX	C-549/19	16 July 2020	Spain	N/A
LP	C-567/19	17 July 2020	Spain	N/A
U.Q. + SI	Joined cases C- 503/19 and 592/19	3 September 2020	Spain	ES
V.R. VS INPS	C-303/19	25 November 2020	Italy	IT
LAND OBERÖSTERREICH (AIDE AU LOGEMENT)	C-94/20	10 June 2021	Austria	-
ASGI, APN, AND NAGA	C-462/20	28 October 2021	Italy	IT
Z.K.,	C-432/20	20 January 2022	Austria	AU
E.K. VS STAATSSECRETARIS VAN JUSTITIE EN VEILIGHEID	C-624/20	7 September 2022	Netherlands	NL, DK, DE
EP	C-752/22	14 March 2024	Finland	FI

NAME	CJEU CASE NUMBER	DATE OF DECISION	COUNTRY	INTERVENING MEMBER STATE
CU AND ND	Joined Cases C-112/22 and C-223/22	29 July 2024	Italy	IT
NW AND PQ	Joined cases C-420/22 and C-528/22	25 April 2024	Hungary	HU, FR
STADT FRANKFURT AM MAIN	Joined cases C-829/21 and C-129/22	29 June 2023	Germany	-

10. Reception Conditions I and II

Council Directive 2003/9/EC of 27 January 2003 laying down minimum standards for the reception of asylum seekers; Directive 2013/33/EU of the European Parliament and of the Council of 26 June 2013 laying down standards for the reception of applicants for international protection

NAME	CJEU CASE NUMBER	DATE OF DECISION	COUNTRY	INTERVENING MEMBER STATE
CIMADE AND GISTI	C-179/11	27 September 2012	France	FR, CZ, EL, IT, PL, CH
SACIRI AND OTHERS	C-79/13	27 February 2014	Belgium	BE, FR, PL
J.N.	C-601/15 PPU	15 February 2016	Netherlands	NL, BE, CZ, EL, IT, CY, PL,
K.	C-18/16	14 September 2017	Netherlands	NL, BE, EE, IE,
D.H.	C-704/17	8 March 2019	Czech Republic	N/A
HAQBIN	C-233/18	12 November 2019	Belgium	BE, HU, NL, UK
FW AND GY V U.T.G.	C-726/18	28 April 2020	Italy	N/A
K.S.	Joined cases C-322/19 and C-385/19	14 January 2021	Ireland	IE
MINISTERIO FISCAL V VL	C-36/20	25 June 2020	Spain	ES
MINISTERO DELL'INTERNO	C-422/21	1 August 2022	Italy	IT, BE, CZ, DE, NL

11. Single Permit Directive

Directive 2011/98/EU of the European Parliament and of the Council of 13 December 2011 on a single application procedure for a single permit for third-country nationals to reside and work in the territory of a Member State and on a common set of rights for third-country workers legally residing in a Member State

NAME	CJEU CASE NUMBER	DATE OF DECISION	COUNTRY	INTERVENING MEMBER STATE
MARTINEZ SILVA	C-449/16	2 June 2017	Italy	IT
WS	C-302/19	25 November 2020	Italy	IT
O.D. AND OTHERS VS INPS	C-350/20	2 September 2021	Italy	IT

12. Visa Code

Regulation (EC) No 810/2009 of the European Parliament and of the Council of 13 July 2009 establishing a Community Code on Visas; Regulation (EU) 2019/1155 of the European Parliament and of the Council of 20 June 2019 amending Regulation (EC) No 810/2009 establishing a Community Code on Visas

NAME	CJEU CASE NUMBER	DATE OF DECISION	COUNTRY	INTERVENING MEMBER STATE
MINH KHOA VO	C-83/12 PPU	10 April 2012	Germany	DE, GR
KOUSHKAKI	C-84/12	19 December 2013	Germany	DE, BE, CZ, DK, EE, GR, NL, PL, CH
X AND X	C-638/16	7 March 2017	Belgium	BE, CZ, DK, DE, EE, FR, HU, MA, NL, AU, PL, SL, SK, FI
EL HASSANI	C-403/16	13 December 2017	Poland	PL, CZ, EE
SUMANAN VETHANAYAGAM, SOBITHA SUMANAN ET KAMALARANEE VETHANAYAGAM	C-680/17	29 July 2019	Netherlands	NL, CZ, DK, EE, FR, IT, PL
R.N.N.S. AND K.A.	Joined cases C-225/19 and C-226/19	24 November 2020	Netherlands	NL, CZ, DE, IT, LI, PL
MINISTER VAN BUITENLANDSE ZAKEN	C-121/20	26 March 2021	Netherlands	N/A

13. Passport Regulation

Council Regulation (EC) No 2252/2004 of 13 December 2004 on standards for security features and biometrics in passports and travel documents issued by Member States

NAME	CJEU CASE NUMBER	DATE OF DECISION	COUNTRY	INTERVENING MEMBER STATE
SCHWARZ	C-291/12	17 October 2013	Germany	DE, PL

14. Transit through Switzerland

Decision No 896/2006/EC of the European Parliament and of the Council of 14 June 2006 establishing a simplified regime for the control of persons at the external borders based on the unilateral recognition by the Member States of certain residence permits issued by Switzerland and Liechtenstein for the purpose of transit through their territory

NAME	CJEU CASE NUMBER	DATE OF DECISION	COUNTRY	INTERVENING MEMBER STATE
KQIKU	C-139/08	2 April 2009	Germany	-

15. Researchers and Students Directive

Commission Directive 2004/14/EC of 29 January 2004 amending Directive 93/10/EEC relating to materials and articles made of regenerated cellulose film intended to come into contact with foodstuffs; Directive (EU) 2016/801 of the European Parliament and of the Council of 11 May 2016 on the conditions of entry and residence of third-country nationals for the purposes of research, studies, training, voluntary service, pupil exchange schemes, or educational projects and au pairing

NAME	CJEU CASE NUMBER	DATE OF DECISION	COUNTRY	INTERVENING MEMBER STATE
BEN ALAYA	C-491/13	10 September 2014	Germany	DE, PL, UK, EL, BE, EE
SAHAR FAHIMIAN	C-544/15	4 April 2017	Germany	DE, IT, PL, EL, BE, FR

16. Social Security for TCN Regulation

Council Regulation (EC) No 859/2003 of 14 May 2003 extending the provisions of Regulation (EEC) No 1408/71 and Regulation (EEC) No 574/72 to nationals of third countries who are not already covered by those provisions solely on the ground of their nationality; Regulation (EU) No 1231/2010 of the European Parliament and of the Council of 24 November 2010 extending Regulation (EC) No 883/2004 and Regulation (EC) No 987/2009 to nationals of third countries who are not already covered by these Regulations solely on the ground of their nationality

NAME	CJEU CASE NUMBER	DATE OF DECISION	COUNTRY	INTERVENING MEMBER STATE
XHYMSHITI	C-247/09	18 November 2010	Germany	DE
WIELAND AND ROTHWANGL	C-465/14	27 October 2016	Netherlands	ES, NL
BALANDIN	C-477/17	24 January 2019	Netherlands	NL, CZ, FR
KOPPÁNY 2007	C-523/20	3 March 2021	Hungary	N/A

17. Border Traffic Regulation

Regulation (EC) No 1931/2006 of the European Parliament and of the Council of 20 December 2006 laying down rules on local border traffic at the external land borders of the Member States and amending the provisions of the Schengen Convention

NAME	CJEU CASE NUMBER	DATE OF DECISION	COUNTRY	INTERVENING MEMBER STATE
SHOMODI	C-254/11	21 March 2013	Hungary	HU, PL, RO, SK

18. Facilitation Directive

Council Directive 2002/90/EC of 28 November 2002 defining the facilitation of unauthorised entry, transit and residence

NAME	CJEU CASE NUMBER	DATE OF DECISION	COUNTRY	INTERVENING MEMBER STATE
PAOLETTI AND OTHERS	C-218/15	25 May 2016	Italy	AU, IT

19. Mutual Recognition of Expulsion Decision

Council Directive 2001/40/EC of 28 May 2001 on the mutual recognition of decisions on the expulsion of third-country nationals

NAME	CJEU CASE NUMBER	DATE OF DECISION	COUNTRY	INTERVENING MEMBER STATE
ORREGO ARIAS	C-456/14	3 September 2015	Spain	N/A

20. Port State Control

Directive 2009/16/EC of the European Parliament and of the Council of 23 April 2009 on port State control

NAME	CJEU CASE NUMBER	DATE OF DECISION	COUNTRY	INTERVENING MEMBER STATE
SEA WATCH	Joined cases C-14/21 and C-15/21	1 August 2022	Italy	IT, ES, NW

21. Trafficking Victims

Council Directive 2004/81/EC of 29 April 2004 on the residence permit issued to third-country nationals who are victims of trafficking in human beings or who have been the subject of an action to facilitate illegal immigration, who cooperate with the competent authorities

NAME	CJEU CASE NUMBER	DATE OF DECISION	COUNTRY	INTERVENING MEMBER STATE
O.T.E	C-66/21	20 October 2022	Netherlands	NL, CZ, DE

22. Morocco–EEC Agreement

Euro-Mediterranean Agreement establishing an association between the European Communities and their Member States, of the one part, and the Kingdom of Morocco, of the other part, and related protocols

NAME	CJEU CASE NUMBER	DATE OF DECISION	COUNTRY	INTERVENING MEMBER STATE
BAHIA KZIBER	C-18/90	31 January 1991	Belgium	BE, DE, FR
YOUSFI	C-58/93	20 April 1994	Belgium	BE, DE, FR
A. HALLOUZI-CHOHO	C- 126/95	3 October 1996	Netherlands	NL, FR
NOUR EDDLINE EL-YASSINI	C-416/96	2 March 1999	UK	UK, DE, FR
FATNA MESBAH	C-179/98	11 November 1999	Belgium	BE, DE, FR, UK
FAHMI AND ESMORIS CERDEIRO-PINEDO	C-33/99	20 March 2001	Netherlands	NL, ES, FR, AU, UK
MOHAMED ALAMI	C-23/02	12 February 2003	Belgium	N/A
YAMINA HADDAD	C-358/02	27 April 2004	Belgium	N/A

23. Tunisia–EEC Agreement

Cooperation Agreement between the European Economic Community and the Republic of Tunisia

NAME	CJEU CASE NUMBER	DATE OF DECISION	COUNTRY	INTERVENING MEMBER STATE
GATTOUSSI	C-97/05	14 December 2006	Germany	DE, EL
E.P.	C-905/19	8 July 2020	Germany	N/A

24. Algeria–EEC Agreement

Cooperation Agreement between the European Economic Community and the People's Democratic Republic of Algeria

NAME	CJEU CASE NUMBER	DATE OF DECISION	COUNTRY	INTERVENING MEMBER STATE
KRID	C-103/94	5 April 1995	France	FR, UK
HENIA BABAHENINI	C-113/97	15 January 1998	Belgium	BE
DJABALI	C-314/96	12 March 1998	France	N/A
X	C-549/22	29 February 2024	Netherlands	NL

Bibliography

Acosta Arcarazo D, 'The Good, the Bad and the Ugly in EU Migration Law: Is the European Parliament Becoming Bad and Ugly? (The Adoption of Directive 2008/15: The Returns Directive' (2009) 11 European Journal of Migration and Law

Adam R, 'Il Rinvio Pregiudiziale Tra Tutela Dei Diritti Soggettivi e Controllo Delle Inadempienze Statali' (2023) 1 Il Diritto dell'Unione Europea

Adinolfi A, 'I Fondamenti Del Diritto Dell'UE Nella Giurisprudenza Della Corte Di Giustizia: Il Rinvio Pregiudiziale' (2019) I I Post di AISDUE 197

Alberti J, 'I rinvii pregiudiziali italiani dall'entrata in vigore del trattato di Lisbona al 31.12.2021: uno studio sulla prassi e sulle sue prospettive' [2022] Eurojus

Albors-Llorens A, 'Remedies against the EU Institutions after Lisbon: An Era of Opportunity?' (2012) 71 The Cambridge Law Journal 507

Allan TRS, *The Sovereignty of Law: Freedom, Constitution and Common Law* (OUP 2013)

Alter K, 'The European Court's Political Power' (1996) 19 West European Politics 458

Alter K, 'Who Are the "Masters of the Treaty"? European Governments and the European Court of Justice' (1998) 52 International Organization 121

Alter K, *Establishing the Supremacy of European Law: The Making of an International Rule of Law in Europe* (OUP 2002)

Alter K, *The New Terrain of International Law: Courts, Politics, Rights* (Princeton University Press 2014)

Alter K and Vargas J, 'Explaining Variation in the Use of European Litigation Strategies: European Community Law and British Gender Equality Policy' (2000) 33 Comparative Political Studies 452

Amadeo S and others, *Il diritto dell'immigrazione e dell'asilo dell'Unione europea* (Giappichelli Editore 2022)

Amato G, 'Un Sistema Incompatibile Con La Direttiva Ue Perché Non Privilegia Il Rimpatrio Volontario' (2011) 5 Guida al Diritto 24

Ambrosini M, 'NGOs and Health Services for Irregular Immigrants in Italy: When the Protection of Human Rights Challenges the Laws' (2015) 13 Journal of Immigrant & Refugee Studies 116

Amnesty International, 'Greece: A Blue Print for Despair. Human Rights Impact of the EU-Turkey Deal' EUR 25/5664/2017

Anagnostou D, *Rights and Courts in Pursuit of Social Change: Legal Mobilisation in the Multi-level European System* (Hart Publishing 2014)

Anagnostou D, 'Judicial Activism in the Name of the Nation: Reneging on the Integration of Immigrants in Greece' (2016) 43 Journal of Law and Society 596

Anagnostou D, *The European Convention of Human Rights Regime: Reform of Immigration and Minority Policies from Afar* (Routledge 2022)

Anastasio S and Centonze S, *Ingresso e Soggiorno Illegale Nel Territorio Dello Stato* (Key Editore 2016)

Andersen EA, *Out of the Closets and into the Courts: Legal Opportunity Structure and Gay Rights Litigation* (University of Michigan Press 2006)

Angeli D and Anagnostou D, 'A Shortfall of Rights and Justice: Judicial Review of Immigration Detention in Greece' (2022) 14 European Journal of Legal Studies 97

Anrò I, 'L'amicus Curiae Presso La Corte Di Giustizia Dell'Unione Europea: Qualche Riflessione per l'apertura Delle Porte Del Kirchberg' [2023] 1 Rivista del Contenzioso Europeo 62

Arena A, 'From an Unpaid Electricity Bill to the Primacy of EU Law: Gian Galeazzo Stendardi and the Making of Costa v. ENEL' (2019) 30 European Journal of International Law 1017

Arena A, 'The "Unsung Heroes" of Costa v Enel: Enabling "Supremacy by Judicial Fiat"' *EUI Webinar, The Court in the Archives* (2021) <https://www.iris.unina.it/handle/11588/873314>

Arena A and Rosanò A, 'Nicola Catalano (1910–1984): Padre del rinvio pregiudiziale d'interpretazione e apostolo del primato del diritto comunitario' [2024] Eurojus 89

Baldaccini A, 'The EU Directive on Return: Principles and Protests' (2009) 28 Refugee Survey Quarterly 114

Barnard C, 'A European Litigation Strategy: The Case of the Equal Opportunities Commission' in J Shaw and G More (eds), *New Legal Dynamics of European Union* (Clarendon Press 1995)

Barnard C, 'Brexit and the [Rule of] Law' (Bennett Institute for Public Policy 2019) Policy Brief.

Bascherini G, 'A Proposito Delle Più Recenti Riforme in Materia Di Trattenimento Dello Straniero Nei Centri Di Identificazione Ed Espulsione' (2012) 1 Rivista Associazione Italiana dei Costituzionalisti

Baubock R and others (eds), *Acquisition and Loss of Nationality, Volume 2: Country Analyses: Policies and Trends in 15 European Countries* (Amsterdam University Press 2010)

Baumgärtel M, *Demanding Rights. Europe's Supranational Courts and the Dilemma of Migrant Vulnerability* (CUP 2019)

Bell M, 'Civic Citizenship and Migrant Integration' (2007) 13 European Public Law 311

Benhabib S, *The Rights of Others: Aliens, Residents, and Citizens* (CUP 2004)

Besselink LFM, 'Integration and Immigration: The Vicissitudes of Dutch "Inburgering"' in E Guild, K Groenendijk, and S Carrera (eds), *Illiberal Liberal States: Immigration, Citizenship, and Integration in the EU* (Ashgate 2009)

Bonjour S and Vink MP, 'When Europeanization Backfires: The Normalization of European Migration Politics' (2013) 48 Acta Politica 389

Bornemann J, 'Reviving the Promise of Schengen' (*Verfassungsblog*, 28 April 2022) <https://verfassungsblog.de/reviving-the-promise-of-schengen/> accessed 29 October 2024

Börzel TA, 'Participation Through Law Enforcement. The Case of the European Union' (2006) 39 Comparative Political Studies 128

Bowcott O and legal affairs correspondent, 'Tens of Thousands Lose Support as Immigration Advisory Service Closes' *The Guardian* (11 July 2011) <https://www.theguardian.com/law/2011/jul/11/immigration-advisory-service-closes-blames-government> accessed 17 December 2024

Brake D, 'When Equality Leaves Everyone Worse Off: The Problem of Leveling Down in Equality Law' (2004) 46 William and Mary Law Review 513

Broberg M, 'Preliminary References as a Means for Enforcing EU Law' in A Jakab and D Kochenov (eds), *The Enforcement of EU Law and Values: Ensuring Member States' Compliance* (OUP 2017)

Broberg M and Fenger N, 'Variations in Member States' Preliminary References to the Court of Justice—Are Structural Factors (Part of) the Explanation?' (2013) 19 European Law Journal 488

Burley A-M and Mattli W, 'Europe Before the Court: A Political Theory of Legal Integration' (1993) 47 International Organization 41

Bürli N, *Third-Party Interventions before the European Court of Human Rights: Amicus Curiae, Member-State and Third-Party Interventions* (Intersentia 2017)

Callewaert J, 'Convention Control Over the Application of Union Law by National Judges: The Case for a Wholistic Approach to Fundamental Rights' (2023) 8 European Papers—A Journal on Law and Integration 331

Caputo A, 'Diseguali, Illegali, Criminali (Una Guida Alla Lettura)' (2009) 1 Questione Giustizia 83

Caputo A and Pepino L, 'Giudice Di Pace e Habeas Corpus Dopo Le Modifiche al Testo Unico Sull'immigrazione' [2004] Diritto, Immigrazione e Cittadinanza 13

Carrera S, '"Integration" as a Process of Inclusion for Migrants? The Case of Long-Term Residents in the EU' (CEPS 2005) No 219/March 2005 <https://www.ceps.eu/ceps-publications/integration-process-inclusion-migrants-case-long-term-residents-eu/>

Carrera S, *In Search of the Perfect Citizen? The Intersection between Integration, Immigration, and Nationality in the EU* (Martinus Nijhoff 2009)

Carrera S and Wiesbrock A, 'Civic Integration of Third-Country Nationals. Nationalism versus Europeanisation in the Common EU Immigration Policy' [2009] The CEPS 'Liberty and Security in Europe' publication series

Cebulak P and Morvillo M, 'The Guardian Is Absent' (*Verfassungsblog*, 25 June 2021) <https://verfassungsblog.de/the-guardian-is-absent/> accessed 29 October 2024

Cebulak P and Morvillo M, 'Backtracking or Defending Free Movement within the Schengen Area? *NW v. Landespolizei Steiermark*' (2023) 60 Common Market Law Review

Chalmers D, Davies G, and Monti G, *European Union Law: Text and Materials* (3rd edn, CUP 2014)

Cichowski RA, 'Women's Rights, the European Court, and Supranational Constitutionalism' (2004) 38 Law & Society Review 489

Cichowski RA, *The European Court and Civil Society: Litigation, Mobilization and Governance* (CUP 2007)

Cichowski RA, 'Mobilisation, Litigation and Democratic Governance' (2013) 49 Representation 321

Claes M and De Witte B, 'Report on the Netherlands' in Anne-Marie Slaughter, Alec Stone Sweet, and JHH Weiler (eds), *The European Court and National Courts—Doctrine and Jurisprudence: Legal Change in its Social Context* (Hart 1997)

Cohen A and Vauchez A, 'The Social Construction of Law: The European Court of Justice and Its Legal Revolution Revisited' (2011) 7 The Annual Review of Law and Social Science 417

Collins M, 'Immigration and Opinion Polls in Postwar Britain' (2016) 18 Modern History Review 8

Cometti M, 'La risposta della Commissione europea al "deterioramento" del diritto di asilo in Grecia: riflessioni sull'attenuato attivismo dell'Istituzione "guardiana dei Trattati"' [2022] Freedom Security and Justice 175

Conant LJ, *Justice Contained: Law and Politics in the European Union* (Cornell University Press 2002)

Conant L and others, 'Mobilizing European Law' (2017) 25 Journal of European Public Policy 1

Condinanzi M, 'La partecipazione al pregiudiziale: tertium non datur' (2023) 1 Rivista del Contenzioso Europeo 1

Cornelius WA, Martin P, and Hollifield JF (eds), *Controlling Immigration: A Global Perspective* (1st edn, Stanford University Press 1994)

Cortner RC, 'Strategies and Tactics of Litigants in Constitutional Cases' (1968) 17 Journal of Public Law 287

Costamagna F and Montaldo S, 'Social Integration in EU Law: Content, Limits and Functions of an Elusive Notion—Introduction' (2018) 3 European Papers 659

Coughlan J, Opravil J, and Heusel W, 'Judicial Training in the European Union Member States' (European Parliament's Committee on Legal Affairs 2011) PE 453.198 EN

Craig P and de Búrca G, *EU Law: Text, Cases, and Materials* (6th edn, OUP 2015)

Cummings SL, *Lawyers and Movements: Legal Mobilization in Transformative Times* (OUP 2025)

Damato A, 'L'incidenza Sul Terzo Pilastro Di Principi e Regole Di Diritto Comunitario', in Andrea Cannone and others (eds), *Studi in onore di Vincenzo Starace* (Editoriale Scientifica 2008)

Darian-Smith E, *Bridging Divides: The Channel Tunnel and English Legal Identity in the New Europe* (University of California Press 1999)

Davio V, 'Detention in the Hungarian Transit Zones: A Case of Higher Fundamental Rights Protection by EU Law Vis-à-Vis the ECHR' [2022] European law review 393

De Búrca G, 'The Evolution of EU Human Rights Law' in Paul Craig and Gráinne de Búrca (eds), *The Evolution of EU Law* (OUP 2021)

De Fazio G, 'Legal Opportunity Structure and Social Movement Strategy in Northern Ireland and Southern United States' (2012) 53 International Journal of Comparative Sociology

De Witte B, 'The Impact of Van Gend En Loos on Judicial Protection at European and National Level: Three Types of Preliminary Questions' in Antonio Tizzano and Sacha Prechal (eds), *50th Anniversary of the Judgment in Van Gend en Loos, 1963–2013* (Office des Publications de l'Union Européenne 2013)

Di Martino A and others, *The Criminalization of Irregular Immigration: Law and Practice in Italy* (Pisa University Press 2013)

Di Pascale A, 'Italy and Unauthorized Migration: Between State Sovereignty and Human Rights Obligations' in Ruth Rubio-Marín (ed), *Human Rights and Immigration* (OUP 2014)

Dia Anagnostou, *Rights and Courts in Pursuit of Social Change: Legal Mobilisation in the Multi-Level European System* (Hart Publishing 2014)

Dixon D, 'Thatcher's People: The British Nationality Act 1981' (1983) 10 Journal of Law and Society 161

Donini M, 'Il cittadino extracomunitario da oggetto materiale a tipo d'autore nel controllo penale dell'immigrazione' (2009) Fascicolo 1 Questione giustizia 101

Donnelly C and De la Mare T, 'Preliminary Rulings and EU Legal Integration: Evolution and Continuity' in Paul Craig and Gráinne de Búrca (eds), *The Evolution of EU Law* (OUP 2021)

Dougan M, 'The Constitutional Dimension to the Case Law on Union Citizenship' (2006) 2006 Inter Alia: University of Durham Student Law Journal 77

Drzemczewski A, 'A "Non-Decision" of the Committee of Ministers under Article 32 (1) of the European Convention on Human Rights: The East African Asians Cases' (1978) 41 Modern Law Review 337

Duffy H, *Strategic Human Rights Litigation: Understanding and Maximising Impact* (Hart Publishing 2018)

Dyer C, 'Ruling Exposes Immigration Loophole' *The Guardian* (20 October 2004) <https://www.theguardian.com/uk/2004/oct/20/eu.immigrationandpublicservices> accessed 17 December 2024

ECRE, 'Asylum in Greece: A Situation Beyond Judicial Control?' (2021) 9

Elsuwege PV, 'Court of Justice of the European Union European Union Citizenship and the Purely Internal Rule Revisited. Decision of 5 May 2011, Case C-434/09 Shirley McCarthy v. Secretary of State for the Home Department' (2011) 7 European Constitutional Law Review 308

Epp C, *The Rights Revolution: Lawyers, Activists, and Supreme Courts in Comparative Perspective* (1st edn, University of Chicago Press 1998)

Epp C, 'Implementing the Rights Revolution: Repeat Players and the Interpreting of Diffuse Legal Messages' (2008) 71 Law and Contemporary Problems 41

European Commission, 'Investor Citizenship and Residence Schemes in the European Union, COM(2019) 12 Final' (2019) COM(2019) 12 final

European Union Agency for Fundamental Rights (FRA), 'Coping with a Fundamental Rights Emergency—The Situation of Persons Crossing the Greek Land Border in an Irregular Manner' (2011)

Evans JM, 'Immigration Act 1971' (1972) 35 The Modern Law Review 508

Extra G and Spotti M, 'Testing Regimes for Newcomers to the Netherlands' in G Extra, M Spotti, and P Van Avermaet (eds), *Language Testing, Migration and Citizenship* (Continuum 2009)

Farkas L, *Mobilising for Racial Equality in Europe: Roma Rights and Transnational Justice* (EUI Law PhD Thesis 2020)

Favilli C, 'L'attuazione in Italia Della Direttiva Rimpatri: Dall'inerzia All'urgenza Con Scarsa Cooperazione' (2011) 3 Rivista di Diritto Internazionale 695

Favilli C, *Migration Law in Italy* (Kluwer Law International 2013)

Favilli C, 'Le Politiche Di Immigrazione e Asilo: Passato, Presente e Futuro Di Una Sovranità Europea Incompiuta' [2022] Annali AISDUE Sezione "Atti convegni AISDUE" 227

Felstiner WLF, Abel RL, and Sarat A, 'The Emergence and Transformation of Disputes: Naming, Blaming, Claiming . . .' (1980) 15 Law & Society Review 631

Ferrajoli L, 'La Criminalizzazione Degli Immigrati (Note a Margine Della Legge n. 94/2009)' [2009] Questione Giustizia 9

Focardi F, 'Ancora Sull'impatto Della Direttiva Comunitaria 2008/115/CE Sui Reati Di Cui All'artt. 14 Co. 5-Ter e 5-Quater d.Lgs. 286/1998' [2011] Diritto Penale Contemporaneo < https://archiviodpc.dirittopenaleuomo.org/d/313-ancora-sull-impatto-della-direttiva-comunitaria-2008115ce-sui-reati-di-cui-all-artt-14-co-5-ter-e-5> accessed 17 December 2024

Fokas E, 'Comparative Susceptibility and Differential Effects on the Two European Courts: A Study of Grasstops Mobilizations around Religion' (2016) 5 Oxford Journal of Law and Religion 541

Fornalé E, 'The European Returns Policy and the Re-Shaping of the National: Reflections on the Role of Domestic Courts' (2012) 31 Refugee Survey Quarterly 134

Freeman GP, 'Britain, the Deviant Case' in W Cornelius, P Martin, and J Hollifield (eds), *Controlling Immigration: A Global Perspective* (Stanford University Press 1994)

Galanter M, 'Why the "Haves" Come out Ahead: Speculations on the Limits of Legal Change' (1974) 9 Law & Society Review 95

Galanter M, 'The Radiating Effects of Courts' in KO Boyum and L Mather (eds), *Empirical theories about courts* (Longman Inc 1983)

Gallo D, 'Rethinking Direct Effect and Its Evolution: A Proposal' (2022) 1 European Law Open 576

Gammeltoft-Hansen T and others (eds) *The Rights of Others: Essays in Honour of Jens Vedsted-Hansen* (DJØF Forlag 2013)

Ganty S, 'Les Tests d'intégration Civique Sous Le Contrôle de La Cour de Justice de l'Union Européenne: Un Exercice d'équilibriste Périlleux Entre Marge d'appréciation Des États Membres et Protection Des Ressortissants de Pays Tiers' [2016] Journal européen des droits de l'homme 32

Gatta FL, 'Enough is enough! La Corte di Giustizia interviene sull'(il)legittimità delle proroghe "a catena" dei controlli alle frontiere interne. Ma lo Spazio Schengen rimane a rischio' (*Diritti Comparati*, 18 May 2022) <https://www.diritticomparati.it/enough-is-enough-la-corte-di-giustizia-interviene-sullillegittimita-delle-proroghe-a-catena-dei-controlli-alle-frontiere-interne-ma-lo-spazio-schengen-rimane-a-rischio/> accessed 29 October 2024

Gatta GL, 'Art. 10 bis T.U. Imm. e "Direttiva Rimpatri": un'altra ordinanza di rimessione alla Corte di Giustizia' (2012) Diritto Penale Contemporaneo <https://archiviodpc.dirittopenaleuomo.org/d/1229-art-10-bis-tu-imm-e--direttiva-rimpatri--un-altra-ordinanza-di-rimessione-alla-corte-di-giustizia> accessed 17 December 2024

Givens T and Case R, *Legislating Equality: The Politics of Antidiscrimination Policy in Europe* (OUP 2014)

Givens T and Luedtke A, 'EU Immigration Policy: From Intergovernmentalism to Reluctant Harmonization' in TA Börzel and RA Cichowski (eds), *The State of the European Union, 6: Law, Politics, and Society* (OUP 2003)

Gkliati M, 'The Application of the EU-Turkey Agreement : A Critical Analysis of the Decisions of the Greek Appeals Committees' (2017) 10 European Journal of Legal Studies 80

Glavina M, 'Reluctance to Participate in the Preliminary Ruling Procedure as a Challenge to EU Law: A Case Study on Slovenia and Croatia' in C Rauchegger and A Wallerman (eds), *The Eurosceptic Challenge: National Implementation and Interpretation of EU Law* (Hart Publishing 2019)

Golub J, 'The Politics of Judicial Discretion: Rethinking the Interaction between National Courts and the European Court of Justice' (1996) 19 West European Politics 360

Goluboff RL, *The Lost Promise of Civil Rights* (Harvard University Press 2010)

González-Ocantos EA, *Shifting Legal Visions: Judicial Change and Human Rights Trials in Latin America* (CUP 2016)

Groenendijk K, 'Family Reunification as a Right under Community Law' (2006) 8 European Journal of Migration and Law 215

Groenendijk K, 'Pre-Departure Integration Strategies in the European Union: Integration or Immigration Policy?' (2011) 13 European Journal of Migration and Law 1

Groenendijk K, 'Waarom Rechters Niet Naar Luxemburg Gaan: Dialoog of Weerstand, Politieke Structuur of Rechtscultuur?' in R Baas and others (eds), *Rechtspleging en rechtsbescherming. Liber amicorum voor prof. dr. Leny E. de Groot-van Leeuwen* (Kluwer 2015) 187

Groenendijk K and Heijs E, 'Immigration, Immigrants and Nationality Law in the Netherlands, 1945–98' in R Hansen and P Weil (eds), *Towards a European Nationality, Citizenship, Immigration and Nationality Law in the EU* (Palgrave 2001)

Groenendijk K and Strik T, 'Family Reunification in Germany, Netherlands and the EU since 2000: Reciprocal Influence and the Role of National and EU Actors' in S Beichel-Benedetti and C Janda (eds), *Hohenheim Horizons, Festschrift für Klaus Barwig* (Nomos 2018)

Groenendijk CA, Rondhuis M, and Strik MHA, "Klagen Bij de Europese Commissie. Effecten van Tien Jaar Juridische Belangenbehartiging Door Het Inspraakorgaan Turken in Nederland" (2015) 6 Asiel & Migrantenrecht 22

Guarnieri C, 'Courts and Marginalized Groups: Perspectives from Continental Europe' (2007) 5 International Journal of Constitutional Law 187

Guild E, 'Competence, Discretion and Third Country Nationals: The European Union's Legal Struggle with Migration' (1998) 24 Journal of Ethnic and Migration Studies 613

Guild E, 'European Developments. The EC Directive on Race Discrimination: Surprises, Possibilities and Limitations' (2000) 29 Industrial Law Journal 416

Guild E, Peers S, and Tomkin J, *The EU Citizenship Directive: A Commentary* (OUP 2014)

Guiraudon V, 'European Integration and Migration Policy: Vertical Policy-Making as Venue Shopping' (2000) 38 JCMS: Journal of Common Market Studies 251

Guiraudon V, Phalet K, and Wal JT, 'Monitoring Ethnic Minorities in the Netherlands' (2005) 57 International Social Science Journal 75

Hammarberg T, 'It Is Wrong to Criminalize Migration' (2009) 11 European Journal of Migration and Law 386

Hansen R, *Citizenship and Immigration in Postwar Britain* (OUP 2000)

Hansen R, 'Paradigm and Policy Shifts: British Immigration Policy, 1997–2011' in J Hollifield, P Martin, and PM Orrenius (eds), *Controlling Immigration, a Global Perspective* (3rd edn, Stanford University Press 2014) 199

Hansen R, 'Commentary'in WA Cornelius and others (eds.) *Controlling Immigration: A Global Perspective* (2nd edn, Stanford University Press, 2003) 338

Harby C, 'The Experience of the AIRE Centre in Litigating before the European Court of Human Rights' in T Treves (ed), *Civil Society, International Courts and Compliance Bodies* (2005)

Harlow C and Rawlings R, *Pressure Through Law* (Taylor and Francis 1992)

Harms L, 'Claiming Religious Freedom at the European Court of Human Rights: Socio-Legal Field Effects on Legal Mobilization' (2021) 46 Law & Social Inquiry 1206

Hartley B, 'Taking the Integration Test: How Do You Deal with a Noisy Party next Door?' [2016] *Dutch News* <https://www.dutchnews.nl>

Hatzopoulos V, 'Casual but Smart: The Court's New Clothes in the Area of Freedom, Security and Justice (AFSJ) after the Lisbon Treaty' in J Monar (ed), *The Institutional Dimension of the European Union's Area of Freedom, Security and Justice* (Peter Lang 2010)

Hawkins O, 'Migration Statistics' (House of Commons Library 2017) No SN06077,

Hilson C, 'New Social Movements: The Role of Legal Opportunity' (2002) 9 Journal of European Public Policy 238

Hilton M, *A Historical Guide to NGOs in Britain: Charities, Civil Society and the Voluntary Sector Since 1945* (Palgrave Macmillan 2012)

Hinsliff G and Bright M, 'Labour Fuels War on Asylum' *The Guardian* (6 February 2005) <https://www.theguardian.com/politics/2005/feb/06/immigration.immigrationandpublicservices> accessed 17 December 2024

Hoevenaars J, 'A People's Court? A Bottom-Up Approach to Litigation Before the European Court of Justice' (Radboud University 2018)

Hofmann A, 'Left to Interest Groups? On the Prospects for Enforcing Environmental Law in the European Union' (2019) 28 Environmental Politics 342

Hofmann A, 'The Legal Mobilisation of EU Market Freedoms: Strategic Action or Random Noise?' (2024) 0 West European Politics 1

Hollifield J, Martin PL, and Orrenius P, *Controlling Immigration: A Global Perspective, Third Edition* (Stanford University Press 2014)

Home Office and Office for National Statistics, 'Immigration Patterns of Non-UK Born Populations in England and Wales in 2011' (2013)

Hoogenboom A, 'Moving Forward by Standing Still? First Admission of Turkish Workers: Comment on Commission v Netherlands (Administrative Fees)' (2014) 35 European Law Review 707

Höpner M and Schäfer A, 'A New Phase of European Integration: Organised Capitalisms in Post-Ricardian Europe' (2010) 33 West European Politics 344

Hoskyns C, *Integrating Gender: Women, Law and Politics in the European Union* (Verso 1996)

Human Rights Watch, 'The Netherlands: Discrimination in the Name of Integration. Migrants' Rights under the Integration Abroad Act' (*Human Rights Watch*, 13 May 2008) <https://www.hrw.org/report/2008/05/13/netherlands-discrimination-name-integration/migrants-rights-under-integration> accessed 19 August 2019

Independent, 'Controversial Filmmaker Shot Dead' *The Independent* (2 November 2004) <http://www.independent.co.uk/news/world/europe/controversial-filmmaker-shot-dead-18345.html> accessed 17 December 2024

Israël L, 'Rights on the Left? Social Movements, Law and Lawyers after 1968 in France' in Dia Anagnostou (ed), *Rights and Courts in Pursuit of Social Change: Legal Mobilisation in the Multi- Level European System* (Hart Publishing 2014) 79

Iliopoulos-Strangas J and Koutnatzis S-IG, 'Greece: Constitutional Courts as Positive Legislators' in AR Brewer-Carías (ed), *Constitutional Courts as Positive Legislators: A Comparative Law Study* (CUP 2011)

Ioannidis M, 'The Judiciary' in K Featherstone and DA Sotiropoulos (eds), *The Oxford Handbook of Modern Greek Politics* (OUP 2020)

Jaremba U and Kappé M, 'The Unfolding Story of Judicial Dialogue in the EU: The Coercive and Persuasive Motives Behind the Participation of Belgian Highest Courts in the Preliminary Ruling Procedure' [2024] German Law Journal 1

Jaremba U and Mayoral JA, 'The Europeanization of National Judiciaries: Definitions, Indicators and Mechanisms' (2019) 26 Journal of European Public Policy 386

Jesse M, 'Integration Measures, Integration Exams, and Immigration Control: P and S and K and A' (2016) 53 Common Market Law Review 1065

Joppke C, 'Why Liberal States Accept Unwanted Immigration' (1998) 50 World Politics 266

Joppke C, *Immigration and the Nation-State: The United States, Germany, and Great Britain* (OUP 1999)

Kapotas P, 'Greek Council of State' (2014) 10 European Constitutional Law Review 162

Karatani R, *Defining British Citizenship: Empire, Commonwealth and Modern Britain* (Frank Cass 2003)

Kelemen D, *Eurolegalism: The Transformation of Law and Regulation in the European Union* (Harvard University Press 2011)

Kilpatrick C, 'Effective Utilisation of Equality Rights: Equal Pay for Work of Equal Value in France and the UK' in F Gardiner, *Sex Equality Policy in Western Europe* (Routledge 1997)

King A, *The British Constitution* (OUP 2010)

Kochenov D and Lindeboom J, 'Breaking Chinese Law—Making European One' in F Nicola and Bill Davies (eds), *EU Law Stories* (CUP 2017)

Kosińska AM, 'The Problem of Criminalisation of the Illegal Entry of a Third-Country National in the Case of Breaching an Entry Ban. Commentary on the Judgment of the Court of Justice of 1 October 2015 in Case C 290/14, Skerdjan Celaj' (2016) 18 European Journal of Migration and Law 243

Krenn C, *The Procedural and Organisational Law of the European Court of Justice: An Incomplete Transformation* (CUP 2022)

Krommendijk J, 'The Preliminary Reference Dance between the CJEU and Dutch Courts in the Field of Migration' (2018) 10 European Journal of Legal Studies 101

Krommendijk J, 'De Lagere Rechter Aan Banden. Is Er Nog Ruimte Voor de Lagere Rechter Om Te Verwijzen Naar Het HvJ?' [2018] Sociaal-Economische Wetgeving 183

Krommendijk J, 'The Highest Dutch Courts and the Preliminary Ruling Procedure: Critically Obedient Interlocutors of the Court of Justice' (2019) 0 European Law Journal

Krommendijk J, 'Why Do Lower Courts Refer in the Absence of a Legal Obligation? Irish Eagerness and Dutch Disinclination' (2019) 26 Maastricht Journal of European and Comparative Law 770

Krommendijk J, 'It Takes Two to Tango: An Introduction' (2020) 5 European Papers 745

Krommendijk J, *National Courts and Preliminary References to the Court of Justice* (Edward Elgar Publishing 2021)

Krommendijk J and van der Pas K, 'To Intervene or Not to Intervene: Intervention before the Court of Justice of the European Union in Environmental and Migration Law' (2022) 26 The International Journal of Human Rights 1394

Labayle H and Pascouau Y, 'Study on the "Conformity Checking of the Transposition by Member States of 10 EC Directives in the Sector of Asylum and Immigration" Done for DG JLS of the European Commission End 2007' Contract JLS/B4/2006/03 <http://odysseus-network.eu/wp-content/uploads/2015/03/2003-86-Family-reunification-Synthesis-.pdf>

Layton-Henry Z, 'Britain: The Would-Be Zero-Immigration Country' in W Cornelius, Philip Martin and J Hollifield (eds), *Controlling Immigration: A Global Perspective* (Stanford University Press 1994)

Layton-Henry Z, 'Britain: From Immigration Control to Migration Management' in WA Cornelius and others (eds), *Controlling Immigration: A Global Perspective* (Stanford University Press 2003)

Lehoucq E and Taylor WK, 'Conceptualizing Legal Mobilization: How Should We Understand the Deployment of Legal Strategies?' (2020) 45 Law & Social Inquiry 166

Leijon K, 'Active or Passive: The National Judges' Expression of Opinions in the Preliminary Reference Procedure' (2020) 5 European Papers 871

Leijon K and Glavina M, 'Why Passive? Exploring National Judges' Motives for Not Requesting Preliminary Rulings' (2022) 29 Maastricht Journal of European and Comparative Law 263

Lenaerts K, 'The Court's Outer and Inner Selves: Exploring the External and Internal Legitimacy of the European Court of Justice' in Maurice Adams and others, *Judging Europe's Judges: The Legitimacy of the Case Law of the European Court of Justice* (A&C Black 2014)

Lenaerts K, Gutman K and Nowak JT, *EU Procedural Law* (2nd edn OUP 2023)

Lenaerts K, Maselis I, and Gutman K, *EU Procedural Law* (1st edn OUP 2014)

Luzzatto R, 'L'Unione Europea in Quanto Comunità Di Diritto: Il Ruolo Del Sistema Giurisdizionale' in M Maresca (ed), *Valori e Principi nella costituzione europea: Il diritto alla mobilità* (Il Mulino 2004)

Madsen MR, Nicola F, and Vauchez A (eds), *Researching the European Court of Justice: Methodological Shifts and Law's Embeddedness* (CUP 2022)

Mańko R, 'The EU as a Community of Law: Overview of the Role of Law in the Union' (2017) PE 599.364 <https://www.europarl.europa.eu/RegData/etudes/BRIE/2017/599364/EPRS_BRI(2017)599364_EN.pdf>

Marin L and Spena A, 'Introduction: The Criminalization of Migration and European (Dis) Integration' (2016) 18 European Journal of Migration and Law 147

Marletta A, 'Nulla di più definitivo del provvisorio? La Corte di giustizia sui limiti alla reintroduzione temporanea dei controlli alle frontiere interne' (*ADiM Blog*, 31 May

2022) <https://www.adimblog.com/2022/05/31/nulla-di-piu-definitivo-del-provvisorio-la-corte-di-giustizia-sui-limiti-alla-reintroduzione-temporanea-dei-controlli-alle-frontiere-interne/> accessed 29 October 2024

Masera, L, 'Immigrazione' in O Mazza and F Viganò (eds), *Misure urgenti in materia di sicurezza pubblica* (Giappichelli 2008)

Masera L, 'Costituzionale il reato di clandestinità, incostituzionale l'aggravante: le ragioni della Corte costituzionale' (2010) 3 Diritto, Immigrazione e Cittadinanza 37

Masera L and Viganò F, 'Addio articolo 14' (2011) Diritto Penale Contemporaneo <https://archiviodpc.dirittopenaleuomo.org/d/572-addio-articolo-14> accessed 17 December 2024

Massey DS, 'Why Does Immigration Occur? A Theoretical Synthesis' in C Hirschman, P Kasinitz, and J De Wind (eds), *The Handbook of International Migration: The American Experience* (Russell Sage Foundation 1999)

Masterman R and Leigh I (eds), *The United Kingdom's Statutory Bill of Rights: Constitutional and Comparative Perspectives* (1st edn, OUP 2013)

Matevžič G and Juhász K, 'Implementing Judgments in the Field of Asylum and Migration on Odd Days' (2022)

Mayoral J, Nowak T, and Jaremba U, 'Creating EU Law Judges: The Role of Generational Differences, Legal Education and Judicial Career Paths in National Judges' Assessment Regarding EU Law Knowledge' (2014) 21 Journal of European Public Policy 1120

McCann M, 'Litigation and Legal Mobilization' in GA Caldeira, RD Kelemen, and KE Whittington (eds), *The Oxford Handbook of Law and Politics* (OUP 2008)

McCann M, *Rights at Work: Pay Equity Reform and the Politics of Legal Mobilization* (University of Chicago Press 1994)

McDonough P and Tsourdi E (Lilian), 'The "Other" Greek Crisis: Asylum and Eu Solidarity' (2012) 31 Refugee Survey Quarterly 67

Melting Pot R, 'Speciale "Pacchetto Sicurezza" - Le Nuove Norme Tra Applicabilità Ed Efficacia' <http://www.meltingpot.org/Speciale-pacchetto-sicurezza-Le-nuove-norme-tra.html>

Merlino M, 'The Italian (In)Security Package: Security vs. Rule of Law and Fundamental Rights in the EU' [2009] CEPS research paper

Merry SE, *Human Rights and Gender Violence Translating International Law into Local Justice* (University of Chicago Press 2006)

Merry SE, 'Transnational Human Rights and Local Activism: Mapping the Middle' (2006) 108 American Anthropologist 38

Miazzi L, 'Detriti di una legislazione: cosa resta della normativa sull'immigrazione' (2013) 5 Questione Giustizia 129

Migration Law Clinic, 'De Wet Inburgering in Het Buitenland in EU-Rechtelijk Perspectief' (2014) <https://migrationlawclinic.files.wordpress.com/2014/08/expert-opinion-de-wet-inburgering-in-het-buitenland-in-eu-rechtelijk-perspectief.pdf>

Milella L, 'Roberti: "Il reato di immigrazione clandestina? Legge che ha solo ostacolato le indagini sui trafficanti"' *La Repubblica* (Rome, 8 January 2016) <https://www.repubblica.it/politica/2016/01/08/news/roberti_il_reato_di_immigrazione_clandestina_legge_che_ha_solo_ostacolato_le_indagini_sui_trafficanti_-130835471/> accessed 7 June 2024

Miller J, 'Explaining Paradigm Shifts in Danish Anti-Discrimination Law' (2019) 26 Maastricht Journal of European and Comparative Law 540

Miller J, *The European Disability Rights Revolution* (EUI Law PhD Thesis 2020)

Miller J, 'Peering Inside the Preliminary Reference Box: Coleman v Attridge Law' (2022) 2021 6 European Papers—A Journal on Law and Integration 1553

Minderhoud P, 'Directive 2004/38 and Access to Social Assistance Benefits' in E Guild, CG Rotaeche, and D Kostakopoulou, *The Reconceptualization of European Union Citizenship* (Brill Nijhoff 2014)

Ministero dell'Interno, Dipartimento di Pubblica Sicurezza, 'Cittadini Stranieri in Posizione Di Soggiorno Irregolare'

Moffatt R and Thomas C, 'And Then They Came for Judicial Review: Proposals for Further Reform' (2014) 28 Journal of Immigration, Asylum and Nationality Law 237

Montaldo S, 'Freedom of Movement, Social Integration and Naturalization: Testing Reverse Discrimination in the Recent Case Law of the Court of Justice' (2018) 2018 3 European Papers—A Journal on Law and Integration 2499

Mügge L, *Beyond Dutch Borders: Transnational Politics among Colonial Migrants, Guest Workers and the Second Generation* (Amsterdam University Press 2010)

Muir E and others, *How EU Law Shapes Opportunities for Preliminary References on Fundamental Rights: Discrimination, Data Protection and Asylum* (European University Institute 2017)

Nascimbene B, 'Lo Spazio Di Libertà, Sicurezza e Giustizia a Due Anni Dall'entrata in Vigore Del Trattato Di Lisbona' (2011) 4 Diritto, Immigrazione e Cittadinanza 13

Natale A, 'La direttiva rimpatri, il testo unico immigrazione ed il diritto penale dopo la sentenza El Dridi' (2011) 2 Diritto, Immigrazione e Cittadinanza 17

Nicola F and Davies B, *EU Law Stories* (CUP 2017)

Oomen B, *Rights for Others: The Slow Home-Coming of Human Rights in the Netherlands* (CUP 2013)

Orgad L, *The Cultural Defense of Nations: A Liberal Theory of Majority Rights* (OUP 2015)

Pagano M, 'Overcoming Plaumann in EU Environmental Litigation: An Analysis of NGOs Legal Arguments in Actions for Annulment' [2019] Diritto e processo 311

Pannick D, 'The Primary Purpose Rule: A Rule with No Purpose' (Young JUSTICE 1993)

Papagianni G, *Institutional and Policy Dynamics of EU Migration Law* (Martinus Nijhoff 2006)

Papapanagiotou-Leza A and Kofinis S, 'Can the Return Directive Contribute to Protection for Rejected Asylum Seekers and Irregular Migrants in Detention? The Case of Greece' in M Moraru, G Cornelisse, and P De Bruycker (eds), *Law and Judicial Dialogue on the Return of Irregular Migrants from the European Union* (Hart Publishing 2020)

Pascouau Y, 'Measures and Rules Developed in the EU Member States Regarding Integration of Third Country Nationals - Comparative Report' (European Policy Centre 2016)

Passalacqua V, 'Legal Mobilization Via Preliminary Reference: Insights from the Case of Migrant Rights' (2021) 58 Common Market Law Review 751

Passalacqua V, 'Who Mobilizes the Court? Migrant Rights Defenders Before the Court of Justice of the EU' (2022) 15 Law and Development Review 381.

Passalacqua V and Costamagna F, 'The Law and Facts of the Preliminary Reference Procedure: A Critical Assessment of the EU Court of Justice's Source of Knowledge' (2023) 2 European Law Open 322

Pavone T, 'From Marx to Market: Lawyers, European Law, and the Contentious Transformation of the Port of Genoa' (2018) 53 Law & Society Review

Pavone T, 'Putting European Constitutionalism in Its Place: The Spatial Foundations of the Judicial Construction of Europe' (2020) 16 European Constitutional Law Review 669

Pavone T, *The Ghostwriters: Lawyers and the Politics behind the Judicial Construction of Europe* (CUP 2022)

Perlmutter T, 'Italy. Political Parties and Italian Policy, 1990–2009' in James Hollifield, Philip Martin and Pia Orrenius, *Controlling Immigration: A Global Perspective, Third edition* (Stanford University Press 2014)

Peršak N, 'Principles of EU Criminalisation and Their Varied Normative Strength: Harm and Effectiveness' (2021) 27 European Law Journal 463

Pescatore P, *Court of Justice of the European Communities: References for Preliminary Rulings under Article 177 of the EEC Treaty and Cooperation between the Court and National Courts* (Office for Official Publications of the European Communities 1986)

PICUM, 'Cases of Criminalisation of Migration and Solidarity in the EU in 2023' (2024) <https://picum.org/wp-content/uploads/2024/04/Cases-of-criminalisation-of-migration-and-solidarity-in-the-EU-in-2023.pdf>

Pijnenburg A and Pas van der K, 'Strategic Litigation against European Migration Control Policies: The Legal Battleground of the Central Mediterranean Migration Route' (2022) 24 European Journal of Migration and Law 401

Pilgram L, 'Tackling "Sham Marriages": The Rationale, Impact and Limitations of the Home Office's "Certificate of Approval" Scheme' (2009) 23 Journal of Immigration Asylum and Nationality Law 24

Pollack MA, *The Engines of European Integration: Delegation, Agency, and Agenda Setting in the EU* (OUP 2003)

Protopapa V, 'Shaping Equality for Migrants. Legal Mobilisation in Italy and the Race Equality Directive' (2019) 1 Journal européen des droits de l'homme 3

Psychogiopoulou E, 'European Courts and the Rights of Migrants and Asylum Seekers in Greece' in Dia Anagnostou (ed), *Rights and Courts in Pursuit of Social Change: Legal Mobilisation in the Multi-Level European System* (Bloomsbury Publishing 2014)

Pugiotto A, 'La "galera Amministrativa" Degli Stranieri e Le Sue Incostituzionali Metamorfosi' (2014) 34 Quaderni costituzionali

Raffaelli R, 'Criminalizing Irregular Immigration and the Returns Directive: An Analysis of the El Dridi Case' (2011) 13 European Journal of Migration and Law 467

Raffaelli R, 'Immigration and Criminal Law: Is There a Judge in Luxembourg?' in Bruno de Witte and others (eds), *National Courts and EU Law: New Issues, Theories and Methods* (Edward Elgar Publishing 2016)

Rasmussen H, 'Why Is Article 173 Interpreted against Private Plaintiffs?' (1980) 5 European Law Review 112

Reale MC and Borraccetti M, *Da Giudice a Giudice. Il Dialogo Tra Giudice Italiano e Corte Di Giustizia Delle Comunita' Europee.* (Giuffrè Editore 2008)

Refugee Support Aegean and Greek Refugee Council, 'CJEU Ruling on the Concept of "Safe Third Country"' <https://rsaegean.org/en/cjeu-ruling-on-the-concept-of-safe-third-country/> accessed 16 October 2024

Reuters, 'Hungary Passes Anti-Immigrant "Stop Soros" Laws' *The Guardian* (20 June 2018) <https://www.theguardian.com/world/2018/jun/20/hungary-passes-anti-immigrant-stop-soros-laws> accessed 6 October 2024

Réveillère V, 'Family Rights for Naturalized EU Citizens: "Lounes"' (2018) 55 Common Market Law Review 1855

Romano A, '"Circumstances . . . Are Clearly Distinct": La Detenzione Dello Straniero per Il Delitto Di Illecito Reingresso Nella Sentenza Celaj Della Corte Di Giustizia' (2015) 2 Diritto, Immigrazione e Cittadinanza 109

Rosenberg GN, *The Hollow Hope: Can Courts Bring about Social Change?* (University of Chicago 1991)

Rozenberg J, 'EU Backing for Chinese Mother's Right to Live in Britain' *The Telegraph* (19 October 2004) <https://www.telegraph.co.uk/news/uknews/1474555/EU-backing-for-Chinese-mothers-right-to-live-in-Britain.html> accessed 17 December 2024

Salomon S and Rijpma J, 'A Europe Without Internal Frontiers: Challenging the Reintroduction of Border Controls in the Schengen Area in the Light of Union Citizenship' (2023) 24 German Law Journal 281

Sartori G, 'Concept Misformation in Comparative Politics' (1970) 64 The American Political Science Review

Savino M, *Le Libertà Degli Altri. La Regolazione Amministrativa Dei Flussi Migratori* (Giuffrè Editore 2012)

Savino M, 'Irregular Migration at the Crossroads, between Administrative Removal and Criminal Deterrence: The Celaj Case' (2016) 53 Common Market Law Review 1419

Savio G, 'Prime riflessioni sulle modifiche penali introdotte dalla legge n. 271 del 2004' (2004) 3 Diritto, Immigrazione e Cittadinanza 71

Savio G, 'La nuova disciplina delle espulsioni dopo la legge 129/2011' (*Melting Pot*, 30 August 2011) <http://www.meltingpot.org/La-nuova-disciplina-delle-espulsioni-dopo-la-legge-129-2011.html> accessed 17 December 2024

Schepel H and Bankenburg E, 'Mobilizing the European Court of Justice' in G De Búrca and JHH Weiler (eds), *The European Court of Justice* (OUP 2001)

Sharma P, *The Human Rights Act and the Assault on Liberty: Rights and Asylum in the UK* (Nottingham University Press 2011)

Shaw J, Miller N, and Fletcher M, *Getting to Grips with EU Citizenship: Understanding the Friction Between UK Immigration Law and EU Free Movement Law* (Edinburgh Law School Citizenship Studies 2013)

Small ML and Cook JM, 'Using Interviews to Understand Why: Challenges and Strategies in the Study of Motivated Action' (2023) 52 Sociological Methods & Research 1591

Small S and Solomos J, 'Race, Immigration and Politics in Britain: Changing Policy Agendas and Conceptual Paradigms 1940s–2000s' (2006) 47 International Journal of Comparative Sociology 235

Spaventa E, 'Earned Citizenship: Understanding Union Citizenship through Its Scope' in Dimitry Kochenov (ed), *EU Citizenship and Federalism: The Role of Rights* (CUP 2017)

Special Rapporteur on the situation of human rights defenders, Mary Lawlor, 'Report on the Visit to Greece' (2023) A/HRC/52/29/Add.1

Spena A, 'Resisting Immigration Detention Special Issue: Crimmigration and Human Rights in Europe: Exclusion, Alternatives and Resistance' (2016) 18 European Journal of Migration and Law 201

Spitaleri F, *Le discriminazioni alla rovescia nel diritto dell'Unione europea* (Aracne 2010)

Spitaleri F, 'L'interpretazione della direttiva rimpatri tra efficienza del sistema e tutela dei diritti dello straniero' (2013) 1 Diritto, Immigrazione e Cittadinanza 15

Statham P, 'Political Opportunities for Altruism? The Role of State Policies in Influencing Claims-Making by British Antiracist and Pro-Migrant Movements' in M Giugni and F Passy, *Political Altruism? Solidarity Movements in International Perspective* (Rowman & Littlefield 2001) 133

Sterett S, 'Judicial Review in Britain' (1994) 26 Comparative Political Studies 421

Sterett S, 'Caring about Individual Cases: Immigration Lawyering in Britain' in A Sarat and SA Scheingold, *Cause Lawyering: Political Commitments and Professional Responsibilities* (OUP 1998)

Sterett S, 'Legal Mobilization and Juridification: Migration as a Central Case' (2016) 38 Law & Policy 273

Stone Sweet A, *The Judicial Construction of Europe* (OUP 2004)

Stone Sweet A and Brunell TL, 'The European Court and the National Courts: A Statistical Analysis of Preliminary References, 1961–95' (1998) 5 Journal of European Public Policy 66

Tan NF and Gammeltoft-Hansen T, 'A Topographical Approach to Accountability for Human Rights Violations in Migration Control' (2020) 21 German Law Journal 335

Tarrow SG, *Power in Movement: Social Movements and Contentious Politics* (3rd edn, CUP 2011)

Tezcan-Idriz N, 'Dutch Courts Safeguarding Rights under the EEC-Turkey Association Law. Case Note on District Court Rotterdam Judgments of 12 August 2010, and District Court Roermond Judgment of 15 October 2010' (2011) 13 European Journal of Migration and Law 219

Thierse S and Badanjak S, *Opposition in the EU Multi-Level Polity: Legal Mobilization against the Data Retention Directive* (Palgrave Pivot 2021)

Thomas R, 'Immigration and Access to Justice: A Critical Analysis of Recent Restrictions' in E Palmer and others (eds), *Access to Justice: Beyond the Policies and Politics of Austerity* (Hart Publishing 2016)

Thomas R and Tomlinson J, 'A Design Problem for Judicial Review: What We Know and What We Need to Know about Immigration Judicial Reviews' (*UK Constitutional Law Association*, 16 March 2017) <https://ukconstitutionallaw.org/2017/03/16/robert-thomas-and-joe-tomlinson-a-design-problem-for-judicial-review-what-we-know-and-what-we-need-to-know-about-immigration-judicial-reviews/> accessed 17 December 2024

Thym D, 'Towards a Contextual Conception of Social Integration in Eu Immigration Law. Comments on P & S and K & A' (2016) 18 European Journal of Migration and Law 89

Thym D, 'Institutional and Constitutional Framework' in E Tsourdi and P De Bruycker (eds), *EU Migration and Asylum Law* (Edward Elgar 2022)

Tilly C, 'Speaking Your Mind Without Elections, Surveys, or Social Movements' (1983) 47 Public Opinion Quarterly 461

Trabucchi A, 'L'effet "erga Omnes" Des Decisions Prejudicielles Rendues Par La Cour de Justice Des Communautes Europeennes' (1974) 10 Revue trimestrielle de droit europeen 56

Triandafyllidou A, 'Migration in Greece' in K Featherstone and DA Sotiropoulos (eds), *The Oxford Handbook of Modern Greek Politics* (OUP 2020)

Tsourdi E and De Bruycker P, 'The Evolving EU Asylum and Migration Law' in E Tsourdi and P De Bruyckere (eds), *EU migration and asylum law* (Edward Elgar 2022)

Tuo CE, 'Regolamento di procedura della Corte di giustizia. Titolo III, Capo IV, Gratuito patrocinio' in C Amalfitano, M Condinanzi, and P Iannuccelli (eds), *Le regole del processo dinanzi al Giudice dell'Unione europea. Commento articolo per articolo* (Editoriale Scientifica 2017)

UNHCR, 'Legal Considerations on the Return of Asylum-Seekers and Refugees from Greece to Turkey as Part of the EU-Turkey Cooperation in Tackling the Migration Crisis under the Safe Third Country and First Country of Asylum Concept' (2016)

Usherwood S and Startin N, 'Euroscepticism as a Persistent Phenomenon' (2013) 51 Journal of Common Market Studies 1

Van den Eynde L, 'An Empirical Look at the Amicus Curiae Practice of Human Rights NGOs Before the European Court of Human Rights' (2013) 31 Netherlands Quarterly of Human Rights 271

van der Pas K, *The 'Strategy' in Strategic Litigation: The Why and How of Strategic Litigation by Civil Society Organizations in the Field of Asylum Law in Europe* (Europa Law Publishing 2024)

van der Pas K, 'All That Glitters Is Not Gold? Civil Society Organisations and the (Non-) Mobilisation of European Union Law' 62 Journal of Common Market Studies 525

Van Oers R, 'Justifying Citizenship Tests in the Netherlands and the UK' in E Guild, K Groenendijk, and S Carrera, *Illiberal Liberal States* (Ashgate 2009)

Van Oers R, *Deserving Citizenship: Citizenship Tests in Germany, the Netherlands and the United Kingdom* (Martinus Nijhoff Publishers 2013)

Van Oers R, De Hart B, and Groenendijk K, 'The Netherlands' in R Baubock and others (eds), *Policies and Trends in 15 European States*, vol 2 (Amsterdam University Press 2006)

Van Oers R, De Hart B, and Groenendijk K, 'Report on The Netherlands' (Robert Schuman Centre for Advanced Studies 2013) RSCAS/EUDO-CIT-CR 2013/1

Vanhala L, *Making Rights a Reality? Disability Rights Activists and Legal Mobilization* (CUP 2010)

Vanhala L, 'Legal Opportunity Structures and the Paradox of Legal Mobilization by the Environmental Movement in the UK' (2012) 46 Law & Society Review 523

Vanhala L, 'Legal Mobilization' <http://www.oxfordbibliographies.com/abstract/document/obo-9780199756223/obo-9780199756223-0031.xml>

Vanhala L, 'Is Legal Mobilization for the Birds? Legal Opportunity Structures and Environmental Nongovernmental Organizations in the United Kingdom, France, Finland, and Italy' (2018) 51 Comparative Political Studies 380

Vassallo Paleologo F, 'Direttiva Rimpatri e Stato Di Diritto - Un Commento Alla Luce Della Circolare Manganelli Del 17 Dicembre' (*Melting Pot Europa*, 7 January 2011) <http://www.meltingpot.org/Direttiva-rimpatri-e-stato-di-diritto-Un-commento-alla-luce.html> accessed 17 December 2024

Vauchez A, 'The Transnational Politics of Judicialization. Van Gend En Loos and the Making of EU Polity' (2010) 16 European Law Journal 1

Vauchez A, *Brokering Europe: Euro-Lawyers and the Making of a Transnational Polity* (CUP 2015)

Vauchez A, 'The Map and the Territory: Re-Assessing EU Law's Embeddedness in European Societies' (2020) 27 Maastricht Journal of European and Comparative Law 133

Vauchez A and de Witte B (eds), *Lawyering Europe: European Law as a Transnational Social Field* (Hart Publishing 2013)

Vavoula N, 'The Interplay between EU Immigration Law and National Criminal Law—The Case of the Return Directive' in V Mitsilegas, M Bergström, and T Konstadinides (eds), *Research Handbook on EU Criminal Law* (Edward Elgar Publishing 2016)

Viganò F, 'Direttiva Rimpatri e Delitti Di Inosservanza Dell'ordine Di Allontanamento Del Questore' [2010] Diritto Penale Contemporaneo <http://www.penalecontemporaneo.it/area/3-/26-/-/284-direttiva_rimpatri_e_delitti_di_inosservanza_dell__ordine_di_allontanamento_del_questore/>

Viganò F, 'Il Dibattito Continua: Ancora in Tema Di Direttiva Rimpatri e Inosservanza Dell'ordine Di Allontanamento' [2011] Diritto Penale Contemporaneo <http://www.penalecontemporaneo.it/area/3-/26-/-/328-il_dibattito_continua__ancora_in_tema_di_direttiva_rimpatri_e_inosservanza_dell___ordine_di_allontanamento/>

Viganò F and Masera L, 'Illegittimità Comunitaria Della Vigente Disciplina Delle Espulsioni e Possibili Rimedi Giurisdizionali' [2010] Rivista Italiana Diritto e Procedura Penale 560

Vink MP, 'Dutch "Multiculturalism" Beyond the Pillarisation Myth' (2007) 5 Political Studies Review 337

Visscher Q, 'De Politieke Wortels van de WRV' (2009) 9/10 Migrantenrecht 459

Vitale G, *Principi generali e diritto derivato. Contributo allo studio del sistema delle fonti dell'Unione europea* (Giappichelli Editore 2013)

Voermans W, 'A 200-Year-Old Constitution: Relic or Enigma?' in GF Ferrari, R Passchier, and W Voermans (eds), *The Dutch Constitution beyond 200 years: Tradition and Innovation in a Multilevel Legal Order* (Eleven International Publishing 2018)

Weiler JHH, 'A Quiet Revolution. The European Court of Justice and Its Interlocutors' (1994) 26 Comparative Political Studies 510

Wiesbrock A, *Legal Migration to the European Union* (Martinus Nijhoff Publishers 2010)

Wind M, 'The Nordics, the EU and the Reluctance towards Supranational Judicial Review' (2010) 48 Journal of Common Market Studies 1039

Wray H, 'An Ideal Husband? Marriages of Convenience, Moral Gate-Keeping and Immigration to the United Kingdom' in E Guild and P Minderhoud (eds), *The First Decade of EU Migration and Asylum Law* (Martinus Nijhoff Publishers 2011)

Wray H, Kofman E, and Simic A, 'Subversive Citizens: Using EU Free Movement Law to Bypass the UK's Rules on Marriage Migration' (2021) 47 Journal of Ethnic and Migration Studies 447

WRR—The Netherlands Scientific Council for Government Policy, 'Ethnic Minorities' <https://english.wrr.nl/publications/reports/1979/05/09/ethnic-minorities> accessed 30 August 2018

Zalan E, 'Hungarian Judge Claims She Was Pushed out for Political Reasons' *EUobserver* (6 July 2021) <https://euobserver.com/rule-of-law/arfcdab903> accessed 17 December 2024

Zemans FK, 'Legal Mobilization: The Neglected Role of the Law in the Political System' (1983) 77 The American Political Science Review 690

Ziniti A, 'Il procuratore di Agrigento, Renato Di Natale: "Con il reato di clandestinità abbiamo gli uffici ingolfati"' *La Repubblica* (Palermo, 29 May 2016) <https://palermo.repubblica.it/cronaca/2016/05/29/news/il_procuratore_di_agrigento_renato_di_natale_con_il_reato_di_clandestinita_abbiamo_gli_uffici_ingolfati_-140854592/> accessed 7 June 2024

Index

For the benefit of digital users, indexed terms that span two pages (e.g., 52–53) may, on occasion, appear on only one of those pages.

Tables are indicated by an italic *t* following the page number.